TRAFALGAR

GREAT BATTLES

TRAFALGAR

JOHN B. HATTENDORF

OXFORD
UNIVERSITY PRESS

OXFORD
UNIVERSITY PRESS

Great Clarendon Street, Oxford, OX2 6DP,
United Kingdom

Oxford University Press is a department of the University of Oxford.
It furthers the University's objective of excellence in research, scholarship,
and education by publishing worldwide. Oxford is a registered trade mark of
Oxford University Press in the UK and in certain other countries.

Published in the United States of America by Oxford University Press
546 Fifth Avenue, New York, NY 10036, United States of America

British Library Cataloguing in Publication Data
Data available

Library of Congress Control Number: 2026941864

ISBN 9780199679263

DOI: 10.1093/oso/9780199679263.001.0001

Printed and bound by
CPI Group (UK) Ltd., Croydon, CR0 4YY

The manufacturer's authorized representative in the EU for product safety is
Oxford University Press España S.A. of Parque Empresarial San Fernando de Henares,
Avenida de Castilla, 2 – 28830 Madrid (www.oup.es/en or product.safety@oup.com).
OUP España S.A. also acts as importer into Spain of products made by the manufacturer.

MIX
Paper | Supporting responsible forestry
FSC® C013604

FOREWORD

The phrase 'great battle' carries four immediate connotations. The first relates to time. The standard narrative, whether applied to Marathon or Waterloo, Salamis or Trafalgar, assumes that the events occurred on a single day—or at most over two or three days. Secondly, a battle has to be on a scale large enough not to be deemed a skirmish. Fighting may characterize war but fighting itself does not constitute a battle. If the forces involved are too small or the commitment to engage by one or both sides too slight, then what happens is not a great battle. At least one side, and possibly both, must want to fight. Third, a battle occurs in a defined, and in some cases a confined, space. On land it is sometimes so geographically limited that it takes its name from an otherwise little-known geographical feature, such as Bunker Hill, or an obscure village or hamlet. At sea, its name may be more capacious but as often it gains precision by adopting the name of the nearest landfall. Lastly, a 'great battle' implies that the consequences are commensurate with the commitment; in other words, that the result proves decisive.

The infrequency with which all these four conditions have been met helps explain why 'great battles' have been rare. Great battles need to be infrequent or they lose their cachet. Calling some forms of combat battles may be no more than a rhetorical device, coined for effect, or, more pragmatically, to give shape to otherwise seemingly inchoate episodes. Since the nineteenth century the word battle has been applied to events that are not concentrated in time and space. Persistent fighting in all seasons and all weathers combined with technological innovation and full social and economic mobilization to make outcomes more cumulative than singular. In the Second World War, the 'battle' of the Atlantic was decisive, both in the economic war and in enabling the D Day landings, but it was not clearly defined in time or space. It lasted nearly four years and, although largely restricted to the North Atlantic, still embraced an expanse of sea larger than any major continent.

At sea especially, battle in a traditional sense was rarely decisive. As the British naval theorist Julian Corbett observed in 1911, man lives upon the land, and so 'it scarcely needs saying that it is almost impossible that a war can be decided by naval action alone'. The Greeks may have checked the Persians at Salamis in 480 BC but they did not topple the Persian Empire. The Christian victory over the Turks at Lepanto in 1572 was similarly a great defensive success, which checked the Ottoman advance into the Mediterranean but not into continental Europe. On 21 October 1805 Nelson 'decisively' defeated the French and Spanish fleets at Trafalgar but war with France continued for another decade. In the short term too, while Nelson's victory ended the danger of a French invasion of Britain, it did not end Napoleon's freedom of manoeuvre within Europe. Just over six weeks after Trafalgar the French emperor won possibly his greatest victory, defeating the armies of Austria and Russia at Austerlitz on 2 December 1805. However, even in land warfare 'decisiveness' can be a relative, rather than an absolute, term. At Austerlitz Napoleon smashed the continental alliance which threatened him in the short term but he did not prevent its resuscitation in 1813. Nor did he win the economic and commercial war waged by Britain and underpinned by its maritime power.

In Corbett's day, the ability of warships to cope with adverse weather conditions enabled by the invention of steam power and the end of sail ought to have made naval battle more possible, but it did not necessarily do so, partly because improved navigation and advanced technology opened up more of the world's oceans and so created greater space in which an opponent could hide. Since the beginning of the twentieth century, war at sea has been increasingly fought under and over the surface, as well as on it. In the Second World War 'great battles' were fought in the Pacific simultaneously at sea and in the air with devastating effects—at Pearl Harbor in December 1941, the Coral Sea in May 1942, and Midway in the following month. Each was conducted at scale and was limited in time, if less so in space. Each was more clearly a 'great battle' in the classical definition than the whole of the battle of the Atlantic, but the war against Japan was also won by sustained economic warfare conducted by submarines and by island-hopping amphibious assaults. The Second World War did not end in a climactic battle like Waterloo in 1815. That final defeat of Napoleon, for many then and since, embodies the concept of decisiveness, not least because it introduced nearly a century of comparative European peace, but its outcome too rested as much on the exhaustion of France, and of its enemies, after two decades of conflict as it did on the results of a single day on a confined battlefield, however sanguinary the fighting.

For those who practise war in the twenty-first century the idea of a 'great battle' can seem no more than the echo of a remote past. The names on regimental colours or the events commemorated at mess dinners bear little relationship to patrolling in dusty villages or waging 'wars amongst the people'. Contemporary military doctrine downplays the idea of victory, arguing that wars end by negotiation not by the smashing of an enemy army or navy. Indeed, it erodes the very division between war and peace, and with it the aspiration to fight a culminating 'great battle'.

And yet to take battle out of war is to redefine war, possibly to the point where some would argue that it ceases to be war. Carl von Clausewitz, who experienced two 'great battles' at first hand—Jena-Auerstedt in 1806 and Borodino in 1812—wrote in *On War* that major battle is 'concentrated war' and 'the centre of gravity of the entire campaign'. Clausewitz's remarks related to the theory of strategy. He recognized that in practice armies might avoid battles, but even then the efficacy of their actions relied on the latent threat of fighting. Winston Churchill saw the importance of battles in different terms, not for their place within war but for their impact on historical and national narratives. His forebear, the Duke of Marlborough, fought four major battles and named his palace after the most famous of them, Blenheim, fought in 1704. Battles, Churchill wrote in his life of Marlborough, are 'the principal milestones in secular history'. For him, 'Great battles, won or lost, change the entire course of events, create new standards of values, new moods, new atmospheres, in armies and nations, to which all must conform.'

Clausewitz's experience of war was shaped by Napoleon. Like Marlborough, the French emperor sought to bring his enemies to battle. However, each lived within a century of the other, and they fought their wars in the same continent and even on occasion on adjacent ground. Winston Churchill's own experience of war, which spanned the late nineteenth-century colonial conflicts of the British Empire as well as two world wars, became increasingly distanced from the sorts of battle he and Clausewitz described. In 1898 Churchill rode in a cavalry charge in a battle which crushed the Mahdist forces of the Sudan in a single day. Four years later the British commander at Omdurman, Lord Kitchener, brought the South African War to a conclusion after a two-year guerrilla conflict in which no climactic battle occurred. Both Churchill and Kitchener served as British Cabinet ministers in the First World War, a conflict in which battles lasted weeks, and even months, and which, despite their scale and duration, did not produce clear-cut outcomes. The 'battle' of Verdun ran for all but one month of 1916 and that of the Somme for five months. The potentially decisive naval action at Jutland spanned a more traditional twenty-four-hour timetable but was not conclusive and was not replicated during the war.

Clausewitz would have called these twentieth-century 'battles' campaigns, or even seen them as wars in their own right. The determination to seek battle and to venerate its effects may therefore be culturally determined, the product of time and place, rather than an inherent attribute of war. The ancient historian Victor Davis Hanson has argued that seeking battle is a 'western way of war' derived from classical Greece. Seemingly supportive of his argument are the writings of Sun Tzu, who flourished in the warring states period in China between two and five centuries before the birth of Christ, and who pointed out that the most effective way of waging war was to avoid the risks and dangers of actual fighting. Hanson has provoked strong criticism: those who argue that wars can be won without battles are not only to be found in

Asia. Eighteenth-century European commanders, deploying armies in close-order formations in order to deliver concentrated fires, realized that the destructive consequences of battle for their own troops could be self-defeating. After the First World War, Basil Liddell Hart developed a theory of strategy which he called 'the indirect approach', and suggested that manoeuvre might substitute for hard fighting, even if its success still relied on the inherent threat of battle.

The winners of battles have been celebrated as heroes, and nations have used their triumphs to establish their founding myths. It is precisely for these reasons that their legacies have outlived their direct political consequences. Commemorated in painting, verse, and music, marked by monumental memorials, and used as the way points for the periodization of history, they have enjoyed cultural afterlives. These are evident in many capitals, in place names and statues, not least in Paris and London. The French tourist who finds himself in a London taxi travelling from Trafalgar Square to Waterloo Station should reflect on his or her own domestic peregrinations from the Rue de Rivoli to the Gare d'Austerlitz. Today's Mongolia venerates the memory of Genghis Khan, while Greece and Macedonia scrap over the rights to Alexander the Great.

This series of books on 'great battles' tips its hat to both Clausewitz and Churchill. Each of its volumes situates the battle which it discusses in the context of the war in which it occurred, but each then goes on to discuss its legacy, its historical interpretation and reinterpretation, its place in national memory and commemoration, and its manifestations in art and culture. These are not easy books to write. The victors were more often celebrated than the defeated; the effect of loss on the battlefield could be cultural oblivion. However, that point is not universally true: the British have done more over time to mark their defeats at Gallipoli in 1915 and Dunkirk in 1940 than their conquerors on both occasions. For the history of war to thrive and be productive it needs to embrace the view from 'the other side of the hill', to use the Duke of Wellington's words. The battle the British call Omdurman is for the Sudanese the battle of Kerreri; the Germans called Waterloo 'la Belle

Alliance' and Jutland Skagerrak. Indeed, the naming of battles could itself be a sign not only of geographical precision or imprecision (Kerreri is more accurate but as a hill, rather than a town, it is harder to find on a small-scale map), but also of cultural choice. In 1914 the German general staff opted to name their defeat of the Russians in East Prussia not Allenstein (as geography suggested) but Tannenberg, in order to claim revenge for the defeat of the Teutonic Knights in 1410.

Military history, more than many other forms of history, is bound up with national stories. All too frequently it fails to be comparative, to recognize that war is a 'clash of wills' (to quote Clausewitz once more), and so omits to address both parties to the fight. Cultural difference and even more linguistic ignorance can prevent the historian considering a battle in the round; so too can the availability of sources. Levels of literacy matter here, but so does cultural survival. Often these pressures can be congruent but they can also be divergent. Britain enjoys much higher levels of literacy than Afghanistan, but in 2002 the memory of the two countries' three wars flourished in the latter, thanks to an oral tradition, much more robustly than in the former, for whom literacy had created distance. And the historian who addresses cultural legacy is likely to face a much more challenging task the further in the past the battle occurred. The opportunity for invention and reinvention is simply greater the longer the lapse of time since the key event.

All historians of war must, nonetheless, never forget that, however rich and splendid the cultural legacy of a great battle, it was won and lost by fighting, by killing and being killed. The battle of Waterloo has left as abundant a footprint as any, but the general who harvested most of its glory reflected on it in terms which have general applicability and carry across time in their capacity to capture a universal truth. Wellington wrote to Lady Shelley in its immediate aftermath: 'I hope to God I have fought my last battle. It is a bad thing to be always fighting. While in the thick of it I am much too occupied to feel anything; but it is wretched just after. It is quite impossible to think of glory. Both mind and feelings are exhausted. I am wretched even at the moment of victory, and I always say that, next to a battle lost, the greatest misery is a battle gained.'

Readers of this series should never forget the immediate suffering caused by battle, as well as the courage required to engage in it: the physical courage of the warrior, the soldier, sailor, or airman, and the moral courage of the commander, ready to hazard all on its uncertain outcomes.

HEW STRACHAN

PREFACE

The Battle of Trafalgar took place on 21 October 1805, near the middle of the multiple phases of the Wars of the French Revolution and Empire that spanned the years 1793 to 1815. It took place twelve years from the outbreak of the series of wars and eleven years from the end of that span.

When one examines the actual events of Trafalgar side by side with the changing dimensions of memory, commemoration, and historical interpretation, a new understanding of the battle emerges. First, one can see that the British side of the Trafalgar campaign involved false and misleading intelligence at various points as well as failure in command coordination. Similarly, modern practitioners and students of maritime campaign planning and warfare find Napoleon's reputation as a military genius tarnished by the tale of Trafalgar. He failed to meet a fundamental aspect of modern thinking by having too many objectives during the Trafalgar campaign. His changing and overly detailed orders often left his naval commanders in confusion and with little discretion of their own as he attempted to micromanage naval affairs.

The occurrence of the battle at a point more than a decade before Napoleon's final defeat becomes a major historical problem that seems to belie the traditional claim for Trafalgar as one of the world's decisive naval battles. At the same time, modern historical scholarship now qualifies many past notions that proclaimed Nelson's tactics as innovative and flawlessly executed.

The study of the cultural afterlife of the battle of Trafalgar demonstrates how, over two centuries, commemoration has adapted, fragmented, and endured as political and social contexts have changed. The multiple meanings of the battle remain mutable, repeatedly reshaped to serve shifting political, cultural, moral, and emotional needs. For navies, Trafalgar has served as a framework for identity, learning, commemoration, and practice. In the long transformation from living memory to distant history, Nelson's enduring example of leadership, rather than imperial triumph, anchors modern remembrance and future relevance.

During the commemorative Nelson decade, 1995-2005, when professional historians analysed Admiral Lord Nelson's battles in the lead-up to the international bicentenary commemoration in 2005, the field of naval history was transformed, gained academic authority, and developed multi-disciplinary approaches that incorporated political, economic, cultural, and social history. For modern historians, understanding the battle of Trafalgar demands integrating maritime, military, logistical, organizational, and economic interpretations over the nineteenth-century idea embodied in the myth of decisive battles. Drawing on this broader intellectual background, modern historians conclude that the Battle of Trafalgar was tactically decisive but strategically limited, while its long-term influence lies in its cultural power and global naval legacy.

ACKNOWLEDGEMENTS

At first glance, specialists in naval history might think that there is little excuse for publishing another book on the Battle of Trafalgar. This seems particularly true after the vast outpouring of so many books, pamphlets, and articles on both the battle and the life of Admiral Lord Nelson in the years between 1995 and 2005. In those years, much new scholarly research was done during the bicentennial decade on the naval aspects in the period of the Wars of the French Revolution and Napoleon that took place between 1795 and culminated at Trafalgar in 1805. The impetus of the research interests that arose during the bicentenary carried over into the following decade with the publication of important additional works that have also carried the naval theme forward to the end of the Napoleonic Wars in 1815.

A series such as this one—designed to provide a succinct look at a wide range of battles through the multiple perspectives of war history, culture, and memory—would have a gaping hole if Trafalgar were to be omitted. Nevertheless, that alone is an insufficient excuse for this book. What does provide a rational purpose is that this volume can attempt to be both an introduction to a vast and complex literature in several languages from differing national perspectives, while at the same time serving to summarize the state of scholarly understanding in the wake of such a large and diverse body of publications.

With that humble purpose in mind for this book, the first acknowledgement must be to the several hundred writers, scholars, and naval professionals who over two centuries have worked to portray, to elucidate, and to commemorate in numerous efforts to better understand the events and the meaning of the Battle of Trafalgar. This little volume rests on their shoulders.

ACKNOWLEDGEMENTS

I am grateful to the constructive criticism of several scholars who read various chapter drafts. These include Roger Knight and Agustín Guimerá and the members of the Naval War College's Hattendorf Historical Center Working Group, particularly Tim Demy, Bill Leeman, Craig Symonds, Geoff Till, and Evan Wilson. In addition, the anonymous readers' reports from Oxford University Press provided further valuable guidance.

JOHN B. HATTENDORF
Newport,
Rhode Island 2024

CONTENTS

LIST OF ILLUSTRATIONS

LIST OF DIAGRAMS, TABLES, AND GRAPHS

Figure 1.1 (Upper right) Vice Admiral Pierre Charles Silvestre de Villeneuve (1763–1806), French Navy, commander-in-chief of the Combined Franco-Spanish Fleet. Portrait by Edmé Quenedey des Ricets (1756–1830) and engraved by Gilles Louis Chretien (1754–1811); (Upper left) Captain-General Federico Gravina y Napoli (1756–1806), Spanish Navy. Bust by Gaetano Merchi, 1799. (Bottom) Vice-Admiral Horatio Lord Nelson (1758–1805), Royal Navy, at Merton House in early September 1805. Engraving of a chalk drawing by John M. Whichelo. The Print Collector/Alamy Images; INTERFOTO/Alamy Images; MUSEO NAVAL/Alamy Images.

1

The Trafalgar Campaign, January–August 1805

On 1 September 1805, Emperor Napoleon Bonaparte left Boulogne on the English Channel. He had just learned that the combined Franco-Spanish fleet had arrived at Cádiz on 20 August, but a week before, he had abruptly cancelled his Grand Dessein to invade England. Consequently, between 23 and 25 August, his newly named Grande Armée began leaving its coastal camps at Ambleteuse, Boulogne, and Étaples, and Napoleon turned his attention to military operations on the Rhine and in southern Germany. There, he planned a pre-emptive strike to defeat Austria's armies before a Russian army could support them.[1]

Napoleon possessed a keen understanding of naval command. During the early years of his reign, his primary emphasis was on utilizing the navy as a means of power projection to transport armies and weapons across the sea; he also developed plans for offensive operations against overseas colonies.[2] The news from Cádiz angered Napoleon. He had come to despise the admiral commanding the combined fleet, Vice-Admiral Pierre Charles Silvestre de Villeneuve. Napoleon had previously ordered him to go north to the Channel along with the Spanish squadron under Rear-Admiral Don Federico Carlos Gravina y Nápoli. Napoleon had wanted Villeneuve and Gravina to join with the Brest squadron to support his plan to invade England. Instead, Villeneuve's delays and adverse winds, along with a changing strategic situation, forced Napoleon to move in a different direction. 'Villeneuve is a wretch who must be ignominiously chased,' Napoleon wrote. 'Without plans, without courage, without public interest, he would sacrifice everything so that he saves his skin. Nothing is comparable to the ineptitude of Villeneuve.'[3] He angrily directed the minister of the French Navy, Admiral Denis Decrès, to order Villeneuve into action.

Writing from Boulogne on 1 September 1805, Decrès laid out for Villeneuve the emperor's new expectations. Decrès explained that Napoleon wanted to end the French Navy's typically defensive approach. A defensive attitude kills audacity and doubles that of the enemy, Decrès wrote. The French Navy's admirals, captains, officers, and sailors all need to show boldness in action. Decrès explained that those who carry audacity to excess and do not hesitate to attack superior or equal forces could fight battles of extermination. The loss of our ships means nothing if lost with glory. Decrès told Villeneuve that if an inferior, or even a comparable, enemy squadron blockades the squadron at Cádiz, he should not hesitate to attack it.[4]

Although typical of the kind of orders he often issued to the army, Napoleon's directive to Villeneuve through Decrès was exceptional for the French Navy. It was perhaps the first time in French naval history that a French government had ordered an admiral to seek a battle to destroy an enemy as a primary objective rather than to protect a convoy or carry out some other naval mission. Both the French Navy and the Spanish Navy had successfully employed a defensive strategy that avoided combat and concentrated on specific missions. This strategy had been particularly effective for them during the American War of Independence.[5] Napoleon typically ordered his naval commanders to engage only smaller British naval forces and avoid combat against forces that were equal to or superior to their own. In this case, however, Napoleon's frustration with Villeneuve produced an angry, rash directive.

The tension between Napoleon, the navy, and Villeneuve had grown for months. When Napoleon undertook his expedition to Egypt in 1798, his favourite admiral was Vice-Admiral Honoré Joseph Antoine, Comte de Ganteaume, who remained a naval advisor to the emperor for years to come. While Ganteaume was serving in the administrative role as prefect at Brest, Napoleon respected his advice that an unsupported invasion flotilla was not feasible and suggested instead the use of a light squadron to release the Brest squadron from the British blockade, allowing the Brest squadron to seize control of the Channel. He soon moved Ganteaume to command the Brest squadron. In 1804, with rumours of an attack and impending invasion of Martinique, Napoleon turned to the charismatic Vice-Admiral Louis-René Levassor, Comte de Latouche-Tréville, to command the Toulon squadron. As a frigate captain, Latouche-Tréville had distinguished himself during the American War of Independence, and later, as an admiral commanding the naval defence at Boulogne in 1801, he had successfully frustrated Vice-Admiral Horatio Nelson's attack on that port. Napoleon's hopes for the highly popular and optimistic Latouche-Tréville evaporated suddenly with the admiral's fatal heart attack on board his flagship in Toulon harbour on 19 August 1804.[6] Napoleon and Decrès debated the choice of a successor. After considering several senior flag officers, Decrès advised Napoleon that the best option in the current state of things was Villeneuve. 'But,' Decrès lamented, 'our admirals are rare, old, and one must use the word, a little lukewarm.'[7] Contrasting starkly with Latouche-Tréville's energy and charismatic leadership, Villeneuve's outlook was one of profound pessimism.[8]

Four major issues mark the story of the Trafalgar campaign. First, Napoleon tended to assume that fleets—like army corps—could be easily manipulated and moved about on a map without sufficient regard for weather and logistical problems. He tended to attribute a naval commander's inability to adhere to his arbitrary schedule to a failure of will and capability. Second, the generally slow speed of communication in the age of sail meant that weeks or even months might pass from the time an order was issued to when a deployed commander received it. Napoleon gave his naval commanders little discretion in implementing his intentions. It was nearly impossible to micromanage a complex campaign by detailed written orders to forces hundreds and even thousands of miles away. Often, the circumstances that had triggered the orders in the first place had already changed by the time the orders arrived. The situation was further complicated as Napoleon increasingly used the semaphore system that Claude Chappe had developed and installed between Paris and Brest in 1798 to communicate rapidly with the admirals in port at Brest, while similar lines were not in place for other major naval ports. Third, intelligence on enemy movements was often challenging to obtain, and misleading information led commanders astray. The matter was complicated further if the system of communication and sharing intelligence among commanders was inefficient. Fourth, Napoleon often undermined the effectiveness of his naval strategic moves by ordering his commanders to pursue multiple objectives rather than focusing on a single central goal. Napoleon's inclusion of troops in his overseas expedition to the West Indies took up space on board the ships that might otherwise have been used for much-needed supplies in those areas. However, Napoleon's decision to include troops was a key part of his strategy of deception and misinformation to lead British forces astray to his advantage. Always optimistic, Napoleon gave his commanders secondary and tertiary objectives to accomplish in the West Indies, which gave them something to occupy themselves usefully while still focusing on his primary objective of controlling the Channel. Always optimistic, he expected his commanders to accomplish all their objectives.[9] Despite these issues, Napoleon's Grand Dessein to invade Britain came close to success, but the outcome depended heavily on contingencies.

Napoleon's Initial Naval Plans

In late September 1804, shortly after Latouche-Tréville's death, Napoleon directed Decrès to prepare three major naval expeditions for 1805. First, Napoleon planned to launch an attack on Surinam on the coast of South America. Then, he planned an attack on Martinique in the West Indies, followed by aiding the French West African colony of Sénégal, and continuing on to seize the distant British outpost of St Helena in the South Atlantic. He soon abandoned the idea of sending a squadron to West Africa and the South Atlantic. In December 1804, he assigned the two other campaign objectives jointly to Vice-Admiral Édouard-Thomas de Burgues, Comte de Missiessy, who commanded the squadron at Rochefort on the Atlantic coast, and to Villeneuve, who led the squadron at Toulon in the Mediterranean.[10]

Napoleon ordered Villeneuve to proceed to the West Indies to force British forces to relinquish the Dutch and French colonies that they occupied: Surinam, Berbice, Demerara, Essequibo, Trinidad, Dominica, and Saint Lucia. Then, Villeneuve was tasked with protecting the French colonies of Martinique and Guadeloupe while also dispatching reinforcements to Saint-Domingue. The orders spelled out exactly how and in what order Villeneuve should undertake these operations and where to join Missiessy. Napoleon also sent similar orders to Missiessy.[11]

Napoleon's orders directed Villeneuve to stay no longer than sixty days in the West Indies after he arrived at Surinam. When this mission was complete, Napoleon directed that Villeneuve and Missiessy should return across the Atlantic together. Having diverted British forces to the West Indies, they were to proceed to Spain's northern coast and raise the British blockade of El Ferrol that held in check four French warships and a Spanish squadron. Then, all available French naval forces were to rendezvous at the anchorage off the Îsle d'Aix near the mouth of the Charente River in preparation for Napoleon's planned invasion of Britain.

Meanwhile, in May 1804, William Pitt succeeded Henry Addington as prime minister with Henry Dundas, Viscount Melville, as First Lord of the Admiralty. At about the same time, Rear-Admiral Alexander F. I. Cochrane succeeded Rear-Admiral Sir Edward Pellew in command of the blockading force off El Ferrol. Lacking Pellew's skill in maintaining cordial diplomatic relations in the local area, Cochrane concluded inaccurately that Spain was bent on going to war with Britain, awaiting only the arrival of a squadron of frigates carrying silver from South America. Based on Cochrane's assessment, Pitt and his ministry decided on a pre-emptive strike to prevent the silver from reaching Spain, justifying it as a refusal to tolerate the subsidy treaty that Napoleon had forced Spain to accept the previous year. Captain Graham Moore, with four frigates, intercepted the Spanish frigates as they approached Cádiz and captured three with a fourth exploding, killing the wife and daughters of a returning governor. As a result of Britain's unannounced, unprovoked, and illegal attack on its neutrality, Spain's government, under its First Secretary of State Manuel de Godoy, decided, following a break in relations, on 14 December 1804 to declare war on Britain. In doing so, Spain withdrew her neutrality and joined Napoleon, Spain's ideological enemy, who represented revolutionary and imperial France. The Spanish declaration of war transformed Napoleon's naval capability, doubling his fleet and providing several superior Spanish ships and naval officers to those in the French Navy.[12]

As the French military and naval preparations were underway and Spain was entering the war, Napoleon wrote two goading letters. The first was to King George III in January 1805, offering a peace proposal. 'Oh, what a sad prospect for people to fight just to fight! The world is big enough for our two nations to be able to live there, and Reason has enough power to find the means to reconcile everything if both sides have the will.'[13] The next day, Napoleon wrote to his new ally, King Carlos IV of Spain, encouraging him to use his navy: 'It is neither fair nor consistent that Spain has the best colonies in Europe, if it cannot show energy or put its squadrons in readiness,' Napoleon told the king.[14] Shortly after that, he directed Decrès to send a letter that Napoleon had prepared to pass to the Spanish Ambassador in France, Rear-Admiral Gravina. This letter informed Gravina of the status of French forces and requested that Spain have twenty-five to twenty-nine warships and 4,700 troops ready to deploy with French forces for purposes that he would reveal later.[15]

Following orders to sail as soon as possible, Missiessy was the first to sea on 11 January from Rochefort. He sailed with five ships of the line and two frigates, carrying the expeditionary force under General Joseph Lagrange. Although two frigates under Rear-Admiral Sir Thomas Graves, commanding the Royal Navy's Western squadron, sighted Missiessy's squadron from a distance, Missiessy successfully slipped through the British blockading force. On receiving Graves's report of Missiessy's movement, the Admiralty in London wondered whether the French admiral's destination was the West Indies or the Mediterranean. A violent storm from the south-west prevented the British frigates from following Missiessy's squadron, and he arrived undetected off Martinique on 20 February 1805 after a fourteen-day passage. Eventually, the Admiralty ordered Sir Alexander Cochrane to pursue Missiessy, but only after Missiessy had been in Martinique for a week.[16]

At Toulon, Villeneuve had also prepared to sail in response to the same orders that Missiessy had received but he was far less successful. Vice-Admiral Horatio Lord Nelson had been commander-in-chief of Britain's Mediterranean squadron since June 1803. The Admiralty had ordered him to take up a station off Toulon that 'was most proper for enabling you to take, sink, burn, or otherwise destroy, any Ships or Vessels belonging to France'.[17] The primary purpose was for the British Mediterranean squadron to play a key role in defending Sicily, Naples, and Sardinia against a French attack, as well as to prevent a French attack on the eastern Mediterranean.

On 10 January 1805, Nelson's squadron watching Toulon had left its station temporarily to resupply in the Maddalena Islands, between Corsica and Sardinia. Taking the opportunity provided, Villeneuve sailed at dawn on 18 January.[18] Two of Nelson's frigates trailed Villeneuve's movements from Toulon until they reached the latitude of Ajaccio, Corsica. As Villeneuve sailed onward in a south-south-westerly direction, the British frigates broke off, shadowing the French fleet. Mistakenly assuming that Villeneuve would remain on course, both frigates sailed for Maddalena to report the news to Nelson. Based on the frigates' report and other intelligence, Nelson concluded that Villeneuve was heading to attack Sardinia, Naples, or Malta, all places of crucial importance for the British position in the Mediterranean. In response, Nelson ordered his squadron to sail from its anchorage in Agincourt Sound in the Maddalena Islands, despite a north-westerly gale, on the evening of 19 January. Passing along the eastern coast of Sardinia to block an attempt against Naples and Sicily, Nelson reached Sardinia's southern tip, where a westerly gale prevented him from sailing further until the weather moderated on 26 January.

Unbeknownst to Nelson, Villeneuve's squadron had not been able to cope with the storm and turned back to Toulon on 19 January, the day that Nelson had sailed from Agincourt Sound. Having found no active threat to Sicily, Naples, and Sardinia, and with no further intelligence about Villeneuve's squadron's other movements, Nelson turned his attention to the next most important areas for the defence of British interests in the Mediterranean. These were Malta, the Peloponnesian peninsula (then known as the Morea), and Egypt. Hearing a report that Napoleon had recalled the French ambassador in Constantinople, Nelson deduced that Egypt was Villeneuve's objective. With assurances from the Morea and Malta, Nelson set sail directly for Alexandria, where he arrived on 7 February.

Finding no sign of Villeneuve in Near Eastern waters, he returned to the western Mediterranean. He sailed via Malta, Sicily, and the south coast of Sardinia. There, he learned that Villeneuve had gone back to Toulon but was now planning to leave port again. Therefore, between 12 and 19 March, Nelson's squadron returned to its patrol off Toulon.[19]

Villeneuve had returned to port discouraged and demoralized by his inability to get his squadron to sea. He betrayed his defeatist attitude as well as frustration with the numerous practical problems his squadron faced. He explained to Decrès, 'It was impossible to manoeuvre because of the broken yards, sails carried away, because of all our damage, there have been as many faults of awkwardness and inexperience as defects in the quality of things delivered by the arsenals.'[20] Napoleon, who had little understanding of practical naval matters, saw this as just another example of ineptitude and inexperience.

Napoleon's 'Grand Dessein'

As always, Napoleon was impatient, continually revising his plans and orders to achieve his strategic objectives. The constant flow of changes created ongoing challenges for the commanders attempting to implement his changing strategies. Napoleon's new alliance with Spain brought additional forces and, at the same time, presented him with new strategic options to consider. On 2 March 1805, he issued new orders to his naval commanders that encapsulated his 'Grand Dessein' to invade Great Britain. He sent detailed orders both to Vice-Admiral Ganteaume, commanding the Atlantic squadron at Brest, and to Villeneuve, who was still in port at Toulon.[21] Napoleon's new strategic idea was, first, to concentrate the available Franco-Spanish naval forces in the West Indies to draw British naval forces away from blockading the French naval arsenals. Then, the combined Franco-Spanish fleet would return to the eastern Atlantic and appear in the English Channel. They would then escort Napoleon's invasion army from its camps in the Pas-de-Calais across the Channel to the shores of England.

Napoleon's new plan required the French Navy's strongest squadron, the Brest squadron under Ganteaume, to proceed to El Ferrol without engaging British forces. There, he wanted to evade the British blockade, which held nine Spanish warships and five French warships in port. Then, all these ships would sail together to the rendezvous at Martinique to accomplish Napoleon's objectives in the West Indies. Simultaneously, Napoleon ordered Villeneuve's squadron to leave Toulon without engaging Nelson's squadron and sail to the West Indies. After passing through the Strait of Gibraltar, Villeneuve was to raise the British blockade off Cádiz. Then, he would bring with him to the West Indies the one French warship there, along with the squadron of six Spanish warships commanded by the former Spanish ambassador to France, Rear-Admiral Gravina. To further strengthen this naval force, Napoleon ordered Vice-Admiral Missiessy to keep his Rochefort squadron in the West Indies and rendezvous with the other two squadrons. Napoleon envisioned that all three squadrons, operating together under the overall command of Vice-Admiral Ganteaume, would, on their return, create the massive naval force necessary to facilitate the French invasion of Britain.[22]

Both France and Spain had significant navies (Tables 1.1, 1.2). If they had joined their navies in 1793, as they had done during the American War of Independence between 1779 and 1783, they would have been more than one third larger than the British Navy.[23] For financial reasons, both countries scaled back their naval building programmes in the 1790s due to a lack of sufficient funding. In France, the navy's budget between 1793 and 1810 remained at 15–17 per cent of the total military budget. No new major Spanish warships were launched after 1798. By 1805, the margin of superiority in numbers over the Royal Navy had largely disappeared. French warship building averaged six to seven ships a year. In the 1790s, King Carlos IV and Godoy planned to expand the Spanish Navy from 200 to 310 ships, including seventy-six new

Table 1.1 French naval forces in commission at the opening of the 1805 campaign.

	118 guns	80 guns	74 guns	Total
Brest	4	5	17	26
Lorient		1		1
Rochefort	1		4	5
El Ferrol			5	5
Cádiz			1	1
Toulon	3	8		11
TOTAL	8	14	27	49

Table 1.2 Spanish ships of the line at the opening of the 1805 campaign.

	Armed and Ready	Disarmed	Total
El Ferrol	7	8	15
Cádiz	6	16	22
Cartagena	2	9	11
TOTAL	15	33	48

Note: Of the thirty-three disarmed ships, eighteen could be mobilized within a few months.

Table 1.3 The Royal Navy's stations worldwide.

Ports and anchorages at home: Portsmouth, Plymouth, Nore, Leith, Cork
Leeward Islands
Jamaica
North America
Newfoundland
South America
Lisbon
Mediterranean
Cape of Good Hope
East Indies

ships of the line; however, this would have required more than 110,000 men, far beyond what was available. The number of Spanish seamen remained static through the early 1800s.[24]

Lacking knowledge of Napoleon's new plan, British naval forces were deployed strategically in key locations worldwide. British warships were spread across fourteen stations, each with a commander in chief (Table 1.3).

The number of warships, particularly the ships of the line that Britain, France, and Spain were able to put to sea, was a key factor in the Battle of Trafalgar. Britain's naval superiority in achieving this was a close-run competition that involved much more than just global reach and the number of ships. There were extensive logistical requirements necessary to maintain the fleet at sea and to provide essential food and water for the men manning the ships. The timely repair and maintenance of warships by a skilled and dedicated labour force in the dockyards and in private yards were crucial factors that involved substantial changes in methodology during 1805. Lord Melville's success in quickly reversing the decline in the dockyards that Admiral Lord St. Vincent had initiated as First Lord of the Admiralty between 1801 and 1804 was a significant aspect. New ship construction as well as repair depended upon the dependable arrival of the key naval stores from the Baltic ports. Britain's ability to finance and obtain the resources for these ends was another critical aspect behind the Trafalgar campaign. Beyond defence industrial support, a further significant British advantage lay in the area of seamanship, facilitated by the extensive and uninterrupted experience of British seamen in staying at sea in all types of weather, manoeuvring fleets, and handling individual ships.[25]

All the foregoing issues combined to enable Britain to substantially increase the number of warships the Royal Navy could maintain on station during the campaign and leading up to the Battle of Trafalgar, as shown in Graphs 1.1 and 1.2. During these years, the overall number of British warships on station increased by a total of forty-five vessels, while the number of ships of the line increased by twenty during 1805 alone.[26]

Within the geographical areas close to France, British naval forces concentrated at the western approaches to the Channel. They blockaded the principal French and Spanish naval ports of Brest, Rochefort, El Ferrol, Cádiz, Cartagena, and Toulon. The purpose of these concentrations was more than to defend Britain's maritime and imperial interests at home and abroad. It was to neutralize and ultimately

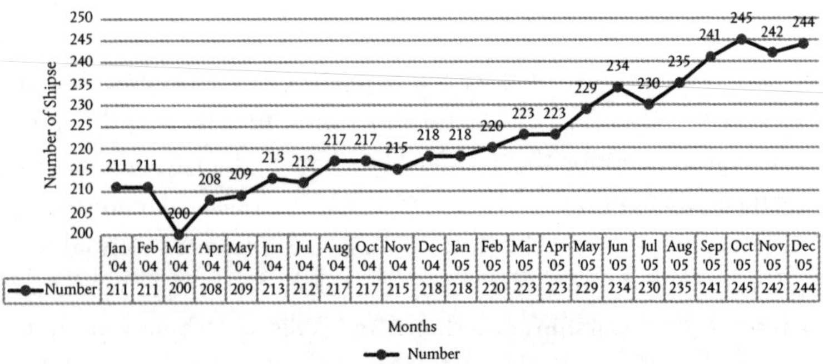

Graph 1.1 The rise in the number of British warships on station worldwide from January 1804 to December 1805.

Admiralty List Books. TNA, ADM 8/87–90. With thanks to Roger Knight, who supplied the raw data he also used in 'The Fleets at Trafalgar: The Margin of Superiority', in Canadine, ed., *Trafalgar in History*, p. 73.

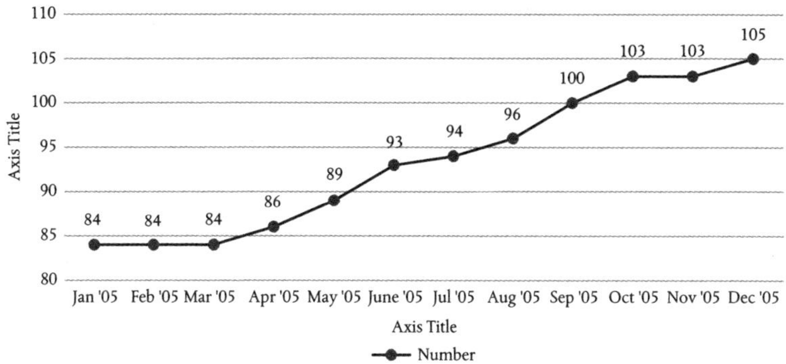

Graph 1.2 The rise in the number of British ships of the line on station worldwide during 1805.

Admiralty List Books. TNA, ADM 8/87–90. With thanks to Roger Knight, who supplied the raw data he also used in 'The Fleets at Trafalgar: The Margin of Superiority', in Canadine, ed., *Trafalgar in History*, p. 73.

destroy French and Spanish naval forces as part of the broader effort to defeat Napoleon definitively on land and at sea.[27]

Despite the vagaries of wind and weather, by late March 1805, the various French squadrons had completed their preparations and were ready for sea. But all was not quite going according to Napoleon's plan. In the West Indies, Missiessy carried out his orders and attacked Dominica with the 3,400 troops he had brought with him under General Lagrange. He also used additional forces under Admiral Louis-Thomas Villaret-Joyeuse, the captain-general of Martinique and St Lucia. The British troops were cornered but managed to hold out during the siege. Eventually, the British governor of Dominica ransomed the island, and French forces departed. When Missiessy's forces attacked Nevis, St Kitts, and Montserrat, the British residents of those islands also ransomed themselves. After debarking the troops that had accompanied him from France as reinforcements for Saint-Domingue, Martinique, and Guadeloupe, Missiessy concluded that Ganteaume had been unable to break out of Brest. He did not receive Napoleon's new orders dated 27 February to remain on station until the end of June. So, following his original orders, he dutifully sailed for France on

28 March. After a slow fifty-three-day passage across the Atlantic, Missiessy and his squadron returned to Rochefort on 21 May. While Missiessy felt that he had done very well, Napoleon was irritated with him for failing to take Dominica. Feigning ill health, Missiessy resigned, and Rear-Admiral Zacharie Allemand took command of the Rochefort squadron.[28]

Meanwhile, Ganteaume wrote to Napoleon from Brest that he and his squadron were ready to sail, but fifteen British warships were blocking the harbour entrance. It would be necessary to fight his way out.[29] Napoleon responded forcefully by telegraph on 23 March, 'A naval victory in that circumstance would lead to nothing. You have only one goal, which is to fulfil your mission. Sortie without combat. What should join you [Villeneuve's squadron] is gone.'[30] In fact, Villeneuve's squadron had not yet left Toulon, and Ganteaume was in a quandary as to what he should do.

On 26 March, Ganteaume thought that a misty day with poor visibility might allow him to elude the British blockade off Brest, and he sailed out through the narrow Goulet passage with twenty-one ships of the line. A vigilant British blockading force of eighteen or nineteen ships of the line, temporarily under the command of the unassuming but highly professional Vice-Admiral Sir Charles Cotton, prevented Ganteaume from getting further than the outer harbour. Anchoring in Camaret and Bertheaume bays, Ganteaume soon found these exposed anchorages untenable as the weather worsened. Unable to get to the open sea without a battle, Ganteaume and his squadron retreated to the safety of Brest on 27 March.[31]

Villeneuve's Second Departure and Nelson's Reaction

Meanwhile, at Toulon, Villeneuve's squadron continued its preparations. Finally, on 30 March, his fleet put to sea in the late afternoon with eleven ships of the line with Rear-Admiral Pierre Dumanoir Le Pelley as second in command. The squadron included four 80-gun ships, five frigates, a corvette, a brig, and 3,411 embarked soldiers. With a north-east wind, Villeneuve sailed in a south-west direction, trailed by two British frigates, *Active* and *Phoebe. Active* immediately sailed to give the intelligence to Nelson, whose main force was patrolling off the south coast of Sardinia in the Gulf of Palmas. There, *Active* found him on 4 April. During the night, *Phoebe* lost sight of Villeneuve and left to report to Nelson. That night, the wind shifted to the east, and Villeneuve turned to pass north of Majorca, heading towards the coast of Spain. Villeneuve, hereby, evaded Nelson's waiting squadron as well as the frigate that Nelson had placed between Sardinia and North Africa. Undisturbed, Villeneuve sailed south, paralleling the coast to the Spanish naval base at Cartagena, where he arrived on 7 April. The British frigates' failure to observe these movements brought the French a decisive advantage, again leaving Nelson entirely in the dark as to French intentions.[32]

Nelson's cruisers spread out to guard Naples, Malta, Sicily, and the coast of Tunisia. Nelson himself took a central position in the area between the Sardinian and the North African coast. As the days passed without any intelligence of the French, he fretted, 'I must not make more haste than good speed, and leave Sardinia, Sicily, or Naples for them to take, should I go either to the eastward or westward, without knowing something more about them.'[33]

On 10 April, Nelson received intelligence that a Russian squadron of seven ships of the line was entering the Mediterranean through the Bosporus and that British transport ships had brought the long-awaited additional troops under Lieutenant-General Sir James Craig. This news led Nelson to imagine that Villeneuve had headed west to attack the convoy of troopships. He, therefore, immediately sailed west against strong westerly and north-westerly winds, leaving five frigates off Sardinia. He made slow headway against the contrary winds. Finally, on 16 April, he learned that sixteen warships had been seen nine days earlier off Cape de Gata between Cartagena and Gibraltar. Subsequent reports verified that Villeneuve had passed through the Strait of Gibraltar on 8 April.[34]

The news gave Nelson great anxiety. He suddenly realized that his fears of a French attack on Italy or in the eastern Mediterranean were misguided. He saw clearly that his critics and service enemies would use this double failure against him. At the same time, he still did not know Villeneuve's intentions. Weighing the possibilities, he thought that the French might have gone west to attack British possessions in the West Indies or sailed north to intercept Craig's troops, attack Ireland, or even the Channel. At this point, Nelson first began to favour the interpretation that Villeneuve's objective might be to join with the Brest squadron for the invasion of Britain. Among all the possibilities, this one presented the existential threat. He believed that the intelligence reports that confirmed Villeneuve's conjunction with the Spanish warships at Cartagena suggested something more than a raid in the West Indies. He could, of course, also obtain additional Spanish reinforcements at Cádiz.

When Nelson arrived at Rosia Bay, Gibraltar, on 6 May, it was nearly a month since Villeneuve had passed through the strait. Nelson had heard nothing from Vice-Admiral Sir John Orde, commanding the British blockade off Cádiz. The blockading duty off Cádiz had previously been part of the Mediterranean command. In October 1804, the Admiralty decided to make it an independent command, as Orde was senior to Nelson. As a result, Orde did not report to Nelson and, therefore, chose not to share any information with him.[35]

The Rendezvous of French and Spanish Warships

Villeneuve reached Cartagena on 7 April and immediately contacted the local commander of the Spanish naval squadron, Lieutenant-General of the Navy José Justo Salcedo y Arauco. At that moment, Salcedo was readying six ships of the line, although none of them were yet in a condition to sail. The naval headquarters in Madrid had sent no orders for Salcedo and his squadron to join the French. After discussions with local authorities, Villeneuve decided to continue to Cádiz. The French squadron passed Gibraltar's fortress on the morning of 9 April and entered the Strait of Gibraltar with an easterly wind.

Villeneuve sent a frigate ahead with dispatches to advise the Spaniards at Cádiz of his imminent approach.[36]

Captain Lord Mark Kerr, commanding the British frigate *Fisgard* undergoing a major repair at the Gibraltar dockyard, sighted the French passing. So, too, did Captain Sir Richard Strachan, in command of the 74-gun *Renown*, off Cape Spartel in the Atlantic at the south-western entrance to the strait. Both took immediate action to warn Orde, whose squadron was anchored 9 miles off Cádiz. By four that afternoon, Orde saw the French approaching. Quickly realizing that the French outnumbered him, Orde sailed west with his squadron, then turned north towards the Channel, sending news ahead to the Admiralty. He did not, however, attempt to alert Nelson despite Strachan's recommendation that he do so.[37]

On the evening of 9 April, Villeneuve anchored off Cádiz and contacted Gravina, now commanding the Cádiz squadron, consisting of two 80-gun ships of the line, one 74, two 64s, a frigate, and a brig, along with a French 74-gun ship of the line, a brig, and a corvette.[38] Having received his orders from Madrid, Gravina quickly began bringing his six ships out of port to join Villeneuve in the offshore anchorage. Not waiting until all the Spanish ships were out of the port, Villeneuve impatiently ordered the combined Franco-Spanish fleet on its transatlantic passage for Martinique at two o'clock in the morning on 10 April 1805.[39]

The Combined Franco-Spanish Fleet in the West Indies

With their combined fleet of eighteen ships of the line—twelve French and six Spanish—Villeneuve and Gravina crossed the Atlantic in five weeks. They arrived on 14 May, without incident, at Fort-de-France, Martinique. Heralding their arrival, a French frigate and three Spanish ships of the line arrived slightly in advance of the main body. Their first action was to request the impressment of sailors serving in local

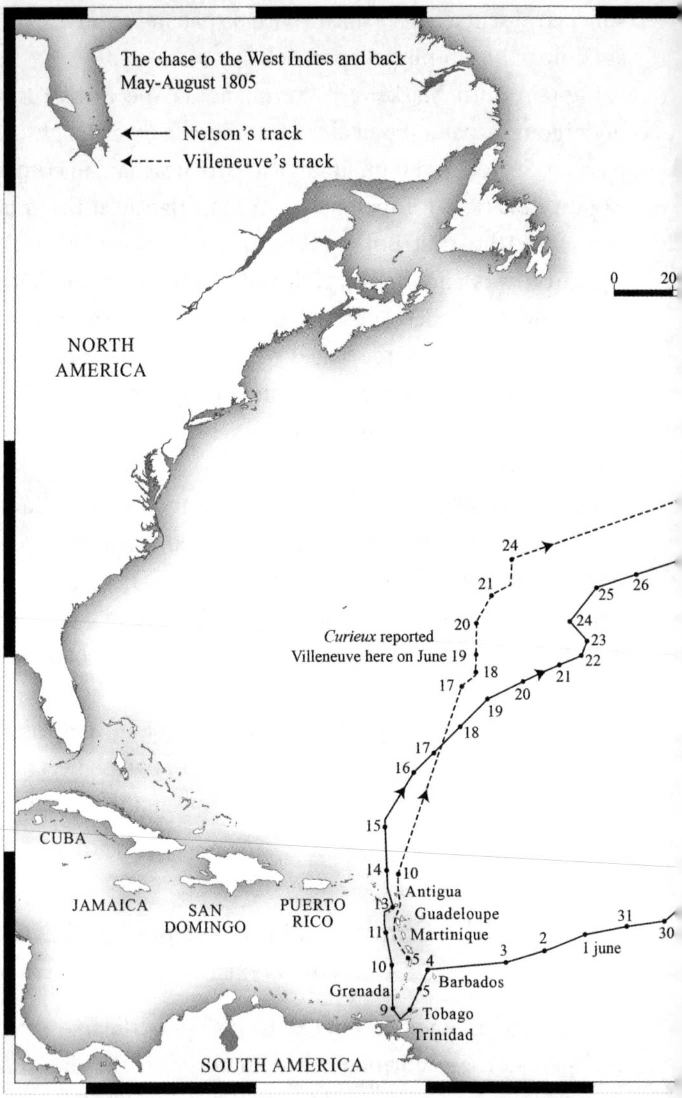

Diagram 1.1a The chase to the West Indies and back, May–August 1805 © 2025, Mappa Mundi Cartography.

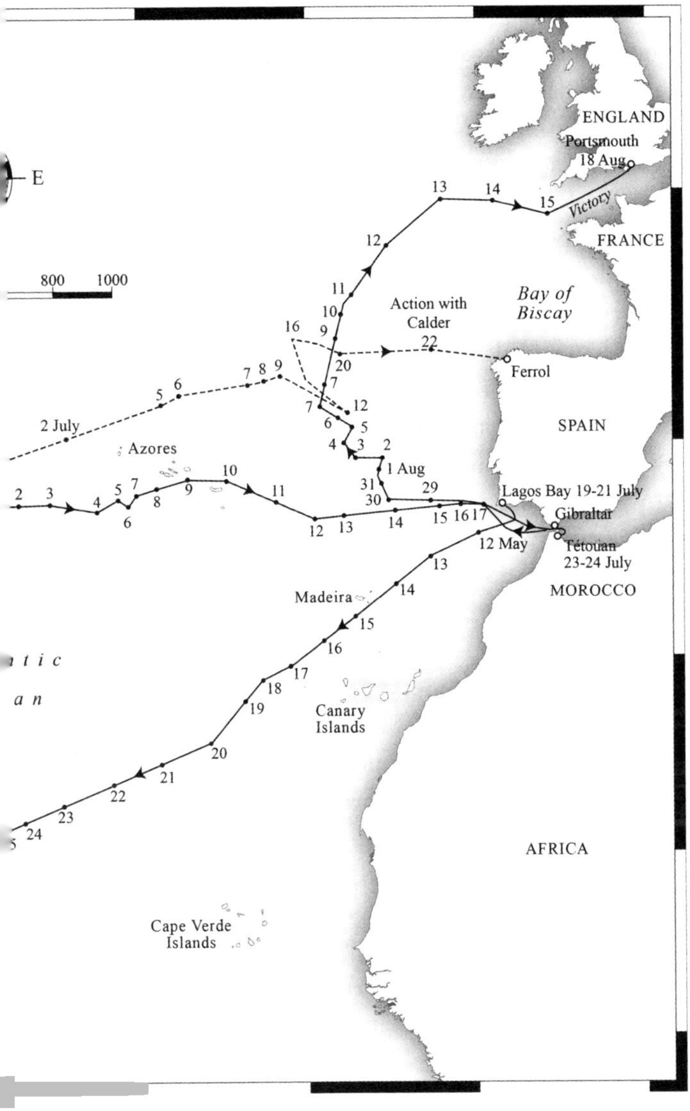
ENGLAND
Portsmouth
18 Aug
Victory
FRANCE
Bay of Biscay
Action with Calder
Ferrol
SPAIN
2 July
Azores
1 Aug
Lagos Bay 19-21 July
Gibraltar
Tétouan 23-24 July
12 May
MOROCCO
Madeira
Canary Islands
AFRICA
Cape Verde Islands
E
800
1000

Diagram 1.1b

Martinican and Guadeloupian privateers and merchant vessels to serve in the undermanned Spanish warships that had left Cádiz in haste. For the remainder of May, the squadron remained at anchor at Fort-de-France, replenishing its water and food supplies. During this period, Villeneuve began planning an attack on Dominica and dispatched two frigates to Guadeloupe to seek additional troops (Diagram 1.1).[40]

Meanwhile, Napoleon's active mind had been developing new plans. On 14 April, he ordered Rear-Admiral Charles René Magon de Médine to leave Rochefort with two 74-gun ships of the line carrying 860 troops and additional orders for Villeneuve. Magon left Rochefort on 1 May and arrived at Martinique on 3 June. A fast frigate, *Didon,* departed Lorient three days after Magon's departure and arrived at Martinique two days ahead of him with duplicate orders on 30 May. This was the first news that Villeneuve had of Napoleon's altered plans.

From Magon's arrival, Napoleon gave Villeneuve thirty-five days to carry out his earlier orders to attack British possessions. If, by that time, Admiral Ganteaume had not arrived in the West Indies, Villeneuve was to sail by the quickest route to El Ferrol in northern Spain. He was to evade the British blockade and join up with the fifteen Spanish and French ships of the line there. With the addition of these warships, Napoleon calculated that Villeneuve would have a squadron of thirty-five ships of the line. With this force, he was to appear before Brest and, without entering port, join the twenty-one ships of the line under Ganteaume. Now, with Villeneuve in overall command, rather than Ganteaume as previously planned, the fifty-six-ship fleet was to enter the Channel and rendezvous off Boulogne.[41]

When the frigate with these new orders arrived, Villeneuve was beginning to undertake his first action in the West Indies. Only after repeated requests from the captain-general at Martinique, Admiral Villaret-Joyeuse, Villeneuve moved to reduce H.M. Sloop-of-War Diamond Rock, the 600-hundred-foot-high rock pinnacle that Rear-Admiral Sir Samuel Hood had fortified in 1804, a mile off the entrance to Fort-de-France. By 29 May 1805, Villeneuve had assembled a large assault force to take the rock, but during that night a squall with heavy rain forced the attacking French and Spanish forces to the south of St Lucia. The defending British force erroneously sent a fast sloop to St Lucia and Barbados to alert the islanders of Trinidad and Tobago that Villeneuve was en route to attack them. The weather conditions prevented the British from seeing the same Franco-Spanish force return to support the attack on Diamond Rock. During the three-day siege that followed, the small British force exhausted all its available resources atop the rock and finally surrendered on June 2.[42]

Two days after the capture of Diamond Rock, Admiral Magon arrived from Rochefort on 4 June with his two-ship reinforcement that brought Villeneuve's squadron up to twenty ships of the line. Villeneuve now undertook the more extensive operations that Napoleon's orders required. His first and most important objective was to capture Barbados.[43]

The British Search for Villeneuve

While Villeneuve, Gravina, and Magon were making their way to the West Indies, Nelson and the British squadron in the Mediterranean were in the dark as to their whereabouts. At the same time, the Admiralty in London was in disarray as domestic politics obscured war operations. The same day that Villeneuve approached Gibraltar on 8 April, a financial management scandal forced the First Lord of the Admiralty, Henry Dundas, first Viscount Melville, to resign. It took three weeks for Pitt to establish Melville's replacement, Admiral Charles Middleton, first Baron Barham.

At two o'clock in the morning after Barham's first day in office, the news arrived from Orde that the French Toulon squadron and the Spanish squadron at Cádiz had combined. In London, the immediate concern was for the convoy carrying Sir James Craig's troops in the Mediterranean for operations with the Russians. No one at the Admiralty knew where Nelson was. The ministry immediately ordered Vice-Admiral Cuthbert Collingwood to take fourteen ships of the line from the Channel fleet and take whatever action was necessary to secure the sea area off Cádiz.[44]

When Nelson arrived at Lagos Bay, near Cape St Vincent on the south-west coast of Portugal on 6 May, it was twenty-seven days after the French had passed. He still had no firm intelligence as to where the Franco-Spanish squadron had gone. Sir John Orde had withdrawn from blockading Cádiz and headed north to report to the Admiralty. He had failed to assign a frigate to shadow the Combined Squadron and determine their likely route. For both the Admiralty and Nelson, their first concern was for the convoy carrying Craig's troops. There was no indication that Villeneuve had gone to the far side of the Atlantic, although some flag officers considered it a possibility. In London, British officials thought it more likely that Villeneuve might have doubled back to enter the Channel or to stand off and attack the approaching convoy.

Given the uncertainty, Rear-Admiral John Knight escorted Craig's troop transport convoy into the Tagus estuary at Lisbon for safety. Meanwhile, word arrived that Nelson's squadron was waiting to escort the convoy past Cádiz. To do that, Nelson added the 100-gun *Royal Sovereign*, the flagship of Rear-Admiral Sir Richard Bickerton, to Knight's 98-gun *Queen* and 74-gun *Dragon* and directed Bickerton to command the squadron in his absence. The diversion of the twenty-one-year-old *Royal Sovereign*, a slow ship but one of Nelson's most powerfully armed, reduced Nelson's squadron to ten ships of the line—half the number of Villeneuve's Combined Fleet. Additionally, while anchored in Lagos Bay on 10 May, Nelson's squadron took on board the provisions from the convoy that were intended to support Craig's troops.[45]

After making these arrangements, Nelson immediately sailed in pursuit of Villeneuve. Nelson sent three frigates out ahead on 11 May 1805, then sailed with the ships of the line the following day. Nelson was 38 leagues (about 114 nautical miles) off Madeira when Villeneuve reached Martinique on 14 May. At this point, Nelson thought that the French were undertaking a concerted attack on British possessions in the West Indies. He did not yet suspect that it was a feint to obscure Napoleon's principal objective of invading England. He circulated his thoughts to his captains about the decisive fleet battle that he anticipated during the crossing. The circumstances would be different from those at the Nile in 1798 or at Copenhagen in 1801. This time, he thought it likely that the opposing fleets would manoeuvre in open water. Nelson encouraged all to think about a decisive action involving few signals, uncomplicated manoeuvres, and the concentration of force with sustained close-range gunnery with ships supporting each other. Over many years, Nelson had given considerable thought to naval tactics in fleet battles. In the process, he also examined Kempenfelt's, Rodney's, and Howe's tactical ideas while gaining his own extensive command experience in fleet actions. Nelson's thinking reflected some of the ideas of Scottish writer John Clerk of Eldin in his influential 1790 book, *An Essay on Naval Tactics*, which had earlier influenced Admiral Richard Lord Howe in the Battle of the Glorious First of June in 1794 (Bataille du 13 Prairial, An 2).[46]

Nelson and Villeneuve in the West Indies

Nelson arrived in Barbados on 4 June. There, he found Rear-Admiral Alexander Cochrane with two ships of the line, having earlier followed Missiessy across the Atlantic. There, too, he learned that Missiessy had returned to France but that Villeneuve was still at Martinique with many sick sailors. Then he saw the report from Brigadier General Robert Brereton, commanding at St Lucia, that a large French fleet was sailing south, apparently for an attack on Trinidad and Tobago. Nelson immediately acted on this intelligence. He took aboard two thousand foot soldiers and 150 artillerymen for a landing force. Sailing the next morning, he soon found, upon arrival at the Port of Spain, Trinidad, that there had been no French attack. However, a dispatch boat from Barbados brought the news that the French had taken Diamond Rock. This news came with the inaccurate intelligence that the French and Spanish squadron at El Ferrol had reinforced Villeneuve, bringing his fleet up to thirty-two ships of the line.[47]

Early on the morning of 5 June, Villeneuve and the Franco-Spanish squadron embarked 780 soldiers, got underway from Fort-de-France, and sailed north to Guadeloupe, where they embarked an additional six hundred men before continuing north. He intended to capture the smaller British outposts on Montserrat and Antigua before turning south-east to attack his main objective: Barbados. En route north on 8 June, Villeneuve sighted a convoy of fourteen British colonial merchant ships with the 28-gun *Barbadoes* and armed schooner *Netley* as escorts. He immediately ordered a pursuit and captured the entire convoy, except for the escorts. This was the first convoy that the British lost entirely.[48]

On interrogating his British prisoners, Villeneuve learned for the first time that Nelson had arrived at Barbados. Villeneuve and Gravina thought that Nelson had twelve ships and that Cochrane's small squadron would add four more. They thought carefully about their choices in light of this and several other factors. First, their capture of the convoy had taken the combined fleet further north and to the leeward than they had initially planned. It would take them considerable time to beat back against the prevailing wind to Martinique. Napoleon's orders had explicitly stated that they should wait for Ganteaume until 9 July. Their logistical support was limited, and the health of the seamen was not good. Considering all these factors, Villeneuve and Gravina came to a joint decision. They reasoned that even if they could win a battle against Nelson's squadron, the West Indies' local logistical support would not be able to sustain the Combined Fleet after a battle. With their understanding of Napoleon's priorities and the uncertainty of Ganteaume joining them in the Caribbean, they jointly decided to leave the West Indies immediately. After offloading the local troops into four frigates for their return to their respective islands, the Combined Squadron sailed on 11 June. Following Napoleon's order, the Combined Squadron set its course for the Bay of Biscay and Spain's northern coast to release the Franco-Spanish squadron at El Ferrol from the blockade. At the same time, Villeneuve dispatched five frigates to report his impending return.[49]

Nelson's intelligence on Villeneuve's position remained either vague or inaccurate. After ascertaining that Trinidad was not in danger, he began to sail north. On 12 June, he reached Antigua, where Villeneuve had been just two days previously. Concluding that Villeneuve must have left the West Indies, the next day Nelson ordered his squadron to sail back across the Atlantic to Gibraltar. He did not know precisely where the Franco-Spanish fleet was going, nor whether they were sailing together as a single unit or separately. He suspected that the French would once again attempt to invade Egypt, and he sent warning dispatches ahead to the Admiralty and to British commanders cruising off El Ferrol, Cádiz, and Cape St Vincent to cover all the most likely options.[50]

The Return to European Waters

Heading north from the West Indies until 24 June, Villeneuve then turned to the east-north-east on his great circle route towards El Ferrol to pass north of the Azores. Nelson, heading for Cádiz, took a more southerly arc that took him directly through the Azores. On 2 July, the Combined Fleet captured and burned a British privateer, recapturing from her a Spanish merchant ship with valuable cargo. Both Villeneuve and Nelson had sent frigates ahead to inform their governments and responsible commanders of their imminent return. Before this information arrived, however, strategic viewpoints had already begun to change in both France and Great Britain. Napoleon continued to reconsider and modify his thoughts, eager to speed up the operation to invade Britain. At the same time, he convinced himself that Britain's weakness lay in its fatal flaw of depending on naval defences. He kept adjusting his timetable of operations. In mid-June, he thought that Villeneuve should be at El Ferrol between 20 and 29 July, then off Brest between 29 July and 8 August, and then off Boulogne between 8 and 18 August.

In London, officials expected that Nelson's presence in the West Indies would likely bring the Combined Fleet back to European waters, but no one knew precisely when or where this would occur. Lord Barham at the Admiralty thought it would be to the Mediterranean.

The Admiralty achieved some clarity on 7 July when H.M. brig *Curieux*, Commander George E. B. Bettesworth, arrived at Plymouth from Antigua after a twenty-four-day passage carrying dispatches from Nelson. En route, *Curieux* had sighted Villeneuve's Combined Squadron, making first to the north and then to the north-north-east, its track suggesting a landfall in the Bay of Biscay. Commander Bettesworth rushed overland from Plymouth with the news, reaching the Admiralty late on 8 July. Barham was already in the process of making new dispositions for the fleet and with this new intelligence he quickly became Britain's 'master-mind and director of the whole campaign'.[51]

Barham ordered Admiral Sir William Cornwallis, commanding the Channel fleet, to send the ships under Rear-Admiral Charles Stirling, then blockading Rochefort, as reinforcements to Vice-Admiral Sir Robert Calder, off El Ferrol. He then ordered Cornwallis to instruct Calder to cruise for the enemy 30 or 40 leagues (about 90 to 120 nautical miles or 167 to 222 km) to the west of Cape Finisterre for six to eight days. Cornwallis took the rest of the fleet under his immediate command to cruise at the same distances west and south of the Channel. Cornwallis received Barham's order off Brest on 11 July and moved to take station. Calder and Stirling joined forces and, with their combined fifteen ships of the line, proceeded to take their station. With these two sea barriers in place, the Royal Navy waited.

Meanwhile, oblivious to all this, Nelson landed at Gibraltar on 17 July and resupplied his fleet. By 25 July, he had heard the news of Villeneuve's northerly track and immediately sailed with his squadron back into the Atlantic, where he made slow progress against northerly winds.[52]

Combat du Cap Finisterre—Combat des Quinze-Vingt—Calder's Action, 22 July 1805

On 9 July, just as Barham was issuing his orders, a violent storm hit Villeneuve and Gravina's Combined Fleet as it was on course for Spain's northern coast. The high north-east winds and heavy seas forced the fleet off its planned track and onto a south-east course for three days. The French 80-gun *Indomptable* lost her mainmast, while other ships were damaged. The storm aggravated the sickness among the already ill sailors of the Spanish squadron and in the two French ships that Admiral Magon had brought to Villeneuve at Martinique.

Meanwhile, at Rochefort, Allemand had observed Stirling's departure on 15 July. Taking advantage of the opportunity, Allemand put to sea with five ships of the line on 17 July. On the same day in Paris, Decrès sent orders to Allemand *not* to leave port until Villeneuve appeared. Missing that order, Allemand followed his earlier orders to make a demonstration by appearing off the coast of Ireland. At the same time, Cornwallis stood offshore in preparation for Villeneuve's arrival. Out of sight at Brest, Napoleon and Decrès sent Ganteaume new orders to sail to the Channel to begin the invasion operation. This time, they ordered him to fight, but only if the British had no more than sixteen ships of the line.

Once again, Napoleon's naval plan was frustrated. Just as Ganteaume received his new orders, the British blockading force returned within sight of Brest. Sighting seventeen or eighteen British sail in the offing, Ganteaume followed his orders precisely and cancelled the plan to get under weigh from Brest.[53]

The storm drove Gravina and Villeneuve south to the latitude of Oporto, Portugal. On 12 July, they were finally able to reverse their course to the north-west. Three days later, they had reached latitude 44 degrees, where they turned east. Approaching in three columns with the Spanish to the right and leeward, Villeneuve's fleet of twenty ships of the line sighted the fifteen ships of Calder's squadron about 16 miles away to the south-west at about one o'clock in the afternoon on 22 July (Diagram 1.2).

The number of the ships of the line in the two opposing lines gave the rationale for the first of the two French names for the battle: le combat des Quinze-Vingt. The encounter took place nearly 300 miles (556 km) west-north-west of Cape Finisterre. In the same vicinity, fifty-eight

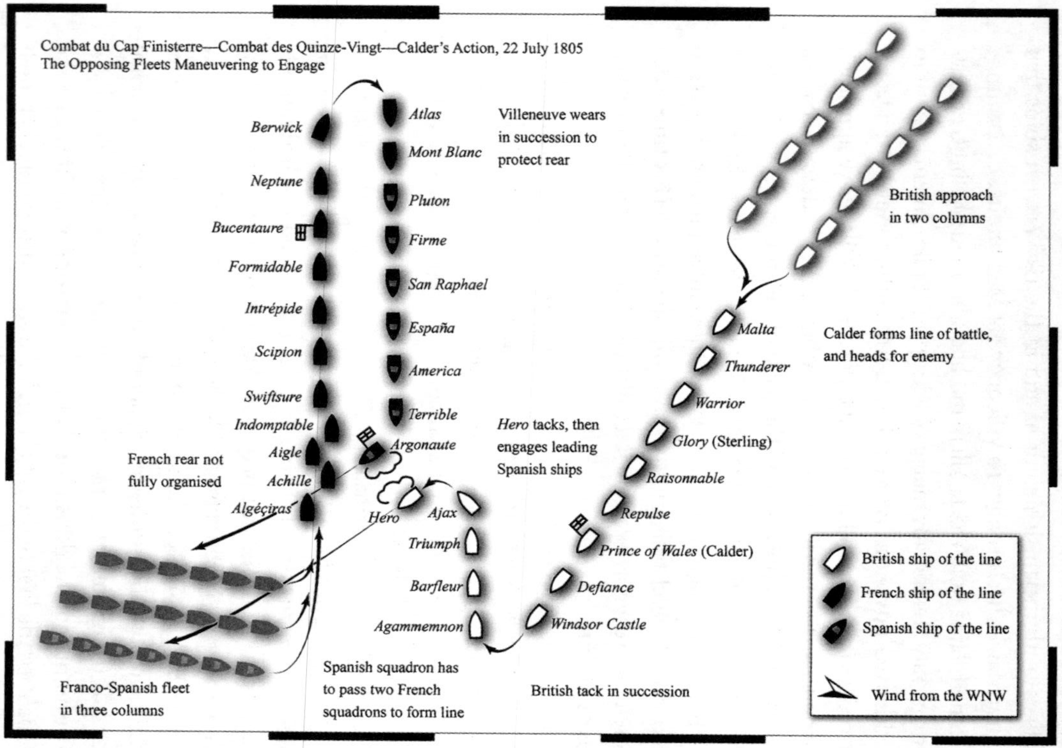

Diagram 1.2 Combat du Cap Finisterre—Combat des Quinze-Vingt—Calder's action, 22 July 1805 © 2025, Mappa Mundi Cartography.

years earlier, British Vice-Admiral George Anson had captured the French squadron under Admiral the Marquis de la Jonquière in the First Battle of Finisterre on 14 May 1747.

On sighting the British ships through the fog, Villeneuve altered course towards Calder's squadron and ordered the three columns into a battle line with the Spanish squadron in the van and Gravina's flagship, the 80-gun *Argonauta*, leading the entire line. Both sides manoeuvred into lines of battle. As they did so, they caught only occasional glimpses of each other through the fog. When the fog lifted about 3.15 in the afternoon, they found each other sailing in parallel lines but on opposing courses, just beyond gunshot range. The British were sailing north-east to the leeward, while the French were heading south-west to windward. Calder was no enthusiast for tactical innovation but had a clear idea of concentrating on the French centre and rear, leaving the Spanish squadron alone. Villeneuve, however, expected Calder to use the tactics that Nelson had used at the Battle of the Nile in 1798 and to double the French rear.

In the event both presuppositions were off the mark. As the vans of the two fleets approached, Villeneuve prepared the fleet to wear in succession. Anticipating that manoeuvre, Gravina wore immediately, bringing the Combined Fleet's van to engage Calder's van, thus parrying the British attempt to pass on an opposite course to attack the French centre and doubling its rear. Calder ordered his ships to concentrate on the French centre as it came into range. Calder's lead ship did not see the signal, and Gravina's move forced Calder to wear and parallel the French on a west-south-west course. This move forced Calder to engage the Spanish van and French centre with his shorter battle line, allowing the French rear to create a counter-concentration. The fog soon returned to blanket both sides, preventing them from seeing one another.

The engagement, nevertheless, lasted four hours until nightfall. Both Calder and Villeneuve reported a victory despite the British capture of two ships from the Combined Fleet. There is no consensus about the exact number of casualties. Still, they were moderate on all sides as the action was fought at a distance.[54]

At the end of the action, Calder notified his ships that he intended to continue the next morning. When the sun rose on 23 July, the opposing ships were scattered but could still see each other at a distance. Neither side made a significant effort to close the distance to reengage. Calder was concerned that the El Ferrol squadron, with its reported sixteen ships of the line, might use the opportunity to come out and reverse the situation. Thinking it wiser to prevent the conjunction of the Combined Fleet with the El Ferrol squadron, Calder moved to block their way. In doing so, he prevented Napoleon's planned invasion of Britain but also failed to force a battle to neutralize the Combined Fleet.

Many of the French and Spanish officers wanted to continue the fight and recover the Spanish prizes, as well as inflict further damage on Calder's ships. However, the next morning, the rising wind and seas made it difficult for either side to initiate an action. With the wind increasing and shifting to the north-east, Calder moved towards El Ferrol. Meanwhile, Villeneuve and Gravina, concerned about their wounded and the health of the large number of seamen afflicted by scurvy and dysentery, sailed south towards Cádiz. After six hours in worsening weather on 28 July, they sought refuge at Vigo Bay in Galicia, 50 miles south of Cape Finisterre.[55]

Calder sent a ship to investigate El Ferrol and was surprised to learn that Villeneuve was not there. Concluding that the Franco-Spanish fleet had gone to Cádiz, Calder reconstituted the blockade at El Ferrol. He assumed that Nelson and Collingwood would engage the Combined Fleet as it approached Cádiz. Once again, Calder did not advise Nelson or Collingwood of the situation.

Far to the south, Nelson was now aware that Villeneuve had returned to the Bay of Biscay with the possibility of supporting a French invasion across the Channel. He saw that the critical strategic juncture was in the Channel, not off Cape Finisterre. He decided to take the fastest route to the Channel and sail further to the west in search of better wind. He, therefore, waited until 30 July to turn north, when he was some 400 miles off the Spanish coast.[56]

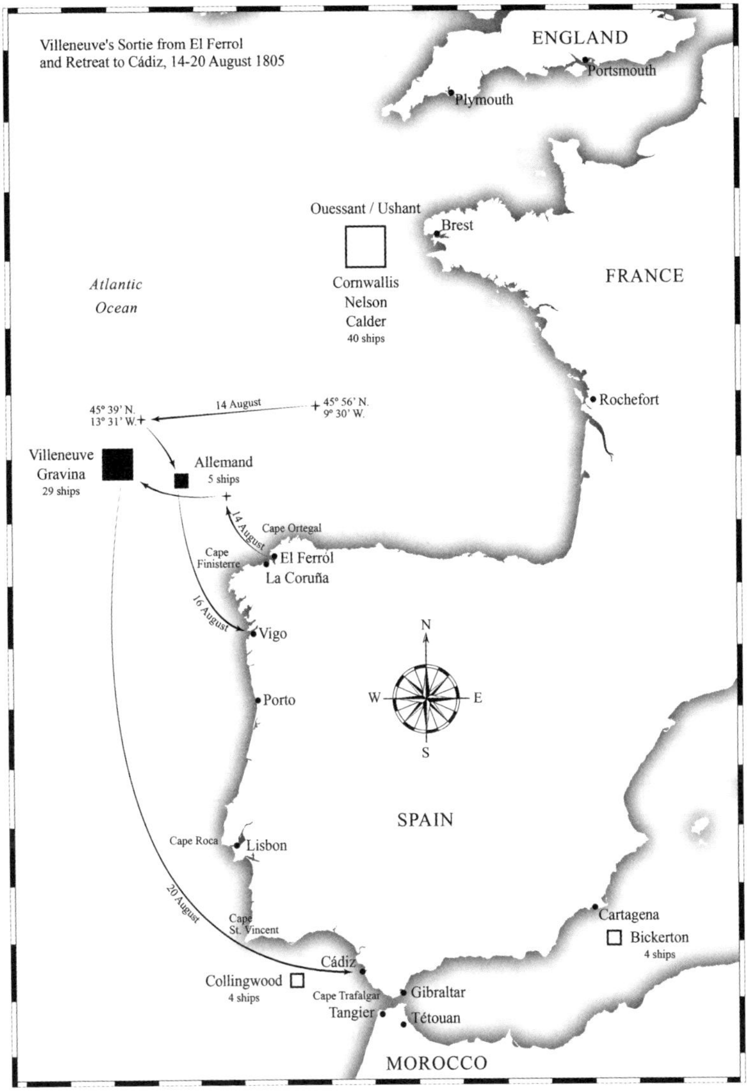

Diagram 1.3 Villeneuve's sortie from El Ferrol and retreat to Cádiz, 14–20 August 1805 © 2025, Mappa Mundi Cartography.

Missed Opportunities and the End of Napoleon's Grand Dessein

On 31 July, Villeneuve and Gravina sailed from Vigo and headed north around Cape Finisterre towards El Ferrol. Having left several ships at Vigo, and with the battle losses, the Combined Fleet now numbered only fifteen ships of the line. Gravina proceeded to El Ferrol and entered that port on 1 August. Following close behind, Villeneuve had just arrived at the entrance to El Ferrol when Napoleon's new order reached him. Dated 16 July, the new order directed him not to enter Ferrol. To avoid being trapped in harbour, Napoleon ordered Villeneuve to wait at nearby La Coruña for Rear-Admiral Antoine-Louis Gourdon, with his five French ships, and the former Spanish naval minister, Lieutenant-General of the Navy Domingo Pérez de Grandallana y Sierra, with his nine ships of the line, to come out of El Ferrol and join the Combined Fleet.[57]

By now, Villeneuve was in deep despair at what he saw as an impossible task. Gourdon reported that they could not get out due to the reconstituted British blockade. The only opportunity now was to meet up with Allemand's squadron. Although Napoleon had ordered Allemand to rendezvous with Villeneuve between 29 July and 3 August, that meeting had failed to materialize. Napoleon returned to the Channel coast at Boulogne on 3 August, ready to make the invasion. Villeneuve decided that there was no point in staying longer at La Coruña as he had lost all elements of a surprise move on the Channel. He decided to sail on 10 August and head north to the Channel, if possible, or, if prevented, sail south to Cádiz, as his most recent orders permitted. In preparation for this, Villeneuve debarked the many seamen who were ill into a ship that he planned to leave behind.

On 8 August, Gourdon and Grandallana sailed out of El Ferrol with five French and eight Spanish ships of the line. Three Spanish ships had initially remained behind in port but were able to join the rest of the squadron three days later. Many of the Ferrol squadron ships had been in port for several years, leaving them highly unprepared for fleet operations. Nevertheless, they rendezvoused with Villeneuve, who continued to hope that Allemand's squadron would join them. At this juncture, Nelson was at the same latitude but far out of reach, heading north some 400 miles (741 km) directly west of Vigo and La Coruña.[58]

On 13 August, Villeneuve and Gravina sailed from Spain's northern coast with a Combined Fleet of thirty-nine vessels that included twenty-nine ships of the line—eighteen of them Spanish—plus six frigates, one of which was Spanish, and four corvettes, of which one was Spanish. Villeneuve led them westward to gain position for an eventual turn north-eastward towards Brest, where he hoped to add Ganteaume's squadron. Early on, he sighted some of the frigates that Calder had left behind north-west of Finisterre. Apprehensive of encountering the overpowering combination of Calder's and Nelson's squadrons, Villeneuve proceeded with caution.

Aware that Villeneuve might attempt to reach Brest and the Channel, the Admiralty directed Cornwallis to concentrate British naval forces off Brest and the Île de Ouessant. Cornwallis quickly brought Calder's and Stirling's ships together with Nelson's on 15 August. This massive concentration of naval force to defend the entrance to the Channel lasted only twenty-four hours. Should Napoleon's invasion scheme be a ruse, Cornwallis feared that the defensive concentration compromised Britain's ability to defeat the Franco-Spanish fleet if its real intent were to strike in the Mediterranean. With this in mind, he quickly divided the fleet as a contingency to counter French squadron moves. Nelson returned to England with two other ships; Calder returned to blockade Ferrol with twenty ships; and Cornwallis retained seventeen to blockade Brest.

As Villeneuve sailed further to the west, the wind shifted to the north-east, blocking a direct passage to Brest. Early in the afternoon of 14 August, one of Villeneuve's frigates sighted several unidentified sails on the horizon. Suspecting that this might be Calder and Nelson, Villeneuve missed an opportunity and opted not to investigate the unknown ships, which were, in fact, part of Allemand's squadron.

Simultaneously, Allemand compounded the lost opportunity when he sighted several of Villeneuve's ships and incorrectly concluded that they were enemy ships. Not wanting to engage a superior enemy force, Allemand continued to Vigo. On the following evening, 15 August, Villeneuve decided not to continue towards Brest. Instead, he ordered the Combined Fleet to turn south and to make for Cádiz (Diagram 1.3). Villeneuve made this decision not for the aggressive reasons the British suspected but rather to avoid 'disaster, confusion, and a vain demonstration'.[59]

Failing to find Villeneuve at the rendezvous or Vigo, Allemand returned to the north. Villeneuve reflected his sense of despair as he reported to Decrès that he had no confidence in his ships' ability to fight or manoeuvre in a significant battle. Villeneuve's decisions created missed opportunities that compromised Napoleon's prospects for invading England.[60] As a result, he had failed to join forces with either Allemand or Ganteaume. Moreover, Villeneuve shifted the strategic stance of the two competing forces. Until he decided to return to Cádiz, Villeneuve had been operating in an offensive position despite his notably defensive conduct during the campaign. At Cádiz, he positioned the worn-out combined Franco-Spanish fleet in a defensive formation, enabling the Royal Navy to respond quickly by shifting from an offensive–defensive stance to an aggressive offence.

At Brest on 21 August, Ganteaume responded to Napoleon's repeated orders and brought his twenty-one ships of the line to anchor outside Brest, between Camaret and Bertheaume. He was still hoping for Villeneuve's arrival but planning to avoid a premature battle. A British frigate sighted Ganteaume's movement and alerted Cornwallis, whose squadron of seventeen ships immediately stood in towards Ganteaume's squadron at 4.30 on the morning of 22 August. As they moved within gun range, the French set sail. One French ship of the line fired a broadside at the British and then, with the remainder of the French squadron, refused battle and headed back into Brest's inner harbour.[61]

Napoleon's plan for Villeneuve had required him to build an overwhelming naval force by uniting the combined Franco-Spanish fleet with the Brest, Rochefort, and El Ferrol squadrons. Then, he was either to evade or defeat Cornwallis and Calder and seize local sea control of the Channel so that the French army could cross to England. Had Villeneuve persisted, he might have successfully combined French naval forces, and the campaign's climactic battle could conceivably have taken place in August in the English Channel rather than off the coast of southern Spain and the entrance to the Mediterranean in October. This did not happen; other events intervened to alter the geostrategic situation.

Napoleon's Pivot

Since 3 August, Napoleon had been at Boulogne waiting for Villeneuve 'like the Messiah'.[62] To demonstrate his power and intent publicly, Napoleon staged a spectacular pass-in-review parade on 4 August with some 112,000 infantrymen. Three days later, some 2,343 landing craft passed in review. Meanwhile, on the larger stage of European affairs, the strategic situation was rapidly changing. Napoleon's aggressive policies in Europe had served to strengthen the British and Russian alliance against France. On 11 April, an Anglo-Russian agreement laid the basis for a Third Coalition against Napoleon. In July, Austria ignored Napoleon's demand to disarm and began concentrating troops in the Veneto and Tyrol. On 8 August, Austria joined the coalition for its protection. Three weeks later, on 31 August, Sweden signed a troop subsidy treaty with Britain for supplying troops in Swedish Pomerania. The war for Central Europe had begun. Prussia and other smaller states now faced a decision either to join Napoleon or to fight in concert with Austria, Britain, and Russia.[63]

2

The Battle

While the Third Coalition was gathering its forces on the wider European stage to fight land actions against Napoleon in Central Europe, the naval focus of the war shifted to the waters off southern Spain. That focus stretched between Cape St Vincent, Cádiz, and the Strait of Gibraltar. The change created a range of geostrategic questions and opportunities for both sides in the conflict, with the Royal Navy now in an offensive stance and the Combined Fleet on the defensive.

Sailing south from the Bay of Biscay, Villeneuve and the Combined Fleet anchored in Cádiz roads on the evening of 20 August.[1] As they approached their anchorage, Villeneuve ordered sixteen of his ships of the line to chase Collingwood's four that had been blockading the entrance to Cádiz. Collingwood retreated to the entrance to the Strait of Gibraltar, where Villeneuve's ships left off the chase and returned to Cádiz. Three days later, Sir Richard Bickerton's squadron of four ships of the line abandoned the blockade off Cartagena in the Mediterranean and joined Collingwood to re-establish the Cádiz blockade. Meanwhile, with no clear indication of Villeneuve and Gravina's whereabouts, Calder began to move south along Portugal's coast. On 24 August, as Calder approached Cape St Vincent, he grasped the operational circumstances when a cutter delivered a report from Sir James Gambier, the British consul-general at Lisbon. Within a week, Calder joined his eighteen ships of the line to Collingwood's and Bickerton's, bringing the total British blockading force off Cádiz to twenty-six.[2]

On 1 September, Napoleon learned that Villeneuve had gone to Cádiz, but he momentarily hoped that the admiral would return to the Channel. He briefly contemplated ordering him to do precisely that. Although the army was already on the march away from the coast, Napoleon gave some thought to re-establishing a force of five hundred boats and eighty thousand men at Boulogne to keep Britain in fear of invasion while also distracting British naval forces.[3] Two new factors diverted his intention. First, Minister of the Navy Decrès implored the emperor not to order the Combined Fleet back from Spain. With only two months' rations available for the fleet, Decrès reminded Napoleon that in 1780, the Comte d'Estaing's fleet had taken fifty-eight days to sail from Cádiz to the Channel during the last invasion attempt. Second, Napoleon learned that Baird's British expeditionary force of six thousand men had reached Malta. In the context of the developing situation in Central Europe with Russia and Austria, Baird's small force could threaten Napoleon's plans there. With this mobile amphibious force, Britain could establish a position of strength and attack some unexpected points where Napoleon's forces were weak. All these factors combined to confirm Napoleon's decision to order the Grande Armée to march from their camps on the shores of the English Channel to Central Europe, thereby strengthening his positions against British amphibious operations in the Mediterranean. To mask his sudden change of strategic intentions, Napoleon himself remained at Boulogne until 2 September. His army marched eastwards, hoping to gain two weeks' advantage before the Austrians noticed the impending French attack.[4]

On 2 September, the Admiralty in London first learned the news that Villeneuve and the Combined Fleet had entered Cádiz harbour when Captain Henry Blackwood of the 36-gun frigate *Euryalus* arrived with the news along with the latest reports from Collingwood's squadron. En route overland from Portsmouth to London, Blackwood stopped at five o'clock in the morning at Merton, Nelson's home, to alert the admiral before going on to central London. Later in the day, Nelson arrived there for meetings at the Admiralty. On 4 September, the First Lord of the Admiralty, Lord Barham, recommended to Prime Minister Pitt that Nelson return immediately in his flagship, the 100-gun *Victory*, to his station as commander-in-chief of the Mediterranean. At the same time, Barham restored the western boundary of the Mediterranean station to include Gibraltar and the area as far west as Cape St Vincent, as it had been since at least the time of Sir John Jervis's command in 1795–9. This action resolved the coordination issue that had arisen earlier in the year between Nelson and Orde due to Orde's seniority over Nelson. Even so, the extension helped to assuage Nelson's concern about confronting 'the increasing sea power of the enemy'.[5] Barham also pointed out to Pitt some additional advantages of a more comprehensive British strategic naval stance. He suggested that British naval forces could be reinforced by the Swedish Navy assisting Admiral Keith in blockading the Texel and a Russian squadron joining Nelson's Mediterranean squadron. The Admiralty issued orders on 5 September for Nelson to sail. Quickly completing repairs and loading supplies, he sailed for Cádiz on 14 September from Portsmouth with his flag in *Victory*.

From the British perspective, the presence of the Combined Fleet at Cádiz raised various possible threats. On the one hand, the Franco-Spanish force could break out and move north again to Brest and the Channel. Alternatively, it could attack the West Indies or even the British convoys from the East Indies. If the Combined Fleet sailed into the Mediterranean, it would endanger Gibraltar.

Knowledgeable British officers were thinking more broadly. Since there was no major French naval force at Toulon, and since the Spanish were unlikely to sail into the eastern Mediterranean, the Russian squadron could deal with the privateering and other threats to trade at the entrance to the Adriatic. They thought Egypt could still be a likely target of a surprise attack. Even more importantly, if the Franco-Spanish fleet at Cádiz entered the Mediterranean and joined the Spanish squadron at Cartagena, it could threaten all British interests in the region, including Sardinia, Naples, Sicily, the Morea, Malta, and Egypt, as well as Craig's expeditionary force.

If the Royal Navy could defeat and destroy the Franco-Spanish Combined Fleet before any of those threats became a reality, Britain could secure control of the Mediterranean. By regaining that control, Britain would regain the regional naval superiority that Spain's entry into the war as a French ally had jeopardized.[6]

Above all, Napoleon wanted his navy to *act*. On 15 September, he repeated his order to Decrès for Villeneuve's fleet to join the squadron at Cartagena. Napoleon had ordered him to get under weigh two weeks earlier, but Villeneuve had declined to take action due to the size of the British blockading force. Now, Napoleon repeated his order for the Combined Fleet to put to sea and proceed to Naples, where it would debark troops for the army under General Claude Carra Saint-Cyr. Napoleon also tasked the fleet with capturing the Russian frigate and the British ship of the line stationed at Naples, as well as intercepting any convoys bound for Malta. After achieving those objectives, the Combined Fleet would sail to Toulon for resupply and repair. Napoleon saw his Mediterranean fleet's principal function was as a fleet in being. 'The existence of so considerable a squadron at Toulon would have incalculable effects,' he wrote to Decrès. 'It makes a powerful diversion for me. That will be the most useful part that I am able to give this squadron in these circumstances.'[7] Napoleon directed Decrès to send this order to Villeneuve by special courier. At the same time, he told Decrès that Villeneuve's 'excessive pusillanimity will prevent me from undertaking it.'[8] In this action, he was replacing him in command with Vice-Admiral François Étienne de Rosily, comte de Mesros, who had served as director of the Navy's Depôt of Charts and Plans in Paris for the past ten years.[9]

The Situation at Cádiz

Despite Napoleon's desires and British estimates of the strategic situation, the Combined Fleet at Cádiz could not undertake operations in its condition. The fleet had not even been able to repair fully the battle damage from the action with Calder on 25 July. Masts and yards needed replacement. The ship's biscuit and other food supplies were inedible, and the food supply was slow and difficult. Despite the earlier period in port at El Ferrol and La Coruña, where many of the Combined Fleet's sailors and soldiers were sent ashore to hospitals, health issues remained a continuing major problem at Cádiz. For budgetary reasons, Madrid had not fully funded the Spanish naval shore facilities. The Spanish naval base at Cádiz was unable to handle permanent repairs for the large number of French vessels in addition to the Spanish warships. There were no French arrangements to fund extensive logistical support through Spanish naval facilities. The Spanish government had recently reduced the manning in the dockyard, and supplies for both repairs and victualling were limited.[10]

Beyond these logistical problems at Cádiz, there was also some discord among some Spanish and French senior officers. Villeneuve and General Jacques Lauriston, who commanded a contingent of the embarked troops, had come to despise one another. Lauriston's extremely critical opinion of Villeneuve and the navy helped fuel Napoleon's criticism, further depressing Villeneuve's fighting spirit and general morale. Admiral Gravina also complained to the Spanish government about Villeneuve's propensity for indecision. At times, Gravina felt the Spanish government did not have confidence in him and considered resigning. However, Gravina hewed to his orders to collaborate with Villeneuve to the best of his ability.[11]

Meanwhile, Napoleon and Decrès ordered Rosily to proceed to Cádiz to relieve Villeneuve, promoting him to full admiral and command of the combined land and sea forces. But they did not tell either Gravina or Villeneuve of the impending change of command. Napoleon ordered Rosily to get all, or part, of the Combined Fleet to sea when the weather permitted to create a powerful diversion in the Mediterranean, acting with Salcedo's squadron at Cartagena. He was not, however, to risk action against superior forces.[12]

Despite the growing strength of the British blocking force off Cádiz, Villeneuve decided that he had no choice but to obey Napoleon's orders to get to sea, enter the Mediterranean, and land troops at Naples. The

French troops re-embarked on board the fleet ships on 2 October while other preparations for getting to sea continued. On 8 October, a council of war met on board Villeneuve's flagship, *Bucentaure*, in Cádiz harbour. Villeneuve explained to the council that the emperor had ordered the fleet to sail at the first favourable opportunity and attack the enemy without hesitation to force a decisive action. The council members unanimously advised that it was not an auspicious time to leave port. The British fleet was far more potent than the Combined Fleet, whose men were still suffering from illness. The health problems of the men in the Combined Fleet had reduced its capabilities. Spanish Rear-Admiral Antonio Escaño pointed out British superiority in three-decked ships and the disadvantage in practical seamanship that the French and Spanish faced due to their prolonged periods in port.

Additionally, Escaño pointed out that bad weather was approaching. Even after the repairs, several key ships were not yet ready for combat. Moreover, Gravina, who was born in Palermo, Sicily, was not in favour of an attack on Naples, which was part of the Kingdom of the Two Sicilies. The council advised Villeneuve that to leave port in these circumstances was 'an act of despair'.[13] While all agreed that they would follow orders, the council members emphasized that it was an 'unpropitious moment' to leave port.[14] They hoped that a better opportunity might present itself if the Spanish Cartagena squadron could get to sea. They reasoned that the British blockading force off Cádiz would need to divide and reduce their strength to deal with both squadrons.

British Preparations off Cádiz

Shortly after Nelson's arrival and taking command from Collingwood off Cádiz on 29 September, he explained to his commanding officers the approach that he would take for a battle with the Combined Fleet. Most of the ship captains off Cádiz had not been on the chase to the West Indies and back. Nelson had not had an opportunity to train them thoroughly in his way of thinking. On 9 October, he summarized his thoughts in a long memorandum. He wanted his ships to operate under the general plan he outlined and to do so simultaneously and independently. He focused his plan on three key factors: speed, surprise, and close engagement.[15] Nelson proposed, first, that the order of sailing was to be the order of battle. He initially envisioned the fleet in two lines, each consisting of sixteen ships, one led by Nelson and the other by his second in command, Collingwood. In addition, he planned to have an advanced squadron of eight of the fastest sailing two-decked ships, which could be added to either line as needed. He planned to cut through the enemy line in two places and engage them from both sides while simultaneously separating the enemy's van from the remainder of the enemy fleet. 'The whole impression of the British fleet', Nelson wrote, 'must be to overpower from two to three ships ahead of their commander in chief…to the rear of the fleet. I will suppose twenty sail of the enemy's line to be untouched. It must be some time before they could perform their manoeuvre to bring their force compact [enough] to attack any part of the British force…'.

Additionally, to minimize the exposure of his ships' vulnerable bows to enemy gunfire, Nelson planned to mislead the enemy as to his intentions. He would have his division feint towards the enemy van, then, at the last moment, turn to attack the centre and rear of the enemy line. Having already inspired his captains to act independently, Nelson explained, 'Captains are to look to their particular line as their rallying point. But in case signals can neither be seen or perfectly understood, no captain can do very wrong if he places his ship alongside that of an enemy.'[16]

Combined Fleet Preparations at Cádiz

Not far away, inside the blockaded harbour at Cádiz, Villeneuve had prepared his instructions to the Combined Fleet. These were a slight variation to the circular letter sent to his captains ten months earlier on leaving Toulon in December 1804. Significantly, Villeneuve had correctly imagined how a British fleet might engage him. 'The enemy will not confine himself to forming on a line of battle parallel with our own and with engaging us in an artillery duel, in which success lies frequently with the more skilful but always with the more fortunate,' Villeneuve wrote. 'He will endeavour to envelop our rear, to break through our line and to direct his ships in groups upon such of ours as he shall have cut off, so as to surround them and defeat them.'[17] Similar to Nelson, Villeneuve ordered, 'Any captain commanding who is not under fire will not be at his post; any, whose next ahead or next astern is closer than he to the enemy will not be doing his duty and a signal recalling him to his post will be a reflection on his honour.'[18]

On 18 October, Villeneuve heard for the first time that Rosily had been in Madrid and was en route to relieve him in command of the Combined Fleet. At the same time, he learned that Nelson had detached Rear-Admiral Sir Thomas Louis with several ships to get supplies for the fleet at Gibraltar. Upon receiving these reports, Villeneuve concluded that this was the opportunity he had been looking for. He wrote immediately to Decrès that he welcomed Rosily as his senior if he could retain second in command. 'It would be too terrible to me to lose all hope of having an opportunity of showing that I was worthy of a better fate...if the wind will allow me to work out, I shall put to sea tomorrow.'[19]

Disregarding the lack of readiness in the Combined Fleet, Villeneuve put to sea. He sought to save his honour and justify himself to Napoleon by obeying the emperor's 4 September instructions to dispatch troops to Naples.[20] In taking this action, Villeneuve was also acting on faulty intelligence. He believed that Nelson's fleet had been reduced to a manageable twenty-two ships of the line. He was aware that Sir Robert Calder had taken the 98-gun *Prince of Wales* to England, where he faced a court martial for the July action. Louis's subsequent departure with six ships for Gibraltar seemed to present the opportunity Villeneuve had sought. His primary objective was not to fight but to circumvent the British blockade and carry out his mission of deploying troops to Italy. Villeneuve did not know that during the preceding fortnight, the 100-gun *Royal Sovereign*, along with two additional 74s and two 64s, had reported to Nelson.

Preliminary Movements, 18–20 October

As his first move on 18 October evening, Villeneuve ordered Rear-Admiral Magon to sea with three Spanish and four French ships. Their task was to capture some of the British frigates off the entrance to Cádiz and to ascertain Nelson's location. The next day, Villeneuve ordered seven more French and one Spanish ship to sail. As they emerged from the harbour, they reported seeing several British frigates in the distance firing guns and making signals.

Patrolling off Cádiz at dawn on 19 October, the British frigate *Sirius* first observed the French ships raising sail. Captain the Hon. Henry Blackwood, who commanded the British squadron of frigates stationed off Cádiz in the frigate *Euryalus*, reported that the ships in harbour had their 'topgallant yards across and eight ships had their topsails at the masthead'.[21] At 07:20 that morning, Blackwood ordered the frigates *Phoebe* and *Naiade* to repeat signals between *Euryalus* and the main British fleet. Nelson, located fifty miles away to the west, received the signals within two hours. After reporting to Nelson, Blackwood ordered the brig-sloop *Weazel* to take the intelligence to Gibraltar and then to Tétouan on the Moroccan Mediterranean coast, a few miles south of the Strait of Gibraltar, where British ships often watered and took on victuals. From only two to four miles distance, Blackwood observed the first dozen ships slowly and laboriously come out of Cádiz.

At dawn on Sunday 20 October, the remainder of the French and Spanish ships were under sail and leaving Cádiz with a light morning breeze from the south-south-east. Four and a half hours after Villeneuve signalled the fleet to sail, they reached the open sea about eleven in the morning. Villeneuve sent off a dispatch to Decrès, reporting that his entire fleet of thirty-four ships of the line and five frigates was under sail. As they sailed, Blackwood's lookouts could see the British fleet in the distance from *Euryalus*'s masthead. As the wind freshened to nearly gale force from the south-south-west, Villeneuve ordered his fleet to form into three primary columns with a two-column squadron of observation. At first, the changing wind direction forced the Combined Fleet on to a west-north-west course, the opposite direction intended. Villeneuve signalled for the fleet to come about and change course to head south to round Cape Trafalgar and enter the Strait of Gibraltar. The rising seas and rain squalls reduced visibility, making it difficult for the ships to manoeuvre into formation. By four in the afternoon, the fleet had finally completed the manoeuvre, but it was still 10 miles off Cádiz and remained disorganized. In light wind, Villeneuve ordered the fleet to make a line of battle on the starboard tack, taking station as convenient, without regard to the pre-planned order, and forming up on the leeward-most ship in the line. Finally, they all managed to get on the same course, but they were still trying to form their battle line.[22]

While the Combined Fleet was manoeuvring into formation, it lost sight of the British ships. During the night, Nelson had moved his fleet of twenty-seven ships of the line and four frigates from a point west of Cádiz on a south-east course towards the Strait of Gibraltar, with the idea of cutting off Villeneuve's passage into the Mediterranean. At dawn on 20 October, Nelson's fleet was about 18 miles south of Cape Trafalgar, far ahead of Villeneuve. Seeing no sign of the Franco-Spanish fleet in the strait at 06:00 that morning, Nelson ordered the fleet to sail to the west for ten hours, initially fearing that Villeneuve had already returned to port. By 16:00 in the afternoon, Nelson was 40 miles directly south of Villeneuve but still did not know his location. At 19:30, Gravina sighted eighteen enemy ships, and Villeneuve ordered the Combined Fleet from a formation of five columns in a single line of battle. Then, at 20:30 that evening, when the two fleets were only 15 miles apart, *Achille*, a ship of the line in the French squadron of observation, confirmed the sighting of eighteen British ships. The French and Spanish ships struggled anxiously and with much confusion throughout the night to form the battle lines. At the same time, the wind dropped, leaving heavy swells.[23]

Aware now that he was close to the Combined Fleet, Nelson did not want to fight a night action. At 20:30, he ordered the British fleet to sail south until 04:00 in the morning. Then, the fleet turned to the north-north-west. The 64-gun *Africa* missed the signal to turn south, continuing north until midnight. At dawn, she was alone, approximately 6 or 7 miles north-east of Nelson's flagship.

Manoeuvring into Battle, 21 October

The two opposing fleets sighted each other at dawn on 21 October, about 9 to 10 miles apart. With light westerly winds, a heavy swell, and hazy visibility, the Franco-Spanish fleet was sailing south about 8 miles west of Cape Trafalgar. During the night, the Combined Fleet's ships had become mixed in the light winds and were far from their intended order.[24] For the first time, Villeneuve could see and comprehend the actual strength of the British fleet. It was not the smaller and more manageable force of eighteen to twenty-two ships that he had expected. Now he saw twenty-seven ships of the line, seven of which were heavily armed three-decked warships that the British used for the intimidating effect of its higher third tier of guns.[25] As Napoleon commented after the July action, 'The advantage of three three-deckers against a squadron that has none is equal to a difference of eight ships of the line, all accustomed to the sea and perfectly trained.'[26]

For Nelson, his fleet was considerably smaller than the forty he had envisioned having for a battle in early October. At 06:15, shortly after sighting the Franco-Spanish fleet, Nelson ordered the British fleet to divide into two divisions. Then, at 06:30, he ordered two more signals: to bear up for the enemy and prepare for battle. At 07:30, he ordered the frigate captains to come on board *Victory* for their instructions. Nelson's fleet, carrying approximately 17,237 men and 2,148 guns, was moving slowly at a speed of less than 1.5 knots. It gradually closed with Villeneuve and Gravina's thirty-three ships of the line carrying about 26,020 sailors and soldiers and 2,636 guns. As they approached, the twenty-seven British ships of the line had a theoretical gunnery advantage over the seventeen French and sixteen Spanish ships due to the presence of seven three-deck British ships and the British carronades, which served as short-range, anti-ship, and anti-crew weapons. While the French had no three-deckers, the four three-deckers in the Combined Fleet were all Spanish and armed with howitzers that served similar functions to the British carronades for devastating close-range firing.[27]

At 07:10, Villeneuve ordered the remainder of the fleet to take up its prescribed positions in the line of battle on the starboard tack. With many ships still out of position, this required extensive manoeuvring in the light winds and heavy swell. Ten minutes later, with his ships randomly spaced, Villeneuve signalled for each of his ships to close the distance between them to a cable length (200 yards or 182.8 metres). Meanwhile, as he observed the British fleet, Villeneuve concluded that 'they appeared to me to be standing in a body for my rear, with the double intention of attacking it advantageously and of cutting off the retreat of the Combined Fleet on Cádiz'.[28] To thwart what he thought was Nelson's intention at 08:00, Villeneuve signalled the fleet to 'wear together', thereby reversing course to sail towards Cádiz, about 30 miles away. As each ship put its stern to the wind to change direction by 180 degrees, Dumanoir's squadron, which had been the rear of the formation, became the van, and Gravina's squadron of observation became the rear. With the wind and sea conditions, this manoeuvre created further complications for forming a battle line that was not yet in place. Half of the Combined Fleet, the sixteen ships from the Spanish *Santa Ana* in the centre to *San Juan Nepomuceno* in the rear, were in a confused situation, not in a line of battle, and trying not to collide with one another. The other half of the fleet had formed a rough line of battle, with some gaps and some ships falling to leeward. This situation presented crucial opportunities for the British to launch an attack.[29]

At 11:40, Nelson signalled to his fleet, 'I intend to push or go through the enemy's line to prevent them from getting into Cádiz.'[30] He soon followed this signal at 11:56 with 'England expects every man to do his duty.'[31] The British fleet bore down on the Combined Franco-Spanish Fleet in two roughly formed, ragged divisions. Nelson, in *Victory*, led the windward division, and Collingwood, in *Royal Sovereign*, led the leeward division less than 2 miles (3 km) to the south of Nelson. Four minutes later, at noon, Nelson ordered signal 63: 'Prepare to anchor during the ensuing night.'[32]

Many French and Spanish ships had been unable either to reach their assigned station or to establish the close distance between ships that Villeneuve had ordered. Each of the four divisions contained both French and Spanish ships. The ships were doubled in several places and scattered widely in the rear. Overall, the Combined Fleet formed, as one participant described it, a 'curve with the convexity turned towards the enemy, in which the bend was accentuated towards the head of the line'.[33] Perhaps justifying the confusion, Villeneuve commented, 'This very irregularity in our line did not appear to me to be a drawback if each ship had continued to close to windward on her next.'[34] Nevertheless, he signalled to the lead ship to make more sail and keep close to the wind. At 11:00, he signalled 'to the rear to keep to the wind' to cover the centre of the fleet, which appeared to be the point on which the enemy was desirous of concentrating his greatest efforts.[35]

About noon, Villeneuve ordered the action to begin as soon as the enemy came into range (Diagram 2.1). The weather was hazy, with light winds from the west and a persistent swell. The Combined Fleet was sailing in the trough of a long Atlantic swell, a harbinger of a storm to come. The swell made the ships roll and often forced their gunfire to be too high or too low. The two fleets began to engage less than 5 leagues (17.26 miles or 27.8 km) south-south-east of Cape Trafalgar. At the rear of Villeneuve's line but ahead of Gravina's squadron, the French 74-gun *Fougueux* and the Spanish 112-gun *Santa Ana*, flying the flag of Gravina's second in command Vice-Admiral Ignacio María de Álava y Sáenz de Navarrete, fired the first shots of the engagement at Collingwood's flagship *Royal Sovereign*. At this point, Collingwood's ships were slowly approaching from the south-west on a ragged line of bearing, rather than Nelson's planned perpendicular approach, which laid ships open to raking gunfire.

Two miles to the north, at about the same time that the Álava engaged with Collingwood, the British 64-gun *Africa* was returning to the fleet but unable to get to her assigned position towards the end of

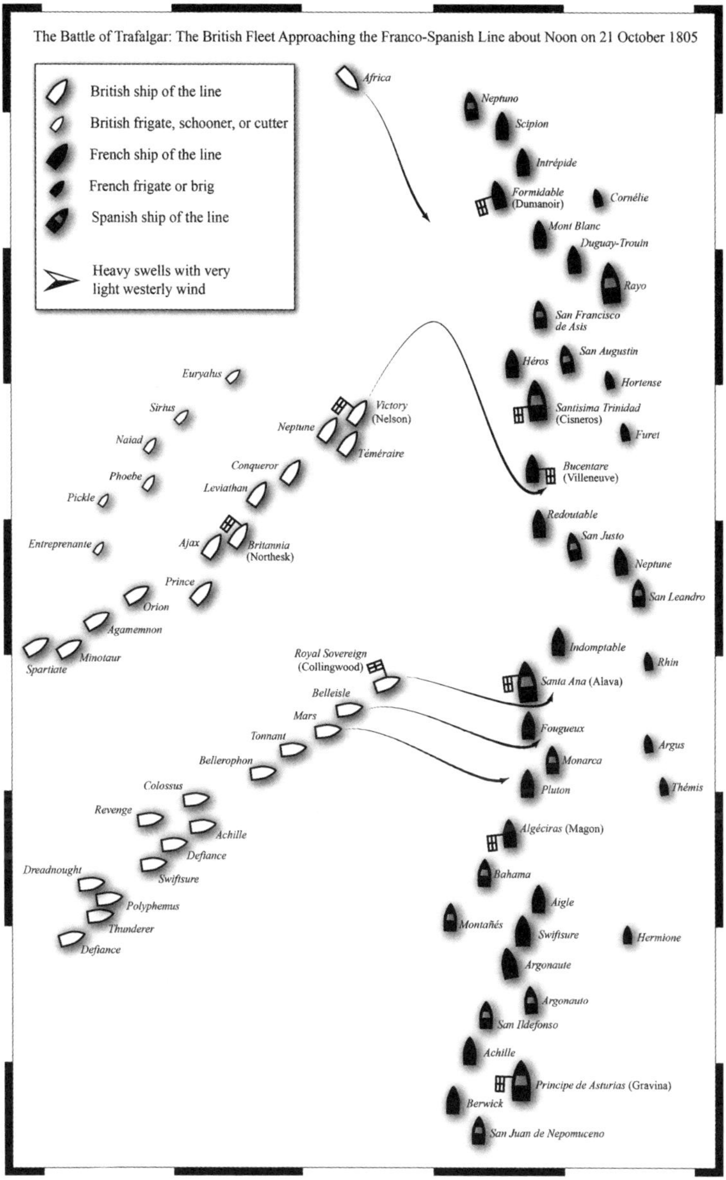

Diagram 2.1 The Battle of Trafalgar: The British Fleet–approaching the Franco-Spanish line about 12 noon, 21 October 1805 © 2025, Mappa Mundi Cartography.

Collingwood's column. *Africa* had missed Nelson's signal to turn during the previous night. Sailing south parallel, but in the opposite direction, to the Combined Fleet, she exchanged gunfire at a distance with the lead ships in Dumanoir's van, the Spanish 80-gun *Neptuno*, and the French 74-gun *Scipion* and *Intrépide*. *Africa* continued her course to join Nelson. As Nelson closed the Combined Fleet, he was unsure in which ship Villeneuve was located. Collingwood mistook the signalling activity on board one of the French frigates as an indication that Villeneuve was commanding from the frigate. Unable to identify Villeneuve's actual location on board the 80-gun *Bucentaure*, Nelson hoisted his last signal at 12:20, Signal 16: 'Engage the enemy more closely.' The signal remained flying until shot away some hours later. Turning away from Villeneuve's van to engage the Franco-Spanish centre, *Victory* ran briefly in the opposite direction to the Franco-Spanish ships, passing the huge four-decked, 136-gun *Santísima Trinidad*, flying the flag of Rear-Admiral Baltasar Hidalgo de Cisneros y de la Torre. When Nelson's flag captain, Thomas Hardy, told the admiral that *Victory* could not break the Franco-Spanish line without colliding with one of the enemy ships, Nelson replied, 'I cannot help it: it does not signify which we run on board of. Go on board which you please: take your choice.'[36] Then, seeing a narrowing gap in the Franco-Spanish line, Hardy turned towards it under heavy gunfire.[37]

Breaking the Line

The two British columns followed their respective leaders: *Royal Sovereign* broke through the line astern of *Santa Ana* at about 12:20. About 25 minutes later, *Victory* cut in closely astern of the twelfth ship in the Franco-Spanish line, not immediately aware that it was Villeneuve's flagship, *Bucentaure*, then turned to sail on a parallel course running onboard the port side of the French 74-gun *Redoubtable*. Both columns broke through the Franco-Spanish line at a higher point than initially planned in early October, giving them a larger group of enemy ships to deal with than anticipated. Each ship in the two columns followed at her best speed without regard to the sailing order. As a result, gaps developed in the British lines. Ships entered combat in small groups rather than as the concentrated force that Nelson envisaged. The plan had been for Collingwood's line to break the line twelve ships from the rear. In the event, he broke through astern of *Santa Ana*, the sixteenth ship from the rear. Moreover, due to light winds and foul bottoms, the slow arrival of the ships following Collingwood prevented a rapid concentration of force on the Franco-Spanish rear.

Nevertheless, Collingwood's line fanned out and split into three groups according to their speed. Collingwood's first eight ships were in action within 20 minutes; the remaining seven took 50 to 170 minutes to open fire. Two of Collingwood's ships steered to starboard and doubled the Franco-Spanish rear. After *Royal Sovereign* and *Victory* had opened fire, the very last ship in each column—the 98-gun *Prince* in Collingwood's line and the 74-gun *Spartiate* in Nelson's line—took 2 hours and 28 minutes and 2 hours and 50 minutes, respectively, before they opened fire.[38] Among those who followed *Victory*, Rear-Admiral Lord Northesk, Nelson's third in command flying his flag in the slow-sailing *Britannia*, took in her studding sails as he approached the enemy line and fired from a distance but did not engage closely or pass through the line.[39]

During *Royal Sovereign*'s 35-minute approach, an estimated 170 guns from four French and Spanish ships fired at Collingwood's flagship. After getting off three to five broadsides, they fired an estimated 743 rounds, with about 15 per cent or 111 balls hitting their target. About 70 per cent of those, seventy-eight shots, hit *Royal Sovereign*'s sails and rigging, and 30 per cent, or thirty-three shots, hit the hull and upper decks. During Nelson's 25-minute approach, eight French and Spanish ships fired an estimated 349 guns at *Victory*. Firing two to three broadsides each, they fired a total of about 846 rounds. Approximately 15 per cent, or 130 rounds, hit *Victory*, with about ninety rounds hitting the sails and rigging and some forty shots hitting the hull and upper decks.[40]

With so many guns firing in such a short time in light wind, a shroud of acrid white gun smoke quickly enveloped the battle scene. Once engaged, participants could see less than 90 metres and often could not identify their opponents beyond their nationality. A midshipman in Collingwood's *Royal Sovereign* reported that 'The smoke was so thick in the action we could hardly make out the French from the English. The *Belle Isle* fired into us until the admiral stopped her; we fired into *Victory* once.'[41]

From *Fougeux*'s opening shots, until *Intrépide* surrendered, the battle took the entire afternoon, lasting some five and a half hours. As soon as Collingwood and Nelson broke through the Combined Fleet's line at the centre and the rear, the action devolved into a confusing mêlée and artillery duel between single ships and small groups of ships. Nelson and Collingwood had fewer ships in their separate columns than Nelson had wanted to have in early October. This situation, combined with the fact that they both cut through the Franco-Spanish line at points higher up than anticipated, reduced their numerical superiority over the sections of the enemy line that they sought to overwhelm. This proportional reduction meant that the British needed the remainder of the fleet to come up rapidly to support their leaders and overwhelm the Combined Fleet completely. For the ships in the rear of the two columns, the intervening slow sailing ships created a tailback effect, slowing those astern as they maintained their assigned stations. The delay of the British ships coming within gun range jeopardized the outnumbered ships ahead of them and forced the impatient captains among them to start firing their guns at too great a distance to have any effect. Some of the ships that did not engage quickly also got in the way of those who were more aggressively trying to reach the action. These circumstances prevented the overwhelming desire that Nelson had and made it impossible for the British fleet to annihilate the Combined Fleet.[42]

To counter the British attack, Villeneuve attempted to maintain his fleet in a rough line of battle formation, but as each ship came into range, she manoeuvred independently to be in an advantageous position to fire a broadside at an enemy ship. At the same time, each captain also sought to prevent the enemy's broadsides from sweeping their decks, fore and aft. The scene was a nightmare of crashing guns and constant fire. Wooden splinters flew across the decks as cannonballs whistled past. Masts and rigging fell, and ships collided. Men fought hand-to-hand to fend off enemy boarders, surrounded by screams of the dying and wounded. Under such terrifying, seemingly chaotic circumstances, courage, self-discipline, prior training, experience, and effective leadership were the elements that kept officers and men focused on their responsibilities and functions. The most intense fighting during the mêlée occurred over the two-and-a-half-hour span between 12:30 and 15:00.

There were two large notable movements within the context of the mêlée and its numerous dramatic separate fights. First, there was the action around the opposing commanders-in-chief at the opening of the battle. The second movement was towards the end of the fight when Dumanoir's van turned around to support Villeneuve and the centre.

The Fight around the Commanders-in-Chief

After Nelson turned away from Dumanoir's van, he led the first ships of his column to the south on the opposite course to the Combined Fleet. Followed directly by the British 98-gun ships *Téméraire* and *Neptune*, *Victory* exchanged heavy gunfire with *Santísima Trinidad* and *Bucentaure*. She manoeuvred to pass through the line astern of *Bucentaure* and ahead of the 74-gun *Redoubtable*, whose jib boom was nearly touching *Bucentaure*'s taffrail. The three French ships were the primary resistance at the Combined Fleet's centre. As *Victory* turned to break through the line, her main yard touched the vangs of *Bucentaure*'s gaff. *Victory* fired a broadside, raking *Bucentaure* from astern. At the same time, *Victory* purposely collided with *Redoubtable*, moving the French ship bodily to leeward to open a gap astern of *Bucentaure*. *Redoubtable* then grappled *Victory* and attempted to board her. Simultaneously, sharpshooters fired and threw grenades onto *Victory*'s main deck as she fired broadsides into the French ship. The three-decked *Victory* was the larger ship with a defensive advantage against boarding over the lower-lying, two-decked *Redoubtable*. This height difference also meant that *Victory*'s main deck was closer to sharpshooters in the French ship's rigging. Shortly after 13:15, at a range of about 50 yards, a French sharpshooter in *Redoubtable*'s mizzen top mortally wounded Nelson.[43]

About 45 minutes later, Captain Jean Lucas of *Redoubtable* determined that his sharpshooters had sufficiently cleared *Victory*'s main deck to launch his boarding parties. As *Redoutable*'s men took up their positions on her main deck, the three-decked British *Téméraire*, now nearly dismasted and adrift, collided with *Redoubtable* on her starboard side, trapping the French ship between two British three-deckers. *Téméraire*'s initial broadside into *Redoubtable* swept the main deck, killed some two hundred men in the boarding parties, and wounded the commanding officer. Shortly afterwards, a third British ship came in astern of *Redoubtable*. She fired a raking broadside into her at pistol range. With a total of 300 men killed and 222 wounded, *Redoubtable* surrendered.[44] Like Nelson and *Victory* for Britain, *Redoubtable* later became a symbol of French fighting spirit. The 74-gun French ship had successfully managed to take out of action a British first- and second-rate warship and kill Nelson.[45]

Meanwhile, about five minutes after Nelson had opened the gap astern of Villeneuve's flagship *Bucentaure*, the British *Neptune* followed. She gave *Bucentaure* another raking broadside and then rounded up to leeward. *Leviathan* and *Conqueror* followed with two more raking broadsides for *Bucentaure*, then moved up the Franco-Spanish line to attack *Santísima Trinidad* from the leeward side.

At about 14:00, Villeneuve signalled Dumanoir to reverse course with the van and come to the centre's aid. By this time, four British ships had raked *Bucentaure* from astern. Shortly after Villeneuve's signal to Dumanoir, *Bucentaure*'s remaining masts fell. He now had no means of manoeuvring or signalling the fleet. He then attempted to shift his flag to *Santísima Trinidad*. He tried to notify the Spanish ship to send a boat for him, as *Bucentaure*'s boats had all been destroyed. *Santísima Trinidad*, heavily engaged, did not respond to Villeneuve's request as the British

Neptune and the 74-gun *Leviathan* and *Conqueror* fired close broadsides into her. As this occurred, *Africa* arrived and fired a raking broadside from ahead, while *Britannia* and *Ajax* fired on *Santísima Trinidad* from a distance. With no assistance available, Villeneuve surrendered to *Conqueror*. It was only when a boat from *Conqueror* boarded *Bucentaure* to accept her surrender that the British learned that Villeneuve was on board. Since *Conqueror* had moved on to deal with *Santissima Trinidad*, he ended up as a prisoner with four other French officers on board *Mars*. With Villeneuve's surrender and Nelson mortally wounded, the fight at the centre of the Franco-Spanish battle line around the commanders-in-chief ended about 14:35.[46]

Further to the south in the rear of the Combined Fleet, Collingwood in *Royal Sovereign* and Álava's flagship, *Santa Ana*, had battered each other for nearly two hours. Nelson had hoped that Collingwood's division would have won the battle by quickly overwhelming the Franco-Spanish rear, but it had arrived piecemeal rather than en masse. The first British ships to engage soon found themselves outnumbered and surrounded until the rest slowly moved up to join the fight. Due to the light wind, Gravina was unable to move forward to support Villeneuve. Still, he retained his position to protect the rear of Álava's division. As a result of the effective Franco-Spanish gunfire, Collingwood's division took more than twice the casualties: Collingwood's lee line had 1,128 killed and wounded to 577 in Nelson's weather line. Of all the ships in the British fleet, the 74-gun *Colossus*, under Captain James N. Morris in Collingwood's column, had the most casualties, with 209 killed or wounded, accounting for about a third of the ship's company.[47] At the same time, Collingwood made more captures, taking eleven of the eighteen that the Combined Fleet lost, including one that blew up. At about 15:00, the dismasted *Santa Ana* surrendered, with Álava seriously wounded and some four hundred casualties. The damage to the British ship forced Collingwood, now aware of Nelson's mortal wounds, to shift his flag from the dismasted *Royal Sovereign* to the 36-gun frigate *Euryalus*.[48]

The Attempt of Dumanoir's Van to Support the Centre

Dumanoir had not immediately replied to Villeneuve's signal at 14:00 to engage. At 14:30, *Formidable*, Dumanoir's flagship and lead ship in the van, eventually repeated the signal. Several ships attempted to turn, but the light winds, swell, and current made this manoeuvre extremely difficult. *Scipion* tacked, but only with the help of her boats pulling her through the wind's eye. The other ships were surrounded by two French ships, *Duguay Trouin* and *Mont Blanc*, which collided in the process. *Intrépide* and *San Augustin* sailed straight to the assistance of *Bucentaure* and*Santísima Trinidad*. Dumanoir was more cautious as he led the three other ships in the van to the windward of the battle.

Aware of the approaching van, Captain Thomas Hardy was able to disengage *Victory* from the shattered *Redoubtable* and move to the north. Taking the initiative as Nelson lay wounded below, Hardy signalled for available ships to create a defensive line to her windward, larboard side. *Ajax*, *Agamemnon*, and *Britannia* responded. *Minotaur* and *Spartiate*, which had been at the end of Nelson's approach line, were coming within firing range at 15:30. As these ships engaged Dumanoir's approaching ships, *Leviathan* engaged and captured *San Agustín*, while *Africa* blocked and engaged *Intrépide*. Observing that *Intrépide*'s heavier guns were punishing *Africa*, Captain Edward Codrington wore his 74-gun *Orion* around *Intrépide*'s stern. He came to on her lee bow between *Africa* and *Intrépide* and forced the French ship to surrender after a 45-minute cannonade. Meanwhile, Dumanoir observed the situation and concluded that his further intervention would make little difference. 'It was therefore my duty in this painful situation to endeavour to effect the repairs of my division in the hope of more favourable chances on the morrow.'[49]

About 16:30, some three hours after being wounded, Nelson died on board *Victory*, aware that a victory was won. The 98-gun *Prince* finally reached the battle area and raked the French *Achille*, setting her on fire. She burned for an hour. Just as the evening sky drew dark, the flames reached the French ship's magazine, and the ship exploded at about 17:30, marking the battle's end. The heavily gunned *Prince* was unique among the twenty-seven British ships of the line, reporting not a single person killed or wounded at Trafalgar.[50]

Other Actions, Other Admirals

While the actions of Nelson, Collingwood, Villeneuve, and Dumanoir represented the principal broad movements of the action at Trafalgar and are often emphasized to the exclusion of others, numerous other actions and several other admirals were also involved. Among them, French Rear-Admiral Magon de Médine and Spanish admirals Gravina and Escaño hold notable places.

Rear-Admiral Magon flew his flag in the 74-gun *Algéciras* and was initially part of Gravina's squadron of observation. When the action began, Magon and his flagship were ninth from the rear in ragged battle formation of the Combined Fleet. Astern of the Spanish 74-gun *Montañez*, ahead of the 80-gun *Argonauta*, and to windward of the 40-gun frigate *Thémis*, Magon's flagship crowded on all sail to block the British 80-gun *Tonnant* from breaking through the line. As *Algéciras* turned sharply to rake the British ship from astern, *Tonnant* parried by turning in the opposite direction. These manoeuvres caused *Algéciras* to collide with *Tonnant* and entangled *Algéciras*'s bowsprit in *Tonnant*'s amidships rigging. *Tonnant* then fired a volley of grapeshot that stripped *Algéciras* of her rigging. While locked together, the French responded with a steady fire that reduced the British ship to the same state. At that point, with three more ships attacking him at pistol range, Magon ordered his sailors to board *Tonnant*. Repulsed by musket fire and grapeshot that cleared the French ship's upper decks, *Algéciras* swung broadside alongside *Tonnant* and continued to fire at point-blank range. Throughout the action, Magon, as his flagship's commanding officer reported, 'feeling our position to be critical went about everywhere encouraging us by his presence and displaying the most heroic coolness and courage'.[51] Magon had refused repeatedly to go below to treat his wounds, having been wounded by a bullet in the right arm and a splinter in the thigh. At 15:15, as Magon remained on deck undeterred, he took a bullet in the chest and died instantly.[52]

Admiral Gravina was embarked in the 112-gun *Príncipe de Asturias,* the principal ship of the squadron of observation. When the squadron merged into the Combined Fleet's line of battle, Gravina was in the van. Then, when Villeneuve ordered the battle line to reverse course to head north on the morning of 21 October, Gravina unexpectedly found his flagship was the third ship from the rear. At the start of the battle, *Príncipe de Asturias* was to the leeward between two French ships, the 74-gun *Achille* ahead of her and the 74-gun *Berwick* astern. As soon as Gravina came within firing range soon after 12:15, he opened fire on a group of British ships trying to break through the line. The British 74-gun *Revenge* succeeded in breaking the line ahead of *Achille.* As *Defiance* attempted to break through ahead of *Príncipe,* Gravina's flagship crowded on sail and fired heavy broadsides. Forced back, *Defiance* then engaged *Berwick* directly astern of *Principe de Asturias.* As the smoke cleared, *Dreadnought* rounded and raked the stern of the last ship in the Combined Fleet's battleline, *San Juan Nepomuceno,* and moved up past *Berwick* to attack *Principe de Asturias* on the lee quarter. As *Revenge* rounded *Achille*'s bow and passed through the line, *Principe de Asturias* turned to starboard on a north-north-east course and engaged her with a broadside. Gravina was seriously wounded in the exchange but retained command. By 16:00, the British three-decker *Prince* passed on the port side of *Principe de Asturias.* Shrapnel from *Prince* wounded Gravina again. This time, the loss of blood prevented him from continuing to command, and Escaño took charge, but he too was wounded. Then, a French and another Spanish ship came to *Principe*'s support. As the firing died down about 17:15 after a gallant defence against numerous attacks, Escaño made the signal for recall, and the nearby ships joined *Principe de Asturias* in sailing for Cádiz.[53]

Immediate Aftermath

Fifteen (52 per cent) of the twenty-nine ships in the Franco-Spanish fleet survived the battle. Dumanoir sailed to the south with four of them, Gravina and Escaño, with eleven anchored for the night in Cádiz Bay. One French ship, *Achille*, had been destroyed by an explosion, and the British captured seventeen French and Spanish ships. Prize crews took charge of all the captured ships. Only two ships, *Algéciras* and *San Juan Nepomuceno*, were initially able to sail by themselves, and British ships took the remaining fifteen under tow. Six British ships, including Collingwood's *Royal Sovereign* and Nelson's *Victory*, also had to be towed (Table 2.1).[54]

The Storm

With the battle between men and ships at an end, all now faced a struggle with the elements. Every seaman would have recognized that the long swell that had persisted for several days was a harbinger of a brewing storm. As Nelson lay dying, he told Hardy again to anchor the fleet for the night after the battle. It is questionable whether anchors could

Table 2.1 Approximate number of casualties in the Battle of Trafalgar and the storm following.

Nationality	Killed	Wounded	Prisoners
French	3,499	1,138	2,200
Spanish	1,050	1,390	
Subtotal	4,549	2,528	
British	449	1,214	260[55]
TOTAL	4,998	3,742	

Note: The 260 British taken prisoner were not taken during the battle but were prize crews wrecked on the coast in the storm after the battle.

have held in the exposed waters around Cape Trafalgar. Many ships were still unable to comply, having lost their anchors or cables during the battle.[55] Those ships that could sail on their own made necessary repairs to their rigging and sails and manned their pumps while temporary repairs dealt with the hull damage. Some took dismasted ships under tow, while other dismasted ships anchored as they could. As the French and Spanish ships headed towards Cádiz Bay, British ships slowly moved towards Gibraltar. After reaching Cádiz, Gravina and Escaño led ten ships to the safety of the inner harbour, while Dumanoir's four French ships weathered the storm at sea.

At approximately 08:00 on 22 October, the storm struck the fleets with heavy rain and a strong south-west wind at Force 10 or 11, preventing the British ships from reaching Gibraltar. On 22 October, during a lull in the storm, Escaño and the war council strongly supported Cosmao-Kerjulien's initiative in taking the French 74-gun *Pluton* with four other ships of the line, four frigates, and two brigs from the Combined Fleet out of Cádiz harbour early on the morning of 23 October to recapture vessels from the British. The wind rose to storm force again, and two of the ships that sortied on this heroic, honour-saving, but highly costly mission subsequently wrecked, as did one of the recaptured ships.[56] The French 80-gun *Indomptable* managed to rescue five hundred survivors from *Bucentaure*, but on the following day ran aground off Rota with the loss of a thousand men. During the high winds, the British tow hawsers broke or had to be cut from the dismasted ships. Under the pressure of the Franco-Spanish ships and the weather, Collingwood decided to scuttle some of the captured ships rather than let them escape. One ship sank under tow, two were burned to prevent their escape, five scuttled, and nine others went aground on the Spanish shore, with a total of some 2,700 men drowned.

There was another lull in the storm on the morning of 24 October that allowed the 74-gun *Donegal* to join Collingwood from Gibraltar for the first time. The storm returned the next day. With intermittent heavy rain and squalls, it continued until 29 October.[57] In the city of Cádiz, the Spanish created temporary hospitals in convents and churches to care

Figure 2.1 *La Santísima Trinidad* (1803). A British naval officer, who had boarded the Spanish ship *La Santísima Trinidad* after the battle, rescued this depiction of the Holy Trinity just before the ship sank on 24 October 1805. This painting fulfilled a 1778 Spanish royal decree that stipulated that every warship in the Spanish Navy should have in its main cabin a 'decent painting, of a suitable size, and in a gilded frame' depicting the ship's patron saint. Fuente: Museo Naval de Madrid / Biblioteca Virtual de Defensa.

for the wounded. It took more than ten days to bring all the wounded ashore as the streets filled with families looking for survivors amongst the shell-shocked seamen.[58]

On 26 October, amid a fresh gale with squalls, Collingwood, still in the frigate *Euryalus*, dispatched the 8-gun schooner *Pickle*, Lieutenant John Lapenotière, to take his dispatch reporting the results of the battle and Nelson's death to the Admiralty. The news that she carried reached London on 6 November. Meanwhile, on 27 October, Collingwood, with some thirty ships in sight, ordered *Prince* to collect all disabled ships and make their way to Gibraltar. Collingwood remained to windward and north-west of Sanlúcar de Barrameda through 30 October. Under a flag of truce, English officers and men whose ships were driven ashore at Cádiz were exchanged for captured and wounded men from Spanish and French ships. On the evening of 30 October, Rear-Admiral Louis arrived from Gibraltar with six ships that had not participated in the battle. Taking advantage of the opportunity provided, Collingwood shifted his flag from *Euryalus* to the 98-gun *Queen*, one of the new arrivals. He brought some of his officers and the French officers he retained as prisoners, including Villeneuve. Collingwood remained on station directing the blockade of Cádiz and Sanlúcar along with the rotation of ships for water, provisions, and repairs.[59]

The Battle of Cape Ortegal—Sir Richard Strachan's Action—Action of Brumaire 13, Year XIV

Meanwhile, Dumanoir, with his four ships, had weathered the storm and eluded the British fleet. On 29 October, they rounded Cape St Vincent and sailed north, standing as far to seaward as the light and variable south-westerly winds allowed. On 2 November, they reached the latitude of Cape Finisterre. Two of his ships, *Scipion* and *Formidable*, were severely damaged and had difficulty maintaining speed. While Dumanoir was making for Cape Ortegal on Spain's northern coast and then for the Isle d'Aix in France, two 36-gun British frigates, *Boadicea* and *Dryad*, sighted them. They alerted Commodore Sir Richard

Strachan, cruising off Ferrol in *Caesar*, commanding a detached squadron of four 74s and four frigates under Admiral Sir William Cornwallis.

Strachan initially thought that these ships were Rear-Admiral Allemand's Rochefort squadron. Strachan took four ships of the line and four frigates with him and sailed to their reported location. He sighted them in the moonlight on the night of 2 November. Strachan's squadron chased Dumanoir's four ships and blocked their attempt to reach a safe port without a fight. By noon on 4 November, Dumanoir, seeing the impossibility of avoiding an action, formed his battle line as Strachan's ships approached with the wind astern of them. As the French formed their line, two of Strachan's frigates, *Phoenix* and *Santa*

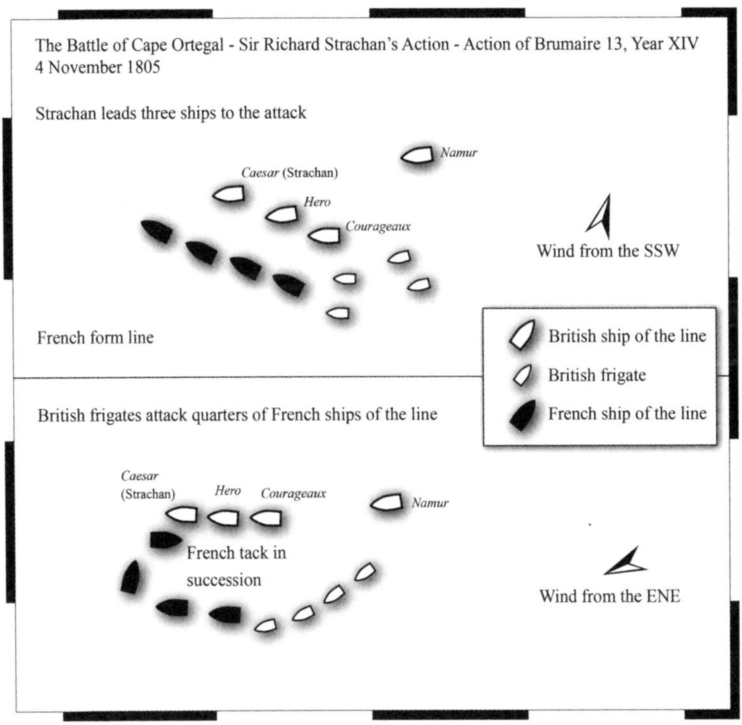

Diagram 2.2 The Battle of Cape Ortegal—Sir Richard Strachan's Action—Action of Brumaire 13, Year XIV—4 November 1805.

Margareta, fired broadsides into the already damaged *Scipion*. Just before noon, *Caesar* and *Hero* exchanged broadsides with *Scipion* and *Mont Blanc* as the British frigates continued to fire into *Scipion*. Shortly after noon, Dumanoir's line tacked in succession to pass Strachan's squadron on the opposite course. A hot, intense fight ensued between the two squadrons, during which the four British frigates positioned themselves to fire broadsides from the leeward of the French squadron while Strachan's 74s fired from windward. By 1600, Dumanoir's four ships, dismasted and in a shattered condition, surrendered to Strachan.[60]

The Curtain Comes Down on Trafalgar

The Trafalgar campaign's dramatic events on the world stage came to an end some three weeks after the battle. On 6 November, Collingwood sent Villeneuve, with the officers accompanying him, on board *Euryalus* as prisoners of war to England, where they arrived on 29 November. On 10 November, Strachan's squadron brought the four captured French ships to Plymouth, where they refitted for service in the Royal Navy.[61] Along with Villeneuve, Dumanoir and his surviving officers and men became part of the French prisoners of war in England. As a result of Strachan's action, the statistics for the Combined Franco-Spanish Fleet's losses rose by 3,700 men killed or wounded, with 5,300 more made prisoners.[62]

Long after the last vestiges of the battle washed up on the shore, the restless waves rolled past Cape Trafalgar. The survivors suffered from their memories and mourned their losses. In contrast, others celebrated their actions or defended their conduct against critics. Throughout the participants' remaining lives, their memories gradually transformed into a public commemoration. In turn, commemoration gave rise to differing national and patriotic narratives and memories. Eventually, after two centuries, the historical debate about Trafalgar is leading towards a broader, more dispassionate understanding of the battle's meaning within the wider context of European and world history.

3

The News of Trafalgar

Understanding the cultural legacy of the Battle of Trafalgar today involves several broad themes, including its artistic and formal commemoration, its place in popular culture, its role in naval culture, and, finally, its changing interpretation in history over time. Before the Battle of Trafalgar became settled in these themes, it was the news of the day. Although the sentiment is often attributed to the American writer Mark Twain in the late nineteenth century, it was Jonathan Swift who wrote more than a century before Trafalgar, 'if a Lie be believ'd only for an Hour, it has done its Work, and there is no farther occasion for it. Falsehood flies, and the Truth comes limping after it; so that when Men come to be undeceiv'd, it is too late; the Jest is over, and the Tale has had its Effect . . .'.[1] As news of the Battle of Trafalgar spread, it carried both truths and falsehoods, depending on one's location. On the Continent, where Napoleon's deputies were reluctant to deliver bad news, and the emperor preferred to emphasize his contrasting great victories on land, both the official reports and the newspapers minimized the importance of the battle, lied about the extent of the defeat, and emphasized the death of Nelson rather than the loss of French or Spanish ships. In Britain, on the other hand, naval officers quite literally raced one another to be the first to deliver the news.

Trafalgar as News in Spain and France

As might be expected, the immediate contemporary newspaper accounts on the Continent differed significantly from those published in British newspapers. The first reports of the sea battle arrived at Cádiz during the late evening on the day of the battle, with Gravina's return. The following day, 22 October, the commandant at Cádiz, Lieutenant General of the Navy Juan Joaquín Moreno, submitted the initial report to Godoy in Madrid.[2] The news travelled quickly to the Spanish capital and across Spain. The information also travelled overland to Lisbon, where it arrived three days later. At the naval bases in northern Spain, La Coruña, and El Ferrol, where seven of the Spanish ships that had fought in the battle had been outfitted and manned, official news arrived on 5 November. On that same day, Admiral Escaño's dispatches on Trafalgar appeared in the official *Gazeta de Madrid*.[3] By mid-December, even Collingwood's dispatch was translated and published in Spain.[4]

In Madrid, General Pierre Riel de Beurnonville, Napoleon's ambassador to Spain, wrote immediately to Decrès at the Ministry of Marine in Paris. He first reported that an inconclusive battle had taken place. Two days later, he provided a more detailed account that arrived in Paris on 7 November. Decrès forwarded Beurnonville's information to Napoleon but couched it in vague terms that evaded telling the extent of the losses. Napoleon received Decrès's report ten days later, on 17 November, the day the Grande Armée occupied Znaim in Moravia. It was a moment of crisis in the 1805 military campaign. Napoleon was stretching the logistical extremity of his army as he marched to Vienna; he was about to unleash his improvised manoeuvre at Hollabrun, and he was debating whether to pursue the retreating Russian Army.[5] His reply, on 18 November, revealed how little he understood what had happened. 'I hasten to let you know that this does not change anything for my naval plans; I am sorry that everything is not ready. They must leave without delay. Order all the troops on board the squadron ashore and to come over land; they will await my orders in the first city of France.'[6]

A few days later, on 21 November at Brünn (modern-day Brno, Czech Republic), Napoleon received Decrès's further details. Napoleon's chamberlain and aide de camp, General Auxonne-Marie-Théodose de Thiard de Bissy, confirmed the new information for Napoleon by translating excerpts from the *London Gazette*. According to details that Napoleon's chief of staff and minister of war, Marshal Louis-Alexandre Berthier, provided to Fouché, the Minister of Police, Napoleon was outraged and agitated by the news. Napoleon exclaimed with disgust, 'I can't be everywhere.'[7] Talleyrand, Napoleon's Minister of Foreign Affairs, helped overcome the emperor's discouragement and despair by assuring him that his genius and future lay in Germany, not at sea. Accepting this alternative, Napoleon set his sights on revenge by preparing for what would be one of his most significant victories, the Battle of Austerlitz on 2 December 1805. That dramatic victory effectively destroyed the British-led Third Coalition. Although Russia continued fighting until the Treaty of Tilsit in 1807, the battle effectively knocked Austria out of the war, leading to the Peace of Pressburg, which contributed to the collapse of the Holy Roman Empire.[8]

Publicly, Napoleon chose to ignore the defeat at Trafalgar. Officials issued orders directing journalists not to publish any accounts of the battle. The French government's official journal, the weekly *Gazette Nationale ou Le Moniteur Universel*, followed the instructions and was completely silent on the subject until after the end of Napoleon's reign. Other French newspapers did not strictly conform but treated Trafalgar very differently than they reported Napoleon's victory at Austerlitz. The Austerlitz report contains details on the forces engaged and the losses involved, but they treated Trafalgar elliptically. *Le Journal de l'Empire* emphasized only Nelson's death and funeral on 1 December but provided no details on the battle.[9] In this, *Le Journal de l'Empire* led its readers to associate Trafalgar with French success in killing Nelson rather than the general outcome of the battle. The following week, the *Journal de Paris* published a translation on 7 December of a false Spanish report claiming that the British had been defeated at Trafalgar with six ships sunk, one burned, and another aground. Among the ship casualties that the newspaper mentioned was *Prince of Wales, Spencer*, and *Tigre*, none of which had participated in the battle.[10] This information originated from a report published on 19 November in the *Gazeta de Madrid*.[11]

Two other themes appeared in *Le Journal de l'Empire*. The first of them celebrated the bravery of the French and Spanish in combat. On 13 January, the paper reported from Madrid on the publication of an ode by the young poet Don Manuel José Quintana in honour of the Spanish sailors who showed such courage at Trafalgar.[12] The front page of the 19 January issue reported news from Cádiz of Admiral Gravina's recovery from his severe wounds. 'For 50 days, they hesitated whether the amputation of his arms would have happened or not; it was finally decided that they would save them both, these arms which he knows so well to use for the honour of our flag and the example of our sailors.'[13] On 6 May, the newspaper reported that the audience at St. Cloud included Admiral Decrès, who presented Captain Jean-Jacques Lucas of the *Redoubtable* and Captain Louis-Antoine Infernet of the *Intrépide* to Napoleon. The emperor named them both commandants of the Legion d'Honneur and told them, 'If all of my ships had been conducted as you commanded yours, victory would not have been uncertain.'[14] Continuing in a more threatening manner, Napoleon declared, 'I know there are several who have not imitated you; I have ordered that information be gathered on this matter. Ship captains who, instead of engaging the enemy, have remained out of cannon range will be prosecuted, and if necessary, a striking example will be made of them.'[15]

The second theme in the *Journal de l'Empire* was to attack Prime Minister William Pitt as a failed leader. In the 25 January 1806 issue, *Le Journal de l'Empire* not only obscured Trafalgar and emphasized Austerlitz but also attacked Pitt. Quoting from 'An extract from a letter from London', the newspaper reported, 'Now Mr Pitt realizes that by taking personal responsibility for this war, he has become personally responsible for all events; all defeats have fallen on him; humiliation pursues him; and his name, which for some time had such great credit in Europe, will become in our country even the surest means of designating the ambitious without capacity.'[16] Similarly, on 12 March, the newspaper published a translation of an article from the British newspaper *Bell's Messenger* that reacted to the British capture of the Cape of Good Hope, noting: 'It was neither at Trafalgar nor at the Cape of Good Hope that the great trial which exists between France and England could be decided; and if from now on we only want to sign a peace that will lower the preponderance of our enemy, we must resolve to shake all the states of the Continent, which are now either won to its cause, or chained by his power.'[17]

The situation was quite different in Britain. The news first reached a British territory at Gibraltar. The schooner *Flying Fish* moored at Gibraltar on Wednesday, 23 October, with a letter from Collingwood to Gibraltar's Lieutenant-Governor, General Henry Edward Fox. *The Gibraltar Gazette* printed an 'Extraordinary' edition, just three days after the battle on Thursday, 24 October, which contained the first report, including Collingwood's letter.[18] Soon, British warships sailed into Gibraltar Bay with their prizes. The wounded and prisoners were brought ashore and taken to the naval hospital at the southern end of the Rock. Two men who died of their wounds were interred in a small cemetery consecrated in 1798 and then known as the Southport Ditch Cemetery (now the Trafalgar Cemetery), just south of the Charles V wall and near the Southport Gate.[19] *The Gibraltar Gazette* gathered more information and printed a much longer and more detailed account on 26 October. Among the additional sources used were the official Spanish reports published just across Gibraltar Bay in the *Algeciras Gazette*, as well as information from the Spanish sailors held as prisoners of war in Gibraltar. In light of that information, *The Gibraltar Gazette* expressed the view that Spanish ships and sailors bore the heaviest losses while bringing honour to Spain. 'They were unwillingly dragged into this contest, by their *good and faithful* allies, the French, who, as usual, were the first to fly, and desert them in the middle of the action; it appears from every account, that four of the French ships were seen running away from the fight, about two hours and a half after the battle began.'[20]

Then, on 2 November, the *Gibraltar Gazette* published its regular issue, accompanied by an additional supplement that provided further detailed and corrected information from Spanish, French, and British sources.[21] A week later, another, even more detailed, report appeared. This issue included the form of Thanksgiving prayer given by the Rev. I. Hughes in the King's Chapel, Gibraltar, on Sunday, 27 October: 'We thine unworthy servants do, this day, most heartily and devoutly offer up unto THEE our praise and Thanksgivings, for that THOU hast endued the Officers and Seamen of the Fleet of thy Servant, our Sovereign, with wisdom and courage and hast blessed them with success; that with inferior strength and numbers they have fought and overpowered a mighty Host, and disconcerted the counsels of our Enemies.'[22]

On 9 November, the *Gibraltar Gazette* included more information the newspaper had acquired from Spanish officers held as prisoners. They reported that Villeneuve had sailed with the Combined Fleet to seek battle out of a feeling of personal resentment and wounded honour, contrary to what they understood Napoleon's intentions to have been. According to the *Gibraltar Gazette*, the Spanish officers believed that the emperor wanted the Combined Fleet to unite with the Cartagena squadron in a French port and to retain control of a significant portion of the Spanish Navy in case Spain tried to shake off the yoke of French rule. The following week, the *Gazette* published this information in French, as the news dispersed from Gibraltar.[23]

The News Reaches Great Britain

Meanwhile, on 26 October, Admiral Collingwood dispatched the schooner *Pickle*, commanded by Lieutenant John Lapenotière, to take his dispatch, reporting the results of the battle and Nelson's death, to the Admiralty. For the first two days, *Pickle* beat against fresh westerly winds and a heavy swell before she was able to round Cape St Vincent and head north. Soon after changing course, Lapenotière sighted a ship standing towards him. He recognized her as the British 18-gun ship-sloop *Nautilus*, commanded by Commander John Sykes. As the two ships came within hailing distance, they hove-to. Sykes came on board *Pickle* at four in the afternoon. While the two vessels resumed their course northward, side by side, the two captains conferred until sunset when Skyes returned to *Nautilus* and veered off towards Lisbon.

At dawn the next morning, 29 October, Sykes was off the mouth of the Tagus. He decided not to enter the river as the wind was preventing any departures. Instead, Sykes hailed a Portuguese boat and paid the skipper to deliver the information to authorities ashore that he had gleaned from Lapenotière. Then he returned to a northerly course. Sykes now took it upon himself to protect *Pickle*, ensure the arrival of the news in England, and, perhaps, share in the glory. Despite his efforts, there is no clear evidence that Sykes's information reached the shore at Lisbon.[24]

Nevertheless, a third opportunity for the news to reach Lisbon appeared. On 28 October, Collingwood sent the 10-gun cutter *Entreprenante*, commanded by Lieutenant Robert Benjamin Young, to Faro on the southern coast of Portugal with dispatches for the British ambassador at Lisbon, Lord Robert Stephen Fitzgerald, and the Admiralty. *Entreprenante* went aground entering Faro, but the messages came ashore on 2 November. Following Lord Fitzgerald's receipt of the news, 'Grand Illuminations took place at Lisbon for three nights.'[25] Meanwhile, *Pickle* and *Nautilus* continued their race to reach England with news of the battle.

Pickle reached Falmouth on the south coast of Cornwall, the first English port inside the Channel, early on the morning of 4 November. Lapenotière went ashore, leaving his ship under the temporary command of her acting second master and pilot, George Almy, who took the schooner on to Plymouth. With great discretion, he made no mention of the news he carried. By landing at Falmouth instead of Plymouth, Lapenotière avoided delays with quarantine and naval protocol, which would likely have both delayed him and required him to turn over Collingwood's dispatch to a more senior, politically favoured officer. As he travelled overland for 270 miles by post-chaise, he avoided Plymouth, taking the northern route across Bodmin Moor to Okehampton, Exeter, Salisbury, and Basingstoke to reach London in thirty-seven hours.

Meanwhile, George Almy took *Pickle* further up the Channel to Plymouth. They arrived there on 4 November, just a few hours after *Nautilus*. On arrival in Plymouth, Sykes also sent off in a post-chaise to London to report what Lapenotière had verbally told him on board *Pickle* off Lisbon. The next day, a printer in Plymouth published a handbill with the news of Trafalgar and the death of Nelson. That handbill was the first report of the battle printed in England, although it was neither authoritative nor entirely accurate. The actual report, Collingwood's official dispatches of 22 and 24 October, were in Lapenotière's safe hands as he raced to London, only about seven miles ahead of Sykes. Lapenotière arrived at the Admiralty in Whitehall about 0100 in the early morning of 6 November with Sykes only an hour behind him. At that late hour, the Admiralty Secretary, William Marsden, was finishing his work in the Admiralty Board Room when Lapenotière burst in, blurting out, 'Sir, we have gained a great victory, but we have lost Lord Nelson.'[26]

Marsden immediately woke the First Lord of the Admiralty, Lord Barham, and they discussed how to present the information to the public. Marsden worked through the remainder of the night to censor Collingwood's dispatches. Collingwood had already exercised great reserve in writing those dispatches. He took particular care to obscure the criticism that officers within the fleet were already making about others who had been overly slow to engage in battle or who had been inefficient or ineffective with their gunnery. Collingwood had bitter memories of the injustice of Lord Howe's dispatch after the Battle of the Glorious First of June 1794, when Howe had omitted his name, thereby incorrectly implying fault on his part. At the same time, he wanted to avoid the public disputes and personal feuds between senior naval officers that had become far too common in the past. The earlier disputes had severely damaged public perceptions of the navy as well as individual reputations and morale within the service.[27]

Collingwood was wary not only of officers who claimed too much credit but also of those who criticized others. Shortly after the battle and the ensuing storm, the wounded Captain Philip Durham had gone onboard *Euryalus* to explain to Collingwood what he and his ship, the 74-gun *Defiance*, had been doing. Collingwood had asked Durham for information in a comment that seemed to slight Durham. During that conversation, Durham praised the conduct of the frigate captains during the battle. At that point, *Euryalus*'s commanding officer, Henry Blackwood, interrupted with a remark that suggested that one of the frigate captains, probably Captain Thomas Dundas of *Naiad*, had not been exemplary. Collingwood immediately shot back, 'Sir, this has been a glorious victory for England and for Europe—don't let there be a reflection against a cabin boy.'[28] The officers in the British fleet quickly took Collingwood's point and withheld their criticism. William Pringle Green, a master's mate from Halifax, Nova Scotia, in the 74-gun *Conqueror* during the battle, later repeated the rumoured understanding that 'So great was the joy of all the people of England and the remaining Admiral [Collingwood], that all was hushed up.'[29]

Adding to the reticence of Collingwood's dispatches, Marsden carefully revised them to present an even more positive image to the public while also avoiding the disclosure of sensitive information to the enemy and unnecessarily worrying the families of men serving in the ships. He removed Collingwood's comment that he had no idea where the vessels that had escaped under Dumanoir had gone. He also removed Collingwood's concerns about his ships' poor state, including his description of *Royal Sovereign, Temeraire, Tonnant,* and *Victory* being 'in a very decrepit condition'. Marsden also removed Collingwood's observation that the fleet had lost control of the French and Spanish prizes during the storm. Later that same day, *The London Gazette* published the revised version of Collingwood's dispatch in an 'Extraordinary' edition.[30]

The Admiralty immediately promoted Lapenotière to Commander, with his date of rank as 6 November 1805, the day he delivered the dispatches. The story was long told that, later the same day, he also provided the news to King George III at Windsor Castle and that the King gave him the first thing to hand at his breakfast table—a muffineer—as a reward. No evidence has been found to substantiate that tale.[31] Later, Lapenotière also received a reward of £500 gratuity and a 50-guinea sword from Lloyd's Patriotic Fund (Figure 3.1), as well as a share of the prize money awarded to all who fought at Trafalgar.

At Edinburgh in Scotland, the *Caledonian Mercury* reprinted Collingwood's dispatch from the *London Gazette* on 9 November. 'It gives us gives us great pleasure to announce to our readers the most GLORIOUS, the most DECISIVE VICTORY, ever obtained by the Navy of Great Britain——it has been obtained at a very dear rate——the Gallant NELSON, who has so often led the fleets of his country to victory, was killed in the action, an event which must fill every Briton with anguish. Thus has fallen one of the greatest ornaments of our country, but his name and heroic actions will be remembered to the remotest posterity in the hearts of his grateful and lamenting countrymen.'[32]

Meanwhile, two British packets brought copies of the *London Gazette* across the Irish Sea on 9 November to Dublin, where *Saunders's News-Letter* also published Collingwood's dispatch.[33]

In northern Europe, the news travelled by a variety of means. By 11 November, the information had reached Rotterdam. 'On 19 November,' the *Naval Chronicle* reported, 'all the Ships in the road of Elsineur [Elsinor, i.e. Helsingør, Denmark] fired three discharges in celebration of the Victory off Cadiz. Immediately afterwards, their flags were lowered and three minute-guns fired on account of the death of Lord Nelson.'[34]

Figure 3.1 Lieutenant Lapenotière's Lloyd's Patriot Fund £100 Trafalgar Sword. National Maritime Museum, Greenwich: NMM (Greenwich Hospital Collection) WPN 1045.

The News Transmitted to North America

The different ways that people on the western shores of the North Atlantic learned of the battle is indicative of multiple ways in which the news travelled further across the seas and around the globe. During the latter half of December 1805, the story was transmitted by two means. First, the oral transmission of news from one ship to another, and second, the delivery of newspapers and reports by ship, most importantly newspapers that had printed Collingwood's dispatches to the Admiralty.[35]

The first news of Trafalgar to reach North America arrived in Portland, Maine, on Friday, 13 December 1805, nearly two months after the battle. The brig *Fox*, Captain Lee, arrived at Portland, thirty-five days from Nantes, having spoken the ship *Neptune* of New York, fifteen days out from Liverpool en route to New York. On the day of his arrival, Captain Lee told the news to the *Portland Gazette and Maine Advertiser*. The newspaper first printed a handbill with the information, then repeated it in its next regular issue on Monday, 16 December.[36]

That same day, Captain March arrived in Newburyport, Massachusetts, forty-six days out from Amsterdam. He had been boarded in the English Channel on 7 November by an armed brig, which informed them of dispatches received at the Admiralty the day before the armed brig left port. This news appeared in the *Boston Gazette* on 19 December.[37] Seventy miles away in Newport, Rhode Island, the *Newport Mercury* repeated the same report.[38]

Further south at New York City, the ship *Neptune*, Captain Stanton, arrived that same day, thirty-five days out from Liverpool, with news from London papers, including the *London Gazette Extraordinary* on Wednesday, 6 November 1805, which contained Collingwood's dispatch. After that, Collingwood's dispatch appeared over the next twelve days in a dozen other newspapers ranging from New York to Philadelphia, Easton, Maryland, and Washington, DC, as well as Hartford, Connecticut; Rutland, Vermont; Newport, Rhode Island; Montreal; and Quebec.[39]

To the north, the brig *Good Intent*, Captain Davis, arrived at Halifax, Nova Scotia, on Thursday, 17 December 1805, with the *London Gazette Extraordinary*. Newspapers in Halifax and St. John's quickly published Collingwood's dispatch.[40]

A week later, on Monday, 23 December 1805, the ship *Hare*, Captain Chew, arrived in New York City, having left Gibraltar on 25 October, where, two days earlier, a schooner carrying Collingwood's dispatches had arrived. On leaving Gibraltar, *Hare* was initially under convoy of the US Brig *Vixen*, Lieutenant George Cox, and had sailed to Málaga, 70 miles east of Gibraltar. There, Chew obtained the report of the American consul, Mr Kirkpatrick. This appears to be the same information that his informant at Cádiz sent to Captain Hugh G. Campbell, US Navy. On 30 October, Campbell, commanding USS *Essex*, forwarded it on to the Secretary of the Navy.[41]

Then, Chew went on to obtain additional information. On 5 November, after parting from the convoy, *Hare* was 40 miles ESE of Cape Spartel when she fell in with Collingwood's fleet and fourteen British ships of the line. H.M. Sloop *Martin* boarded *Hare* and provided further details of Nelson's death and the Trafalgar action. The New York City newspapers printed Chew's and Consul Kirkpatrick's reports on Tuesday, 24 December, and the *Alexandria* [Virginia] *Daily Advertiser* copied them on 27 December 1805.[42]

Further south in Charleston, South Carolina, the brig *Mary*, Captain Wood, arrived on 28 December 1805, thirty-four days from Gibraltar, with a passenger who was at Cádiz during the action and then at Algeciras and Gibraltar. His account appeared in Charleston's *City Gazette*.[43]

The News Reaches the West Indies

Meanwhile, in the West Indies, which had been directly involved in part of the Trafalgar campaign earlier in 1805, the first news arrived at Barbados. The ship *Venerable*, Captain Lewtas, arrived at Bridgetown, Barbados, on Saturday, 14 December 1805, forty-five days out from

Liverpool. En route on 28 November, she spoke the ship *Pandora* from Bremen bound to St. Thomas, which on 16 November had been boarded off Madeira by Lieutenant Brown of H.M. frigate *Tartar* and given the news. Two days later, on Monday, 16 December, the American brig *Sally*, Captain Boardman of Wiscasset, Maine, arrived in Bridgetown, Barbados. On 4 December, he had fallen in with the American brig *Nancy*, Captain Orgood, thirty-one days out from Cádiz and bound for New York, with the news. Both reports appeared in the same issue of the Barbados newspaper.[44] Several days later, on Friday, 20 December 1805, the packet *Princess Elizabeth* arrived at Bridgetown, Barbados, thirty-eight days from Falmouth, carrying the *London Gazette Extraordinary* with Collingwood's dispatch, which was printed the following day in the *Barbados Mercury and Bridgetown Gazette*.[45]

The News in the Wider World

The news of Trafalgar reached other parts of the world at various points during 1806. Those living in Calcutta, West Bengal, first learned of the battle from reports published in Italian newspapers that reprinted a story from Gibraltar dated 25 October. The *Calcutta Gazette* published this on 20 March 1806. Nearly a month later, the Honourable Company's ship *Princess of Wales* arrived at Calcutta carrying copies of the *London Gazette*. Using that source, the *Calcutta Gazette* immediately published on 24 April Collingwood's dispatches from the 6 November 1805 issue of the *London Gazette Extraordinary*.[46]

Further to the east in Australia, *The Sydney Gazette and New South Wales Advertiser* reported on 13 April 1806 that Captain George Byng of the 64-gun *Belliqueux* had brought two essential pieces of news to the Governor of New South Wales, Captain Philip Gidley King. Byng reported that he had participated in the capture of the Cape Colony on 10 January 1806 with the forces of Commodore Sir Home Popham and Major-General Sir James Baird. He provided Governor King with a verbatim copy from the *Cape Gazette Extraordinary* of Sunday, 26 January 1806. 'His Excellency the Major-General Commanding in Chief seizes with transport the occasion of announcing the signal and glorious success of His Britannic Majesty's Arms in a Naval action, over the combined fleets of France and Spain. This splendid atchievement [sic] is however obscured by the loss of Vice Admiral Lord Viscount Nelson, whose deathless name could scarcely acquire new lustre by heroic exploits.'[47]

Baird had also ordered detailed information placed in *The Cape Gazette* that Captain Higginson of the American ship *Laura* had reportedly obtained from H.M. schooner *Pickle* at 4 p.m. on the afternoon of 28 October as she was carrying Collingwood's dispatch to England. *The Cape Gazette* noted that Captain Sykes of HMS *Nautilus* confirmed Higginson's information at Lisbon, where Higginson had departed on 4 November for the Cape. Historians now know that *Laura* did not directly encounter *Pickle*, but Higginson's statement suggests that he likely gathered the information at Lisbon when his ship was wind-bound in the Tagus, a period that included the three nights of 'grand illuminations' that took place. His statement is the only indirect evidence that Sykes's report about Trafalgar, which he sent to Lisbon from *Nautilus* after meeting at sea with Lapenotière in *Pickle*, may have reached shore.[48]

The news arrived at Hobart Town, Tasmania, ten months after the battle in August 1806. Colonel David Collins was the founding Lieutenant-Governor of the convict colony at Sullivan's Cove on the Derwent River's west side. The two-year-old isolated colony was facing starvation in 1806 when Collins ordered a quiet day of prayer and thanksgiving for 'the news of the great Naval victory'. There was little merriment in their dire condition, but Collins ordered his garrison—a single company of Royal Marines—to pray in the chapel, followed by a parade and the firing of a royal salute. In honour of the occasion in which the Royal Marines had played a significant part, Collins freed Royal Marine Job Stokes from his confinement for a misdemeanour in 'hopes that he will in future feel in common with his Brother Soldiers that he belongs to a Corps that will not suffer any disgrace brought upon it'.[49]

Individual Reactions

As the public versions of the news of Trafalgar spread across the world from one gazette or newspaper to another, individuals who participated in the action had their own stories to tell. Some of these were the required official after-action reports from commanding officers or the senior surviving officer on board the participating warships. Others were private letters to family and friends.

The surviving official naval reports, logbooks, and other documents are readily available among naval records in their respective national archives. Numerous scholars have subsequently consulted them and published them.[50] An exception to this was the original copies of Collingwood's dispatches on Trafalgar, whose existence was brought to the broader public's knowledge only in 2013. In 1821, King George IV ordered the Admiralty to gather the key original dispatches from each of the seven major naval victories during the wars of the French Revolution and Empire, leaving only copies in the files. The Admiralty had these original documents bound with portraits of the admirals and maps in a colossal volume measuring more than 2 feet long, 18 inches wide, and several inches thick. The volume, covered in blue velvet and decorated with silver-gilt symbols of naval warfare, was placed in a satin-lined wooden box. These original British records of events, written in the immediate aftermath of the battles, within the span of living memory of the events—Trafalgar among them—had become a totem of naval memory and a display of British naval heritage. In 1859, the Admiralty presented the volume to the British Library, where it has been housed and displayed since then.[51]

Collingwood's dispatch from Trafalgar was the same that Lieutenant Lapenotière had brought in the schooner *Pickle*, and the *London Gazette* had printed in edited form, and that newspapers around the world had copied. Unusually, in the collection, the Trafalgar material also includes several other dispatches recounting the battle's aftermath, including Collingwood's order to Lapenotière.[52]

Collingwood's dispatch was significant because it was written by the senior surviving British naval officer and a major figure in the action. However, like any other participant in the sprawling action at Trafalgar, he saw and understood many aspects of the event but not all of them. As the new commander-in-chief, others who saw the action from different aspects gave him their reports, but he had not yet received them all when he wrote his dispatch, as illustrated by the example of Captain Durham of *Defiance*.

Much remained to be understood and analysed after the fact. Every commanding officer shared the same problem: the smoke and intensity of the action obscured a great deal. Like all such action reports, much depends on the individual reactions and mentality of those who wrote them as they needed to reconcile their experiences and put them into words. Throughout history, it has often been a challenging task for a sailor of decisive action who has little time for reflection or analytical writing. Official reports can also provide writers with the opportunity to publicize and even justify their actions, with an eye to their promotions or reputations, rather than producing a bland, unemotional, strictly factual narrative. At the same time, the observer's facts or conclusions may be wholly or partially mistaken. In comparing reports, it is difficult, if not impossible, to explain all the discrepancies between them.[53]

In the case of the French dispatches, those of Villeneuve and his flag captain, Magendie, and those of Dumanoir were written while they were prisoners of war in England. They may have intended to influence the perceptions of their captors.[54] At the same time, Villeneuve gathered accounts of the battle from both British and French sources that he could use to defend himself when he returned to France.[55] Other than Collingwood's dispatches, most contemporary reports were unknown or unavailable to the public, but they gradually came to light only later through historians' efforts to analyse and explain the actions.[56] There were, however, official uses of this material. For example, four years after the battle, Napoleon ordered two courts of enquiry to examine the conduct of Rear-Admiral Dumanoir, one for Trafalgar and another for the subsequent action between 11 and 13 November 1805. In the first case, the court cleared Dumanoir of any misconduct; in the second, it found that he 'had showed too much indecision in all his manoeuvres' but concluded that 'there is nothing but praise to be bestowed upon the constant courage of the captains, officers, and crews'. In the second case, the court of enquiry resulted in a court-martial that eventually cleared Dumanoir on 8 March 1810. He returned to active service the following year.[57]

In contrast to the official communications and records that informed official enquiries and courts-martial, personal communications were never meant to be a permanent record but rather to inform relatives and loved ones at home that they had survived the conflict. The British descriptions tended to be dry, factual, and reticent, with only hints of emotion. Twenty-four-year-old Quartermaster Benjamin Stevenson of HMS *Victory* described to his sister 'a Verrey hard ingagement', with seven ships attacking *Victory*. 'Dear Sister I shall say but little more about it For it is too Cruel for your feelings but I dare say you will here Enough of it in the Newspaper.'[58] After lamenting Nelson's death and wishing for peace between France and Britain, Stevenson went on to say, 'I can not Express it with Pen and Ink but the sorrow liyes all at my hart . . . it is most time fore me to have a little pleasure in my life for this is A miserable one at Present.'[59] James West, a twenty-nine-year-old able seaman in *Britannia*, wrote to his parents that his ship had captured the Spanish *Santísima Trinidad* with a pun on his ship's name and a patriotic song. 'We took the largest ship belonging to any Nation in the world: she carried 140 guns. I am happy to inform you of such a glorious victory over such a Fleet, never was before. We went to our guns like sons of Britain, *Britania* struck home that day.'[60] Like many others, West felt the loss of Nelson deeply. 'I am sorry and every British Seaman too for the Noble Hero Lord Nelson is no more. He died in the arms of victory, the glory of the World around Him. They came out of Cadiz to take us, but the English Hero defied them. They do forget the *Victory* got her Guns to bear upon them and their 4 decker and played *Britons Strike home*.'[61] Chaplain John Greenly, serving in *Revenge*, hinted at the carnage of naval battle more explicitly when he wrote to his father, 'There has been a dreadful slaughter on board the *Revenge* and *Victory, Belleisle, Tonnant* & *Royal Sovereign*. I was wounded in twenty places by splinters of shot that came close to me, but mere scratches; its rather an unusual thing for a Chaplain to be wounded in action, but mine were so slight that I would not be put on the list of wounded.'[62]

Royal Marine Lieutenant Paul Nicholas, serving under Captain William Hargood in HMS *Bellisle*, supporting Collingwood's flagship, remembered his training and felt the leadership of his commanding officer as he first experienced the battle:

> My eyes were horror struck at the bloody corpses around me, and my ears rang with shrieks of the wounded and the moans of the dying. At this moment seeing almost everyone lying down, I was half disposed to follow the example and several times stooped for the purpose, but—and I remember the impression well—a certain monitor seemed to whisper, 'Stand up and do not shrink from your duty.' Turning round, my much esteemed and gallant senior [Captain Hargood] fixed my attention; the serenity of his countenance and the composure with which he paced the deck, drove more than half my terrors away; and joining him I became somewhat infused with his spirit, which cheered me on to act the part it became me.[63]

French and Spanish personal accounts of the battle typically had more graphic descriptions of the face of naval battle, perhaps to explain and justify their actions. Don Pedro Galdós wrote, 'The scene on board the *Santísima Trinidad* was simply infernal. She could not move. The English shot had torn our sails to tatters. It was as if huge invisible talons had been dragging at them. Fragments of spars, splinters of wood, thick hempen cables cut up as corn is cut by the sickle, fallen blocks, shreds of canvas, bits of iron, and hundreds of other things that had been wrenched away by the enemy's fire, were piled along the deck. Blood ran in streams about the deck, and in spite of the sand, the rolling of the ship carried it hither and thither until it made strange patterns on the planks. The ship creaked and groaned as she rolled, and through a thousand holes and crevices in her hull the sea spurted in and began to flood the hold.'[64]

A French Army officer in *Pluton* reported, 'A cannonball piercing the second battery killed three men and wounded several others, of whom I was one. I fell, bathed in my own blood and that of the dead men, I remained there for some time unconscious.' Others left him lying on the deck where he fell, thinking him dead, but when he regained consciousness, his shipmates took him to the surgeon, who dressed his three wounds. He continued, 'After that, when I was laid out on a mattress, I was again wounded in the head in two places by the splinters thrown up by a cannon ball as it passed through the orlop deck. What made me worse was that yet again I could not see, and that afterwards a dozen wounded men fell on my body and made me suffer considerably.'[65]

The broad differences between these reactions reflect characteristics of national social practices and temperaments as well as in the responses of each to winning and losing situations. The different ways in which participants from the three countries recorded their personal experiences revealed three distinct patterns for the broader, initial official, and historical accounts of the battle, as well as the inspiration for the initial commemorations of Trafalgar. For the British, it was a focus on a hero's death in the moment of victory. For the French, it was an event best ignored except to highlight brave exploits. Simultaneously, for the Spanish, it was an opportunity to celebrate bravery and professional competence in a battle against an overwhelming enemy. These three different patterns, created by the initial distribution of news about the Battle of Trafalgar, carried forward into artistic and formal commemoration, popular and professional naval cultures, as well as subsequent interpretations in history. The interpretation created through the widespread distribution of the edited version of Collingwood's dispatch in the press set the tone for memory, commemoration, and historical understanding in English-speaking lands around the world. Similarly, French reticence about the battle, as well as Spanish efforts to obtain recognition for their effective contributions, characterized memory, commemoration, and historical understanding in France and Spain.

4

The Battle of Trafalgar in Painting, Sculpture, and Monuments

Artists commemorated the Battle of Trafalgar in various high art forms, including traditional paintings, sculptures, and architectural monuments. In France, the state allocated extensive funding to support monuments commemorating Napoleon's imperial military victories; however, there was little mention of naval activities, as state policy primarily emphasized Napoleon's military victories on land.[1] At the time of the Battle of Trafalgar, the Royal Navy was the leading symbol of British society and its national identity. Naval victory, warships, naval commanders, and 'Jack Tar'—the ordinary sailor—were symbols of British patriotism. British state funding supported several key sculpture and architectural projects, while others, along with painters and other artists, were left to private commissions, competitions, and public exhibitions. Trafalgar symbolized the relationship between the navy and the nation in the context of all British naval victories in the war. Yet, the arts and funding for it reflected broader public opinion as the navy's reputation fluctuated. At the same time, the British Army gained higher regard during the last five years of the war, particularly through its successes in the Peninsular War and Waterloo. The reputation of Britain's hero, Horatio Nelson, also fluctuated in the light of revelations about his liaison with Lady Hamilton.[2]

Among the various art forms, painting emerged as a powerful method of commemoration. Nearly every contemporary British artist interested in painting naval battles has painted some version of the Battle of Trafalgar. As a result, numerous paintings emerged, contributing to an understanding of the battle and becoming an integral part of British national self-esteem.

The first visual image of the battle was a print that appeared from Laurie & Whittle in December 1805 entitled 'An Accurate Plan of the Positions of the British Fleet' with a cartouche that showed the wounded Nelson on the quarterdeck of *Victory* and the legend 'Ever Memorable Battle off Cape Trafalgar: 21 October 1805'. The publisher gave credit to Lieutenant Lapenotière and Captain Henry Blackwood for the information they provided as the first officers to reach London after the battle. A bird's-eye view diagram that was part map, showing the Spanish and African coasts and the entrance to the Strait of Gibraltar, appears to have been based on the diagram that accompanied Collingwood's dispatches, which Captain Magendie, Villeneuve's flag captain, had attested was an accurate depiction. These and several others that followed portrayed the approaching two British lines as close and orderly. Modern research has demonstrated that the two lines were far more ragged and scattered than depicted in the diagrams, leading to the difficult, bloody, and protracted battle that ensued. Nevertheless, these early diagrams influenced both the popular image of the battle and the battle as depicted in paintings.[3]

British Painting

The Royal Academy of Arts, established in 1768, made a notable contribution to the development of a distinctively British style in art and cultural patriotism.[4] Art depicting warships stretched back to the images in the Bayeux Tapestry, completed around 1077. It was, however, the Dutch who, in the early seventeenth century, developed a distinctive skill in creating a maritime atmosphere in their art. The two Willem van de Veldes, father and son, brought the Dutch approach to England in 1673. The style inspired and dominated English maritime painting for half a century. By the mid-eighteenth century, distinctly English characteristics began to emerge.[5] As these trends developed, the primary source for commissioning and purchasing maritime paintings were the ship captains and admirals who wanted to preserve the memory of their ships and the events in which they had participated. This audience demanded detailed technical accuracy from the artists in portraying warships and their equipment, as well as realistic representations of wind on the water, the sea, and the sky.[6]

In this tradition, Captain Henry Digby, who had commanded HMS *Africa* at Trafalgar, commissioned the experienced ship captain and artist John Thomas Serres to paint two large views of Trafalgar, one at the opening of the battle and one in the storm that followed. Both

Figure 4.1 *Neptune Engaged, Trafalgar, 1805*, by Francis Sartorius, Jr. (*c.*1782–*c.*1808). HMS *Neptune*, shown bow on, exchanges broadsides with the four-decked Spanish ship *Nuestra Señora de la Santísima Trinidad*. In the background to the right of the painting HMS *Conqueror* fires into the dismasted French flagship *Bucentaure*. The Picture Art Collection/Alamy Images.

works emphasized the distinctive role that Digby and HMS *Africa* played, having been separated from the main fleet the night before the action. Emphasizing Nelson's general guidance to his captains 'to place his ship alongside that of the enemy', Serres reflected Digby's view of *Africa*'s role as a kind of heroic single-handed action against the van of the Franco-Spanish fleet. In doing this, he did not depict *Africa* but instead painted the scene that Digby saw as he viewed both the battle and the storm from her quarterdeck.[7]

Another participant who commissioned work was Charles Middleton, Lord Barham. He had been the First Lord of the Admiralty and the strategic director on the British side of the campaign and battle. Barham employed another experienced mariner-artist, Nicholas Pocock, to paint two significant works showing the beginning (Figure 4.2) and the end of the Battle of Trafalgar as well as two other events relating to the broader Trafalgar campaign: Sir Robert Calder's action on 22 July 1805 and Sir Richard Strachan's action on 4 November 1805.

Figure 4.2 *The Battle of Trafalgar, 21 October 1805*, by Nicholas Pocock. IanDagnall Computing / Alamy Stock Photo.

After completing the paintings in 1812, Pocock prepared an accompanying notebook that contained illustrated watercolour sketches and descriptions of the painting, what art historian David Cordingly termed 'the almost obsessive care taken by the artist to achieve accuracy in his battle pieces'.[8] For each painting, he drew a schematic diagram of the battle that showed the wind and compass directions, the position of the ships, and a concise verbal description of the moment illustrated, all based on eyewitness reports and even questions the artist posed.[9]

The commissioned painting played a unique role in preserving visual versions of individual memories and notable actions, but it was not the only approach to commemorating the battle. As part of the broader attempt to promote a distinctively British form of art and to create a market for British artists, wealthy British collectors established the British Institution for the Encouragement of British Artists in 1806. It commissioned some works for public collections and awarded prizes. For example, in 1824, the British Institution offered a £200 and a £100 prize for the best sketches of the battles of the Nile and Trafalgar. The following year, the prize was £500 for a finished painting that would be donated to the recently established National Gallery of Naval Art in the Painted Hall at Greenwich Hospital, the first gallery devoted to any aspect of national history and one of the first national, rather than royal or aristocratic, collections of art in Britain.[10] The competition produced more than thirty paintings. The Institution awarded its second prize to William Daniell, a recently elected member of the Royal Academy, for his finished painting of the Battle of Trafalgar. Surprisingly, however, for a competition designed to emphasize the arts of sea painting and naval victory, the first prize in the Trafalgar competition went to Samuel Drummond. His image looked aft on *Victory*'s main deck with the ladder to the quarterdeck crowded with sailors to show the spot where Nelson fell. Another artist, Denis Dighton, created a notable painting of *Victory*'s deck, depicting the moment when a sniper's bullet struck Nelson.[11]

This reaction was no surprise in the context of the typical British response to Trafalgar. When the news arrived in Britain, it was not greeted with joy and dancing in the streets but rather in a mood of sorrow and loss at the death of a great leader. Nelson's sacrifice of his life at the moment of victory did not affect the battle's outcome, but it did demonstrate the virtues of effective leadership and decentralized naval command. The charismatic Nelson had already inspired his men to do what was necessary to gain victory. The focus on Nelson served to reflect popular sentiment towards a national hero and, at the same time, gave the battle a specifically inspirational and heroic meaning.

Arthur William Devis made one of the first such significant paintings in response to Josiah Boydell's offer of a £500 prize for the best oil painting of Nelson's death. Released from debtors' prison to undertake the work, he completed his painting before the deadline of 21 March 1806. Devis's painting was a realistic view of Nelson's death as it happened below in the cockpit of HMS *Victory*. The American-born artist Benjamin West, who had already become famous for his 1770–1 painting of the death of General James Wolfe on the Plains of Abraham at

Figure 4.3 John Constable painted this large and uncharacteristic watercolour of *His Majesty's Ship Victory in the Battle of Trafalgar between Two French Ships of the Line* for the 1806 Royal Academy exhibition. The Picture Art Collection/Alamy Images.

Québec during the Seven Years' War, looked askance at Devis's work. West despairingly commented that he had depicted Nelson 'dying in the gloomy hold of a ship like a sick man in a Prison Hole. To move the mind,' West declared, 'there should be a spectacle presented to raise & warm the mind, and all sh[oul]d be proportioned to the highest idea conceived of the Hero.'[12]

At age sixty-seven in 1805, West undertook a companion piece to his Wolfe painting. He exhibited three versions of *The Death of Nelson* between 1807 and 1811. West's key theme echoed the sentiments that Collingwood had used in his General Order to the fleet that accompanied his widely circulated dispatch: 'The ever to be lamented death of Vice Admiral Lord Viscount Nelson... whose memory will be ever dear to the British Navy, and the British Nation, whose zeal for the honour of his King, and the Interests of his Country will be ever held up, as a shining Example for a British Seaman...'.[13] West envisioned this idea in his painting *The Immortality of Nelson* through the allegorical figures of Neptune and Victory, lifting Nelson's body upward as Britannia receives it in glory. As in his depiction of Wolfe, Nelson's death is reminiscent of traditional religious paintings of Christ's removal from the Cross. The painting represented sacrifice, rather than merely the pursuit of glory, as a distinctively British aspect of victory. The composition included sea monsters, British lions, and winged putti, symbolizing the continuation of Nelson's immortal genius. West initially envisaged this painting as an altarpiece for a proposed memorial.[14]

West painted three other paintings on the theme. His first version appeared as *A Sketch for a Monument to Lord Nelson*, featuring the image of Nelson's death at the centre, with mourning sailors and marines as supporters, along with wrecked hulls of the Spanish warships *San Josef* and *San Nicolas*, which Nelson had captured at the Battle of St Vincent in 1797. His second version showed a realistic image of Nelson's death in the cockpit, while the third showed Nelson on the quarterdeck of *Victory* in a pose reminiscent of his *Death of Wolfe*. Again, he included many officers and seamen. He even paid several of *Victory*'s sailors a guinea apiece to travel from Chatham dockyard to London to sit for the portraits he used. West claimed that thirty thousand people had come to his home to view this immensely popular picture, although the art critics thought it far inferior to his *Wolfe*.[15]

J. M. W. Turner and Trafalgar

Among all the competing British painters, J. M. W. Turner's works dominated British maritime art in the first half of the nineteenth century. Between 1806 and 1839, he produced three major works focused on Trafalgar, spanning over thirty years. Shortly after Nelson's funeral, Turner completed his first Trafalgar painting and exhibited it at his gallery in Harley Street. This painting was a view of the battle from the starboard mizzen shrouds of HMS *Victory*. By including both Nelson's death and the mêlée action of four ships of the line locked in combat—the French ship *Redoubtable* and the British ships *Victory*, *Temeraire*, and *Neptune*—in his image, Turner strove to create for his viewers a vicarious experience of war at sea.[16] The reaction to Turner's first painting was distinctly mixed when it was exhibited in 1806, and it remained so after he reworked it in 1808. One critic wrote, 'It appeared to me a very crude unfinished performance, the figures miserably bad.'[17] Such views echoed several others, but the engraver John Landseer probably understood more clearly than others the artist's intent: 'Mr. Turner, in the picture before us, had detailed the death of *his* hero, while he has suggested the whole of a great naval victory, which we believe has never before been successfully accomplished, if it has been attempted, in a *single* picture.'[18]

In 1822, King George IV commissioned Turner to create another painting of Trafalgar for display in the State Apartments of St James's Palace, paired explicitly with Philip de Loutherbourg's portrayal of *Lord Howe's Action, also known as the Glorious First of June, 1794*. These paintings and images of two of Wellington's victories highlighted George III and George IV as the sovereigns who oversaw Britain's military and naval prowess. Turner's new painting echoed de Loutherbourg's elemental composition, with a ship of the line dominating the upper part of the painting. At the same time, officers and men saved lives in the lower portion. Yet, Turner's work was dramatically different. De Loutherbourg had created a spectacular battle scene that emphasized movement and confrontation.

In contrast, Turner conflated several events to create a static emphasis on HMS *Victory* and her crew gathered in a group in and around small boats in the foreground. Nelson's death is not apparent, but the exaggerated image of his flagship flying parts of the famous signal 'England Expects Every Man to Do His Duty' and the falling foremast carrying his white vice-admiral's flag evokes his dominant but unseen presence. In the foreground, just below the water's surface, a close viewing can make out fragments of Nelson's motto, *Palmam qui meruit ferat*: 'Let him who has earned it bear the palm.' These words appear next to the sailors rescued from the sea, allowing the painting to emphasize the contributions and sacrifices of the ordinary seamen in the battle. Turner's grim presentation of wounded, dying, and drowned sailors in a sea scattered with wreckage prefigured Francisco Goya's *Disasters of War* and *Dos de Mayo*, which Goya would paint a few years later, which reminded viewers of the horrors of war as well as sacrifice and glory.[19]

For the naval audience that preferred precision and detailed technical accuracy in portraying warships, Turner's 1823–4 *Battle of Trafalgar, 21 October 1805* was no more successful than his earlier 1806–8 painting. Naval critics of the day included the Duke of Clarence—the future King William IV—who had served in the Royal Navy and did not appreciate his subordination of technical detail to artistic and emotional values. Turner spent eleven unpaid days adjusting the painting to satisfy the naval critics at Court but felt that the changes had spoiled the effect he wanted. For his part, Turner disliked painting the complex rigging of a warship and preferred, for visual balance, to emphasize the mass of a ship's hull by increasing its apparent size and de-emphasizing the rigging.

Many interpreted the king's failure to award Turner a knighthood, along with his decision in 1829 to remove the paintings from St James's Palace and place them in the National Gallery of Naval Art at Greenwich, as indications of general disapproval and demotion. However, the move from the palace, with its restricted access, to a public space had the opposite effect, increasing the commemorative connections for the painting to the Royal Navy and naval victory. Turner's painting, along with de Loutherbourg's, took pride of place at the entrance to the Painted Hall, where every visitor saw them on both arrival and departure. The paintings were the last of thirty-eight from the Royal Collection to be placed at Greenwich during its first five years as a naval art gallery. They were the culmination of royal approval for making Greenwich the centre for national naval commemoration. In the previous year, the Upper Hall, which had been the place where Nelson's body lay in state before his funeral, had also become a venue to exhibit Nelson's relics when the Duke of Clarence presented to the gallery the coat that Nelson had worn at the Battle of the Nile. The paintings of the first and last great naval battles of the Revolutionary and Napoleonic Wars created symmetry in a visual collection of images that emphasized the commemoration of national naval triumphs.

By 1830, full-length statues of St Vincent, Earl Howe, Duncan, and Nelson flanked the two paintings. These plaster copies of the identical statues, which were memorials in St Paul's Cathedral, contributed to creating a secular monument that emphasized personal heroism and virtues, as well as the hierarchy and authority necessary for national naval success. Soon, many other Trafalgar relics joined the display, including Prince Albert's gift of Nelson's bloodstained coat from the Battle of Trafalgar. This commemoration, along with the physical presence in residence of the naval veterans of these wars as Greenwich Hospital pensioners, added a powerful commemorative dimension for visitors. Acting as guides to the visitors and as repositories of living memory, they established a human and tangible connection to the visual image that Turner had created of duty and sacrifice.[20]

Turner completed his third painting, which touched on the theme of Trafalgar, in 1839: *'The Fighting Temeraire,' Tugged to her Last Berth to be Broken Up, 1838*. While the title did not explicitly reference the battle, describing the ship as the Fighting *Temeraire* immediately evoked the

Battle of Trafalgar in the public mind. Like his two earlier Trafalgar paintings, it is not an accurate historical record but an image that produced broader artistic meaning. Turner pictured the ship, which had played a prominent role at Trafalgar, as a steam tugboat pulled her up the River Thames to the breakers' yard at Rotherhithe. It was a common sight, as at this time about half of the British fleet that had fought at Trafalgar had already been sold off or scrapped. However, Turner made his painting when the fate of *Temeraire* was of great public interest. By 1839, a growing nostalgia and romanticism for the age of sailing ships had emerged. At the same time, there was a notable revival of interest in Nelson's life and the Battle of Trafalgar through him. The navy's sale of the ship and her final voyage to the shipbreakers' yard made headlines in every major news publication. One London newspaper interpreted Turner's meaning in his image of the ghostly ship under a cloudy sky, with a barely visible waning crescent moon, contrasted against the warm colours of the sunrise reflected in the river: 'A gorgeous horizon poetically intimates that the sun of the *Temeraire* is setting in glory.'[21] For some viewers, the painting symbolized the passing of the age of sail, while for others, it represented British postwar decline.[22] For others, the artist was romanticizing a process of technological transformation that was creating a new and potentially threatening world.

Those who had not understood or appreciated J. M. W. Turner's attempt to capture the essence of the naval and artistic world in his Trafalgar paintings continued to want more precise visual images that reflected a lifelike and more literal interpretation of the event. The next major artist to emerge for the subject was Clarkson Stanfield, the last of the British artists who had experienced the Napoleonic Wars. He had served in the merchant navy for eight years and had been an able seaman when the Royal Navy pressed him into naval service during the last years of the war. Upon demobilization, he became a professional painter and initially worked with John Thomas Serres, painting stage sets for the theatre. King William IV noticed one of his works at an exhibition and commissioned him to paint a view of Portsmouth and the opening of the new London Bridge in 1831. His royal commissions swept him quickly into the Royal Academy, bringing a range of new commissions from prominent individuals.[23] He painted three significant works relating to our theme. In 1836, Stanfield completed his version of the *Battle of Trafalgar* for the United Service Club. This highly successful painting soon earned him an appointment as curator of the Naval Gallery at Greenwich, where he advised on acquisitions, the maintenance of the collection, and the Painted Hall. While holding that position in 1853, the railway contractor Sir Samuel Morton Peo commissioned him to paint *HMS Victory with the body of Nelson on board towed into Gibraltar on 28 October 1805, seven days after the Battle of Trafalgar.* Art critics lauded this work for its dramatic power.[24] His melodramatic description of the painting ran in part:

> Battle stained and tempest tossed, a mighty ship comes on,
> no shout of Triumph welcomes here for the glorious victory won,
> For she carries her dead admiral, killed in Trafalgar's Bay...[25]

Stanfield made his last contribution to the theme in 1863 with his *The Situation of His Majesty's Ship, The Defense, and her Prize. Il St. Ildefonso, on the morning following the Battle of Trafalgar, Cadiz, and Rota in the distance, with many of the captured ships ashore on the coast between Cadiz and Cape Trafalgar*. The art critic of *The Times* enthusiastically described his images of the ship 'weltering in the trough of the sea, the union jack flying over the proud flag of Spain'.[26]

Naval Art in France

Meanwhile, landscapes and marine paintings had long been considered marginal subjects in France. However, before the Revolution, Claude-Joseph Vernet painted a masterful series of twenty-four views of French harbours, which his talented pupil Jean-François Hue completed. In the years that followed, the levelling effect of the Revolution and Napoleon's military preferences had reduced the prestige of the French Navy. During that period, there were few significant artists available who could record or commemorate French naval operations.

Figure 4.4 *Le Redoubtable à Trafalgar*, by Louis-Philippe Crépin, 1806. The artist depicted the action with the French tricolour flying high, while HMS *Victory*'s White Ensign lay in the water, symbolizing French success in killing Nelson. Fuente: Musée national de la Marine, Paris.

Louis-Phillipe Crépin was one of those few. In 1806, he painted *Redoubtable at Trafalgar* (Figure 4.4). The artist saw Trafalgar as a stinging defeat that must be avenged. In his painting, he depicted *Redoutable*'s flag at the centre. In contrast, the flag of HMS *Victory* trailed in the water, symbolically replacing the stinging defeat of the battle by celebrating Nelson's death as a victory.[27] This scene resonated widely in France as competing stories circulated about who in *Redoubtable* had fired the bullet that killed Nelson.

There was little subsequent interest in naval art until the restoration of the French monarchy under King Louis-Phillipe from 1830 to 1848 when the Grand Admiral of France appointed Louis Garnerey as his marine painter. A decade later, the French Navy gained widespread popularity within France with the victory of the French, Russian, and British fleets over the Turks at Navarino in 1827 during the Greek War of

Independence. In 1830, the French Navy commissioned for the first time two *peintres officiels de la marine* (official painters of the navy), Crépin and Théodore Gudin, while Auguste Étienne François Mayer became the marine painter and drawing master at the newly established École Navale, the French Naval Academy. During the reign of Louis-Philippe, the French Navy commissioned these three artists, among others, to produce hundreds of paintings over the coming decades for an illustrated version of French naval history for the newly created Musée de l'Historie at Versailles. Among them, Auguste Mayer became a prominent and widely recognized marine artist. In 1836, Mayer exhibited his painting of Villeneuve's flagship titled *Combat Glorieux du vaisseau le Bucentaure contre trois vaisseau Anglais, le 21 octobre 1805*. It was one of six studies that Mayer made of *Bucentaure* during the Battle of Trafalgar. Curiously, at some point in the early twentieth century, the painting was mislabelled at the Musée de la Marine in Paris as *Redoubtable Surrendering*. Scholars eventually corrected this false attribution by closely examining the details of the French ship, identifying her as *Bucentaure*.[28]

Spanish Art

Similarly, in Spain, significant artistic representations of Trafalgar appeared later in the mid-nineteenth century. A work in the Prado's collection by the Catalan artist Francisco Sans Cabot from 1862 depicts the wreck of the ship of the line *Neptuno* on the rocks of Puerto de Santa Maria after the battle. This eclectic work embodies the neoclassical style in depicting the resignation of the officers and men after a glorious defeat while simultaneously presenting the storm in a romantic style.[29]

In 1870, the Spanish artist Rafael Monleón y Torres, newly appointed conservator of painting at the Museo Naval de Madrid, exhibited his *'Battle of Trafalgar.' General View, 21 October 1805* (Figure 4.5). The artist chose to depict the battle's opening, when Admiral Collingwood's flagship, the *Royal Sovereign*, cut through the Franco-Spanish line between the Spanish ship *Santa Ana* and the French *Fougueux*, inflicting

Figure 4.5 *Combate de Trafalgar*, painted by Spanish artist Rafael Monleón y Torres (1853–1900) in 1870. Heritage Image Partnership Ltd/Alamy Images.

significant damage with its first broadside. Ships to the leeward of the Franco-Spanish line of battle are in the foreground. Monleón y Torres became known for his realism and attention to nautical detail, which included a touch of vivid romanticism that brought together history and myth while contributing to the construction of national consciousness in late nineteenth-century Spain.[30] Providing an unusual sculptural response in 1884, Ángel Díez Sánchez created his *Episodio de Trafalgar*, which depicted a warrior standing in grief over a fallen sailor.[31]

Two other artists elaborated on the prevailing Spanish interpretation of the battle as one that saved Spanish honour through valiant conduct in combat. Eugenio Álvarez Dumont painted in 1892 the heroic death of Brigadier Cosme Damián Churruca on board the 74-gun *San Juan Nepomuceno*.[32] In 1903, Ángel Cortellini Sánchez painted the struggle between *Santa Ana*, the flagship of Admiral Ignacio Maria de Álva, and Collingwood's *Royal Sovereign*, in which the Spanish ship suffered heavy casualties and materiel damage.[33]

Modern British Painting

While modern paintings of the Battle of Trafalgar are relatively rare among French and Spanish naval artists, British artists have continued to carry on the theme into the twenty-first century. The most prominent of the later British artists was William Lionel Wyllie, a prolific painter recognized as the most distinguished British maritime artist of his day. He painted an image of HMS *Victory* as early as 1892. Six years later, in 1898, he painted *The Battle of the Nile, 1 August 1798*, to mark the centenary of the battle, then exhibited it as his first historical painting at the Royal Academy in 1899. In painting this work, Wyllie followed the pattern of the earlier artists who had first-hand experience of the sea.

Similarly, in 1905, for the centenary of Trafalgar, he exhibited at the Royal Academy his *Trafalgar. 2:30 p.m., 21 October 1805*. He went on to make a copperplate etching of his Trafalgar painting. Having become keenly interested in the Napoleonic Wars and the Trafalgar period, he was a founding member of the Society of Nautical Research and was actively involved in the society's campaign to save HMS *Victory* in 1910. Over the years, he made several paintings, etchings, and drypoints of *Victory*. Towards the end of his life, he returned to the subject of Trafalgar. He painted a meticulously researched 42-foot (14 m) long *Panorama of the Battle of Trafalgar*, which King George V unveiled in 1930 for what is now part of the National Museum of the Royal Navy, located next to HMS *Victory* in Portsmouth. The navy paid for a special annex to the museum to house the panorama.[34]

In the latter part of the twentieth century, Geoff Hunt came to wide public notice, first as a book cover illustrator and later as a master painter of the sailing navy era. In 1987, the publisher HarperCollins commissioned Hunt to design the book covers for Patrick O'Brian's Aubrey-Maturin series of naval novels, then numbering thirteen volumes. Eventually, he created the covers for all twenty-one volumes published in editions worldwide. He collaborated with several other naval fiction writers and historians who wrote about the same period, including Julian Stockwin and the covers for the Heart of Oak Sea Classic series that Henry Holt published in the United States in the late 1990s. After that, Hunt transitioned from book-cover illustration to creating larger paintings. In 1998, Richard Lucroft Limited Editions commissioned him to make five paintings of 'Nelson's Ships' for sale as prints between 1998 and 1999. One of them was *Victory Races Temeraire for the Enemy Line, Trafalgar, 21 October 1805*, focusing on the period of anticipation as Nelson's line of battle approached the Franco-Spanish ships. A sequel in the same series was *Victory Breaks the Enemy Line, Trafalgar, 21 October 1805*, depicting the moment when *Victory* is about to pass ahead of the French *Redoubtable* and astern of Villeneuve's flagship, *Bucentaure*. As a follow-up to these paintings in 1999, an airline pilot who was passionately interested in the subject commissioned Hunt to paint *HMS Victory on the Atlantic Chase*, illustrating Nelson's voyage with the Mediterranean fleet as they chased Villeneuve across the Atlantic to the West Indies during the first portion of the Trafalgar campaign. In the two decades that followed, Hunt accepted several commissions to paint scenes of the Battle of Trafalgar.[35]

British maritime artists have continually painted images related to the Battle of Trafalgar for two centuries. The expression of other forms of commemorative art is much more limited.

The French Arc de Triomphe

During the Revolutionary and Napoleonic Wars, France maintained a consistent policy of raising monuments, funded by the government, that drew attention to the ideals of the French state and its leaders. Under Napoleon, the ancient Romans inspired the French approach, in which monuments were seen as manifestations of the divine authority of the ruler, who was believed to be able to foresee events and provide for them. Among the many allusions to Roman imperial practice in the Napoleonic period is the Arc de Triomphe at the Place de l'Étoile in Paris, which makes a direct reference to the Roman arch that Emperor Titus built in Rome in 85 AD as well as the last example of the Arch of Constantine from 315 AD. Napoleon selected the site and ordered the construction of the Arc de Triomphe in 1806 to commemorate the growing number of his victories. Like many monuments, however, their construction's time-consuming and costly processes changed as the political and social context around them evolved. Unfinished in

1810, when Napoleon wanted to drive through the Arc de Triomphe to reach the Palais de Louvre on the occasion of his marriage to Marie-Louise of Austria, he ordered a temporary structure of wood and canvas to be constructed. Approximately five hundred workers went on strike to protest their low wages, but the authorities soon rectified their situation. By Napoleon's fall from power in 1815, work on the incomplete Arc stopped entirely. After an eight-year delay, King Louis XVIII ordered work to resume, and the monument was quickly finished. No longer dedicated to Napoleon's Imperial Army, Louis XVIII wanted it dedicated to the Army of the Pyrenees, which had just restored King Ferdinand VII to the throne of Spain. The work continued through the death of Louis XVIII and into the reign of his brother Charles X. On 2 August 1830, some twenty thousand people gathered at the Arc and successfully demanded the abdication of King Charles X. After a hiatus of two years in which Louis-Phillipe came to the throne, work recommenced on the Arc de Triomphe, now to be dedicated to the armies of the French Revolution and the Empire, not just Napoleon's army. At that point, Lieutenant-General St-Cyr Nugues headed a commission that established the three lists of names engraved on the monument. The commission recommended the names of thirty battles of the Revolution and the Empire, ninety-six feats of arms, and the names of 384 generals. Finally completed in 1836, the government cancelled the grand celebration to mark its completion, fearing that a mob might attack Louis-Philippe.

There was also a huge public outcry about the names the commission had chosen to commemorate. The architect immediately added the names of 172 actions and 128 senior officers. Up until 1895, the government continued to add names. Although the Arc de Triomphe did not include the Battle of Trafalgar among commemorated battles, it did display the names of twenty-eight senior officers of the French Navy who fought during the Wars of the Revolution and Empire, including Decrès, the minister of the navy who oversaw the Battle of Trafalgar; Villeneuve, who commanded the Franco-Spanish fleet; Cosmao-Kerjulien, who commanded *Pluton* as a captain at Trafalgar and became

Figure 4.6 *Death of Admiral Magon at the Battle of Trafalgar*, by the Swiss-born history painter at the court of King Louis Philippe of France, Karl Girarde (1813–71). Chronicle / Alamy Stock Photo.

a rear admiral in 1806; Magon de Medine (Figure 4.6), who commanded *Algésiras* and died at Trafalgar as second in command of Gravina's division; and Rosily-Mesrosand, who Napoleon ordered to relieve Villeneuve.[36]

Spanish Memorial

A public monument to the Battle of Trafalgar in Spain stands in the Parque Genovés near the sea at Cádiz, erected at the battle's bicentenary in October 2005,[37] but the most significant memorial is located not far away on a military base. In 1850, a Spanish royal decree ordered the conversion of a late eighteenth-century church within the grounds of the San Carlos military district at San Fernandez, Cádiz, into the Pantheon of Illustrious Sailors (El Panteón de Marinos Ilustres).

'King Carlos III donated royal land to establish a new military base and enclave that extended the defences of Cádiz. To provide for this new community, construction began in 1786 on a neo-classical style parish church. After Carlos III's death, work on the church stalled, but the base soon became home to the Spanish Naval Academy, the headquarters of the Spanish Marines, and provided local offices for the navy. From 1845, the Naval Academy began using the church as its chapel, making it an ideal location for an inspirational place to honour and remember distinguished naval officers from all periods of Spanish naval history. Construction work resumed in 1850 and was completed in 1854. Although the Naval Academy moved from this site to Pontevedra in 1943, the Panteón remains in use as a mixture of naval mausoleum and memorial. Among the Spanish heroes of Trafalgar, Gravina, Alcalá Galiano, Cayetano Valdés, and Uriarte are buried in the Panteón. Stone tablets memorialize Churruca, Alcalá Galiano, and Alsedo.[38]

Gibraltar Cemetery

The oldest surviving memorials associated with the Battle of Trafalgar lie not far from the battle site. In a small cemetery at Gibraltar are the gravestones of thirty-six-year-old Captain Thomas Norman, Royal Marines, who served in HMS *Mars* during the battle, and twenty-year-old naval Lieutenant William Forster, who served in HMS *Colossus* (Figure 4.7). Brought to Gibraltar immediately after the battle, they died of their wounds ashore and were buried in what was then called the South Ditch Cemetery, consecrated in 1798. Most of those who died in the battle were buried at sea; others who died of their wounds at Gibraltar were interred in unmarked graves in the nearby St Jago's Cemetery. Gibraltar restored the South Ditch Cemetery in the 1980s after years of neglect. Formally named Trafalgar Cemetery, a monument to the battle was added in 1992. It is the site where commemorative ceremonies take place annually on 21 October.[39]

Figure 4.7 Grave of Lieutenant William Forster of HMS *Colossus,* who was wounded during the Battle of Trafalgar. Taken ashore at Gibraltar after the battle, he died of his wounds and was buried in the Southport Ditch Cemetery (now known as the Trafalgar Cemetery). David Osborn / Alamy Stock Photo.

British Monuments

During this period, the British approach to monuments was, in one respect, distinctive. Rather than commemorate an event, British monuments tended to follow a tradition of celebrating national genius in terms of individual heroism. For wartime heroes, this merged with the ideal of exemplary death in action. At the same time, Britons shared with the French an admiration for the practices of Classical Rome. There were two main ideas from the ancient Roman tradition that British leaders of the day found attractive. One was to create a mausoleum of heroes, as the French Constituent Assembly had done in 1791 by converting the Church of Saint-Geneviève into a model of the Pantheon in Rome. Another competing idea was commemorating human achievements with a column surmounted by a heroic statue.[40]

Emperor Trajan's column from 113 AD was one of the most famous monuments for Classical military achievements. The first column in Britain was the monument built in the 1670s by Sir Christopher Wren to commemorate the rebuilding of London after the fire. By the beginning of the eighteenth century, the idea of erecting columns to commemorate military achievements had already surfaced in Britain. The idea behind this was that the literal raising of a statue on a column created a spirit of emulation in the viewer, moving the hero from an earthly and ordinary person to a revered figure. This approach created a practical problem because the statue's details became indiscernible at a great height. Still, it had been first used in Britain in 1730, when Sarah, Duchess of Marlborough, raised such a column in Blenheim Park to commemorate her husband, John Churchill, 1st Duke of Marlborough. As early as 1799, the sculptor John Flaxman had proposed a naval victory column in Greenwich Park, but the suggestion found little traction then. By the late eighteenth century, Westminster Abbey had already become a jumble of sculptural monuments. In 1795, Parliament decided to use St Paul's Cathedral for such purposes in the future and to create a kind of British national Pantheon with the Royal Academy appointed to supervise the sculpture and artwork installed. For those reasons,

St Paul's became the obvious place to hold Nelson's funeral and to bury his remains in the crypt.[41]

After news of the battle reached London on 6 November 1805, numerous artists put forward proposals for monuments. However, no state funding was available for such memorials beyond the sculptures traditionally placed in Westminster Abbey and, from 1795, in St Paul's Cathedral. Many privately funded projects faltered after Nelson's public funeral, as the battle receded into memory, while war taxes and debt rose as the conflict dragged on for another decade. Finally, in 1814–15, Napoleon's abdication sparked renewed interest in private funding to create monuments to victory. In the meantime, two national monuments were advanced to commemorate the Battle of Trafalgar through Lord Nelson's exemplary and heroic figure. The first was a sculpture in St Paul's, in addition to the tomb, and the second was a national monument funded by public subscription. The first attempt to raise funds by public subscription failed, and the money was returned to the donors. In March 1807, many artists competed for the commission to create the Nelson sculpture and exhibited their work together at the British Institution. On the day of the exhibition's opening, the Royal Academy selected Professor John Flaxman to produce the sculpture. Flaxman worked on the project for eleven years, finally unveiling it in May 1818 and placing it in the cathedral between one of the great piers between the dome and the choir, opposite a statue of Marquis Cornwallis. A particularly successful blend of classical and modern details, the statue depicted a figure of Britannia pointing up to Nelson, with two small boys looking up to the exemplary figure of Nelson. By the time the monument was put in place, public interest in the project had faded, along with the idea of using St Paul's as a mausoleum. The victory at Waterloo brought demands for new monuments.[42]

In the years that the St Paul's monument was in progress, the City of London also commissioned a memorial for Guildhall. The alderman decided to hold an open competition for the work and select the artist from unsigned proposals. Artists submitted twenty-eight proposals for the project. Among them, a well-known sculptor, Charles Rossi, appeared to be the judges' choice; however, the council ultimately chose the unknown sculptor James Smith. The controversy surrounding this decision ended open competitions as no one wanted to risk the humiliation and unfavourable publicity it had involved. Smith completed the statue in 1810 with an eclectic group of figures, one of whom turned away from the others to inscribe Nelson's victory in an obelisk. There was a minimal positive reaction to what most viewers found a dull and confusing sculpture. As a result, the sculptor faced financial ruin and gained no prestige for his labours.[43]

Throughout Britain and British territories, cities, towns, and even private citizens proposed monuments to Nelson as a sincere response to his heroism and self-sacrifice at Trafalgar. Many of these ideas did not come to fruition, but some did. As early as November 1805, local ironworkers spontaneously erected a monolith at Taynuilt, on the north shore of Loch Etive in Argyll and Bute, Scotland. This work is the oldest surviving monument. The navy built an obelisk on Portsdown Hill overlooking Portsmouth in 1807. Edinburgh constructed a tower at Calton Hill, while Birmingham and Liverpool commissioned statues. Among others, Barbados commissioned a statute, while Dublin, Montreal, and Great Yarmouth erected pillars to Nelson's memory.[44]

The largest memorial to the Battle of Trafalgar in Britain is the Nelson Monument in Trafalgar Square, London. Upon the completion of the National Gallery of Art, built between 1833 and 1837, critics found the modest, low-lying façade of the building to be insufficient, both visually and architecturally, as the envisioned magnificent terminus for Whitehall. However, the area was then undergoing development, and the site of the square in front of the gallery, close to Parliament, Buckingham Palace, and the Admiralty, provided an ideal location for a monument. The area was named William IV Square, but in 1830, a building speculator persuaded the king to rename it Trafalgar Square. The major challenge was to design a suitable monument for the location, situated behind the National Gallery and adjacent to the Church of St Martin-in-the-Fields, with its distinctive spire. In February 1838, a group of prominent citizens proposed building a national monument to Nelson through public subscription and an open competition on the site at no public expense. Two previous attempts to create a memorial by public subscription to the navy and Nelson had failed in 1800 and 1805, but the project went ahead despite these warning precedents.

Artists submitted 140 designs and forty models to the committee charged with selecting the design. In February 1839, the committee approved William Railton's plan for a triumphal pillar featuring a 200-foot-high fluted Corinthian column surmounted by a 17-foot-high statue of Nelson. The base was to have four bronze reliefs depicting scenes from Nelson's life with four couchant lions at each corner of the base. The press complained that the decision was too hasty and the design lacking. To quell the ensuing uproar, a second competition took place. With only a slight improvement in the additional design choices, the committee again chose Railton's proposal. After the public controversy over the selection had subsided, new arguments arose among the architects and builders, while concern also grew for the stability of the tall, slender pillar. A Select Committee convened to consider the criticism and made scathing remarks about the design and location in its report. These criticisms and arguments cast further doubts on the project, reducing the donors' desire to provide funding. As a result, the committee reduced the pillar's height by 30 feet to 170 feet and made the elegant, slender column into a broader structure to withstand high winds. The slow progress of the fundraising initially led to a delay in casting the bronze lions and reliefs. In 1843, Edward Hodges Baily completed Nelson's statue in Portland stone rather than bronze in order to save money. When the artist exhibited the statue, the public initially received it poorly, as it was intended to be viewed at the top of the pillar, not at eye level. Additional problems arose. The failure to raise sufficient funds eventually pushed the monument's completion onto the Treasury.

Contrary to their contract, the foundry workers had mixed plaster into the bronze during the casting of the reliefs. Eventually, convicted of fraud, the Court sent them to prison. In 1844, Tsar Nicholas I was in London and passed through Trafalgar Square. According to *The Times*, 'he observed the unfinished and dreary appearance which the tardily erected memorial to immortal Nelson still presents to the eye. Inquiring the cause, His Majesty was informed that a want of the necessary funds was the only obstacle to its completion. The emperor immediately directed Chevalier Binkhausen to put down his name for a considerable sum,' later revealed to be £20,000.[45] Despite these issues, the Nelson column finally came to fruition in 1867 with the addition of Landseer's lions.[46]

The column's bronze relief representing Trafalgar depicted sailors and marines with muskets looking aloft to return the fire of the sniper whose bullet hit Nelson. The image produced little comment until the twenty-first century. The British-Nigerian historian David Olusoga pointed out in 2016 that the artist John Edward Carew included a black sailor. While unremarkable to the mid-nineteenth-century observer, when significant numbers of black seamen served in the Royal Navy, recent commentators have demanded better explanations of the historical context and even urged the removal of the Nelson column for the admiral's alleged role in promoting white supremacy.[47]

In 1807, writing under the pseudonym of Don Manuel Alvarez Espriella, Robert Southey suggested that if every victory should have a monument, they should be like the ancient monument for Thermopylae, dedicated to the memory of all who died in the battle.[48] After the end of the war, Parliament voted to create memorials for all who died at Trafalgar and Waterloo. In 1817, the Royal Academy's Committee of Taste selected Robert Smirke's design for a naval monument and allocated a budget of £100,000. Although these monuments did not materialize, individual monuments for others began to proliferate. For example, Richard Westmacott produced a memorial to Collingwood in St Paul's. In 1845, Newcastle erected a large statue of Collingwood on a column that served usefully at the entrance to the River Tyne as a seamark. At St Paul's, the monument to Captain George Duff, who died commanding HMS *Mars* at Trafalgar, includes a seaman weeping beside his casket. Other monuments appeared in churches and churchyards across the country.[49] There is even a memorial at the Royal Naval

Barracks at Chatham, England, to the French military and naval prisoners of war who died in captivity.[50]

As time passes, the placement of statues and monuments is constantly threatened, and they become the object of attack. As a result, the purpose can easily be lost or become irrelevant to modern life. Such was the fate of the Nelson Pillar raised in Dublin, Ireland, in 1808 (Figure 4.8). Placed in the centre of a main commercial street, Sackville Street, the monument caused both political and artistic controversy from its construction. As Irish national sentiment grew, the outsized and dominating presence of a memorial to an Englishman in a leading commercial area became increasingly out of place. Gradually, the street name became Gaelicized and renamed, with a monument to Daniel O'Connell, who led the failed 1848 rebellion. Later, other monuments to Irish nationalists followed, including one to the Irish nationalist politician Charles Stewart Parnell. 1916 Irish Republicans first attempted, but failed, to blow up the Nelson Pillar during the Easter Rising. Finally, it was destroyed in 1966. Its place was taken in 2003 by a thin needle entitled 'The Spire of Dublin or Monument of Light'.[51]

Similarly, the planters of Barbados raised a statue of Nelson at Bridgetown in 1813, funded by a grant from the Barbados Colonial Legislature. Traditionally, the explanations for having the figure in the West Indies were that Nelson and his fleet had saved Barbados from French occupation when he chased Villeneuve across the Atlantic during the Trafalgar campaign, or sometimes, more simply, that the Battle of Trafalgar had saved Barbados. The island had become a fully independent country from the United Kingdom in 1966 but chose to remain in the Commonwealth as a constitutional monarchy with Elizabeth II as head of state and Queen of Barbados. Fifty-five years later, on 30 November 2021, Barbados became an independent republic.

The Barbadian government removed the Nelson statue and placed it in storage just a year before the country became a republic. Recent historical research shows that the statue had little to do with honouring Nelson or the men who fought at Trafalgar. Instead, the Colonial Legislature was using it to appease the government in London at a

Figure 4.8 Nelson's Pillar, Sackville (now O'Connell) Street, Dublin, Ireland. The 134-foot-high monument was completed in 1809 and stood until 1966 when the IRA blew up Nelson's statue on the top and the remains of the column were subsequently demolished. https://commons.wikimedia.org/wiki/File:Nelson%27s_Pillar,_Sackville-Street,_Dublin_RMG_PU3914.tiff.

moment of political tension between the colony and the ministry in London, thereby demonstrating its loyalty. At the same time, it objected to the creation of the West Indian Regiment, made up of formerly enslaved men, which destabilized the established colonial order and created an interracial society.[52]

After the living memory of the Battle of Trafalgar transitioned to commemoration, the artistic creations inspired by the event experienced unexpected challenges. The original intentions to honour the British heroes of Trafalgar through monuments in a national mausoleum at St Paul's Cathedral were forgotten as the nineteenth century wore on. While many other projects failed, those that survived typically experienced challenges that altered them or found them out of tune with the changing circumstances of the society that surrounded them. In contrast, historically accurate painted images of battle scenes continued to be in demand for more than two centuries. Although largely ignored until the battle's bicentenary in France and Spain, the English-speaking world has seen widespread interest in the battle and Nelson's life, which has continued to stimulate interest and creativity among artists.

5

The Battle of Trafalgar in Popular Culture

In contrast to painting, sculpture, and other high art forms, popular culture reflects broad understanding within societies. It is typically expressed through the widespread sale of music, verse, printed materials, images, and objects. It involves a wide range of media that varies over time and differs between national and linguistic groups.[1] The public memory of the Napoleonic Wars varied significantly across Europe, differing widely from country to country. The same holds for the Battle of Trafalgar. There were distinct and changing approaches in Britain, France, and Spain over the next two centuries.[2]

Spanish Popular Culture

The initial Spanish response in popular culture was a mixture of grief, denial, and vindictive anger. It echoed a similar Spanish reaction to the failure of King Philip II's 'Invincible Armada' more than two hundred years earlier in 1588 with the belief that the weather had been at fault and Spain would eventually be victorious over Britain.[3]

The earliest appearances of the subject in popular culture occurred shortly after the battle, at Cádiz, the Spanish port from which the Franco-Spanish fleet had sailed and to which it had returned immediately after the battle. There were two notable publications at Cádiz: a poem and a pamphlet. The first was a six-page 'Poem on the "Battle of

21 October 1805"'. In it, the unidentified poet described heroic Spanish sailors, who 'In each clash, they increased their spirit' and described the British king as 'He who abuses the sceptre of the ocean' and should 'Cede that empire to the Hispanic Monarch'.[4] The second was a pamphlet that referred to Greek mythology to describe the *Public Entry of Admiral Nelson in the Court of Pluto on 23 October of This Year*. Nelson gave a speech in poetic form, declaring that 'The motive of the war was weak, null and void.' The climax of the story built on the self-image of the Spaniards, who saw themselves as heroic and humane, while the British were uncivilized, lawless, and brutal, as Nelson described the battle:

> What a well-ordered action!
> What a gentlemanly combat!
> What an action!
> What a butchery!
> What a barbarity!
> What a devastation![5]

Another Spanish publication, Manuel Fernández Varela's fifty-four-page printed *Funeral Oration*, was delivered at El Ferrol in Galicia on 23 December 1805, at the memorial service for those who died at Trafalgar. It was initially published in Madrid and then reprinted in Mexico City in 1807.[6] The preface to the funeral oration explained that 'the sad news of the unfortunate battle on 21 October' had caused a great sensation at El Ferrol, where so many of the Spanish ships that fought in the battle had outfitted. On that December day, the largest church in the area, 'with due pomp and magnificence', dedicated a large cenotaph in the middle of the church 'to the eternal memory of those brave sailors who gave their lives for their country on 21 October'. The cenotaph had three main sections, consecrated to the three classes who served in that fleet: officers, crew members, and soldiers. The orator eulogized Nelson as that 'strong and determined man, who was the terror of the seas and the main support of his nation'. Then, he went on to point out that he was 'overly confident in the multitude of his ships, and in the advantage of his manoeuvres, not counting on the courage and resistance of his opponents, he anxiously awaited the moment to beat them, hoping by this means to be crowned with new laurels.' The priest pointed out the moral of the event. 'This is how our self-esteem deceives us and how it often leads us to our precipice! Heaven wanted to punish us with the horrors of war, and he [Nelson] and his minions were destined for victims of our fury.'[7]

The first Spanish literary responses to Trafalgar did not reflect the enormity of the Spanish Navy's losses. Even from the beginning, there was a tendency to minimize the losses and claim the battle as a victory. Well-known, popular writers of the time, such as Juan Bautista Arriaza, Manuel José Quintana, Leandro Fernández Moratín, and María Rosa Gálvez de Cabrera, wrote poetic praises to the Spanish Navy and its Trafalgar heroes. Some, such as Francisco Sánchez, charged Britain as being the aggressor that caused all the suffering. Franciso Sánchez Barbero and Tomás González verbally attacked Nelson and the Royal Navy. González described Britain's 'unjust dominion of the sea' and compared the British admiral to 'a wolf attacking sheep', who Sánchez Barbero described as the 'most barbaric and tyrannical hero'.[8]

The Anglophobia expressed in such early Spanish writings on the subject contrasted with the humanity that the ordinary Spanish people showed to the shipwrecked British prize crews that came ashore in the storm after the battle. Writing from Gibraltar in November 1805, Captain Edward Codrington of HMS *Orion* related in a letter the story of a British survivor, who 'says, and with very great truth, that had he been wrecked on any part of England he would never have received one-half the attention he did from those poor Spaniards, whose friends we had just destroyed in such numbers'.[9] One might speculate that efforts of the British crews to save the lives of their captured seamen, along with Collingwood's return of wounded French and Spanish prisoners and the exchange of Spanish (but not French) prisoners from his prizes, provided an initial basis for a change of Spanish attitudes towards the British.

British Popular Culture

In contrast to the reactions in Spain, when the first news of the battle reached London on 6 November 1805, the reaction was a mixture of celebration and sorrow over the death of Nelson. As the London *Times* reported the following day, 'We do not know whether we should mourn or rejoice.'[10] In nearly every case, the rejoicing also included an element of mourning for the hero.[11] The theatres of London were among the first to create tributes to the Battle of Trafalgar and Nelson. Typical of such events, Covent Garden added to its last performance of the evening a scene of naval officers admiring a setting of the British fleet riding triumphantly as a medallion portrait of Nelson, surrounded by rays of glory, came down. The theatre company then led the audience in singing a rendition of 'Rule Britannia', to which they added an additional verse: 'Rule, brave Britons, rule the Main, Avenge the god-like hero slain!'[12]

On the day the news arrived, Princess Elizabeth wrote privately to Lady Charlotte Finch 'to congratulate you upon this glorious news. We have lost our hero, but his name & great deeds must ever live[.] Ought we not to be grateful? All I trust is that we ascribe this victory to the Almighty... The dear & beloved king received this news with that pious confidence he always places in the goodness of the Almighty.'[13] On hearing the news in Parliament, Lord Castlereagh wrote to his wife, 'You will weep for Lord Nelson, while you and all around you rejoice in his glories... We have lost no ship, but alas! The first admiral in the universe.'[14] Having received a similar letter from Castlereagh, Lady Londonderry replied to her son-in-law on 13 November 1805: 'Never was there an event so mournfully and so triumphantly important to England as the battle of Trafalgar. The sentiment of mourning the individual more than rejoicing in the victory, shows the humanity and affection of the people of England: but their good sense upon reflection will dwell on the conquest, because no death, at a future moment, could have been more glorious.'[15] *The Times* reported a similar understanding among the people:

> The victory created none of those enthusiastic emotions in the public mind, which the success of our naval arms have in every former instance produced... No ebullitions of popular transport, no demonstrations of public joy, marked this great and important event. The honest and manly feelings of the people appeared as it should have done: they felt an inward satisfaction of triumph of their favourite arms; they mourned with all the sincerity and poignancy of domestic grief, their Hero slain.[16]

The ministry announced a day of public thanksgiving for the battle on Tuesday 5 December 1805. The Church of England provided a special collect for the occasion that clerics throughout the country adapted for their use: 'Let not Thy gracious goodness towards us, in the signal Victory which Thou has given us over the common Enemy be frustrated by a presumptuous confidence in our own might.'[17] Another minister added, 'Let there be no malignity against the enemies with which we contend.'[18]

Nelson's State Funeral

The ministry was careful to leave an appropriate one-month interval between the day of thanksgiving for the Battle of Trafalgar on 5 December 1805 and Nelson's state funeral on 9 January 1806. While Pitt's government intended the funeral as preparing the people for a long war in the wake of the devastating news of Napoleon's victory at Austerlitz,[19] the public may have consciously seen little differentiation between the two. A state funeral in London was an unusual event, with only three since the Restoration of the monarchy in 1660. There had been nothing comparable for a military or naval leader since the state funeral for John Churchill, first Duke of Marlborough, eighty-four years earlier in 1722.[20] The more elaborate event for Nelson consisted of four major parts: first, Nelson's body lay in state at the Painted Hall at Greenwich Hospital, where an estimated thirty thousand people viewed the coffin in three mob-filled days of mourning. Then, there followed a water procession from Greenwich to Whitehall Stairs that halted all other river traffic, consisting of seventeen barges flanked by eighteen River Fencibles boats and sixteen River Marine boats. A land procession followed this from Whitehall Stairs to the Admiralty, where the body remained overnight in the Captain's Room, then continued in procession from the Admiralty to St Paul's Cathedral the next day for evensong and the burial service in the crypt of the cathedral.[21]

Thousands assembled to view the events during all four aspects of the funeral. The occasion brought together a wide range of people from across the country, with different groups representing various layers of British social, regional, economic, religious, and political viewpoints. Nelson's choreographed funeral transcended these divisions to foster loyalty and patriotism. The event was timely, as Trafalgar was the first significant victory for the four-year-old United Kingdom of Great Britain and Ireland. The new Union Flag was a prominent feature throughout all the events, marking them as a symbol of national unity that bridged the divides within the country. Members of the royal family, the aristocracy, the landed gentry, merchants, bankers, shopkeepers, colonial planters, and society wanted to show themselves as part of this national event. While the spectacle honoured Nelson and the victory at Trafalgar, it also served various national, political, commercial, and personal interests.[22]

Commercialization of Trafalgar and Nelson in Britian

From the time of the victory at the Nile in 1798, Nelson's prowess had made him a widely admired figure whose name and image were commemorated in commercial commemorative prints, pottery, and keepsakes. These cheaply available and widely purchased commercial items, including Staffordshire pottery, enabled ordinary people to decorate their mantelpieces and share in the memory of Trafalgar (Figure 5.1).[23]

The items sold in connection with the victory of Trafalgar reflected the profound shock that the public felt upon learning of Nelson's death in battle. These were feelings of personal loss, grief, and public and national loss. The imagery of mourning immediately appeared on the

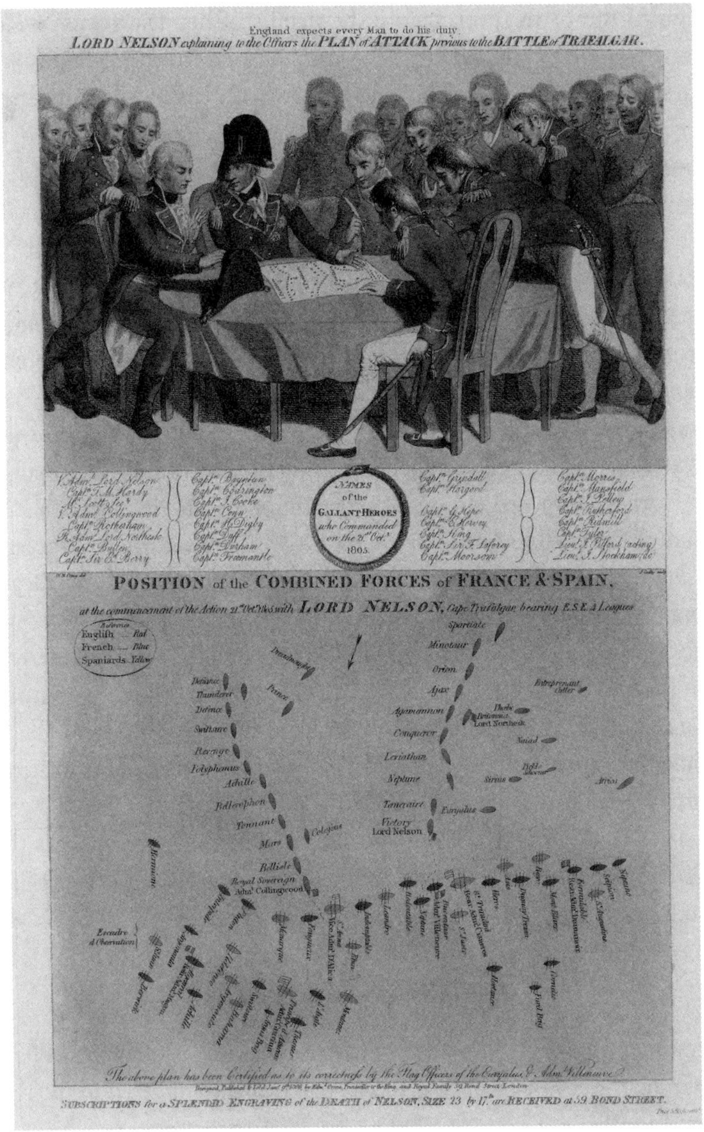

Figure 5.1 'England expects every Man to do his duty; Lord Nelson explaining to the Officers the Plan of Attack previous to Battle of Trafalgar', published by Edward Orme (1806). Popular images such as this one influenced understanding of the battle. images@rmg.co.uk - Sept 24.

news of the battle, even before the details of his death were widely known to the public. Enterprising printers sold inexpensive prints of Britannia mourning Nelson and images of Nelson surrounded by mourning figures. Other artisans transferred such images to glass, ceramics, and textiles, creating jewellery, boxes, and even furniture to commemorate Nelson and Trafalgar.[24]

Even at such a time of national mourning, the satirists were also at work to point out the excesses of the event. Among several satirical graphic images sold, William Holland's *The Sailor's Monument to the Memory of Lord Nelson* depicted a sailor in his garden with a simple monument made from a sea chest, barrels, and an Englishman's heart wrapped in mourning cloth. The print expressed the sailor's devotion to Nelson while simultaneously mocking the elaborate and expensive memorials proposed around the country. In another print, James Gillray's caricature *'Immortality—The Death of Nelson' in the Moment of Victory* mocked Benjamin West's allegorical painting and the City of London's proposed statue. The image depicted Nelson dying on the deck of HMS *Victory* as fame trumpets 'Immortality'. A British tar, with the face of the Duke of Clarence, presents Nelson with a captured French flag as Captain Hardy, with the face of George III, supports him, while Britannia standing behind Nelson, with the face of his mistress, Emma Hamilton, is engulfed in tears. While the sense of public grief was real following Trafalgar, the satirists underscored aspects that bordered on the absurd. Using the event as a cover, they targeted their usual suspects.[25]

British Verse and Poetry

Verse and poetry also became widely popular forms of expression. At least thirty-six poems about Nelson or Trafalgar appeared in the thirteen months between November 1805 and December 1806. Most of these poems sold for about two shillings, but a piece by the chaplain of HMS *Britannia*, Laurence Hynes Halloran, who had been present at the battle and served as secretary to Rear-Admiral Lord Northesk, brought 10s. 6d. Other poems expressed militant loyalty and patriotic fervour in restoring the Bourbons to the French throne in the wake of Trafalgar. In contrast, others suggested that Nelson's death had an enervating effect on national morale. Halloran's long work differed because he could provide an eyewitness account in poetic form. Here, he reflects on the aftermath of the battle:

> 'Mid the victorious fleet, an helpless prey,
> Torn and dismasted, nineteen captures lay;
> Their hulls immense in floating ruins spread,
> Sad prisons of the dying and dead.[26]

Halloran's poem is particularly interesting in how he used it to claim his position within the broader sphere of national patriotism by identifying himself as a learned member of the naval service with a classical education. At the same time, he uses the occasion to critique British society, contrast the suffering of seamen with the ease of the wealthy elite, and even inform the reader how the wartime economy forced him, as a literary man, into naval service to make a living. Other poems by naval officers, particularly those that appeared in *The Naval Chronicle*, demonstrated their writers' patriotism and drew attention to themselves in ways they hoped would promote their naval careers.[27] Sir Walter Scott, one of the most significant literary figures of the day, made several attempts to commemorate the event in poetry. 'Trafalgar is almost too grand in its native simplicity to be heightened by poetical imagery,' he wrote. I have 'repeatedly sat down to the task, [but] it has always completely overwhelmed me'.[28]

Several poems were intended to be recited aloud in public, and some evolved into ballads with a typically simple metre and varied rhyme. Unlike earlier naval actions, there were relatively few ballads relating to Trafalgar. As the Regius Professor of History at Oxford, Sir Charles Firth, noted in 1908, 'The period from the renewal of the war with France in May 1803 to the general peace in 1815 supplies few ballads of any merit, and the more important the event celebrated, the worse, as a rule, is the ballad.'[29] Trafalgar produced about a dozen ballads. Typically descriptive, one began:

> Come, all you British heroes, come listen to my song,
> It is of a noble battle by our brave seamen won;
> 20 October that was the very day
> The combined fleet from Cadiz, my boys, did put to sea;
> The *Euryalus* made the signal, the *Defence* she did repeat,
> The *Mars* and the *Colossus* conveyed it to our fleet.[30]

Another, titled 'Nelson's Glorious Victory at Trafalgar', was a bit more awkward in its wording:

> Arise, arise, brave Britons!
> Perform your loudest lays,
> And join me in a chorus
> To sing Britannia's praise.
> Once more, the hero of the Nile
> Did seek to make Britannia smile
> With another victory on the file—
> O brave Nelson![31]

Songs from earlier naval wars, such as William Boyce's 'Heart of Oak', which had first appeared in 1759 and eventually became a standard patriotic anthem still in use today, were also sung in connection with Trafalgar.[32]

As the war against Napoleon continued over the next decade, the Battle of Trafalgar faded in British public consciousness. The eventual completion of public monuments to Trafalgar and the continued devotion of naval men to commemorating Trafalgar ensured that it did not entirely disappear from public view. In 1822–3, for example, a moving panorama or 'peristrephic' of the battle of Trafalgar was displayed to paying audiences around the country, along with a similar panorama depicting George IV's coronation.[33]

As the heroic icon who had come to symbolize the battle in Britain, Nelson's reputation declined momentarily in 1815 with the publication of *Memoirs of Lady Hamilton*. The book contained several letters from Nelson to Emma that documented that he was not the modest man his earliest biographers made him out to be but a vain egotist with a penchant for decorations. Clarke and McArthur's 1809 *Life of Admiral Lord Nelson* and Robert Southey's 1813 *Life of Lord Nelson* both laid the insecure foundation for numerous myths about Nelson's life while simultaneously creating a biography that ignored documentary evidence to serve as a patriotic manual for young men. Thomas Carlyle added to this trend with his book *Heroes and Hero Worship*, published in 1841, which sought to use biographies as inspiring examples of Christian piety. With the publication of Nicholas Harris Nichols's seven-volume *Dispatches and Letters of Lord Nelson* between 1844 and 1847 and Thomas Pettigrew's *Memoirs of Vice-Admiral Lord Nelson* in 1849, there was clear proof that Nelson's relationship with Emma Hamilton and his illegitimate child disqualified him for inclusion in the Victorian pantheon of highly moral heroes.[34]

By the mid-nineteenth century, several British male military figures were figuring in heroic imperial myths as the British Empire grew. Some naval writers struggled to include Nelson in this pantheon, but, as one historian described, they 'strained and squirmed to prevent moral obloquy falling on their chosen hero'.[35] Nevertheless, one music hall sketch of the period had Nelson and Trafalgar inspiring Wellington in a vision on the night before Waterloo:

> Nelson! My glorious prototype, who ten long years ago
> Died Nobly, in Trafalgar's Bay, to Trash our common foe,
> Great Spirit! Speak! Speak! Counsel me! See, at your feet, I kneel.
> Nerve, nerve my heart! Make strong the hand the hand that grasps the British steel.[36]

Across the British Empire, the victory was commemorated in geographical names in far-flung regions around the world. There is the seaside resort village of Trafalgar in KwaZulu-Natal in South Africa; a village and waterfall in St George Province on the island of Dominica, West Indies; a town in Gippsland, Victoria, Australia; a community in

St Mary's, Guysborough County, Nova Scotia, Canada; a township and a moraine in Ontario, Canada, and a subzone of the town of Hougang in north-eastern Singapore. Additionally, in the United States, there is the town of Trafalgar in Indiana and a neighbourhood in Montrose, Ashley County, Arkansas.

A three-year-old weekly newspaper, *Les Annales politiques et littéraires*, published a long two-page article on the subject for the eighty-first anniversary of the battle. The report was in a section titled 'Forgotten Pages'. Noting at the outset that steam and electricity had fundamentally changed naval tactics since the days of warfare under sail, the editor suggested that it might be interesting for readers to read an account of this 'bloody battle' from the age of sail. The author, much influenced by Adolphe Thiers's history of the period, had much to say in defence of Admiral Villeneuve and explained that the battle was a materiel disaster for France, but 'it in no way harmed the legitimate prestige our intrepid sailors acquired as prodigals of heroism'. Remembering Villeneuve's despairing comment that 'All is lost, save honour', the author noted that 'what ruined him was the discouragement inspired in him by the inferiority of our navy with that of the English'.[37]

Public Interest in France

Meanwhile, in contrast to British and Spanish public mourning and commemoration after the battle, the French had initially ignored the battle. Public interest in the Battle of Trafalgar began to develop in France only after Napoleon's death. In 1826, alongside the first memoirs published by veterans of the Napoleonic Wars, appeared a two-volume work entitled *Mémoires de Robert Guillemard, sergent en retraite*. A popular work, even noticed by Goethe in Germany, and written in a colourful and engaging style, it was quickly translated into English by the publisher.[38] The author claimed to be recounting his life from historical documents, mostly unpublished, that showed he was a conscript who had embarked in the 74-gun *Redoubtable* at Cádiz in 1805. During the Battle of Trafalgar, he described being on the fighting top of the ship's mizzen mast when he saw Nelson on the deck of *Victory* and fired the shot that killed him. Taken prisoner in *Victory*, he accompanied Admiral Villeneuve as a prisoner of war to England, where he became his secretary. Released with him, he claimed to be present when Captain Magendie, the commanding officer of Villeneuve's flagship, *Bucentaure*, assassinated Villeneuve a few months later at Rennes. The book became the source of unfounded legends about Nelson's death and the false accusation of Magendie's guilt that have remained in circulation even to the present. A few years later, the book's author, Joseph Alexandre Lardier, came to regret his fictional presentation in the novel of Magendie as a murderer. A journalist and writer who had served in the French Army, an accountant in the navy, and even a British prisoner, Lardier had the experience and talent to write the tale, likely with assistance from another writer, Charles-Ogé Barbaroux. Lardier published a statement in 1830 that Guillemard was merely a product of his imagination and that his book was historical fiction. Despite Lardier's disclaimer, many accepted his fiction as fact. Guillemard's supposed birthplace in southern France, Six-Fours-les Plages, and the nearby city of Toulon named streets in honour of the fictional Guillemard.[39]

Public Memory in Spain

In Spain, 'the glorious defeat' is remembered today in the names of streets and squares in fifteen provincial capitals. In addition, the names of the Spanish heroes who died in the battle are also commemorated in street names: Federico Gravina in three cities, Cosme D. Churrucca in eleven, and Dionisio Alcalá Galiano in four.[40] From 1808, the commemoration of Spanish participation in the Battle of Trafalgar temporarily disappeared in Spain as the political and military situation dramatically changed. Since 1801, Spaniards had been irritated but compliant with Napoleon's overbearing and demanding attitudes. Suddenly, in 1808, Napoleon decided to occupy Spain as a step on the path for the French Army to reach opposing British forces in neighbouring Portugal. He then replaced Spain's Bourbon king with his brother, Joseph Bonaparte. The ensuing War of Independence for Spain overshadowed its previous reluctant alliance with France, as Spain seized French warships in Spanish ports.[41]

With this revolution in political and military affairs, Britain, the former enemy, became Spain's ally in a move that ended the traditional, centuries-long hostility between the two countries. As a result, in the aftermath of the Peninsular War, the Spanish popular retrospective viewpoint of Trafalgar changed substantially. The new view developed incrementally through the nineteenth century.

Cecilia Böhl de Faber, the writer who published under the name of Fernán Cabellero, first began to publish her work amid the anti-Napoleonic context of the Peninsular War. As a girl of eight, she may have witnessed the battle at a distance from the shore at Cádiz. Later, she wrote a short story that appeared in both French and Spanish entitled 'La madre o el combate de Trafalgar'. In her story, the widowed mother of a naval officer loses her sanity due to the strain of waiting for the return of her three sons from the Battle of Trafalgar. She described it as a battle that 'had no equal in the splendours of history in honour, courage, disgrace, and disaster'.[42] In her work, Fernán Cabellero did not denigrate the British but praised the Spanish heroes of the battle and placed the blame for the defeat on the ineptness of Villeneuve, whose choice of tactics the Spanish officers had opposed. Another who focused on the anguish and grief Trafalgar brought was Antonio Alcalá Galiano, whose father had died in the battle commanding the Spanish 74-gun *Bahama,* which had lost 20 per cent of her crew in combat before being captured. His son, Antonio Alcalá Galiano, was just sixteen years old when his father died, but he went on to have a notable career as an academic, poet, and politician. A key figure in the debate over the rise of Romanticism, he wrote about Trafalgar in two of his works, *Recuerdos de un anciano,* a collection of essays written in the 1860s and first collected in book form in 1878, and his posthumously published *Memorias de don Antonio Alcalá Galiana*, which appeared in 1886, twenty-one years after his death. His work reflected his feeling of losing his father in the battle, remembering vividly, 'The night closed, in horrifying uncertainty, and not only for those immediately interested in the fate of those in the squadron.'[43] As an academic, he also attempted to correct the prevailing popular interpretation by noting that few Spaniards objected to joining the French in 1805 and that Britain was then Spain's enemy.

Galiano's work was notable for commemorating the personal family losses he and many others suffered at Trafalgar. Another writer, Eugenio de Ochoa, reflected the customary anti-French view of his time. In a letter to the editor of *La Illustración de Madrid in 1871*, he wrote:

> And meanwhile, Nelson scorched our squadron at Trafalgar, and we were the toy of France, and we prepared ourselves candidly to open our plazas to their armies so that they plunge us into a war of extermination, which if it ended with glory for us, also cost us rivers of tears and blood...[44]

Benito Pérez Galdós and His Novel

Ochoas's sentiments presaged—or, as some think, inspired—Benito Pérez Galdós to undertake his novel *Trafalgar*.[45] This novel, first published in 1873, is the most important Spanish literary work to deal with the battle. It was the first in a series of ten books that Galdós wrote about various 'national episodes'. Galdós's *Trafalgar* is a historical novel with a typical triangular love story and description of the events surrounding the battle by a fourteen-year-old fictional narrator, Gabriel Araceli, who joined the navy and participated in the action. Drawing on the recollections of actual veterans and historical documents, Galdós crafted a vivid narrative. As the *San Francisco Chronicle* noted on the publication of the English translation in the United States, '[H]is picture of the bloody sea-fight is far more graphic than that of the historians.'[46] With the advantage of hindsight, Galdós also foresaw the technological revolution that navies would experience later in the nineteenth century. At the same time, he laid the groundwork for a new and more nuanced interpretation of the event, demonstrating respect for the Royal Navy and Nelson in the British victory. Presenting a new Spanish perspective, Galdós tamps down the earlier expectations of eventual triumph, anger towards the British, resentment towards the French, and the adulation of Spanish heroes. Expressing disgust at the barbarity and horror of war while questioning its morality, Galdós clarifies that Gravina was at fault for Spain's sacrifice at Trafalgar due to his lack of prudence and forceful decision-making.[47] 'I say it almost dims the halo of prestige with which the popular voice crowned the leader of the Spanish forces on that disastrous occasion,' the protagonist of his novel declared. The praises lavished on Gravina are exaggerated. 'Everything he did proved him to be an accomplished gentleman and a brave sailor, but perhaps too much of a courtier to show the determination which comes of long experience in war; he was deficient too in that complete superiority which, in so learned a profession as the Navy, can only be acquired by the assiduous study of the sciences on which it relies.' Gravina, he concluded, 'was a good commander of a division under superior orders, but nothing more'.[48]

Others soon repeated the conclusions that Galdós reached in his novel. In 1889, a popular drama written by Julio de las Cuevas García and José Caldeiro, with music by Maestro Moreu, appeared. Titled *Glorias españolas; epsisido lírico nacional del combate de ¡Trafalgar! En cinco actos y en verso*, the drama questioned Spanish motives as it contrasted patriotism and the fever of war, calling into question the entire concept of sacrifice in combat, as it extolled the opposing values of peace and family life.[49]

In 2004, the Spanish publisher Alfaguara commissioned Arturo Pérez-Reverte, writer and member of the Royal Spanish Academy, to write the novel *Cabo Trafalgar*. By the time of the bicentenary of the battle in 2005, the author had sold more than 400,000 copies of the book. Inspired by Galdós's work, Pérez-Reverte created his novel around four main characters: three Spanish naval officers and a French naval officer who commanded a small reconnaissance vessel that observed the battle. His use of a French perspective was new in Spanish literature on the subject. The tremendous public success of Pérez-Reverte's book earned him the award of the Spanish Navy's Grand Cross of Naval Merit.[50]

German Popular Interest

In Germany, the topic took varied paths in popular culture. German readers developed an interest in Nelson and Trafalgar only after German unification in 1871 and the establishment of the Kaiserliche Marine. Interest in the battle in Germany initially arose through biographical studies of Nelson. One of the earliest examples was Rudolf von Gottschall's edited multi-volume *Der Neue Plutarch*, a series of biographies on leading characters in history, literature, and art intended for a broad audience. For the contribution on Nelson, von Gottschall engaged Friedrich Althouse, Professor of German Literature at University College, London, a recognized authority on Thomas Carlyle and well known for his writing in German periodicals about English character and notable Englishmen.[51] With the published British sources readily at hand, Althaus wrote of Trafalgar:

> Never in recent history had a more decisive sea battle been fought. And as it turned out later, it was decisive, not just in the sense of the visual image. On the contrary, in England, one rightly referred to it as the great victory of all previous confrontations, for the victory at Trafalgar finally decided England's supremacy at sea.[52]

One of the early writers promoting German naval expansion was Reinhold Werner. He had retired in 1878 as a rear admiral, having served as an officer in the Prussian Navy and later in the Imperial German Navy.[53] In his retirement years, he became a well-known author writing on naval and maritime subjects. In 1884–6, he published a two-volume work on famous sailors from the seventeenth, eighteenth, and nineteenth centuries, *Berühmte Seeleute*. The second volume included essays on John Paul Jones, Nelson, Farragut, and Tegethoff. His 'Nelson' provided a detailed account of Trafalgar. However, his focus in the piece was on comparing Nelson with the Dutch admiral Michel de Ruyter, concluding that Nelson was the greatest admiral of all time.[54] Walter Parow, a senior teacher at the Friedrichs-Werderschen Oberrealschule, took a third approach, suggesting a more aggressive tone. In his thirty-three-page pamphlet of 1890, *Die Seeschlacht bei*

Trafalgar, he concluded that the battle, in terms of numbers and size of ships, was one the most important in world history. In terms of the meaning of the battle in history, Parow declared, 'For the English nation, it forms one of the most beautiful titles of glory since the English were granted the privilege of throwing iron, not gold, on the scales of war, and defending the freedom of their native soil not with foreign but with their own blood.'[55]

Trafalgar and Rising Navalism

In Britain, the Royal Naval Exhibition held on the grounds of the Royal Hospital, Chelsea, from May to October 1891 attracted more than two million visitors. While designed as a 'navalist' political campaign to draw attention to the contemporary navy's needs and strength in its rivalry with the French, German, and Russian navies, it also included a full-sized replica of the hull of HMS *Victory* that included a waxwork scene of the death of Nelson, a polygonal rotunda with a 32-foot high

Figure 5.2 Edmund Richard White's late nineteenth-century painting, *A Relic from Trafalgar*, shows young naval cadets entranced by one of HMS *Victory*'s battle-damaged sails © Look and Learn / Bridgeman Images.

and 310-foot round circular panorama by Chevalier Philipp Fleisher of the battle of Trafalgar as seen from the quarterdeck of HMS *Victory*, and a large display of Nelson relics.[56]

One of the most important organizations in the rise of navalism at the end of the nineteenth and early twentieth centuries in Britain was the Navy League, founded in 1894. The group made a significant contribution to raising public awareness of the Royal Navy and its needs. One of the League's several successful programmes was to transform Trafalgar Day into a national commemorative celebration, as proposed by journalist Arnold White in July 1896. The first celebration took place at the flag-festooned Nelson Column in Trafalgar Square on 21 October 1896 (Figure 5.3). Many provincial and colonial cities followed suit in the years that followed. The Navy League's intention with the Trafalgar Day celebration was to create mass support for the importance of sea power. 'Nelson's life and death, it was foreseen, might be utilized to personify British Sea Power to the children, if not the veterans, of British democracy throughout the world.'[57] In 1898, Rear Admiral Lord Charles Beresford collaborated with the journalist and naval historian Herbert W. Wilson, the chief leader writer of the *Daily Mail*, to produce a large-format, illustrated volume entitled *Nelson and His Times*. In his preface, Beresford explained,

> This Work is... address to the millions of the great British democracy, for whose prosperity and freedom, as that of generations yet unborn, Nelson fought and died... He taught the lesson which all our people should take to heart, that while the British Empire maintains its naval strength, the freedom of its people and the security of its borders may be successfully preserved against any hostile combination of the military powers.[58]

In the years before 1914, British navalism was a remarkably successful movement. Aside from its partisan and political repercussions in developing support for the Royal Navy, it also created a cultural navalism through lantern-slide lectures, public speeches, primary school essays, and the activities of wives' clubs.[59] Along with them came the rise in the use of Nelson- and Trafalgar-related names and images for commercial purposes. Most famously, newspaper advertisements from the late

Figure 5.3 'Nelson Column in Trafalgar Square decorated for Trafalgar Day, 1896', *The Illustrated London News*, 24 October 1896. Look and Learn / Illustrated Papers Collection / Bridgeman Images.

1890s for Pears Soap had a portrait of Nelson and the column in Trafalgar Square, while those for Beecham's Pills employed Nelson's Trafalgar signal. More recently, the association has continued with the name of a travel agency, a brand of tobacco, and Pusser's Rum.

Heroism in Popular British Culture

Mid-Victorian family magazine articles and popular books, such as W. Clark Russell's *Nelson*, had left the impression that the romantic phase of naval history, exemplified by Nelson and Trafalgar, belonged irretrievably to a bygone age. The new sophisticated steam warships with modern weapons seemed personified by a brutish Cyclops rather than a glorious hero of Homeric times. Nevertheless, the Royal Navy remained an organization that fostered and promoted heroism as part of its service culture. With the revival of the Royal Navy during the last decade and a half of Queen Victoria's reign, popular culture reflected the navy's return to some of the older Age of Sail tropes as part of the naval revival.[60]

The most significant aspect in references to Trafalgar at the end of the nineteenth century and the opening of the twentieth century was to build on Nelson's 'Every man should do his duty' signal. The emphasis here was not on the example of Nelson's heroism and leadership but on the ordinary seaman whom the signal called to action. Combined with prevailing Victorian ideas about manly Christian heroes, patriotic duty, hard work, and self-denial, these elements came together to produce an idealized model for the modern naval seaman. In 1898, a boy's newspaper captured the sentiment with a story on 'The True British Sailor-Boy', accompanied by a cover image that showed a twelve-year-old lad hugging the mast of his sinking ship, declaring, 'I did not desert you.' Like Nelson, the boy did his duty even with the sacrifice of his own life. He expressed the *manliness* many Britons believed provided the basis for moral and physical supremacy over others.[61] G. A. Henty, a prolific author of popular historical adventure fiction for boys, employed this theme in his last novel, *By Conduct and Courage: A Story of Nelson's Days,* posthumously published in 1904.[62] Later, the widespread use of the image of Boy 1st Class John Cornwell, who died at the age of fourteen in the Battle of Jutland, served the same purpose, reproduced in newspapers, penny stamps, commemorative medals, and even an oil portrait.[63]

Naval service at sea offered a sense of mystique and adventure that military service on land did not. The realities of modern war did not end the romantic aspects of being afloat as they did ashore. The evocation of Trafalgar and Nelson contributed to the development of a sense of loyalty and patriotism in the early twentieth century. It helped to rationalize and accept the sacrifice and realities of wartime losses.[64]

Trafalgar and Early Twentieth-Century Wars

The end of the nineteenth century and the beginning of the twentieth century brought contemporary wars that echoed Trafalgar. These limited wars in distant parts of the globe were quite unlike the global scope of the Napoleonic Wars with their massive battles. Nevertheless, contemporary observers saw parallels. During the Spanish-American War in 1898, Spain's defeat at Trafalgar became a premonition of its defeat by the United States. During the war, an article in Madrid journal concluded, '[Admiral] Cervera evades [Admiral] Sampson's vigilance, and the weak and valiant squadron of the Philippines sinks into the Ocean, as the *Trinidad* and the *San Juan Nepomuceno* sank at Trafalgar.'[65]

Just five months before the one-hundredth anniversary of the Battle of Trafalgar, the Battle of Tsushima between the Russian and Japanese fleets took place at the entrance to the Sea of Japan on 27 May 1905. As the most significant major naval battle in the century since Trafalgar and one in which the Japanese destroyed the Russian fleet, the British, as well as the Japanese popular press, immediately compared Japanese Admiral Tōgō to Nelson at Trafalgar. A cartoon in the *Chicago Tribune* showed the world pushing Togo up on his plinth as he was 'Taking his Place' between the statues of George Dewey, the victor in the recent battle of Manila Bay, and Nelson.[66] On hearing detailed news of the battle, the President of the United States, Theodore Roosevelt, congratulated the Japanese Ambassador in Washington, declaring,

'Neither Trafalgar nor the defeat of the Spanish Armada was as complete—as overwhelming.'[67]

In England, *Punch* captured the prevailing attitude at the centenary with a cartoon entitled '1805–1905 Admiral Lord Nelson. "MY SHIPS HAVE PASSED AWAY, BUT THE SPIRIT OF MY MEN REMAINS"' (Figure 5.4).[68] At the same time, the author Thomas Hardy featured Nelson and Trafalgar in his three-volume drama in verse, *The Dynasts*, published between 1904 and 1908, an epic retelling of the Napoleonic Wars. The public most widely appreciated the prolific poet, novelist, and historian Sir Henry Newbolt for his nautical and patriotic verse. Charles Villiers Stanford set several of them to music, including 'The Little Admiral' as part of *Songs of the Fleet*.[69] Others appeared only in verse form, such as 'The Fighting Téméraire', 'For a Trafalgar Cenotaph', and 'The Old and the Bold'. Another, 'The Quarter-Gunner's Yarn', became popular with its lower-deck account of Trafalgar:

> We now saw the enemy bearing ahead,
> And to East of them Cape Trafalgar it was said,
> 'Tis a name we remember from father to son,
> That the days of old England may never be done.[70]

A decade later, the First World War also raised the memory of Trafalgar in public discourse (Figure 5.5). At the war's opening in 1914, a Welsh newspaper noted that as Britain moved troops to the uttermost parts of the globe in the new conflict, 'there is none to say us nay, none to hinder or prevent us, such is the sequel of Trafalgar'. The writer declared that the battle taught us a lesson we have never forgotten. However, some have been reluctant to accept it fully, 'to maintain the overwhelming supremacy on which the life, the very existence of country and Empire depend'.[71] Two years later, at Trafalgar Day commemorations in Liverpool in 1916, there was a more sombre note: 'The grateful memory of Nelson's men was mingled with that of those, who 111 years later, gave their lives in the battle of Jutland.'[72]

Figure 5.4 '1805–1905 Admiral Lord Nelson "My Ships have Passed Away, but the Spirit of my Men Remains", *Punch*, 18 October 1905. https://commons.wikimedia.org/wiki/File:%271805-1905_Admiral_Lord_Nelson_%27My_Ships_have_Passed_Away,_But_The_Spirit_of_My_Men_Remains%27_Punch,_October_18,_1905%27_RMG_PT0098.tiff.

DAILY SKETCH, THURSDAY, OCTOBER 21, 1915

GERMANS LOSE HEAVILY AT HULLUCH.

DAILY SKETCH.

GUARANTEED DAILY NETT SALE MORE THAN 1,000,000 COPIES.

No. 2,065. LONDON, THURSDAY, OCTOBER 21, 1915. [Registered as a Newspaper.] ONE HALFPENNY.

THE MESSAGE OF TRAFALGAR DAY TO BRITAIN'S MANHOOD

The British sea-hounds go a-hunting—a recent picture from the North Sea.

Sir John Jellicoe at a fancy dress ball wearing the uniform of a British Admiral of the Fleet of Nelson's time.

A British destroyer ripping along—on patrol duty in the North Sea.

This is Trafalgar Day—and never was anniversary more significant in the history of people than it is to every man of British birth and blood to-day. While our warships guard the coasts of our island-home, mighty Dreadnoughts sentinel the northern waters and swift destroyers patrol the narrows, invincibly maintaining the sea-power won at Trafalgar, there rings through all the land Nelson's immortal message to his countrymen. "England expects"—now more than ever. When the above picture of Admiral Jellicoe was taken he did not dream Fate would call him to be the Nelson of our day.—(Cribb and Lafayette.)

Figure 5.5 'Message of Trafalgar Day to Britain's Manhood', front page of *The Daily Sketch*, 21 October 1915. John Frost Newspapers / Alamy Stock Photo.

Saving HMS *Victory* and Creating Museum Displays

While Trafalgar Square and the Nelson Column in London, built in the early 1840s, remained the symbolic heart of British national memory of the battle and a vision of an enduring maritime empire at the centre of the British government, the centenary celebrations for the Battle of Trafalgar in 1905 launched a significant effort to save Nelson's flagship, HMS *Victory*, as a memorial to both Nelson and the battle.[73] It took nearly two decades for this effort to come to fruition. Since Trafalgar, the public has viewed the ship as an important relic from the battle that the people could occasionally visit, with the Admiralty caring for it at national expense. In October 1831, the Admiralty listed her for disposal, but a public outcry saved her and kept her with various functions at an anchorage in Portsmouth harbour. A group of people concerned about the fate of the ship established the Society for Nautical Research in 1910, with the preservation of the ship as one of its principal objectives. On Trafalgar Day 1922, the Society launched the Save the *Victory* Fund under the chairmanship of Admiral of the Fleet Sir Doveton Sturdee. At the same time, the Admiralty moved the ship into Drydock number 2 at H.M. Dockyard Portsmouth, where the initial restoration work began through a generous donation by the wealthy shipowner and philanthropist Sir James Caird, first Baronet of Glenfarquar.

The Royal Navy provided a steel cradle for the ship and paid for the cost of docking. In addition, the navy paid for the repairs on a reimbursable basis. To meet this cost, the Society's Save the *Victory* Fund raised the requisite £100,000 by 1925. While there was general agreement that the object was to restore the ship to her appearance at the Battle of Trafalgar, a detailed plan for undertaking that required considerable research. As soon as the dockyard completed the repairs, the focus turned to opening the ship to the public, while the Save the *Victory* Fund continued to raise funds for a permanent endowment for the ship. The ship already had a small museum of Nelson and Trafalgar relics. These historical objects, including Nelson's funeral barge, had to be moved to another location to facilitate repairs to the ship. This issue led to the creation of a separate museum to display these objects. As the initial repairs were completed, King George V formally visited the ship to view the progress on 17 June 1928. Plans were laid to build a new museum with an annex to house W. L. Wyllie's panorama of the battle. The Society opened the new museum to the public in July 1938, with temporary financial support from the Admiralty and the Treasury. Second World War dashed the Society's hope that public admission charges to the museum would quickly eliminate the debt. The museum was closed during the war from 1939 to 1945, with the trustees of the newly established National Maritime Museum at Greenwich taking over its management of the collection. After the war, the collection returned to the Society's management from 1948 until 1971, when the Society donated the *Victory* Gallery and its collections to the Ministry of Defence to be part of the new Museum of the Royal Navy located at the same site. Over the years, the drydocked HMS *Victory* and the associated museum, which tells the story of the ship's history and battles, have significantly contributed to tourism in Portsmouth.[74]

Meanwhile, Sir James Caird was also deeply involved in donating to the National Maritime Museum for that museum's collections on Nelson and Trafalgar. Through his generosity, the new museum built further on the foundations laid in the 1820s with the Greenwich Hospital Collection and the curatorial work of Edward Hawke Locker. He contributed to all aspects of the museum but was particularly interested in Nelson and Trafalgar, as evidenced by his addition of ship models, prints, drawings, and manuscripts. Working with the museum's first director, Sir Geoffrey Callendar, Caird funded the purchase of such iconic relics as Turner's painting of *Trafalgar* and Devises's *Death of Nelson*, as well as six paintings by Nicholas Pocock that had been commissioned as illustrations for James Stanier Clarke and John M. M'Arthur's *The Life of Admiral Lord Nelson, K.B.* Among numerous other pieces, Caird also purchased Samuel Drummond's *Battle of Trafalgar*, six studies by John Burnet for his *Greenwich Pensioners' Commemorating the Anniversary of the Battle of Trafalgar*, as well as Thomas Davidson's painting *England's Pride and Glory* and W. L. Wyllie's collection of drawings and watercolours.[75]

The museum collections grew and matured, making a wide range of artifacts and images relating to Trafalgar available to the public and for reproduction in both popular and, eventually, scholarly literature. The addition of an exhibit on Trafalgar boosted visitor attendance and ameliorated early difficulties with visitation.[76]

Popular Fiction

During these same years, people recognized that the Battle of Trafalgar and its era in naval history marked the pinnacle of the golden age of maritime warfare under sail. Popular fiction writers increasingly used the period in their work. By the mid-nineteenth century, writers such as James Fenimore Cooper and Frank Marryatt, as well as works of art including J. M. W. Turner's *Fighting Temeraire* had already romanticized the sailing ship era, while awkward-looking steamships belching sooty coal smoke replaced the graceful beauty of ships under sail. As commercial cargo-carrying sailing ships ended their useful employment, mariners-turned-writers published their adventures at sea under sail in books. Notable among them were the Australian Alan Villers's *Falmouth for Orders* (1929) and the eighteen-year-old English adventure-seeker Richard Brinsley Sheridan's *Heavenly Hell* (1932).

Within this broader context, C. S. Forester (Cecil Scott Forester, the pen name of Cecil Lewis Troughton Smith) published in 1937 *The Happy Return*, the first of his series of eleven popular novels that followed the adventurous and evolving career of a fictional naval officer in the Royal Navy, Horatio Hornblower, during the period of the French Revolution and Napoleonic Wars. The series became immensely popular during Second World War and its aftermath, perhaps as a romantic contrast and relief from the gritty realities of contemporary naval warfare. Deeply grounded in historically accurate contexts, Forester's fresh and new approach to the naval novel sparked numerous imitators. The most successful, widely translated, and read of these books were those written by Patrick O'Brian with his twenty-one-volume

Aubrey-Maturin series. O'Brian's work captivated a considerable audience, ranging from university professors, naval professionals, yachtsmen, and general fiction readers. Nelson and the Battle of Trafalgar were often mentioned in passing and figured, either explicitly or assumed, as background in all these books.[77]

Among the very few authors of this genre who directly dealt with Trafalgar in detail was Richard Woodman, a career Trinity House captain, who created a series of novels following the career of Nathaniel Drinkwater to reflect the sea life of the period more accurately. In the sixth novel in Woodman's series, *1805*, the Spanish Guarda Costa captures the fictional Captain Drinkwater. They take him on board Villeneuve's flagship *Bucentaure* as the Combined Fleet put to sea, giving the Englishman an unusual vantage point on the battle. Woodman paints a sympathetic picture of Villeneuve that vindicates his wisdom and decisions. He suggests that the French admiral foresaw Nelson's tactics and had prepared a feasible counterattack but was reluctant to fight because he knew the outcome.[78] Another writer, Bernard Cornwell, who created a series around a fictional British Army officer named Richard Sharpe during the same period, also involved his hero at Trafalgar. Returning from duty in India, the fictional warship HMS *Pucelle*, in which Sharpe is embarked, becomes part of Nelson's column attacking the Franco-Spanish fleet. The novel follows a storyline in which *Pucelle* takes on the historical role of the real-life HMS *Téméraire* and becomes involved in the intense multi-ship action around HMS *Victory*. Given the command of some marines on board, Sharpe leads a boarding party in a bloody slaughter of the enemy.[79]

Alan Villiers served in the Royal Navy during Second World War and received the Distinguished Service Cross. After the war, he continued to be active in sailing, as well as serving as a film advisor and consultant on sailing ships, and a writer. Among his works, he wrote a vivid, ninety-five-page book for a popular audience that clearly explained many of the technical aspects of naval warfare of the time: *The Battle of Trafalgar: Lord Nelson Sweeps the Seas*. Villiers's conclusion reflected the broad understanding in British popular culture that all French hopes for global expansion and domination 'disappeared in the smoke of the cannon at Trafalgar'.[80]

Even at the end of the first quarter of the twenty-first century, references to Trafalgar seem to be everywhere across the country, not just in the museum ship HMS *Victory*, naval museums, on the walls of innumerable parish churches, or in Trafalgar Square. In the summer of 2002, some thirty thousand people participated in a British Broadcasting Corporation television poll to nominate the 'Greatest Briton of all Time'. In November of that same year, the public voted. Among the hundred names, Nelson came out ninth, immediately following John Lennon and just ahead of Oliver Cromwell.[81] In 2005, the Society for Nautical Research and the Woodland Trust launched a 'Tree for All' campaign, aiming to plant 250,000 trees in twenty-seven new woodlands across the county. The new woodlands each represented a ship at the battle of Trafalgar, with the largest being Victory Wood in Kent. In Britain, two other organizations, with their publications, websites, and activities, serve as ongoing links between the popular, the enthusiast, the scholarly, and the professional: the Nelson Society, established in 1981, and the 1805 Club, established in 1990.[82] Over the past two centuries, popular culture has been only one aspect of understanding the Battle of Trafalgar's cultural legacy. Professional naval cultures, the official centenary and bicentenary celebrations, and the ongoing work of professional historians have each contributed.

6

Trafalgar in World Naval Cultures

For the navies involved, the aftermath of the Battle of Trafalgar followed a typical professional pattern. Immediately after a naval battle, the priority for the navy was always to look to the safety of the ships, then to tend to the wounded, bury the dead, and deal with the prizes and prisoners of war. Then came rewards and punishment. Later, veterans of the action contributed to the development of a specialized, distinctly naval professional commemoration of the battle, which differed from the one in popular culture.

Then, as the veterans of Trafalgar passed from the scene, they left behind them an inheritance that shaped the navy's thinking. This inheritance exemplified a 'naval service heritage': an unspoken understanding of the past that is related to the historical analysis of professional historians but sometimes contradicts it. This concept of heritage involves the unique, inherited sense of service identity created by people and events in the past. It represents the values, traditions, practices, service culture, and artifacts handed down through previous generations of professionals but may incorporate different ideas for different groups within the navy. Those who serve in navies absorb their sense of heritage throughout their service lives as they observe and experience what makes their navy distinctive. Naval heritage, as a concept, is marked by traditional understandings that are typically meant to inspire the best professional performance in officers and ratings,

Figure 6.1 The Trafalgar Vase, designed in 1805–6 by John Flaxman and made in London by Digby Scott and Benjamin Smith. Lloyd's Patriotic Fund presented these sterling silver vases to fifteen of the Trafalgar ship captains. It is inscribed 'Britons Strike Home' and 'Britannia Triumphant'.The Print Collector/Alamy Images.

even if they are not necessarily historically accurate. Naval heritage covers a broad spectrum. At its worst, it is deliberately managed misinformation about the past. More commonly, it is benign in intent, ranging from legend to traditional interpretations meant to inspire higher performance. However, with inventions for facts and slogans for dialogue, it is the *bête noir* of the professional naval historian seeking a broad understanding of context with documented accuracy in detail.

Rewards and Punishments for French Participants

In a series of audiences at Saint-Cloud in May 1806, Napoleon received several key French officers who had commanded ships in the battle, including captains Lucas, Infernet, Magendie, and Villemadrin. The emperor told them, 'You are among those who have fought well; you will have your recompense.'[1] Napoleon promoted them to commander in the Order of the Legion of Honour. As Napoleon reflected on the reports other commanding officers provided, he became increasingly suspicious of the other captains' behaviour. Wanting to understand the defeat, he pressed Decrès to investigate their actions. The result offered little but unleashed a wave of accusations among the interrogated officers in their defence. Among them, only Cosmao refused to denounce his comrades, saying that he had been too busy fighting the English to judge the actions of others.[2] He was the only commanding officer at Trafalgar promoted to rear admiral, while just two frigate commanders became captains. Meanwhile, the senior French admiral, Villeneuve, and the Spanish admiral, Gravina, died in 1806 before the government acted. Villeneuve's death, although determined to be a suicide, has continually raised questions among observers. Napoleon, however, awarded his widow an annual pension of 6,000 francs and later commented on the suicide that Villeneuve 'should never have acted like that; he was brave though he had no talent'.[3]

Upon Rear Admiral Dumanoir's release from his parole as a prisoner of war at Tiverton, England, and his return to France, Napoleon sought to make an example of him and convened a naval inquiry on four charges relating to his conduct at Trafalgar. The court dismissed the charges and absolved Dumanoir in September 1809. Napoleon ordered a second inquiry and court martial in December 1809 related to Dumanoir's conduct following the battle, when Sir Richard Strachan's squadron captured him and his four ships. This time, the second inquiry held him guilty of error in judgement but not of misconduct. Decrès, the Minister of Marine, urged Napoleon to be lenient, but the emperor insisted on proceeding with a court martial in March 1810. To Napoleon's irritation, the court martial acquitted Dumanoir and his officers, allowing him to return to active service in 1811.[4]

Spanish Awards

In contrast to Napoleon's parsimony in promoting or rewarding his naval officers and sailors, the Spanish Navy was much more generous. In November 1805, Admiral Gravina was promoted from Lieutenant-General to Captain-General of the Navy, the highest rank in the navy. His second in command, Antonio de Escaño, who took charge when Gravina was wounded, became a lieutenant-general and, within two years, was Minister of the Navy. Ignacio de Álava, whose flag flew from *Santa Ana* during the battle as a lieutenant-general, received the Grand Cross of the Order of Carlos III. In addition to Escaño, two others were promoted from squadron chief to lieutenant-general, six captains became brigadiers, and five brigadiers became squadron chiefs.[5] In 1808, Spain awarded a medal to all who participated in the capture in June of the six-ship French squadron at Cádiz, then under Rosily, which had been in port seeking repairs following the Battle of Trafalgar. In 1816, after the war had ended, Spain created a medal, the Laureada de Marina, which was renamed and redesigned with a royal crown some months later as the Diadema Real de Marina, to reward the officers and men of the Spanish Navy for having fought in the Napoleonic Wars.[6]

British Awards

The victorious Royal Navy rewarded its men with decorations, promotions, and money. Following the Battle of the Glorious First of June in 1794, the Admiralty established its first service award for senior officers who participated in naval victories. Designed by Lewis Pingo, the Naval Gold Medal came in two versions: a large 2-inch-diameter version for admirals and a smaller, 1.3-inch version for warship captains. This award remained in use until 1815, when widened criteria for the Order of the Bath superseded it. For Trafalgar, three large and twenty-seven

Figure 6.2 Flag Officer's Naval Gold Medal for Trafalgar awarded to Vice-Admiral Collingwood (both obverse and reverse sides).
National Maritime Museum, Greenwich: NMM, Med0159.

small gold medals were awarded. The obverse showed Britannia with a spear in her left hand and shield standing on the prow of an ancient galley with her right foot resting on a helmet, crowned with a wreath by a winged victory. The reverse had a personalized inscription within a wreath of oak and laurel. For example, Collingwood's inscription read, 'Cuthbert Collingwood Esquire, Vice Admiral and second in command on the 21 October MDCCCV. The Combined Fleets of France and Spain Defeated' (Figure 6.2).[7]

The British lost most of the captured French and Spanish ships in the storm that followed the battle. Nevertheless, Parliament authorized £300,000 to be distributed as though it were prize money. In addition, some prize money came from the eight captured ships that had survived the storm and which were sold or brought into service. The government also awarded an annual £5,000 pension to Nelson's elder brother, the Rev'd William Nelson. He was raised to the peerage as Viscount Merton and Earl Nelson and received a grant of £90,000 to purchase an estate. The Patriotic Fund awarded sums of up to £100 to naval lieutenants and Royal Marine captains and below based on rank, the severity of the wounds, and consequent disability.[8]

A wide range of naval promotions occurred, headed by Collingwood, who became a baron and succeeded Nelson in command of the Mediterranean squadron. He and Lord Northesk became vice-admirals of the red, a grade in the Royal Navy recently reinstated in November 1805. Northesk was also appointed Knight of the Bath. In addition, the captains of three ships of the line became rear admirals of the blue by their seniority, but five lieutenants skipped over the rank of commander and became post-captains. Additionally, all the first lieutenants of the frigates and the ships of the line at Trafalgar and in Strachan's action became commanders, as did three additional lieutenants from *Victory* and one from *Royal Sovereign*. Fifteen senior master's mates and four midshipmen were commissioned as lieutenants for their meritorious conduct during the battle.[9]

To supplement the awards and promotions from the government, the wealthy manufacturer Matthew Boulton struck sixteen thousand medals for the veterans of Trafalgar at his own expense in his Soho Mint at Birmingham. Designed by Conrad Heinrich Kückler, the medal was suspended on a dark blue ribbon. The obverse of the medal featured a profile bust of Nelson with a pigtail in uniform with the legend 'HORATIO VISCOUNT NELSON K. B. DUKE OF BRONTE, &C'. The reverse showed a general view of the battle with the legend 'ENGLAND EXPECTS EVERY MAN WILL DO HIS DUTY' and 'TRAFALGAR OCT^{R} 21. 1805'. The edge of the medal was engraved with the inscription 'TO THE HEROES OF TRAFALGAR FROM M. BOULTON'.[10] He made gold medals for the admirals, silver for officers and midshipmen, and pewter for the ratings. As unofficial medals, however, none could be worn on naval uniforms.

Another individual, Alexander Davison—Nelson's good friend, accountant, and prize agent—privately made a pewter medal for the ratings on board *Victory*. Designed by Thomas Halliday, the obverse featured an oval shield with a motto and an inscribed ribbon surmounted by a bust of Nelson. Around the shield were the words 'TRIA. JUNCTA. IN. UNO.', while the ribbon read 'PALMAN QUI. MERUIT FERAT'. An inner line at the top, under Nelson's name, had the quotation 'ENGLAND

EXPECTS EVERY MAN WILL DO HIS DUTY'. At the bottom, the inner line read 'NATUS SEP. 29. 1758' and 'HOSTE DEVICTO REQUIEVIT OCT. 21. 1805' on the outer line. The medal's reverse showed the ship's broadside image at anchor. Below it is the inscription 'VICTORY OFF TRAFALGAR OVER THE COMBINED FLEETS OF FRANCE & SPAIN OCT. 21.1805'. Over the image of the ship is a double entendre biblical quotation referring to God, Nelson, and HMS *Victory*, 'THE LORD IS A MAN OF WAR', and under it, the biblical source, 'EXODUS c.15, v.3'.[11]

More than forty years later, additional British medals were created. The first appeared in 1843 to mark the construction of Nelson's Column and the opening of Trafalgar Square. This medal, designed by Joseph W. Davis, featured a bust of Nelson on the obverse surrounded by 'ENGLAND EXPECTS EVERY MAN WILL DO HIS DUTY' inscribed on a garter. The reverse showed the monument with the National Gallery behind it.[12] In 1845, the governor of Greenwich Hospital, Admiral Sir Robert Stopford, presented the medal during a special ceremony in the Painted Hall to some 340 veterans of Trafalgar.[13]

Following the end of the Napoleonic Wars in 1815, several veteran officers of the Peninsular campaigns had begun to complain privately and publicly in professional journals that they and their men had received no recognition in the form of a medal for their combat service. They noted that the king had awarded gold and silver medals to senior officers for some of the significant victories during the war and that the Battle of Waterloo had led to the creation of the first campaign medal for any of the British armed forces to be awarded to all participants in every grade and rank. In 1840, several army officer veterans petitioned the Duke of Wellington on the matter, but the duke declined to interfere in what he considered a Crown prerogative. By this time, however, the campaign medals were no longer the novelty they had been during the war, when Davison and Boulton had made their private medals for Trafalgar. Foreign and colonial governments, and even the East India Company, had begun to issue medals. The Sultan of Turkey presented his St Jean d'Acre medal to all British naval officers and seamen who had served in Egypt and Syria in the 1840 operation in those waters.[14]

In 1842, Queen Victoria, likely at the suggestion of Prince Albert, intervened in a plan for the government of India to present awards to British soldiers and sailors who had served in thirteen actions in China from 1841 to 1842. The queen suggested to the East India Company that such a distinction 'be derived from the highest fountain of honour'.[15] In the light of this initiative and a more egalitarian and enlightened approach, the issue of a Peninsular War medal re-emerged in Parliament. The subsequent debate on the subject soon led to the conclusion that such a distinction must extend to all who served in the army and the navy and stretch back in time to recognize service that occurred more than fifty years earlier. As Parliament debated, the Duke of Richmond became the champion of the cause, persuading the queen and Prince Albert of its merits. The queen approved the military version in December 1846 and the naval version on 27 May 1847.[16] Over the next three and a half years, public advertisements appeared at intervals announcing the increasing number of qualifying actions. Trafalgar was one of the first listed as a gold medal action. The silver medal was initially known as the Naval War Medal. Designed by William Wyon, the obverse of the medal showed the profile of a bust of Queen Victoria wearing a diadem (Figure 6.3). The reverse featured an image of Britannia seated on a sea horse with a trident in her right hand and an olive branch in her left hand. The recipient's name was inscribed on the edge of the medal, suspended from a plain silver clasp with a white ribbon edged in dark blue. On the ribbon were silver clasps for each action the individual had participated in. Trafalgar was one of 231 separate clasps. After a gap of forty-three years since the battle, 1,613 Trafalgar clasps were awarded, of which 119 went to men who had served in HMS *Victory*.[17]

Naval Service Heritage

In 1824, Rear Admiral Charles Ekins published one of the earliest studies of Trafalgar, specifically designed for teaching young naval officers the fundamentals of naval tactics. He developed his book, *Naval Battles, from 1744 to the Peace in 1814, Critically Reviewed and Illustrated,*[18] to be a

Figure 6.3 Naval General Service Medal with Trafalgar clasp, 1848. PjrStudio / Alamy Stock Photo.

study of all the recent significant fleet actions. A dense and largely impenetrable book for the general reader, with numerous tactical diagrams described in technical detail, it sought to update and critique John Clerk of Eldin's *Essay on Naval Tactics,* which had so influenced Nelson's thinking about fleet tactics. Ekins included descriptions and documents on Trafalgar and later actions up to Pellew's attack on Algiers in 1816.

Ekins's work, however, was soon overshadowed by the changing nature of naval warfare following the last fleet engagement under sail at Navarino in 1827. With the Royal Navy's demobilization after the end of the Napoleonic Wars, it remained nominally the world's superior force, but, in practical terms, it was a force composed of worn-out and dilapidated ships, supported by overwhelmed dockyards, declining financial support, and limited manning resources. The new post-war emphasis was on utilizing small warships for a wide range of imperial duties worldwide.[19] While Ekins's book eventually became only a reference for specialists in the history of naval tactics, it contributed to the long-standing professional emphasis in the navy on large-scale fleet actions, an idea that would eventually re-emerge.

As the navy transformed itself to adapt to a new technological age and time gradually distanced naval veterans from the battle, many still marked the anniversary of the Battle of Trafalgar. John Burnet's best-known oil painting documents a typical gathering of 'Greenwich Pensioners Celebrating the Battle of Trafalgar'. Exhibited at the British Institution in 1837 and made into popular print before the Duke of Wellington purchased it in 1841 for display in Apsley House, it illustrates a group of pensioners in Greenwich Park explaining the tactics at the Battle of Trafalgar to a group of boys from the Greenwich Hospital School (Figure 6.4).[20] Few works went as far as Burnet's in creating nostalgia for the war and romanticizing it as the golden age of overseas heroic naval deeds and harmony at home. The work created a positive image of the veterans, who the artist depicted in a positive and individualized manner, celebrating them for their service under Nelson's command.[21]

In October 1844, Queen Victoria and Prince Albert returned to Portsmouth in the royal yacht and went ashore in a royal barge through a line of procession made up of warship barges. En route, the queen noticed that the trucks of HMS *Victory*'s topmasts were decorated with laurel, as were the ship's figurehead, taffrail, decks, and sides.

Figure 6.4 *Greenwich Pensioners Commemorating the Battle of Trafalgar*, a popular 1836 engraving by John Burnet after his own best-known painting.

Public Domain, Library of Congress.

On enquiring why, the queen was reminded that it was Trafalgar Day. To the astonishment of the attending Lords of the Admiralty and the officers and men manning the warship barges, the queen immediately diverted the royal barge's course to come alongside *Victory*. Boarding the ship with only the second lieutenant on deck to greet her, she viewed the plaque that commemorated the place where Nelson fell and read aloud the words of the famous signal inscribed on the rail over the steering wheel, 'England expects every man will do his duty', and then went below to the cockpit where Nelson died (Figure 6.5). That evening, after the queen's departure, the commanding officer hosted a dinner on board for sixty people where the loyal toasts to the royal family were drunk and 'with deep devotion, in solemn silence, the "memory of Nelson" was received'.[22] Two years later, on Trafalgar Day in 1846, when Captain Pasco, who as a lieutenant had supervised the hoisting of Nelson's signal at the battle, was in command of *Victory*, a similar dinner was held on

Figure 6.5 Deck of the *Victory* on the anniversary of the battle (October 21) after an original sketch by our own artist', *Illustrated News of the World* (1858). Chronicle/ Alamy Images.

board the ship. A newspaper report of this occasion in the *Times* confirmed the exact wording of the toast that had been first used at the Lord Mayor's Dinner in November 1805: 'The immortal memory of Nelson and those who fell with him'. Trafalgar Night dinners that followed the bicentenary in 2005 revived the original wording.[23]

The Last Survivors of Trafalgar

The identity of the last survivors of Trafalgar has been a subject of debate for over a century (Figure 6.6). Newspapers reported that the last French survivor, Henry Blanc, died in 1884. Eight years later, in March 1892, Louis André Manuel (also known as Emmanuel-Louis) Cartigny, a powder monkey in *Redoutable* during the battle, died at Hyères, in southern France, and was posthumously awarded the title 'the last Trafalgar one of all'.[24] Among the veterans of the Spanish Fleet, Don Xavier Ulloa, who died in 1856 at the age of eighty-four, was identified as the last Spanish survivor. A week after Cartigny died in France

Figure 6.6 'The Surviving Officers of the Battle of Trafalgar' engraving by an unnamed artist in *The Graphic*, 1 March 1879, p. 216. Chronicle / Alamy Stock Photo.

in 1892, Don Gaspar Costela y Vasquez, who had been a seaman in *Santa Ana*, died in a home for naval pensioners at San Fernando, Cádiz. No death records have been found to support the claim of the Spanish veteran who reportedly died at the age of 109 in 1898 in Dallas, Texas, ninety-three years after the battle. Pedro Antonio Zia Martinez was reputedly a sixteen-year-old cabin boy in the 74-gun *San Juan Nepomuceno* at the time of Trafalgar. Sir William Laird Clowes wrote in 1895, 'It is not very easy to say who the last [British Trafalgar] survivor is.'[25] Candidates for the distinction began to appear as early as the 1850s, when Charles Bullen, flag captain of *Britannia* and the last of the captains at Trafalgar, died. Among the authentic veterans were several fraudulent or fanciful claimants. Among British officers, the last British survivor was Lieutenant-Colonel James Fynmore of the Royal Marines, who died in 1887. He had been a volunteer first class, serving with his father, who commanded the Marine Detachment on board HMS *Africa*. The closest competitor to Fynmore was the hundred-year-old Joseph Sunderland, a powder monkey in the frigate *Beaulieu*, who died in

March 1890. His ship arrived in the fleet the day after the battle but participated in the aftermath.[26]

Naming Ships

A traditional means by which navies commemorate a battle or a successful admiral is to name a warship after the person or the battle. A ship's name expresses values, pride, and traditions.[27] In the case of a warship, a distinction may be made between ships named for rulers, whose names evoke loyalty, and those named for great victories and heroes, whose exemplary stories inspire valour in future battles. The presence of that name in the fleet is a constant reminder to the officers and seamen who serve in and with that ship of the heritage she bears. In October 1805, the Admiralty ordered the first-rate, 120-gun *Nelson*, the lead ship in a new class of five three-decked warships.[28] She was the first of five ships in the Royal Navy named after the victor of Trafalgar.[29] Later, the Admiralty named four others for Collingwood.[30] A few months later, in January 1806, the Admiralty ordered a 90-gun second-rate named *Trafalgar*. Neither ship was completed in time for service with the fleet during the Napoleonic Wars. In 1867, the Admiralty passed *Nelson*, by then converted to a screw line of battle ship, to the colony of Victoria in Australia to serve as a coastal defence and training ship. She remained there until sold in 1898. In 1841, a new *Trafalgar* was launched. Converted to have auxiliary steam power in 1859, she served with the fleet and eventually became a training ship at Portsmouth. The third ship to be named *Trafalgar* was the lead ship in the two-ship low-freeboard *Trafalgar* class of ironclad battleships with her sister ship, *Nile*. She served as a flagship with the Mediterranean Fleet from 1890 to 1897 and as a guardship at Portsmouth from 1898 to 1902, when she participated in King Edward VII's Coronation Fleet review. She then served in the Home Fleet from 1909 to 1911.[31] In 1945, the battle-class destroyer HMS *Trafalgar* (D77) was commissioned as the fourth ship of the name. She served briefly in the Far East and then in the Mediterranean from 1958 to 1962 before her decommissioning.[32] The fifth and most recent is the nuclear-powered submarine *Trafalgar* (S107), which was in service from 1983 to 2009. In 2001, the boat fired the first British Tomahawk cruise missiles used during Operation Veritas in the Afghan War.[33]

Complementing the navy's system of naming ships is a more inclusive approach, the battle honour system, which is similar to the British Army's much older regimental battle honours system. The Royal Navy formally established its practice in 1954.[34] The motivating idea behind them is to foster *esprit de corps* among the ships' companies and to lead them to take a personal interest in the wartime exploits of their ships and past ships that carried the same name. Since warships do not have regimental colours, battle honours are displayed on a battle honour board. This board is usually made of solid teak wood and mounted on the ship's superstructure. On it are the ship's badge and scrolls with the ship's name and her associated honours. Thirty-two ships' names are authorized to carry the battle honours for Trafalgar, representing every ship that had a role in the battle, not just the major ships of the line.[35] Through ships' names and battle honours, the men and women of the Royal Navy have a daily reminder of Trafalgar, one of the great battles in British naval history.

Twenty Spanish warships have carried the names of the Spanish heroes of Trafalgar. Seven have borne the name of Brigadier Cosme Damián de Churruca y Elorza, who commanded *San Juan Nepomuceno* (Figure 6.7). Five ships have been named for Captain Francisco Alsedo y Bustamante, who died in the battle while commanding the 80-gun *Montañez*. Commodore Dionisio Alcalá Galiano, the commander of the 74-gun *Bahama*, and Lieutenant-General Federico Gravina had four ships in the Spanish Navy named in their honour.[36]

Among French ships at the battle, the most famous was the 74-gun *Redoutable*, one of whose snipers fired the shot that killed Nelson. Seven subsequent ships in the French Navy have borne the name, including the world's first steel-built, central battery ironclad built in 1876 and the

Figure 6.7 Brigadier of the Navy Don Cosme Damián de Churruca y Elorza, who died at Trafalgar while commanding the Spanish 74-gun *San Juan Nepomuceno*. By an unknown artist, ca. 1848.

Museo Naval, Madrid. Alamy 2C875W1.

1971 *Redoutable* (S611), the lead boat of a class of nuclear-powered ballistic missile submarines, now a museum ship in Cherbourg. In addition, a French cruiser and a destroyer bear the name *Magon,* in memory of Rear-Admiral Charles René Magon de Médine, who died on board his flagship, *Algésiras*, while serving as the second in command of the reserve squadron under Gravina.[37]

Developing the Concept of Decisive Naval Battle

In the latter half of the nineteenth century, as sailing warships shifted to steam propulsion, wooden ships gave way to iron and steel hulls, and new naval weapons appeared, navies underwent an intellectual revolution. With visions of the changing character of maritime warfare in a new era, technological and scientific solutions initially dominated the minds of naval officers. Some perceptive observers began to see that technological development, however essential to modern navies, was a never-ending spiral. To control, understand, and direct this spiral, naval officers began to shape their craft into a profession through education, training, and analysis, leading to the establishment of standards that could raise the overall quality of their activities. Some of the hallmarks of this development included the creation of organizations to study and discuss naval and military issues, the publication of journals, and contributions to a growing specialized literature on the subject.[38]

In 1851, Sir Edward Creasy made one of the early contributions to the growing military literature of the period with his widely read book *Fifteen Decisive Battles in World History*. The volume popularized the notion of decisive battles among the public and military thinkers, but Trafalgar was not among the battles Creasy described. The only naval action he recognized as such was the Spanish Armada of 1588. The editors of later editions in the early twentieth century expanded the naval component by including recent battles, such as those at Manila and Santiago in 1898 and Tsushima in 1905. However, the work still ignored Trafalgar.[39] Finally, Fletcher Pratt's 1956 study, *The Battles That Changed History*, looked at four naval battles—Quiberon Bay in 1759, Chesapeake Bay in 1781, Trafalgar in 1805, and Midway in 1942—that 'were turning points after which things would have been a great deal different if the decision had gone the other way'.[40] Ironically, it was a British military historian, Major-General J. F. C. Fuller, who made the most fulsome professional judgement about Trafalgar, even though he had not included it in his earlier study on *Decisive Battles*.[41] In his *Military History of the Western World*, Fuller wrote:

> In every respect, Trafalgar was a memorable battle and its influence upon history profound. It shattered forever Napoleon's dream of invading England. It brought to an end the 100-year struggle between her and France for the lordship of the seas. It gave England the Empire of the Oceans, which was to endure for over half a century and make possible a Pax Britannica. More immediately important, it showed the world of 1895 that Napoleon was not invincible, and it compelled him to fall back on his Continental System, to seek to establish a universal empire which would economically strangle England, and which instead ended by his own political strangulation. Without Trafalgar, there could have been no Peninsular War, and without the Peninsular War, it is hard to believe that there could ever have been a Waterloo.[42]

John Knox Laughton

Until the late nineteenth century, naval officers had focused on strategic and tactical approaches that had proven effective in their own experience and that of their predecessors. Still, they found that technological advances needed clarification in statistics and ship design. They lacked a broad, theoretical doctrinal understanding of naval warfare, unlike military thinkers such as Antoine-Henri Jomini and Carl von Clausewitz, who had developed their perspectives based on experiences and reflections from Napoleon's land campaigns. A step towards such a development came in June 1874, when John Knox Laughton of the Royal Naval College, Greenwich, presented a paper at the Royal United Services Institution on 'The Scientific Study of Naval History'. Laughton understood that in a time of such broad technological change, the navy could not effectively use rigid fighting instructions with its new type of ships but needed to understand the principles that formed naval strategy and tactics. The only way to do this was through the professional study of naval history.[43] Laughton continued his work in this vein for professional naval education and the development of naval tactics. In 1886, he condensed and re-edited Nicholas Harris Nicolas's seven-volume compilation into his version of *Letters and Despatches of Horatio, Viscount Nelson, K.B.*, to make it more useful for naval officers. Laughton dedicated the book to Admiral Sir Geoffrey Phipps Hornby, noting how he had 'recognized in Nelson not only the national hero but the consummate tactician; and how emphatically you have insisted that the principles which he enunciated and illustrated are, in spite of all changes, as true now as they were eighty or ninety years ago'.[44] In Laughton's presentation of the material, he skilfully used selected excerpts from his correspondence to create a biography, arguing that Nelson's tactical ideas were much more profound than aggressively laying your ship alongside the enemy's and engaging in a mêlée action. Laughton emphasized that Nelson's outstanding contribution at Trafalgar was fundamentally based on his command style and that he exercised tactical control of the fleet through his thorough training of his captains in his intentions. Rather than relying on signals that could often be obscured or misread during a smoke-filled action, Nelson relied on what modern navies today call mission command, understanding a senior commander's intent in a way that combines decentralized execution and encourages junior commanders' freedom of action and initiative in carrying out the plan. In Laughton's judgement, Nelson at Trafalgar completed the ultimate development of sailing ship battle tactics with his new and higher level of comprehension and application. Laughton believed that Nelson, the ultimate professional officer, tactician, and leader, provided the best exemplar for modern officers to study.[45]

Laughton's pioneering research and understanding of naval history laid the groundwork for several new lines of development within the Royal Navy and other navies. One of his initiatives, along with Captain Reginald Custance, was the establishment of the Navy Records Society in 1893, aimed at producing authoritative historical sources accompanied by extensive introductions. Over the years, several of these volumes provided new and detailed insights into the campaign and Battle of Trafalgar. Among these were John Leyland's volumes on *The Blockade of*

Brest, 1803–1805 (1899, 1902);[46] Sir Thomas Jackson's *Logs of the Great Sea Fights, 1794–1805* (1900),[47] Julian Corbett's *Fighting Instructions, 1530–1816* (1905),[48] and Laughton's edition of the *Barham Papers* (1907–11).[49] While these volumes remain important published primary sources for historians today, the Society's initial purpose was to inform and educate serving naval officers about historical matters relevant to contemporary concerns in what twenty-first-century historians would term applied history.[50]

Laughton's Influence in the United States

A second line of development of Laughton's influence occurred across the Atlantic in the United States at the U.S. Naval War College in Newport, Rhode Island. In 1870, Captain Stephen B. Luce, U.S. Navy, had commanded the steam sloop of war USS *Galena* on a cruise as a neutral observer of the French naval blockade of Germany during the Franco-Prussian War. During a port call in London, Luce visited the Royal United Services Institution in Whitehall, London, where he met John Knox Laughton and discovered they shared a wide range of interests. By 1875, they were in regular correspondence with each other. The two men exchanged copies of the papers they had written. Among them, Laughton sent Luce a copy of his 'Scientific Study of Naval History' and found in him a ready convert to the idea, as Luce had read widely in naval history. A decade later, Luce referred to Laughton's article in a lecture he gave to the first class at the newly established Naval War College, which he had founded. In this lecture, Luce echoed Laughton's view that Nelson soundly based his tactics at Trafalgar on the principle of concentrating force rather than the simplistic adage of placing warships against warships.[51]

In establishing the Naval War College, Luce conceived it as an institution for educating officers in the highest branches of the naval profession—strategy, tactics, international law, and history—and to prepare them for duties that extended beyond commanding a ship. It was not a place to teach war but to understand how wars began, how they were fought, and how they could be ended. As Luce later defined it, the college was 'a place of original research on all questions relating to war and to statesmanship connected with war, or the prevention of war'.[52]

Naval studies generally had yet to go beyond technological and tactical battle studies. Luce saw the need for a broad theoretical understanding of what navies do. He sought a writer who could create for the navy the theoretical foundation that Jomini had provided for the army. To achieve this, Luce designed the new college's curriculum based on what he called the comparative approach, examining military thought to identify what might be relevant for developing a theoretical understanding of naval warfare. Initially, the college developed a curriculum centred on historical studies, international law, and naval war games, incorporating military works that spanned from Edward Hamley's 1866 textbook, *Operations of War Explained and Illustrated*, to the perspectives Americans had on the approach of the German General Staff during their recent successful wars. Having developed a theoretical basis and understanding of what a navy does through this method, naval officers could choose more wisely which technological courses to take to achieve those ends.

Alfred Thayer Mahan

Luce searched among the bright and articulate officers he knew in the U.S. Navy to find someone who could take up this study as a primary task. His first choice was unavailable to undertake the work. Finally, Luce settled on Commander Alfred Thayer Mahan, who had served under him as a seamanship instructor in 1862–3, when Luce headed the Seamanship Department at the U.S. Naval Academy, then located in Newport, Rhode Island, during the American Civil War. Mahan had published a prize-winning professional article, written an operational naval history, and was the son of the U.S. Military Academy professor Dennis Hart Mahan, who had been the leading early disseminator of Antoine-Henri Jomini's thinking for the U.S. Army. Alfred Mahan soon succeeded Luce as president of the Naval College, where he delivered the lectures assigned to him. Several years later, in 1890, Mahan published these same lectures as *The Influence of Sea Power upon History, 1660–1783*. Two years later, in 1892, he published a second volume of Naval War College lectures, *The Influence of Sea Power upon the French Revolution and Empire, 1793–1812*. Then, in 1897, Mahan published *The Life of Nelson: The Embodiment of the Sea Power of Great Britain* as the capstone to his Sea Power series.[53]

Mahan presented a complex argument in these books that combined political, political-economic, and governmental perspectives. He saw that the British victory at Trafalgar was not inevitable but rather made possible by the economic and industrial forces behind the navy that allowed for the concentration of British naval forces in the eastern Atlantic. In Mahan's view, Nelson's greatest asset as a leader was his willingness to take decisive actions that led to a decisive battle, culminating in the destruction of an enemy force. In the case of Trafalgar, the battle effectively ended significant fleet actions and removed serious challenges to British sea trade. This victory allowed the continuation of the economic blockade of the continent, thereby securing the country's financial strength while weakening France.[54]

The interpretation of Mahan's thinking that a decisive fleet battle was the key to naval success, rather than an attack on trade or an economic blockade, had widespread ramifications in professional naval thought among the great power navies and the naval forces that aspired to become major navies. It was not an obvious conclusion, given that many major naval battles had been indecisive. Nevertheless, in Mahan's hands, the exception proved the rule, although some later historians have thought this an incomplete interpretation of Mahan's thinking.[55]

The Idea of Decisive Battle in Continental European Navies

New weapons and new ship designs had brought about a reconsideration of naval tactical and strategic thinking in all navies. In France, after more than half a century of a nearly continual naval race with Britain in the wake of Trafalgar and the Napoleonic Wars, the situation changed. Germany's defeat of France in 1871, Bismark's subsequent isolation of France, and the possible spectre of German, Austrian, and Italian navies coming together to oppose the French Navy created a new and different threat to France. In those years, it became clear that the French Navy could no longer even think of engaging in a major Trafalgar-like decisive battle with a major power.

Turning away from the idea that the best strategy was to attack the enemy at its strongest point—its battle fleet—French Admiral Louis-Antoine-Richild Grivel reverted to a two-century-old French line of thinking that promoted *guerre de course*, commerce raiding, over *guerre d'escadre*, fleet battle. The near-simultaneous invention of the self-propelled torpedo in 1867 sparked a new line of thinking, creating an argument based on technological and matériel superiority. French followers of this approach—notably Rear Admiral Théophile Aube, Gabriel Charmes, and the Jeune École—saw that Britain's industrial strength ensured naval superiority; however, her growing imperial stance and dependence on overseas trade exposed new vulnerabilities. By 1900, this insight had become the foundation for French naval strategy in a future *guerre industrielle*. Not everyone agreed.[56]

Rather than avoiding a major battle, some theorists, influenced by the recent rise of international law and liberal thought on warfare, argued that the most humane way to fight a war among civilized nations was to use the maximum amount of violence in the shortest time possible. For this approach, a decisive major battle was preferable, as it avoided the casualties among civilians that an attack on commerce and industry would bring. French naval lieutenant Ambroise Baudry explained that wars 'tend to become less barbarous. In the conflict of civilized nations, there are no more sackings and pillage...If the weapons of the field of battle are always improved, war outside the immediate area of their use is becoming or tending to become more humane.'[57] Many agreed with Baudry and his accompanying thought that victory won with gallantry was one of the greatest expressions of the human spirit. In this discussion, the word 'Trafalgar' rarely, if ever, appeared directly. The example of Nelson and Trafalgar was clearly in the back of their minds as the most recent naval battle to exhibit gallantry. Such ideas about future warfare were clearly, but unconsciously, present in the way the British commemorated Trafalgar and Nelson.[58]

Mahan in German Naval Thinking

In Germany, Mahan's work profoundly influenced Kaiser Wilhelm II and Admiral Alfred von Tirpitz. They encouraged translating those of Mahan's books on naval history that emphasized decisive battles such as Trafalgar, but not Mahan's books on international relations or naval strategy. As Secretary of State of the Navy Office, Tirpitz's promotion of Mahan's work widely popularized it among German naval officers, using Mahan's work to present the argument for a battle fleet. Additionally, several officers associated with the German Navy's war college, the Marineakedemie, wrote studies of naval history based largely on Mahan's work.[59] Tirpitz's establishment of a news bureau within the Imperial Navy Office conveyed the message of Mahan's works on the necessity for a battle fleet to the broader German public. Following Mahan's interpretation and influenced by contemporary German military thinking, Tirpitz's view soon solidified into the concept of an *Entscheidungschlacht*—a decisive battle in the spirit of Trafalgar—fought between Helgoland and the River Thames. Such a battle, he believed, would give the command of the sea to the victor, as Trafalgar had done. Such thinking continued in German naval thought, as exemplified by Admiral Erich Raeder's views in the late 1930s regarding a decisive fleet battle involving massive surface battleships. Raeder convinced Adolf Hitler that Germany needed a battle fleet of large surface warships to maintain command of the maritime lanes of communication. This understanding, which successive generations of German naval leaders developed from Mahan, was an incomplete and incorrect version that missed many of the subtleties and qualifications within

Mahan's thought, including his broader understanding of sea power linked to economic productivity and democratic governance.[60]

Japanese Naval Thinking

German naval officers were not alone in making selective interpretations of Mahanian ideas. The Imperial Japanese Navy shared a similar view but saw it vindicated in the 1905 Battle of Tsushima. With the coming of the Meiji era in 1868, the Japanese began to develop a navy. At first, it was a haphazard collection of old vessels inherited from the shogunal navy, which even included an armoured ram originally intended for the American Confederate States Navy. A multinational naval force led by the Royal Navy's Admiral Sir Augustus Kuper had defeated Japanese Chōshū naval and land forces during the Shimonoseki Straits Campaign in 1863 and 1864. As a result, Meiji naval officials concluded that they needed a new Imperial Japanese Navy modelled after Western navies. One of their first steps was establishing a Western-style naval academy in Tokyo, which was later relocated to Etajima in 1888. It soon turned out officers with unquestioned 'professional competence, fanatical courage, and extraordinary *élan*', as the historian Arthur Marder described them.[61] In 1870, the emperor decreed that the Royal Navy was the model for Japan's future naval development. Three years later, a thirty-four-man British naval mission under Lieutenant-Commander Archibald Douglas arrived and remained for six years, making substantial progress in modernizing the Japanese Navy along the British model. The Douglas Mission successfully introduced British uniforms and naval traditions, attitudes, and approaches to seamanship. While such large and expensive naval missions did not long continue, a series of key individual British naval officers made significant contributions at the Naval Academy, where cadets learned English, and at the Naval Staff College, founded in 1888, which became the most important centre for the development of Japanese naval strategic and tactical thought. These early British influences brought to Japan an appreciation of British naval history, including a knowledge of Nelson and Trafalgar. The naval museum at Etajima preserved a bust of Nelson and a lock of his hair embedded in a miniature model of HMS *Victory*'s stern. In 1921, the First Lord of the Admiralty, Lord Lee of Fareham, presented to Admiral of the Fleet Tōgō a photograph of a painting of Nelson making his famous last signal to the fleet at Trafalgar along with reproductions of a Nelson letter and portrait.[62]

Further supporting the general knowledge of Nelson and Trafalgar that British officers taught Japanese naval officers, the Japanese naval line officers' professional organization, Suikōsha, published a translation of Mahan's *Influence of Sea Power upon History* in 1896, and the naval academy subsequently adopted it as a textbook. Japanese versions of *The French Revolution and Empire* and *The Life of Nelson: The Embodiment of Sea Power* appeared in 1900 and 1906.[63] Additionally, Lieutenant-Commander Satō Tetsutarō began to write several books to justify Japanese naval growth based on their understanding of Mahanian ideas with the addition of ideas put forward by the American naval officer Bradley A. Fiske. These included the views of J. V. Chase and Frederick William Lanchester's algebraic theory that explained how concentrated modern gunfire conferred an expanding and cumulative advantage compared to that in the age of sail.[64] The Imperial Japanese Navy's fundamental focus was on decisive and annihilating battles between battleships. They based their thinking on the concepts put forward by Mahan, as illustrated by Trafalgar, and validated them in their battle experiences at the Yalu in 1894 and at Tsushima in 1905. The Japanese approach was a false application of Mahan's sea power theory of global hegemony to a regional power with its land empire close at hand rather than a maritime nation with distant overseas territories. At the same time, like other navies of the day, the Japanese Navy focused on tactical naval thinking rather than developing a comprehensive maritime strategy.[65]

The Limitation of Tactical Thinking

Few naval officers in any navy of the period had the education or insight to see beyond the tactical or operational level of naval warfare.

This is readily understandable, as the tactical level is the environment in which navies operate daily at sea and is the level at which navies fight. The strategic and grand strategic levels involved a much broader level of understanding, which required an appreciation of tactical outcomes and their impact on broader political, military, economic, and other governmental issues. For many naval officers of the day, the ultimate objective of fleet naval operations was merely the annihilation of the enemy in a pitched battle. While the capability to fight and win is an essential attribute for any armed force, the emphasis on battle in this environment has led to overemphasizing and deifying battle for its own sake.[66] Lieutenant Baudry demonstrated this when he wrote that:

> the security of the lines of communication, whether by sea or by land, has its importance, [and] is a factor in making war and achieving victory. But the object, *the sole object,* is the disruption and destruction of the organized forces of the enemy by sea and land. And this object is obtainable by one means only—battle. Neutralization, bottling up, dispersion of the said forces without a battle—I will go farther, and say without a great and decisive battle, are only half-measures and half-successes.[67]

For naval officers in many navies in the late nineteenth and early twentieth centuries, Trafalgar became the apotheosis and premier historical example of the decisive battle. In their understanding, at the tactical level, it met all the criteria for a decisive battle. At the same time, its victorious hero, who gallantly died at the moment of victory, was, as Mahan subtitled his biography of Nelson, 'The Embodiment of the Sea Power of Great Britain'.

The Spell of Trafalgar in the Navy

In the mid-1880s, far-sighted naval officers began to realize that the Royal Navy was not adequately organized for modern naval warfare. Lord Charles Beresford commented, 'The fact was that after Trafalgar, this country had attained to so supreme a dominance upon all seas, with so high a degree of sea training acquired in independent commands that organization for war was taken for granted. We were living on the Nelson tradition.'[68] Nevertheless, when the First World War began in 1914, despite organizational improvements, British and German naval officers still fully expected that the eventual clash would result in another Trafalgar victory.

In Sir Julian Corbett's lectures to the British naval war course and his subsequent book, *The Campaign of Trafalgar*, he aimed to skewer the professional myths that had grown up around Trafalgar with his broad-ranging strategic study and to confront Mahan's emphasis on decisive battle and obsession with concentration of force as well as to quiet the advocates of smaller battleships. Using the example of Trafalgar, he stressed in his lectures the importance of commonly understood and widely employed tactical doctrine, fluidity between attack and defence, dispersed action, and a rapid concentration for battle.[69] As to the battle itself, Corbett concluded, 'By universal assent, Trafalgar is ranked as one of the decisive battles of the world, and yet of all the great victories, there is not one which to all appearance was so barren of immediate result.'[70] Corbett's incisive analysis of the Trafalgar campaign and his excoriating judgement about its limited strategic effects touched on both the place of the battle in professional naval thought and its broader understanding in historiography. (See Chapter 8 below on Corbett's work in historiographical terms.)

In 1911, Corbett published his book *Some Principles of Maritime Strategy*, a work that provided a fundamental British maritime doctrine for the period dominated by Admiral Lord Fisher. Corbett developed the book from a handout that he gave his students on the naval war course: 'The Green Pamphlet' or 'Strategical Terms and Definitions Used in Lectures on Naval History'.[71] *Some Principles* made only a few passing direct references to Trafalgar. Although Corbett used numerous points from the broader Trafalgar campaign as examples in the book, he made no explicit point about the Battle of Trafalgar. Instead, the book laid out a conceptual framework for a maritime strategy that was much more refined and carefully derived from British historical experience than Mahan's. Since the earliest years of the twentieth century,

Carl von Clausewitz's theoretical work had already interested and influenced Corbett's historical analyses. In 1906, the Royal Navy's Naval Intelligence Division provided the naval war course with an English translation of an article by Rear-Admiral Kurt von Maltzahn from the German Navy's professional journal, *Marine Rundschau*. Von Maltzahn's June 1905 article posed the question, 'What Lessons Has General von Clausewitz's Work *On War* for the Naval Officer?' The article stimulated Corbett's thinking and helped crystallize his thoughts on several points. Although Corbett rejected von Maltzahn's emphasis on defeating an enemy's armed forces and his assertion that Nelson belonged to the decisive battle school, he agreed that, despite inherent differences, a general understanding of war could be transferred from land to sea when viewed from the highest perspectives of understanding. Among them—a key point for Corbett—were applications of limited warfare.[72]

Corbett argued that the conduct of wartime naval operations fell into three categories: methods of securing command of the sea, methods of disputing command of the sea, and methods of exercising command of the sea. There were two ways of securing command: by obtaining a decision in battle and blockade. He noted that the British Navy naturally preferred battle because it typically had preponderance over its enemy and, thus, had a high chance of succeeding. 'The idea seems to be rooted in the oldest traditions of the Royal Navy,' Corbett wrote. 'The conviction of the sea service that war is primarily a question of battles, and that battles once joined on anything like equal terms must be pressed to the last gasp, is one that has had nothing to learn from the more recent continental discoveries.'[73] Corbett saw this as the creed enshrined in the Articles of War and in the apotheosis of Nelson that deified the idea of battle in the Royal Navy. He went on to point out that 'devoutly as we may hold the battle faith, it is not always possible or wise to act upon it'.[74] While the careful reader of Corbett's *Some Principles* could see that he had some doubts about the necessity of battle, others who read the text with less care might grasp no more than his opening lines on the subject:

> The only way of securing command by naval means is to obtain a decision by battle against the enemy's fleet. Sooner or later it must be done, and the sooner the better. This was the old British creed. It is still our creed, and needs no labouring. No one will dispute it, no one will care even to discuss it, and we pass with confidence to the conclusion that the first business of our fleet is to seek out the enemy's fleet and destroy it.[75]

This statement suggested and even encouraged the continuing expectations in the fleet that a major Trafalgar-like battle would take place in the next war. A decade later, after studying the experience of the most recent war, Corbett had changed his view. He noted in the introduction to his official *History of Naval Operations* in the First World War, 'by a strange misreading of history, an idea had grown up that its [the main fleet's] primary action is to seek out and destroy the enemy's main fleet. This view, being literary rather than historical, was nowhere adopted with more unction than in Germany, where there was no naval tradition to test its accuracy.'[76] When the occasion for a fleet battle finally arose near the Skagerrak, off the Jutland peninsula's north coast in the North Sea on 31 May 1916, nine battleships in the British Grand Fleet carried names with Trafalgar Honours. With the heritage of Trafalgar entirely in their minds, British seamen had an enormous motivational advantage and confidence that the German fleet sailors did not have. At the same time, it put an immense burden on Admiral Sir John Jellicoe to be another Nelson under entirely different circumstances. Yet, in the end, Jutland produced no decision, and the war continued with a different focus for navies.

For Julian Corbett, Jutland and Trafalgar had similar outcomes, reinforcing his ultimate conclusion that battles were not necessarily important. In the third volume of Corbett's official *Naval Operations* dealing with Jutland, the Admiralty insisted on pointing out its fundamental disagreement on this point with Corbett in its disclaimer. 'Their Lordships find that some of the principles advocated in this book, especially the tendency to minimize the importance of seeking battle and of forcing it to a conclusion, are directly in conflict with its views.'[77] The concept of decisive battle had become such a fundamental element in the Royal Navy's service culture that it could not be swayed by such historical analysis.

During the century between Trafalgar and Jutland—the period one historian characterized as 'the long calm lee of Trafalgar'—naval warfare and the Royal Navy underwent significant changes. The Victorian penchant to regulate and control dominated the Royal Navy during this period. Unlike the situation that Nelson and his captains enjoyed, there was little room for individual initiative. The fleet became centrally organized, with senior admirals sending increasingly explicit signals directing ship manoeuvres and operations in contrast to the practice at Trafalgar. Doctrine tended to become rigid and unchanging in a service known for its anti-intellectualism, smothering the tradition of tactical, individual initiative, and mission command that characterized Nelson and the age of sail. Senior commanders emphasized centralization and direct control of the fleet rather than encouraging initiative.[78]

At the same time, if war should come, the navy expected a great battle in the tradition of Trafalgar. The culture within the Royal Navy continued to preserve the memory of Trafalgar, using Horatio Nelson as the personification of the battle in institutional memory. When the Crimean War was on the verge of interrupting the Pax Britannica, the First Lord of the Admiralty, Sir James Graham, supported the choice of the experienced sixty-seven-year-old Vice-Admiral Charles Napier to command in the Baltic. Writing to the Earl of Clarendon, Graham commented, 'I hope, even still, that the "Nelson Touch" will not be necessary: but if unhappily it should be so, Charley Napier is the boy to administer it.'[79] Admiral Edmund Lyons, Napier's counterpart commanding in the Black Sea, vainly thought he physically resembled Nelson and tried to convince the press and others that he was a similarly active, energetic, and charismatic leader for combat.[80] Such thoughts were common in the Royal Navy at the time, as a sailor who had fought under Nelson reminisced in the 1850s, 'Nelson was considered our Saviour and our God... We gloried that we followed in the wake of Nelson, as the only Jesus Christ or Saviour we acknowledge in the fleet.'[81]

Another prominent officer who promoted the combined memory of Nelson and Trafalgar was Admiral Sir John Fisher. As a boy, Fisher had grown up next door to Admiral of the Fleet Sir William Parker, who had served under Nelson in the Mediterranean. Parker inspired the young lad with his reminiscences of those dramatic times. Later, Fisher had served under Sir Geoffrey Phipps Hornby. Through him, Fisher first learned the professional value of the historical study of naval tactics and the art of an admiral even before coming to know Mahan's books. Later in command of the Mediterranean Fleet, Fisher had Nelson's signal at Trafalgar painted over the guns of his flagship, HMS *Renown*. Selected as the First Sea Lord in 1904, Fisher deliberately took office on Trafalgar Day. He cited Nelson as an example at every turn as he promoted new and innovative ideas. In promoting the design for a new type of warship, he chose the name of a ship that had served at Trafalgar, the 98-gun *Dreadnought*. Serving as First Sea Lord until 1910, he revived the names of nearly every ship that had served at Trafalgar as he built a new fleet to deliver a Trafalgar-like victory.[82] Trafalgar and Nelson also profoundly influenced David Beatty, who kept copies of Nelson's biographies as well as paintings of Trafalgar in his cabin at sea.[83]

When the First World War eventually produced a major naval battle at Jutland in 1916, it was no decisive victory. Neither side destroyed the other. For Germany, it was a tactical victory at sea; for Britain, it was a strategic victory when the German fleet returned to port without contesting further British control. Nevertheless, Kaiser Wilhelm II of Germany proclaimed a German Trafalgar-like victory. Euphorically, he reportedly told the officers and men of his navy: 'The spell of Trafalgar has been broken; the English were beaten. You have started a new chapter in world history.'[84] In the controversy that arose after Jutland, the contrasts between the battles of Jutland and Trafalgar became a significant part of the critique that pointed to the folly of expecting a modern Trafalgar in the machine age.[85]

During the Second World War, German and Japanese naval leaders continued to quest for a decisive Trafalgar-like battle. In the post-war period, however, naval strategists have come to realize that while a major battle may be a turning point, the decisive nature of war is determined by more significant aspects that control warfare: financial strength, industrial production, logistics, and political will.

British Colonial Naval Heritage

While the Battle of Jutland did not turn out to be the Trafalgar-like battle of destruction that many had expected, the commemoration of the 1805 battle had come to have a different meaning in the British colonies and dominions. As shown during the immediate aftermath of the battle, the commemoration and memorialization of Trafalgar also showed loyalty to the king and Britain in general. The statue of Nelson that Barbados erected in 1806, along with the broad participation of diverse groups in Nelson's funeral, demonstrated these aspects.

In the early twentieth century, the rapid expansion of the Imperial German Navy led the Royal Navy to reconsider its global deployment and concentrate its main forces in home waters. This decision held implications for naval defence in British overseas dominions and colonies. It led eventually to the establishment of the Royal Canadian Navy in 1910, the Royal Australian Navy in 1911, and the New Zealand Naval Forces in 1913. Many British naval traditions were continued in those services, as well as a deep knowledge of British naval history, including the Battle of Trafalgar and the legacy of Admiral Nelson. Great Britain transferred some naval assets to promote these new naval services. One of the first two Canadian warships to arrive in Canada from Britain in 1910 was HMCS *Niobe*. The authorities timed her arrival from England at Halifax for 21 October, the 105th anniversary of the Battle of Trafalgar. On that same day, Rear-Admiral Charles Kingsmill, the first director of the Naval Service of Canada, broke his broad pennant in her at the mouth of Halifax harbour, becoming the first Canadian admiral to fly his flag in Canadian waters.[86]

In the years after the First World War, Trafalgar Day had become a minor anniversary no longer observed in some parts of the empire. However, as war threatened again in the 1930s, colonial officials revived

Trafalgar Day celebrations to develop a local naval culture. In 1933, Trafalgar Day marked the first public event of the newly formed Hong Kong Royal Naval Volunteer Reserve.

Meanwhile, on the same day in Australia, one hundred Navy League cadets, accompanied by their band, marched in Sydney from Customs House to the Mayfair Theatre, where they watched the British film *Our Fighting Navy*.[87] In 1935, Allen Wolsey Cardinall, the Commissioner of the Cayman Islands in the West Indies, introduced a Trafalgar Day essay contest in local schools as a means of developing naval interests among schoolchildren and potential recruits. As one student essayist wrote, 'Today, Trafalgar seems to say we are a unit of the greatest nation on

Figure 6.8 '1500 Officers and Men of the Royal Australian Navy Marched Through the City of Melbourne in Commemoration of Trafalgar Day and to Assist the War and Austerity Loan', 21 October 1942. Australian War Memorial. Public Domain. Library of Congress Prints and Photographs Division Washington, D.C. 20540

Figure 6.9 'Once Again I Call Upon Every American To Do His Duty'. The caption to this Second World War era cartoon paraphrases Admiral Lord Nelson's signal to his fleet before the Battle of Trafalgar. Drawn by Clifford Kennedy Berryman, it was published the day after the Japanese attack on Pearl Harbor, 7 December 1941, and shows Uncle Sam urging Americans to come to the defence of their country. Behind him stand the ghostly figures of soldiers from past American wars. *Washington Star*, 8 December 1941. eSales@awm.gov.au - Sept 24.

earth, therefore, we should make ourselves worthy of the greatest and best.'[88] The revived Trafalgar Day and other initiatives helped foster interest in the Royal Navy, develop imperial sentiment, and encourage local volunteers for the British Merchant Navy and the Trinidad Royal Navy Volunteer Reserve.

During the Second World War, newspapers throughout Australia reported that naval cadets from the Australian Naval College marched through the streets of Melbourne to commemorate Trafalgar Day and to support the Victory Loan fundraising drive (Figure 6.8).[89] In the 1950s, the Kenya Royal Naval Volunteer Reserve and its successor, the Royal East African Navy, used Trafalgar Day to their advantage.

Its annual Trafalgar Day Sailing Regatta provided a testing ground for recruiting local petty officers.[90]

More recently, in 1996 and 1999, the first two editions of the Royal Navy handbook *British Maritime Doctrine* opened with a description of how Nelson used doctrine in his Trafalgar memorandum to facilitate the effective use of force.[91]

The professional naval reaction to the battle differed distinctly from the way the public perceived it, as well as from the developing interpretations of professional historians. The merger of the Trafalgar story with professional thinking about decisive battles in Britain, Germany, Japan, and elsewhere resulted from a concentrated and narrow focus on the tactical details of the battle rather than a broad strategic analysis. Sharing this approach during the first century after the battle, both naval service culture and nineteenth-century historians of the battle contributed to the concept that navies existed mainly to fight a decisive fleet battle.

7

National Commemorations

Unlike almost every other great battle, the anniversary of Trafalgar continues to be celebrated, providing an opportunity to observe changes in the British national mood regarding what to commemorate. The national commemoration of the Battle of Trafalgar, which took place for the centenary in 1905, the sesquicentennial in 1955, and the bicentenary in 2005, were each distinctive events that, at once, both embodied and differed from the views expressed in public and naval cultures. The context and attitudes of the times in which each event occurred enormously affected each commemoration. Cumulatively, over time, the public developed a consensus on the meaning of the Trafalgar commemoration as the national mood changed from commemorating a victory over the French to celebrating Nelson and promoting the Royal Navy in public consciousness.

The events of 1905 marked the transition from the remembrance of an event within the living memory of those who had experienced the Napoleonic Wars to the abstract commemoration of a distant historical event. In 1905, the world was a very different place than it had been in 1805. It required some historical imagination and investigation to uncover the connections between the two worlds of experience. Ships and armaments had changed dramatically at sea. Unlike Georgian Britain, the Edwardian United Kingdom was not at war with France and Spain. The Entente Cordiale, signed between France and Britain in April 1904, formalized what had been in place for several decades, officially ending centuries of rivalry and conflict between the two countries.

Britain was at the height of her imperial power over a transoceanic empire that, in the popular imagination of that time, was founded on Nelson's victory at Trafalgar. It was a period of peace but with the looming possibility of war with Germany for France and Britain. A distant war in the western Pacific between Japan and Russia resulted in a Trafalgar-like victory at Tsushima in 1905, reinforcing Mahan's view that decisive naval victories were both possible and strategically significant. Yet, just thirty-four years earlier, Germany had defeated Napoleon III's France in the Franco-Prussian War without any significant naval actions. Spain was still coming to terms with its defeat in its 1898 war with the United States and the loss of Cuba, Puerto Rico, the Philippines, and Guam. These conflicting situations and trends in the early twentieth century made a centenary celebration of the 1805 battle important for some and more abstract and repugnant for others.[1]

Reciprocal Anglo-French Fleet Visits, 1905

The spirit of friendship and cooperation between France and England that the Entente Cordiale engendered dominated the scene. Above all, this new attitude further emphasized the tendency to use Trafalgar to celebrate Nelson as a national hero rather than commemorate a victory over the French. As early as December 1904, the British Foreign Office warned against making any celebration of the Battle of Trafalgar that might upset the French. As a result, the king and queen did not participate in Trafalgar celebrations in the cities, towns, and villages across the country. The Admiralty ordered the fleet not to make any special display for Trafalgar. This reticence was apparent during both the British Channel Fleet's visit to Brest under Vice Admiral Sir Arthur Wilson in July 1905, with twelve battleships and eight cruisers, and the reciprocal visit of the eighteen-ship French Northern Squadron under Vice Admiral Léonce Albert Caillard to Portsmouth from 7 to 14 July. King Edward VII made a royal review of the two combined British and French squadrons on 9 August.

While the British officials remained reticent about Trafalgar during the visit, French naval officers and men coming ashore at Portsmouth typically exclaimed, 'Which ship is the *Victory*? *Ah! Comme ça. La vaisseau de Nelson. Voilà!*'[2] In the moment's enthusiasm, Fred T. Jane, the naval wargamer and founding editor of naval reference books, wrote, 'Nelson's fleet conquered Villeneuve, but Caillard's fleet has done more—it has conquered England.' It was not just the king's official welcome that was impressive, but rather the exceptionally warm welcome that ordinary English people gave to the French. On a spontaneous tour of Hampshire for the French officers, Jane and several others took groups of them on a 27-mile motor car trip to Winchester. En route, a cheering crowd met them along the way, 'animated by one single thought: to make the Frenchmen welcome. This was the real thing, the voice of England,' Jane wrote.[3] A special train took the admiral and French officers to London. Upon arrival at Victoria Station, the French ambassador, Pierre Paul Cambon, greeted them, along with Admiral Sir John Fisher and the British Ambassador to France, Sir Francis Bertie. A procession of fifty carriages took them to the Palace of Westminster, where two hundred Members of Parliament, headed by the Lord Chancellor, the 1st Earl of Halsbury, and the Speaker of the House of Commons, The Rt Hon. James William Lowther, entertained the French officers for dinner in Westminster Hall. En route, enthusiastic crowds cheered the French as they passed Piccadilly and the Duke of Wellington's highly decorated Apsley House. Passing down St James Street and along Pall Mall, they came to Trafalgar Square, where Admiral Caillard and his officers saluted the Nelson statue as they passed, eliciting a warm response from onlookers.[4] The French visitors returned to Portsmouth a few days later, and the fleet sailed home on 14 August. The visit was very successful. *The Spectator* noted that any 'note of provocation or defiance has been entirely absent'.[5] As the French squadron departed, HMS *Victory* rendered honours to the French flagship. As the *Morning Post* reported, 'Whatever memories Trafalgar may have for Frenchmen, they are at one in the acclaim for Nelson as our greatest admiral, and nothing indeed has pleased them more than to have honours paid to them on their visit to our shores by a friendly *Victory*, which a century ago encountered their best and bravest in hostile array off Cape Trafalgar.'[6]

The Trafalgar Centenary Celebration, 1905

While the diplomacy of the Entente Cordiale dampened any tendency that might have existed for overexuberant celebration in Britain and discouraged the king's participation in the events, the public did not ignore the centenary. The Navy League, then at the peak of its activities, went to great lengths to outdo all their previous celebrations at Trafalgar Square. One historian noted, 'Nelson's column was adorned with flags and streamers like some giant stone maypole.'[7] Preparations for decorating the column began nine days before the anniversary. Numerous evergreen ropes decorated the statue's base between the bas-reliefs depicting Nelson's victories. In contrast, a thick rope of leaves spiralled downwards around the column from the entablature on which Nelson's statue stood. A large white ensign and a Union flag were flying from poles mounted at two of the corners of the entablature with lines leading to the ground displaying the flags of Nelson's signal, 'England Expects . . .'. At the base, there were numerous wreaths from all over the empire. The New Zealand government had even shipped its wreath in ice for preservation.[8]

All this seemed to transform Trafalgar Square into the symbolic heart of the British Empire, with Nelson presiding over it on the top of his column. In the morning, before the ceremonies began, the two princes, the future kings Edward VIII and George V, happened to be passing the square and stopped their carriage. They stood quietly for a moment, then saluted and continued their journey. At about the same time, the Portsmouth Naval Brigade arrived and laid a wreath from Admiral Tōgō. The formal events took place in the afternoon. A semi-religious service began with Bishop Welldon, Canon of Westminster Abbey, conducting a brief service as the Union flag fluttered down to half mast. Alexander Watson then recited Rudyard Kipling's

'Recessional', after which the crowd joined a Westminster Abbey singer in a national anthem rendition. Observers estimated that the surging crowd numbered from twenty thousand to a million people at various times, with remnants remaining until midnight.[9]

Centenary concerts, displays, and other celebrations took place in various parts of London. Some organizations had long-running events, such as the Royal United Services Institution, which displayed an exhibition of Nelson relics from 1 May and extended it to the end of November. A week after the centenary, the British Museum opened its exhibition on the history of the Royal Navy from the Armada to Trafalgar. On the morning of the centenary day, the London Society of East Anglians gathered at Nelson's tomb in the crypt of St Paul's Cathedral and laid a laurel wreath from the rectory garden at Burnham Thorpe, where Nelson was born. That afternoon, the Royal Albert Hall was the scene for the British and Foreign Sailors' Society's commemoration, presided over by Lord Brassey with the mayors of London boroughs. The audience joined in singing the 'Old Hundredth' psalm—'All people that on earth do dwell'—and heard a telegram read from Earl Grey, Governor-General of Canada, who assured the audience that all Canadians, both French and English, were honouring Nelson on that day. After a recital of Kipling's 'Recessional' and a display of naval drill, Lady Dimsdale presented a bust of Nelson made from the wood of HMS *Victory* to Admiral Tōgō, represented by the Japanese naval attaché, Captain Kabusaki. The audience greeted the presentation with tremendous cheers and repeatedly interrupted the attaché's acceptance speech with enthusiastic applause. The Albert Hall event ended with all saluting as the Union flag came down solemnly to half mast. Later that evening, the Navy League held a Trafalgar banquet at the Criterion Restaurant in Piccadilly, to which branches of the Navy League throughout the empire sent congratulatory telegrams. Admiral Edmund Fremantle, the grandson of Captain Thomas Fremantle, Nelson's friend who had commanded *Neptune* at Trafalgar, gave the after-dinner address, and W. P. Reeves, the colonial agent for New Zealand, proposed the toast to Nelson's immortal memory.[10]

Elsewhere in Britain, October 1905

With the presence of HMS *Victory* in the harbour, Portsmouth was a natural place to mark the occasion. Despite the centenary, it turned out to be a quiet day with a small crowd of people due to competition from the Welsh football match at Gloucester that drew a much larger crowd. Nevertheless, the ship was flying the famous signal, and the sailors had wreathed her masts with the traditional laurel. The dignitaries laid laurel wreaths at the spot on the deck where Nelson fell and in the cockpit where he died. Incongruously, the modern, one-year-old submarine *B1* lay moored alongside the 140-year-old *Victory*. On the evening of the centenary, the submarine's secondary batteries powered the electric lights that illuminated the masts, yards, admiral's flag, and three decks of gun ports. That evening at the Royal Naval barracks in Portsmouth, the current officers of *Victory* hosted a Trafalgar Night banquet for approximately two hundred attendees. After the loyal toasts, a silent toast was drunk to 'the memory of those who fought and fell, whether friend or foe, in the glorious battle of 100 years ago'.[11] Admiral Sir Cyprian Bridge gave the address on 'Trafalgar and its effects on history'. He pointed out the many personal connections that Nelson had with Portsmouth. In tune with the times, Bridge noted that the government had wisely left it to the people to undertake celebrations of a popular and spontaneous character. 'There was no undignified boasting and no unseemly exultation over the defeat of others. We felt, perhaps without recognizing the feeling, that one of the things that made Nelson great was the greatness of those with whom he had to contend. We could, therefore, grasp in friendship the hands of those great nations which withstood us so manfully on the sea 100 years ago.'[12] In conclusion, Bridge noted that 'we could do full justice to Nelson without being unjust to others. He achieved for us maritime supremacy unchallenged for more than half a century after his death, and perhaps not seriously challenged until now. The supremacy, by the security of our sea communications, which it ensured, made the British not only the first but also a long way the first of maritime commercial nations.'[13]

Another notable provincial celebration occurred at Nelson's birthplace, Burnham Thorpe, Norfolk. The village had already sent the wreath for the East Anglians to lay on the tomb at St Paul's. In early October, the Dominion of Canada offered to donate a tenor bell to All Saint's Church, Burnham Thorpe, where Nelson's father had been the rector, on the condition that other colonies contribute the six other bells at the cost of about £570 to replace the bells in the church tower that had fallen years before.[14] Several days later, the rector, the Revd H. M. Elliot Briscoe-Drake, appealed for the funds in *The Times* to complete the church's restoration.[15] In response, the Prince of Wales (later King George V) donated £30 to the church and £20 to a centenary dinner for the village's inhabitants. Several others soon joined the appeal. The midday dinner for the villagers took place in a barn on a nearby farm, during which toasts were drunk to the health of the Prince of Wales and to 'the immortal memory'. On view were Nelson's relics, including his baptismal register, the font, and his signatures at weddings he had witnessed as a youth. In addition, church members showed visitors the wooden pulpit made of wood from *Victory* and the communion plate that had been in use during his lifetime. Afterward, the Bishop of Newcastle preached at a crowded service of 'Thanksgiving to Almighty God for the great gift to the Empire of Viscount Nelson of the Nile and Burnham Thorpe'. Eleven robed clergy members were in procession for the event, including the Bishop of Newcastle and the Bishop of Thetford.[16]

Smaller events took place across the country during the centenary weekend. Shops and homes displayed flags and bunting from Friday to Sunday. *The Times* had encouraged a 'Sailor's Service' close to Trafalgar Day. An estimated 90 per cent of parish churches across the country complied, with most of them doing so on Sunday, October 22. Many sermons focused on Nelson's life and achievements or his devotion to duty, although a few referred to his relationship with Lady Hamilton as a blot on his character. Other clergymen chose to speak about Nelson's legacy as a century of sea power and peace. Schoolchildren played a significant part in the celebrations, and essay-writing contests were a notable feature of the centenary. Yet not every town and village marked the occasion. The press quickly pointed out places where the editors thought some commemoration should have occurred. The sailor-poet and future Poet Laureate of Great Britain, John Masefield, felt that Portsmouth 'is not taking the centenary very deeply to heart'.[17]

The Celebrations across the Empire, 1905

In Canada, some 250 towns celebrated the event. Australian newspapers noted that the Canadian celebrations were significant in a country united by people from both British and French backgrounds. The Australian newspapers quoted Governor-General Lord Grey's comment that Nelson had fought and died 'not to triumph one race over another'.[18] Generally, however, there was little celebration of the event in Australia out of consideration for the Entente and the potential for insulting the French. In Sydney, a celebration took place in which the great-grandson of Lieutenant Pasco, Nelson's signal officer, raised the signal flags for 'England expects…'. Bands played both the British national anthem and 'La Marseillaise'.[19]

Despite the governor-general's view and the reports received in Britain and Australia, the leading French-Canadian newspaper, *Le Canada*, was highly critical of the British celebrations. The newspaper highlighted that the Corporation of London had not supported the celebration financially and urged Montreal to follow that example. In Ottawa, a large crowd gathered at Parliament Hill to hear the governor-general.[20]

At Halifax, Nova Scotia, the Royal Navy's Second Cruiser Squadron, under the command of Rear Admiral Prince Louis of Battenberg, was in port and decorated for the occasion. On the day of the celebration, all the ships in the squadron hoisted white ensigns to their mastheads at morning colours and remained for the entire day. However, HMS *Drake*, Battenberg's flagship, flew the flags that *Victory* had flown at Trafalgar, including the 'England expects' signal in twelve hoists and the standard signal number 16 to 'engage the enemy more closely'. At 4:30 in the afternoon, the officers and men assembled on the quarterdecks of their ships in their dress uniforms. The squadron marked the hour of Nelson's death with *Drake* firing fifteen-minute guns as a funeral salute to Nelson as a vice admiral and commander-in-chief. At the same time, *Drake* lowered Nelson's vice admiral's flag to half mast as all the ships in the squadron lowered their masthead flags, ensigns, and Union flags to half mast. Following the funeral salute, marine detachments on the quarterdecks of the ships fired the traditional three-volley salute, with a bugler playing the admiral's salute in the intervals between the volleys. After the third volley, they played the last post and the funeral march. Upon completion of the funeral march, the captains of each ship gave a similar short address that Admiral Battenberg had approved, which provided a brief appreciation of Nelson as a man and a seaman. The ceremony ended with a reading of Nelson's prayer from the day of the battle. On Prince Louis's instructions to honour Nelson's memory, the ships' bands did not play again until after nightfall. The next day, the admiral and his staff, along with officers and men representing each squadron ship, attended services at St Paul's Church on the Grand Parade in Halifax, where Nelson reputedly worshipped on his visits to Halifax.[21] In fact, Nelson never visited Halifax, although he sailed along the coast of Nova Scotia, well offshore, three times while in command of *Albemarle* in 1782.[22]

At the same time, the Mediterranean Fleet celebrated at Malta, where the commander-in-chief, Admiral Lord Charles Beresford, held a naval review on shore in Palace (St George's) Square in Valetta in the morning with three thousand officers and men taking part. The 117 captains of guns from the various ships who had hit their targets five or more times in recent gunnery competitions were formed into a company at the right of the line and were the first to march past, leading the entire parade. At four o'clock, the flags came down to half mast on all the fleet ships. Half an hour later, the officers and men had assembled on their ships' quarterdecks and faced aft as each ship slowly and reverently dipped its colours as the bands played the dead march. At its conclusion, the ships slowly re-hoisted their colours, and the ceremony ended.

That evening, the massed bands of the fleet played in Palace Square. At the same time, Beresford gave a dinner to the admirals and senior officers of the fleet, after which ships' commanding officers lectured to their ships' companies on the life of Nelson.[23]

Perhaps the most prominent celebration outside Britain took place in Port Elizabeth, Cape Province, South Africa, where 4,500 children marched in procession from the Donkin Reserve to St George's Park, accompanied by a large model of HMS *Victory*. Another three thousand people either followed the procession or lined the parade route. Employees of the harbour board constructed the model for the occasion and paraded with it. Unfortunately, the main mast of the model was so tall that during the parade it became entangled in some overhead electrical power lines and broke. Despite the damage, the march continued. On its completion, the mayor presented a souvenir medal of *Victory* and a brooch made from the ship's copper to each of the children who had collected five shillings for the Nelson Centenary Fund. As part of the ceremony, the Seaman's Institute presented the mayor with a miniature bust of Nelson.[24]

At Queenstown in Cape Province, the Queen's College Boys' High School students raised funds to obtain a shield from the British and Foreign School Society. Made from copper and wood from *Victory*, the school awarded it for industry, willingness, manliness, devotion to duty, and protection of the weak.[25]

In June 1905, the governor of Barbados, Sir Gilbert Carter, proposed to the Secretary of State for the Colonies, Alfred Lyttleton, that 'A special issue of stamps by this colony on this occasion may not be considered inappropriate when it is known that the first statue in memory of Lord Nelson, which is reproduced in the proposed design, was erected by the people of Bridgewater in the year 1813.'[26] Several years prior, Carter, a widower, had met and married Gertrude Codman Parker, a wealthy and talented American artist who had studied at the Museum of Fine Arts in Boston. Lady Carter had become interested in designing postage stamps and undoubtedly influenced her husband in this project, as well as in creating stamps for Barbados.[27] The novelty of producing such a postage stamp did not impress the Colonial Office. One official noted the 'Centenary of Trafalgar seems to me a lame excuse for a special stamp issue. If Barbados were a Crown Colony, pure and simple, I would be in favour of refusing to sanction the project.'[28] However, considering Barbados's independent finances, other officials recommended that the colony go ahead. However, it seemed doubtful there was enough time to produce the centenary stamp, which might prove too costly. The postage stamp eventually did appear in 1906 and commemorated the centenary of the commissioning of Richard Westmacott's full-length bronze statue of Nelson in Bridgetown. The colonial government of Barbados issued the stamp as part of its first series of postage stamps that depicted local scenes and historical events rather than the previously used images of Britannia or a portrait of the sovereign.[29]

The sentiment heightened by the Entente Cordiale in 1905 to emphasize Nelson continued. In September 1916, during the height of the First World War, *The Daily Graphic* commented, 'Let October 21 be kept under the title Nelson's Day. It is the glorious testament which he wrote there with his blood, rather than the defeat of our gallant foes which we desire to celebrate. It is the word Duty which Nelson's name connotes, rather than the name of the Spanish headland, which nine out of ten of us mispronounce, which is uppermost in our minds.'[30]

The Sesquicentennial, 1955

On Trafalgar Day in 1955, the *Birmingham Daily Post* commented that 'Throughout a century and a half, this anniversary has been accorded special honour by English men and women and in this year 1955 their sense of identity with, and pride in, the seamen that delivered that England from the pride of invasion is probably stronger than at any period since the days immediately succeeding these events. That is because this generation has also experienced the danger of imminent invasion by a continental foe and the deep sense of gratitude for deliverance achieved by the bravery and consummate skill of a few.'[31]

The Bath Festival, organized annually by the City of Bath since 1946, and Messrs Harold Holt Ltd of London, along with Ian Hunter (impresario of the Edinburgh Festival) as festival director, decided to include a Trafalgar theme for the 1955 season. The programme ran from 11 to 21 May and consisted of concerts, plays, an opera, and other musical events following the pattern of the Edinburgh Festival on a reduced scale. Instead of a military tattoo, Hunter decided to re-enact the Battle of Trafalgar as an open-air night review to celebrate the 150th anniversary of the battle. Immediately after this decision, the Royal Navy became involved and appointed Commander Peter J. H. Hoare, RN, on additional duty from the office of the vice controller of the navy, as its festival society liaison officer. Hunter engaged Moran Caplat, the Glyndebourne Opera company's general manager, as as producer for the opera, which was based on a script that Captain John E. 'Jackie' Broome, DSC, RN (ret.) wrote. The opera production involved three hundred people, including twenty-two actors from the Bath Operatic and Dramatic Society, as well as a crowd scene featuring sixty people. The festival created a Trafalgar Room to entertain ten guests of honour attending the event on nineteen different nights of the performance. Among the guests of honour attending were the First Lord of the Admiralty, the First and Second Sea Lords, the Commander in Chief, Plymouth, the Secretary of the Admiralty, the Lord Lieutenant of Somerset, and the Lord Mayor of Bath. The section of the Admiralty Office in Bath (Admiralty Bath) created an annex to the Admiralty Luncheon Club at the Empire Hotel that they furnished in the style of an admiral's day cabin from *c.*1925. It included portraits of Nelson from the First Lord's office and Samuel Pepys from the office of the Secretary of the Admiralty. In addition, there was a display of artifacts from the Admiralty Library and HMS *Victory*.[32]

As planning for the October 150th anniversary continued in 1955, an American schoolboy, Alfred Charles Holden, Jr. of Baltimore, Maryland, wrote to the Admiralty to suggest a series of commemorative stamps. The Post Office once again declined to take up the opportunity to issue a stamp, as they had fifty years before, believing 'that if they signalized the anniversary of Trafalgar, they would be called upon to signalize very many hundreds of other anniversaries and said that the issue of a commemorative stamp in this country was an extremely rare event and normally only associated with the Royal household'.[33] The First Sea Lord, Admiral Lord Mountbatten, replied to Holden, thanking him for his interest in the Royal Navy.

Early on the morning of 21 October 1955, the Admiralty signalled the fleet 'Following received from Her Majesty the Queen: "Splice the Main Brace".'[34]

Among the significant events of the day, Queen Elizabeth II unveiled the statue of her father, King George VI, in his uniform as an admiral of the fleet. Unfortunately for all who attended that morning, the dedication ceremony at Carlton House Terrace, overlooking the Mall and St James's Park, took place in a downpour. Everyone was thoroughly drenched, including the royal family, Prime Minister Anthony Eden, and all the uniformed senior officials.[35]

Amid the celebrations, a note of inter-service rivalry arose between the army and the navy. At 10 Downing Street on Trafalgar Day with the other service chiefs, the commander-in-chief of the Imperial General Staff, Field Marshal Sir Gerald Templar, expressed sorrow to Lord Mountbatten that the request for a wreath to be placed among the others at the Nelson Column on behalf of 'The British Army' should have been turned down. Mountbatten immediately enquired into the circumstances. In November, the Permanent Secretary of the Admiralty reported back to Mountbatten that, shortly before Trafalgar Day, the Military branch received a telephone call from their counterpart in the War Office, stating that an inquiry had been made by a higher authority regarding whether the army should lay a wreath or not. 'The opinion given was that the Army would already be well represented by the three "ex-Marine" regiments (the Queen's Own Royal West Kents, Welch, and East Lancs), which by custom lay a wreath every year, and that therefore there was no necessity for the War Office to do more on this prominently naval occasion. In the light of our further knowledge now,' the Permanent Secretary wrote, 'I think the attitude taken within the

Admiralty was correct, and that the C.I.G.S. was laying it on a bit heavy in weeping on your shoulder (? crocodile tears).'[36]

Later that afternoon at Trafalgar Square, the rain eased somewhat. A journalist noted that the bells of 'St Martin's-in-the-Field' mixed oddly with the 'Early One Morning', played by the Royal Marines School of Music band. The Duke of Edinburgh reviewed the gathered detachments from the Royal Navy, Royal Marines, WRNS, Reserve Forces, and Sea Cadets and delivered a five-minute address to those present. A news reporter recorded that the cadets circled around the fountains where the spray added to their dampness in the rain. The lions around Nelson's Column, which the reporter noted were 'usually so fierce looking, today had the appearance of amiable and frolicsome pets' with laurel wreaths on their heads and holding the anchor ropes for Nelson's signal in their jaws. At the column's base were nearly a dozen wreaths from naval organizations, infantry regiments, Commonwealth countries, Malta, and Gibraltar. Among them, the largest was a huge wreath with yellow roses and yellow and bronze-coloured chrysanthemums inscribed 'From the Government and People of India'.[37]

The British Broadcasting Service covered the events with television broadcasts throughout the day—a newsreel featured images of the church service from Nelson's birthplace in Burnham Thorpe, Norfolk. During the day, BBC radio broadcast the 'Nelson Touch', a play by David Scott Daniel. In the evening, Professor E. E. Rich, the Vere Harmsworth Professor of Imperial and Naval History at the University of Cambridge, broadcast a talk on the battle.[38]

The main televised event was the arrival of the Queen and the Duke of Edinburgh at the Painted Hall in Greenwich for the Trafalgar Night dinner, where they joined the Prime Minister, the current Earl Nelson, and the country's naval leaders, including the senior naval representatives in the country of the Commonwealth navies. It was the first time a reigning queen had dined in the Painted Hall and the first time a Trafalgar Night dinner had been nationally televised.

In response to the loyal toast proposed by the First Lord of the Admiralty, J. P. L. Thomas, the Queen remarked, 'I have been wondering this evening what the correct collective noun should be for Admirals. On the whole, I think I like "a foam of flag officers", though on this unique occasion when nearly a hundred admirals have sat down together for a meal, we should speak of "an ocean of admirals". Whatever the correct name should be for such an awe-inspiring collection of senior officers, it is most appropriate that this gathering with double the number of junior officers should meet in this hall on this very special occasion.'[39] The Queen concluded her remarks by noting, 'It is because the inspiration of Nelson is still a living force, and because of his humanity, that we do him honour tonight.'[40]

The Duke of Edinburgh proposed the toast to 'The immortal memory of our great lord Nelson'. His prefatory remarks focused on the theme that Nelson's role at Trafalgar should neither be overplayed nor misused. He pointed out that hidebound officers, who disapproved of new and forward-looking proposals, often responded by claiming that the new ideas did not fit in with the Nelson tradition. The duke went on to point out that if Nelson is ever quoted 'as an excuse for not facing the future fair and square, it can only be by people who have no idea what he really stood for, or how he was regarded in his own age'.[41] He concluded his remarks with the challenge, 'Let us resolve that we shall never allow the Nelson tradition to become an excuse for timidity, for lack of initiative, for fear of that great adventure which is the new age that confronts us.'[42]

Dinners and celebrations of the event took place across the country and in the dominions and colonies. For example, the Mediterranean Fleet at Malta floodlit the ships and shore stations on the evening of Trafalgar night until midnight. The Royal New Zealand Admiralty Board reported to London that 'Ships dressed overall; guards paraded for the vice admiral's salute. The saluting ships fired a 15-gun salute at noon with "make and mend" on completion.'[43] People all over the world noted the anniversary. The commander-in-chief of the Royal Norwegian Navy, Vice Admiral Peter J. Espeland Jacobsen, sent a personal message to the First Sea Lord: 'I would like... on behalf of the Royal Norwegian Navy to pay tribute to the memory of Vice Admiral Viscount Nelson, the spirit shown on that day has been a shining example throughout the succeeding years for my Navy and one which all people will hope for peace and freedom should be provd [sic] to follow.' Mountbatten replied: 'Although we are very proud in the Royal Navy of the Nelson tradition, it is the progressive views for which he was so distinguished that we hope to emulate now and in the future.'[44]

On the following Sunday, the Admiralty Board, with other senior officers and officials, attended a commemorative service at St Paul's Cathedral, marking the end of the official Sesquicentennial observance in London. Across the country, services took place in parish churches and cathedrals. The sixth Lord Nelson read the lesson at the crowded parish church of St Mary the Virgin in Merton, near Nelson's former home in Surrey. From St Martin's in the Bullring at Birmingham to Chester Cathedral, Sea Cadets, officers, and men and women of the Royal Naval Volunteer Reserve and Royal Navy were on parade. In Scotland, notable services were held at the West Church of Aberdeen, with the officers and men of HMS *Pickle* in attendance. In Glasgow, naval and naval reserve units formed in St Enoch Square and marched to the Nelson Monument on Glasgow Green, and Lord Provost Andrew Hood reviewed the parade. The minister of Glasgow Cathedral held a short service, and Vice Admiral E. W. L. Longley Cook gave an address.[45]

The Bicentenary, 2005

Planning for the Trafalgar bicentenary began an entire decade before the event. On Trafalgar Day 1995, a group of interested naval officers, scholars, and enthusiasts announced the beginning of the 'Nelson Decade'. The group included, among others, Admiral Lord Lewin, the former Chief of Defence Staff and Chairman of the Trustees of the National Maritime Museum; Dr Roger Knight, Deputy Director of the National Maritime Museum, Greenwich; and Colin White, Deputy Director of the Royal Navy Museum, Portsmouth. An Official Nelson Commemoration Committee (ONCC), made up of representatives from a wide range of institutions, laid out a general plan of commemorative events, scholarly conferences, and publications for the 200th anniversaries of each of Nelson's major victories: the battles of Cape St Vincent in 1997, the Nile in 1998, Copenhagen in 2001, and culminating in the Trafalgar bicentenary in 2005.[46]

Although academic historians and museum experts took the lead and focused on academic insights, they built on the fertile ground that the famous British naval novelists, such as C. S. Forester, had been cultivating since 1937 with his Horatio Hornblower books, and Patrick O'Brian, since 1969 with his Aubery-Maturin series. Such writers had successfully popularized fictional accounts inspired by the naval history of the French Revolutionary and Napoleonic Wars, making the names, ships, and battles of the time familiar to an established and growing audience. Such works helped create a growing and widespread fascination for the period that other eras of naval history lacked. They laid the groundwork for a major national commemoration and revitalized academic historical research on the topic.[47]

As 2005 and the culminating focus on Trafalgar drew closer, it merged with another broader initiative, 'SeaBritain 2005', an initiative of the British government's Department of Culture, Media, and Sport to raise the profile of the United Kingdom's maritime interests. A range of views emerged regarding the celebration. In early 2005, right-wing politicians and their supporting media highlighted the coming commemoration. They began to argue that the general public, particularly those under thirty, were profoundly ignorant of the significance of Trafalgar, Nelson, and the Royal Navy and that schools had overemphasized the history of the Nazis and the Holocaust to the detriment of an understanding of national values in British history. From this political perspective, the Trafalgar commemoration needed to focus on patriotism and pride to restore a proper British national identity. Yet, with so many differing groups and viewpoints involved, the event supported a wide range of views and causes. Some were very narrowly and institutionally focused, such as the Norfolk Museum, in the county where Nelson was born, which used the occasion to draw attention to its existence.[48] The business community also took advantage of the occasion and produced a wide range of commemorative items, including books, prints, and ceramics.

The Royal Navy saw the commemoration as a significant opportunity to educate the public about the service and its history with its programme 'Trafalgar 200' as a crucial part of 'SeaBritain 2005'. The First Sea Lord, Admiral Sir Alan West, demonstrated his interest in naval history with his active and energetic participation in the planning and activities. In the middle of his term of office in 2004, the Royal Navy published an overview of its activities for the previous year in its periodical *Broadside*. The report laid out the Royal Navy's objectives in the Trafalgar commemoration:

- To increase public support and advocacy for the Royal Navy;
- To increase awareness of the importance of the UK maritime sector;
- To increase interest in the Royal Navy as a career opportunity and to provide an inspiring experience for serving personnel;
- To promote the inspirational legacy of Nelson for all people;
- To develop international naval links.[49]

The most significant event for the bicentenary occurred in June 2005, when the Solent was the scene for the first fleet review since Queen Elizabeth II's silver jubilee in 1977. 172 warships, manned by more than 25,000 sailors from thirty-five nations, participated in the event. Among them were ships and sailors from the Commonwealth navies of Australia and Canada, which had long commemorated Trafalgar; however, on this occasion, they were joined by warships from Brazil, Germany, India, Italy, Japan, Latvia, Russia, Serbia, South Africa, South Korea, and Turkey, among others. The warships included the modern-day equivalents of those who participated in the Trafalgar battle, as well as twenty-three sail-training ships reminiscent of the Trafalgar period. Britain provided sixty-five vessels for the review, of which twenty-seven were survey vessels, fishery protection ships, and training craft. France sent seven ships, including the largest warship present, the nuclear-powered aircraft carrier FS *Charles de Gaulle*, while Spain contributed two: the Spanish Navy's flagship, *Príncipe de Asturias*, bearing the same name as Admiral Gravina's flagship at Trafalgar, and the frigate *Blas de Lezo*, named in memory of the admiral who had successfully defended Cartagena de Indias from the British in 1741. The United States sent USS *Saipan*, an amphibious assault ship, and the US Coast Guard Cutter *Eagle*. With a royal yacht no longer in service to review the assembled ships, the Queen, accompanied by the Duke of Edinburgh, Defence Secretary Dr John Reid, and First Sea Lord Admiral Sir Alan West in HMS *Endurance*, an Antarctic patrol vessel and icebreaker, steamed through the lines of anchored warships, receiving three cheers from each ship as she passed. To add more action for the spectators, warships from Britain, Australia, and Canada joined together for a sail past at 17 knots. HMS *Cumberland*, HMAS *Anzac*, and HMCS *Montréal* showed off their top-notch seamanship and station-keeping skills.[50]

That evening, seventeen sailing ships from five nations re-enacted a *son et lumière* version of the Battle of Trafalgar with simulated cannon broadside, gun smoke, and ten thousand pyrotechnics. Although an actor playing the part of Nelson figured prominently by sailing in a cutter to join his flagship, the opposing fleets identified themselves only as blue and red rather than Britain versus France and Spain. For some, this was going too far in terms of political correctness, as nationalistic patriotism was largely absent from the events. The right-wing press, notably *The Sun* and *Daily Mail*, were incensed over the decision to play down the British victory, and the BBC only reluctantly covered the event.[51] When questioned about this aspect, Admiral West pointed out that it was an international celebration of the sea and the qualities of Nelson's leadership. 'I don't want a triumphalist thing for the battle of Trafalgar. That's not the point. Trafalgar is a fact of history, but this is a wonderful opportunity for defence diplomacy.'[52] Furthermore, West noted that everyone in Britain and around the world knows Nelson as a naval hero. 'His qualities of leadership, teamwork, humanity, bravery, courage, and compassion—these are as pertinent today as they were 200 years ago.'[53]

Even before the sesquicentennial event in 1955, attitudes towards commemorative stamps and coins were undergoing rapid change. In 1976, Spain had already issued a postage stamp in honour of Churruca, and in 1981, Anguilla issued one for Nelson. By 2005, widespread interest had developed. The British Post Office issued a commemorative set, and twelve other countries issued stamps commemorating Trafalgar in connection with the Crown Agents Stamp Bureau, seven of which were United Kingdom Overseas Territories, requiring the Queen's permission. In 2024, an authoritative stamp catalogue listed seventy-eight stamps associated with Trafalgar and seventy-six with Nelson. The Royal Mint issued two commemorative five-pound coins. Both coins bore a portrait of Queen Elizabeth II by Ian Rank-Broadley on the obverse. The Horatio Nelson Commemorative Crown, designed by James Butler, depicted Nelson in his full-dress uniform on the reverse, while the Battle of Trafalgar Commemorative Crown, designed by Clive Duncan, showed HMS *Victory* leading the fleet into the battle.[54]

For its part, the National Maritime Museum at Greenwich presented its bicentenary exhibition, 'Nelson and Napoléon'. The museum's director, Rear Admiral Roy Clare, explained that 'The exhibition focuses on personal stories as a way of promoting understanding of a complex period in European history. By bringing Nelson and Napoleon together, we avoid a purely Anglo-centric view and consider the impact that the French Wars had on societies at the time.'[55] As N. A. M. Rodger put it, 'Both were distinguished by supreme professional gifts, as leaders, organizers and tacticians, but both had conspicuous personal weakness.'[56]

Among the numerous events that took place on the anniversary and the days leading up to it, Christie's auctioned Captain Thomas Hardy's Naval Gold Medal for the Battle of Trafalgar, fetching the largest amount ever paid up to that time for a British medal, £248,000.[57] British television channel UKTV broadcast the film *The Hero and the Harlot*, an account of Nelson as 'the lover rather than the military man', showing 'how the Lord Admiral shocked society by having an affair with Lady Emma Hamilton'.[58] Across the country, the traditional wreaths were laid at the various monuments, and Trafalgar Night dinners took place. With so many events on the calendar, not all could occur on the precise day. For example, on 20 October, the Duke of Edinburgh attended the Bicentenary Trafalgar Night dinner hosted by the Royal Navy Club of 1765 and 1785 in the Painted Hall at Old Royal Naval College, Greenwich, while the Duke of York attended the Trafalgar Night dinner at Naval Air Station, Yeovilton, in Somerset.[59]

On the morning of the anniversary, the First Sea Lord attended the raising of Nelson's signal on board HMS *Victory* and a service to commemorate the battle and Nelson's death, then rushed to London to lay a wreath on Nelson's tomb in St Paul's Cathedral, before returning for dinner in Portsmouth. Meanwhile, sailors rang the bells on Royal Navy ships worldwide at noon to commemorate the moment when Nelson took the fleet into battle. At Cádiz in Spain, the Spanish defence minister, José Bono, the president of the council of Andalusia, and the ambassadors to Spain from France and the United Kingdom, joined by officers and crew of HMS *Chatham*, paid homage to those who had died at Trafalgar at the Panteón de Marinos Ilustres in San Fernando. Afterwards, *Chatham* with the flagship of the Spanish Navy, the aircraft carrier *Príncipe de Asturias*, the Spanish frigate *Reina Sofía*, and the French frigate *Montcalm*, sailed out of the harbour into Cádiz Bay, where they laid wreaths on the sea. The passengers on board *Príncipe de Asturias* included descendants of heroes of the battle, such as Nelson, Villeneuve, Gravina, and Churruca, among others.[60]

Meanwhile, the most notable Trafalgar Night dinner of 2005 occurred on board HMS *Victory*. The menu for the candlelit dinner in Nelson's cabin on board the ship itself symbolized the battle by including Norfolk roast beef served with French and Spanish wines. The First Sea Lord proposed the loyal toast to Queen Elizabeth, who in response made a short speech and personally proposed the toast to 'The immortal memory of Nelson and those who fell with him', reviving the early nineteenth-century wording. The evening also included the Queen lighting the first of one thousand 'Trafalgar Weekend National Beacon Fires' lit nationwide. In addition, HMS *Victory* fired a fifty-two-gun broadside salute, and the band of the Royal Marines beat the retreat.[61] The Bishop of London, the Rt Rev'd Richard Chartres, gave the Trafalgar 200 Sermon at St Paul's Cathedral the following Sunday. He began his sermon with a teasing quotation from a clergyman on the eve of his retirement, who had written, 'It is about time the clergy of the Church of England gave up the modish obsession with synods and strictures and returned to the real business in life—bee keeping, cricket, and siring Nelsons.' Yet, the bishop's message was more serious: 'A sense of calling, a connection with foundational convictions derived from his belief in God who nerves his worshippers for struggle but also enjoins justice and humanity, a profound sense of the relational element in all great human enterprises—these are Nelson's contributions to a time when we are once more facing people with fire in their minds . . .'.[62]

Among all the traditional, national commemorative events, there was one significant new aspect: a celebration of HM schooner *Pickle*, the dispatch boat commanded by Lieutenant John Lapenotière that had carried Collingwood's dispatch and brought the first news of Trafalgar to the Admiralty. Racing HM sloop *Nautilus* for the honour of being the first to deliver the news, Lapenotière had debarked from *Pickle* at Falmouth and taken a post-chaise overland to London, arriving about 1 a.m. on 6 November, using twenty-one changes of horses to travel the 270 miles from Falmouth to London in thirty-seven hours. Although naval officers had been commemorating Trafalgar Night as early as December 1805, warrant officers and chief petty officers began to celebrate Pickle Night. First held on 6 November 1974 at Portsmouth Barracks, it has since spread worldwide to warrant and chief petty officer messes in Australia, Canada, and elsewhere. From 2004 to 2022, under the leadership of Rear Admiral Joseph F. Callo, USNR (ret.) and Captain Sally McElwreath Callo, USNR (ret.), a prestigious formal dinner was held in the Model Room of the New York Yacht Club. Eventually, the annual event became a fund-raiser in the United States for the National Museum of the Royal Navy. Admiral Sir Mark Stanhope, RN, and the author Martyn Downer were the featured guests at the 2005 bicentenary Pickle Night in New York. Earlier, during the summer of

2005, members of the 1805 Club had played a significant role in creating the 'New Trafalgar Dispatch'. The Sail Training Ship *Lord Nelson* brought a replica of Collingwood's dispatch to Falmouth, where HRH the Princess Royal greeted the actor playing Lapenotière in a replica post-chaise as he set off ceremoniously, recreating the events and establishing a modern 'Trafalgar Way'. Along the route, some thirty-seven permanent plaques stand to commemorate the event.[63]

Over the century of commemoration between 1905 and 2005, the three major British national commemorations of the battle played a significant role in changing the pattern of commemoration and moving public understanding away from the celebration of a victory over enemies and mourning for those lost during the battle, which had characterized most of the century from 1805 when the war was still a living memory. In the twentieth and twenty-first centuries, when the old enemies, France and Spain, had become newfound friends and allies, the exemplary attributes of Horatio Nelson as a great naval leader had replaced the celebration of British imperial victories or national dominance. As the details of the battle faded into the distant historical past, Nelson became, more than ever, a figure whose leadership attributes remained relevant to the present and the future. At the same time, Nelson's surviving flagship, HMS *Victory*, became the most evocative surviving token—and even totem—of the battle, presenting an exhilarating visual image in a physical presence that survived from the time of Nelson and the Royal Navy of his era.

8

The Nineteenth- and Early Twentieth-Century Historians' Trafalgar

The historiography of the Battle of Trafalgar, spanning over two centuries, reflects the evolution of naval historians from untrained naval artisans to modern academics working in a subspecialty that lies within the broader field of maritime history, encompassing its multidimensional humanistic study of human interactions with the sea. As is typical with many other subjects, a range of writers have dealt with the topic. They included popular writers and journalists as well as political and professional commentators who fall within the wider public sphere. The subject here is the specialist naval historians and their early precursors, who made original contributions to knowledge about the topic of Trafalgar and wrote about it after a disciplined study of primary sources that involved empathy for historical actors, respect for interpretive debate, and an evolving set of practices. Such professional naval historians only began to appear on the scene in the mid- to late nineteenth century, reflecting and interacting with developments in German and American universities to develop historical studies as an independent academic discipline rather than as a part of literature.[1]

The writing of history underwent a dramatic change by the mid-1820s, when the first significant naval histories appeared, including studies of the Battle of Trafalgar. Along with poetry, painting, and the novel, the new trend in history was shifting away from a self-conscious rhetorical approach to a transparent style that emphasized accuracy in the description of historical events.[2] This approach, however, required documentary verification, which was not always readily available. In the early eighteenth century, Josiah Burchett had a rare privilege when he readily used the Admiralty archives under his purview to write his *Memoirs of Transactions at Sea*. The Admiralty opened its pre-1793 records to the public only in 1885.[3] Even the major universities of the day had little interest in pushing the limit. Oxford remained focused mainly on classical and medieval history, establishing a professorship in modern history only in 1862 and its Honorary School of Modern History in 1872.[4]

William James and Edward Pelham Brenton

Two multi-volume competing histories emerged within a year of each other in 1822–3. The first to appear was William James's *The Naval History of Great Britain, from the Declaration of War by France in 1793 to the Accession of George IV in January 1820*.[5] It was followed closely the next year by Captain Edward Pelham Brenton's *The Naval History of Great Britain from the Year MDCCLXXXIII to MDCCCXXII*.[6] Over several editions between 1823 and 1837, the two titles competed with one another, creating a bitter controversy between the authors that played out in the books and the press. Both authors were well-acquainted with the naval scene but from quite different perspectives. James, born in 1780 into a family of lawyers, qualified as an attorney at the age of twenty-one. In 1803, he moved to the West Indies, where he began practising before the Supreme Court in Jamaica, becoming a proctor to prepare cases for the Vice-Admiralty Court. In this position, he became well-acquainted with several naval officers and the details of their prize cases while also hearing first-hand reports about naval operations in the Caribbean. In 1812, he happened to be passing through Philadelphia, where American authorities detained him as an enemy. While in the United States, he was appalled to read the American accounts of their victories in the frigate actions during the War of 1812. Viewing them as overdrawn exaggerations that impugned the reputations and character of the British naval officers he knew, James published several works that pointed out their factual inaccuracies and chauvinistic exaggerations. Acting as an advocate for the Royal Navy's history, James applied his legal training in evidence to undermine American accounts. As historian Andrew Lambert wrote, 'He dipped his pen in his finest vitriol to condemn those that he considered had allowed the Americans to gain those advantages of which they boasted.'[7]

Although vilified in America, James's devotion to his subject led him to persevere and write a more extensive work that covered the entire war and its immediate aftermath. Throughout his writings, James developed a distinctive approach to writing history that attempted to balance conflicting sources and establish an objective standard to describe all ships' operations. He developed a methodology to assess the strength of competing ships through a critical comparison of all available accounts, which he evaluated with meticulous reliance on evidence. Soon after completing his revised and expanded second edition of history in six volumes, James died in 1827. The success of the book led his London publisher, Richard Bentley, to purchase the copyright permission from James's widow in 1836 and seek an author to update the work for a third edition. He eventually settled on Captain Frederick Chamier, Royal Navy, who had already seen considerable success writing descriptive novels of naval life for Bentley's publishing house. Earlier, Captain Edward Pelham Brenton had severely criticized James's second edition, even suggesting that James had plagiarized his work. Chamier made a solid rebuttal to Brenton and published a revised third edition in 1837 that remained in print for the following sixty-one years. Reprints and revisions were published in 1847, 1859, 1878, 1886, 1888, 1898, and 1902, making it the dominant history of the naval war and the Battle of Trafalgar for much of the nineteenth century. The *Edinburgh Review* in 1840 called it 'The most perfect and comprehensive naval history ever written'.[8]

James's rival, Captain Edward Brenton, came from a very different background. He was born in colonial North America, in Newport,

Rhode Island, in 1774, to a loyalist and career naval officer who later rose to the rank of rear admiral. He had two brothers who also became naval officers. His elder brother and father's namesake, Jahleel, became a vice-admiral. His younger brother, James Wallace Brenton, died from his wounds received as a lieutenant serving in HMS *Speedy* under Nelson's Mediterranean command in 1799. In their naval careers as officer sons of a serving officer, the three Brentons benefitted from the patronage of Admiral the Earl of St Vincent. At a young age, Edward became fascinated by naval history and read extensively on the subject. While still on active duty, he began preparing for a career as an historian upon his retirement. He wrote private memoranda about every public event that pertained to the navy and the war. Characteristically, he made sketches in every port he visited. Edward Brenton retired from active service at the end of the war in 1815, and within four years, he was actively working on his *Naval History of Great Britain*. The first volume appeared in 1823, dedicated to St Vincent, and with illustrations based on his sketches and those drawn by his brother Jahleel. Like William James, Brenton sought verification for his work through correspondence with eyewitnesses, with whatever official documents he could obtain in print, and through correspondence with their authors within his wide network of professional colleagues who had actively participated in the war. In 1837, Brenton published a revised edition of his naval history, extending it to 1836 in two handy octavo volumes. The book included a six-page response to the criticisms that James and Chamier had made. In 1838, Brenton went on to publish the first biography of the Earl of St Vincent. Then, after turning his attention to charitable work in his last years, he died in 1839.

These two authors are significant in that they represent two distinct visions of writing naval history that have endured. Both represent the new emphasis on facts. Both are highly patriotic and oriented to a Tory viewpoint, like so many working in naval history, focusing on their national navies. Both works contain valuable insights obtained from first-hand observers.[9] James was the proponent of detailed descriptions of specific operations, using his factual evidence as a lawyer presenting a brief seeking judgement in court and aggressively relishing attacking his competitors to his advantage. Brenton was a much more reserved and religious person who deeply regretted involvement in such controversies. He replied forcefully in his defence, but with some restraint. Anticipating the views of some modern historians about the importance of visiting the historical sites they write about, Brenton pointed out an instance in James's criticism, noting that 'This is one of the many errors arising from the want of local knowledge so common to the class of writers who consider that an acquaintance of the subject is a very unimportant part of the business.'[10] A highly experienced officer who clearly understood the navy, he was devoted to the service and deferential to his seniors. In some ways, his work presaged modern ideas by providing general yet concise accounts of detailed actions within the broader context of the war. Suggesting an attitude that persists today among serving naval officers, he recognized the value of naval history as a means to impart professional lessons. In particular, he also wanted to inspire in young people 'the same ardour and zeal' for the service that he felt.[11] This attitude led him to criticize some officers for failing to control their emotions and using excessive force. His judgemental approach brought objections from those he had criticized, seeking to rebut the slurs on their honour.[12]

The result is that the first English histories of Trafalgar differ significantly from one another. James provides a highly detailed account in eighty-five pages, while Brenton compressed and condensed the story into twenty-eight pages.[13] James provides a comprehensive account that attempts to offer a fair assessment of the actions of all the principal officers during the battle. At the same time, Brenton focuses on the death of Nelson, as it was synonymous with the battle and the main event that carried moral meaning in his leadership and death. 'Thus fell the greatest sea officer, of this or any other nation, recorded in history,' Brenton wrote. 'His whole career, from his earliest entrance into service, offers to the youth of the British Navy, the most illustrious examples of every manly virtue; whether we view him as a midshipman, a lieutenant, as the captain of a frigate, or as a commander-in-chief.'[14]

> The battle of Trafalgar will stand, without aid of sculpture or painting, the greatest memorial of British naval valour ever exhibited; no pen can do it justice; no description can convey an adequate idea of the glories of that day; and the event which deprived us of our favourite chief, consummated his earthly fame, and rendered his name for ever dear to his country.[15]

In contrast, James wrote, 'To die in the arms of victory is, of all deaths, that which the true warrior most covets. What then was there so particularly to deplore in the death of Lord Nelson?'[16] However, James then went on to quote more than a page from Brenton's history.

Characteristically, James called out by name any perpetrator of an error of fact that touched on his subject. Referring to Rear Admiral Charles Ekins's recently published manual on naval tactics for young officers, *Naval Battles,* James declared, 'Admiral Ekins has entirely misunderstood the principle upon which the battle of Trafalgar was fought.'[17] Then, he proceeds to several pages of detailed discussion to refute Ekins's view. Ekins had argued that 'The preconcerted plan of attack differed essentially from the real one, inasmuch as that presumes the two lines to have borne up together. In the actual case, they *afterwards* fell into line ahead, the ships in the wake of each other, in obedience to the signal made in conformity with a change of intent on the part of Lord Nelson.'[18] Ekins asserted that the original plan in Nelson's memorandum would have had Collingwood's 'lee division *bearing up together,* followed soon after by the centre, the fleet originally formed in the order of sailing upon a wind on the larboard tack', placing Nelson's entire fleet on a line abreast to attack the rear and the centre of the opposing Franco-Spanish fleet.[19] Ekins went on to point out that the actual approach to the battle was quite different. The primary conditions under which the battle took place replaced the suppositions that Nelson had made before the battle, and the attack was made in two columns in a line ahead.[20]

James then asserts that 'If a printed misstatement upon an important point of history may be justifiably set right, have we not an equal privilege over a painted statement of the same nature; especially when produced under circumstances the most likely of any to inspire confidence in its accuracy?'[21] Here, he turns to J. M. W. Turner's painting of *Trafalgar*. 'Unfortunately for the subject which this splendid picture is meant to represent,' James wrote, 'scarcely a line of truth, beyond perhaps the broadside view of the Victory's hull, is to be seen upon it.'[22] What James called 'These glaring falsehoods and palpable inconsistencies' centred on the artist's conflation of events in time and imprecision as well as the entirely false idea of the foremast falling.[23]

Although Brenton's work presaged several modern historical approaches and was more wide-ranging, providing greater context for the reader than James's, it was James's history, with its overly combative comments and undigested details, that prevailed.[24] It was a significant source for Willaim Laird Clowes's *The Royal Navy: A History from the Earliest Times to 1900*, which stood for a century as the primary, general reference for British naval history.[25]

While these developments were unfolding in narrative naval history, a complementary shift was occurring in the field of biography. The type of romantic biography that contained—sometimes fictional—moral lessons, such as Robert Southey's 1813 *The Life of Nelson*, remained popular and continued to be printed. By the late 1820s, the biographical genre of 'life and letters' began to focus on the participants of the Battle of Trafalgar, bringing historical figures into sharper focus through their own words and letters, although without the rigorous modern standards for documentary editing that are now in place. Among the first was G. L. Newnham Collingwood's 1828 *A Selection from the Public and Private Correspondence of Vice-Admiral Lord Collingwood*.[26] In 1844–6, Sir Nicholas Harris Nicolas followed with seven volumes of *The Dispatches and Letters of Vice Admiral Lord Viscount Nelson*.[27] The final volume contained not only Nelson's official and private correspondence leading up to Trafalgar, but also diaries and correspondence of eyewitnesses at the battle, including the reports of British, French, and Spanish officers, published dispatches, newspaper reports, and even poems and descriptions of monuments.[28]

Adolphe Thiers and Jurien de la Gravière

Meanwhile, in France, the politician and historian Adolphe Thiers published the first significant history of the French Revolution in ten volumes between 1823 and 1827. This achievement earned him a seat in the Académie Française. After serving in various ministerial positions in the French government between 1832 and 1840, including brief terms as Foreign Minister and Prime Minister in 1840, Thiers went on to publish a massive, twenty-volume history of the consulate and empire between 1845 and 1862. This work exhibited a notably anti-British bias, designed to glorify Napoleon's memory.[29] Thiers cast Napoleon as the brilliant strategist who hoodwinked Nelson and the Royal Navy into going to the West Indies. Echoing Napoleon, Thiers was highly critical of Villeneuve, who he described 'had the weakness, like a man whose moral tone is palsied, to exaggerate the capacity of his enemy and depreciate the merits of his own men'.[30] Going on, he provided a detailed description of the Battle of Trafalgar, after which Thiers concluded, 'Such was the fatal battle of Trafalgar. Inexperienced seamen, allies yet more inexperienced, a relaxed discipline, a neglected materiel, in all things precipitation with its consequences.'[31] Thiers noted that there were beneficial consequences that might have been drawn from 'this great disaster to the French fleet'. The actions of *Redoubtable*, *Algeciras*, and *Achille* at Trafalgar were feats of battle mentioned with pride alongside the triumph at Ulm. 'Unfortunate courage is not less admirable than fortunate,' he wrote, 'and is more touching.'[32] The government, too, might have learned from this bloody defeat. 'It might infer that nothing is to be done in a hurry and, particularly in naval affairs, it must see reason to relinquish the idea of presenting squadrons not inured to the sea in line of battle, and meanwhile apply itself to form them by frequent and distant cruises.'[33]

Lamenting the lack of recognition Napoleon gave the French officers and men, Thiers was particularly critical of the Spanish. Wanting to honour service to the flag, the Spanish king promoted all who had served at Trafalgar, the brave as well as the cowardly. 'It was a weakness natural to an antiquated court, but a weakness inspired by benevolence,' Tiers wrote, '…the brave and the cowardly French were confounded in the same treatment, and that treatment was oblivion.'[34]

Thiers went on to explain that Napoleon strove to forget the whole affair of Trafalgar and to make others forget it as well. 'Dating from this day, Napoleon gave less heed to the navy, and desired that it should be generally regarded with the same indifference.'[35] As Thiers evaluated the battle, 'with regard to the battle of Trafalgar, Europe herself willingly observed the silence he [Napoleon] wished. The reverberating tread of his steps on the continent prevented the echoes of the cannon of Trafalgar from being heard. The powers which had Napoleon's sword suspended above them were but little reassured by a naval victory profitable to England only…British glory afforded no consolation for their own humiliation. Trafalgar, therefore, did not efface the effect of Ulm…'.[36]

Just as Thiers's book on the consulate and empire appeared, Nichols's volumes of Nelson's letters sparked interest in a young French naval officer, Capitaine de Corvette Édouard Jurien de la Gravière. He began to write a series of articles for the *Revue des Deux Mondes* between 1845 and 1846, which eventually became the first of his many books in 1847, under the title *Guerres maritimes sous la république et l'empire*.[37] One of the first French naval histories to describe Trafalgar, it remained in print into the twentieth century. Translated into English as *Sketches of the Last Naval War* by Captain the Hon. Edward Plunkett, Royal Navy (later Admiral Lord Dunsany), and published in London in 1848, the book gained a wider audience and contributed to some further understanding of French experience in the battle.[38] Jurien de la Gravière's account of the battle provided a more politically neutral seaman's description of the battle than Thiers's. Using both published English sources and the reports of French participants, he provided a detailed description of the events at sea, accompanied by three engraved diagrams to illustrate the action. For Jurien de la Gravière, Nelson's victories at the Battle of the Nile and Trafalgar were part of the same development. 'Trafalgar and Aboukir explain each other,' Jurien de la Gravière wrote, 'they follow on and complete each other: they are two episodes in the life of the same man, two almost inevitable periods in the life of the same Navy. Since a first test had taught us nothing, the same temerities could succeed again: the enemy had nothing to change in his tactics, since we had not changed our means of defence.'[39] The French naval officer believed that Nelson simultaneously demonstrated at the mouth of the Nile the same strategic revolution that Napoleon had achieved during his campaign in Italy. 'Made to surprise fortune with his audacity rather than to follow through with his manoeuvres, Nelson thus removed our squadrons, so to speak, with the bayonet. He was the Suvarov and not, as has been claimed, the Bonaparte of the seas.'[40]

Marliani and the Spanish Reactions to Thiers

The interpretation that Thiers gave the Battle of Trafalgar insulted and enraged Spanish readers. The Marqués de Molins, Minister of the Spanish Navy from 1847 to 1851, had begun a campaign to expand the Spanish Navy in 1849. At the same time, he initiated a campaign to counter criticisms of the Spanish Navy that stemmed from Spain's performance in the Battle of Trafalgar. He encouraged Manuel Marliani Cassens, a Spanish-born writer, diplomat, and politician of Italian descent, to take up the cause and use Thiers's work as his foil. In 1850, Marliani published his 750-page book, which vindicated the Spanish Navy against Thiers's insulting statements in his *History of the Consulate and Empire*.[41] He dedicated his book 'to the memory of the heroes of Trafalgar [with] respect and admiration'. Published with the authorization of the navy, the book featured a portrait of the Marqués de Molins as its frontispiece. Marliani's work used Jurien de la Gravière's book, the published memoirs of Godoy, and Collingwood's letters to create his detailed description of the battle. Additionally, he included a section of biographies of the principal Spanish naval officers and 110 pages of appendices.[42]

'The battle of Trafalgar was the immolation of our naval forces to the politics of a foreign power; contrary to national interests, the French alliance, imposed by treaties, was fatal,' Marliani wrote.[43] 'Our heroic sailors, as if they sensed that this was the last opportunity in which they would be able to show off their strength and knowledge for many years, showed themselves superior to themselves; they performed prodigies of courage and skill; they died as heroes after having given their opinion as wise men in the council to avoid a catastrophe that in their heightened patriotism they amply foresaw.'[44] Although Marliani's historical methodology was soon outdated, his approach and his conclusions on Trafalgar significantly influenced Spanish historical interpretations of the battle. Rafael Altamira cited his book in his four-volume work *Historia de España y de la civilización española,* published between 1900 and 1911. Even more importantly for naval historians, he influenced the principal work on Spanish naval history that followed: Captain Cesáreo Fernández Duro's authoritative nine-volume *Armada española,* published between 1895 and 1903. Although superseded by modern research on specific subjects, including Trafalgar, Duro's work is still recognized in 2024 as an authoritative general history of the Spanish Navy. It is currently available in digitized form on the Spanish Ministry of Defence website.[45]

A Changing Approach to Naval History

Until the 1890s, naval history in most countries was primarily a narrative describing ship manoeuvres, seamanship, and the accuracy of naval gunfire—the technical crafts mastered by sea officers. Given that emphasis, it was not surprising that writers who were either serving or retired officers dominated the subject. In France, naval historians such as Capitaine de Frégate Onésime Joachim Troude in his *Batailles navales de la France*[46] depended on Brenton's work for some details of the battle. At the time Troude was writing, Emperor Napoleon III had already ordered the publication of Napoleon I's correspondence, which appeared between 1858 and 1870. Historians sharply criticized this edition as hagiographic and incomplete; nevertheless, in 1863, when volume 11 appeared, containing some of Napoleon's correspondence regarding Trafalgar, it provided a range of insights not previously known. Of particular importance, the correspondence revealed in detail Napoleon's relationships with his naval minister, Vice-Admiral Decrès, and Decrès's relationships with senior officers in the fleet leading up to the Battle of Trafalgar and during attempts to recover French naval strength in the years following the battle.[47] Capitaine de vaisseau Louis Édouard Chevalier used this material in his *Histoire de la marine sous le consulate et empire* in 1886.[48]

Mahan

The development in the late nineteenth century within the Royal Navy and the United States Navy of studying naval history for officer education, as well as the creation of naval strategic theory, soon had a broader impact on approaches to writing naval history in general. Mahan's work gained a broad public audience and was translated into several languages. Among his many works, he published three accounts of the Battle of Trafalgar. The first appeared in his 1894 book, *The Influence of Sea Power upon the French Revolution and Empire, 1793–1812*.[49] The second appeared in his biography of Nelson in 1897,[50] and the third was a paper delivered to the Military History Society of Massachusetts in 1898.[51] Mahan was reticent about the sources he used for these works, although the first version of Trafalgar has some sparse annotations. From those notes, one concludes that he relied mainly on Thiers, Napoleon's correspondence, Nelson's dispatches, and Collingwood's correspondence. Although he used Thiers and was unaware of Marliani's work, he did not reflect Thiers's disdain for the Spanish Navy. Having owned and consulted José Ferrer de Couto's 1851 book, *Historia del combate naval de Trafalgar*, Mahan understood the massive number of Spanish casualties during the battle.[52]

While Mahan devoted only twelve pages to describing the Battle of Trafalgar in his two-volume work *The Influence of Sea Power upon the French*

Revolution and Empire, his interpretation of the battle, placing it within the much larger context of national political economy at the strategic level, was a significant contribution to historical understanding.[53] Mahan concluded that Villeneuve's decision to sail from Ferrol for Cádiz was the final blow that frustrated Napoleon's invasion plans for England. 'On the part of the allies, Trafalgar was, in itself, a useless holocaust, precipitated in the end by the despair of an unfortunate admiral, upon whose irresolution Napoleon not unjustly visited the anger caused by the wreck of his plans,' Mahan wrote. Agreeing with popular historians that Trafalgar was the most significant and momentous naval victory of the war, he qualified the judgement by noting that the battle had a restricted result. 'Trafalgar was the cause', he wrote, 'of Napoleon's resolution to crush Great Britain by excluding her commerce from the Continent.'[54] From Trafalgar onwards, the conflict became a trade war, 'ordinarily a secondary operation of maritime war, but exalted in the later years of Napoleon's reign to be the principal, if not the sole, means of action'.[55] In Mahan's *The Life of Nelson*, he devoted three times as much space to Trafalgar as in his book on the *French Revolution and Empire*. Still, his focus in the biography was on Nelson's professional life and his decisiveness in political, military, and administrative areas as a leader, tactician, and agent of the state.[56]

The popularity of Mahan's books around the world reflected the resonance between the historical world of the Napoleonic Wars and the structure of international relations in the late nineteenth and early twentieth centuries. Although several of his ideas were not original and reflected earlier naval thinking, the wide sales of his books significantly contributed to the study of naval history in raising the subject from technical narratives of ship manoeuvres and gunnery to higher levels of understanding. In a curious phenomenon, many people who used Mahan's name and works as a basis for their arguments in contemporary affairs limited their understanding to his emphasis on large fleets and decisive battles and did not engage with his economic arguments.

In 1899, Vice-Admiral Philip Colomb addressed the subject of Nelson's tactics in his final detailed article, published before his death.

The article first appeared in the *United Service Magazine* in 1899 and was reprinted as a pamphlet in 1905. Colomb made the point in his article that despite the numerous diagrams published on the battle, a proper study of the signal books, orders, or ships' logs had yet to be made on either side. Colomb had one great charge that he brought against historians. 'They have one and all combined to destroy Nelson's character as a tactician. They have agreed, despite first-class evidence to the contrary, to show that Nelson on the 21st of October, and practically all his officers, entirely forgot his order of the 9th of the same month and made the attack, in what it is hardly too much to say was in the worst possible way.'[57] Colomb went on to say, 'Without question [the historian William] James is responsible for much of our ineffective thinking over the battle of Trafalgar... It is only within the last few years that we have come to understand his vast incapacity for taking broad and comprehensive views and linking cause and effect in the chain of events.' Noting that the excessive detail in James's work confused and obscured all general conceptions, Colomb pointed out James 'had not misrepresented the action of cause and effect in the battle; he left it out of his account. It is the blind guidance of James that had misled us because it was so long before we became aware that he was blind.'[58]

Mahan's books offered some antidotes to Colomb's complaint and remained dominant through the centenary of the battle in 1905 when few new historical insights emerged. However, commentary on the Battle of Tsushima and the centenary of Trafalgar again raised unanswered questions about Nelson's tactics. These arising questions began to spark research.

In England, the Navy Records Society published Julian Corbett's volume on *Fighting Instructions, 1539–1816*, which placed Nelson's memorandum of 9 October 1805 in a broader perspective.[59] At the same time, the editor of the *Times Literary Supplement* and *The Times*'s leading naval expert, James R. Thursfield, in a series of articles leading up to the centenary, noticed the discrepancies between the simplified tactical diagrams in Mahan's recent work on Nelson and the diagram in Nicolas's *Nelson's Dispatches and Letters* that showed Nelson's ships in a more disordered pattern.[60] In 1906, the British writer Edward Fraser published extensive quotations from translated French and Spanish documents, including some tactical diagrams. Unfortunately, Fraser did not identify his sources.[61]

Desbrière

Meanwhile, in France, the chief of the French Army's Historical Section, Colonel Édouard Desbrière, had completed a four-volume study of French plans for an amphibious assault on Britain between 1793 and 1805.[62] Since Britain had successfully defended herself from these French plans through the Royal Navy's blockade of Brest and in the Trafalgar campaign, Desbrière followed the documents in the archives with two additional studies to discern how this came about, one on the Brest blockade and one on the Trafalgar campaign.[63] During his work, Desbrière first noticed an issue with the tactics in using John Leyland's Navy Records Society volume on *The Blockade of Brest*, which did not align with the standard English descriptions.[64] As Desbrière explained it, 'a legend had sprung up concerning the manoeuvres actually employed by Nelson. For all that, the influence of the erroneous ideas of the English tactics at the battle of Trafalgar, which had been formed in all navies, remained great, and it is permissible to recognize the trace of it in the dispositions adopted by the Russians at the battle of Tsu-Shima.'[65] This 'legend' arose shortly after the battle when two schools of thought emerged regarding whether Nelson had implemented the ideas outlined in his memorandum. Captain Moorsom, who had commanded the 74-gun *Revenge* in Collingwood's division, was among those commanding officers who believed that he had not.[66] Charles Ekins repeated this interpretation in his manual on naval tactics. Desbrière's book made a significant new contribution to French historical literature by providing an extensive collection of transcriptions from British, French, and Spanish archives that detailed the Trafalgar campaign. At the strategic level, Desbrière argued that Nelson had taught the essential strategic lesson that one needed tactical success to make the offensive successful. The Franco-Spanish loss, however, was due not only to a poor defensive position but to a false understanding of naval warfare. Napoleon accused Villeneuve of cowardice yet had given no orders for him to seek a great battle. The emperor's orders to the fleet were quite the opposite of those given to his land forces. He had not even sought command of the sea.[67]

The significant contribution of Desbrière's book was to demonstrate that the conventional view of the time on Nelson's tactics was incorrect. He documented that Nelson had not attacked in two parallel lines at ninety-degree angles to the Franco-Spanish line. The British ships all broke through at various intervals, and, most importantly, Collingwood's Lee squadron had approached on a line of bearing. In 1933, Constance Eastwick published an English translation of the original 1907 edition. Her work in correcting the original French and Spanish transcriptions against the original documents, as well as replacing the French translations of material in English with the original English versions, made her edition the most authoritative source to date.[68]

Julian Corbett

Like Mahan, whose work on Trafalgar had begun through his series of lectures at the U.S. Naval War College, Julian Corbett also started dealing with the subject in his lectures at the Royal Navy's Naval War College and his volumes on tactics for the Navy Records Society. One of the issues that Corbett addressed at the war course was the widespread disagreement over the meaning of Nelson's memorandum and whether he had fought the battle as outlined in the memorandum. New manuscript material from several British collections provided Corbett with sufficient material to develop his work beyond the Navy Records Society volumes into a two-volume analysis of *The Campaign of Trafalgar* in 1910.[69]

In his preface to the new book, Corbett noted a score of works on the Waterloo campaign but not even one on the Trafalgar campaign. 'Of the battle itself,' Corbett wrote, 'there are studies innumerable, serious, fanciful, and anecdotic; but the fact remains that though its centenary is past and gone, no British pen has ever been set to the task of producing from the vast store of material that exists, anything like a reasoned Staff account of that crowning chapter in the history of naval warfare.'[70] Despite all the spade work done in recent years, 'the subject has been left, so far as the Service is concerned, in the same comparative darkness that enshrouds the bulk of our naval history'.[71] Using documents published in recent years and his extensive research in the Public Record Office, the British Library, and elsewhere, Corbett produced a study that stood for more than a century as the definitive account of the Trafalgar campaign. He concluded that it 'not merely secured the British Isles from invasion. The ramparts it built stretched to the ends of the earth. It was not merely that it destroyed French naval power. By securing bases in the Mediterranean and towards the East, it made it impossible for any partial revival of Napoleon's Navy to place any part of British overseas possessions in serious jeopardy.'[72] To answer the question, 'Was the battle fought in accordance with the plan or attack, or was it not? The answer surely is plain and simple enough...in major tactics it was; in its minor tactics it was not.'[73] Corbett ended his book by concluding that this campaign in the War of the Third Coalition might have done more against any other enemy than Napoleon, with any other ally than Prussia, but 'As it was, the sea had done all that the sea could do, and for Europe, the end was a failure.'[74] In making this remark, Corbett was not downplaying the importance of the Continental System or the economic war but engaging Mahan's conclusions in a wider dialogue about the broader questions of the war and the limitations of sea power in dealing with land power.

Despite Corbett's brilliant achievement in his broad view of the policy and strategy of the entire campaign, a group of naval officers challenged his conclusions, as well as those of Desbrière, regarding Nelson's naval tactics and whether Nelson had implemented the concept outlined in his pre-battle memorandum. These men ignored Corbett's strategic argument and focused on the naval details. There were still unresolved issues as to the placement of ships, the interpretation of signals, and the need for an authoritative track chart of ships' movements. In addition, Admiral Cyprian Bridge had succinctly laid out the more significant issue in his 1905 centenary address to the annual meeting of the Navy Records Society:

> The criticism of Nelson's procedure at Trafalgar in its most potent form may be summarised as follows. It is affirmed that he drew up and communicated to the officers under his orders a certain plan of attack; that just before the battle he changed his plan without warning; that he hurried on his attack unnecessarily; that he exposed his fleet to excessive peril; and, because of all this, that the British loss was much heavier and much less evenly distributed among the ships of the fleet than it might need have been.[75]

The Admiralty Inquiry

This critical view drew much from the unresolved issues Rear Admiral Charles Ekins had raised in his manual on naval battles in 1824. For some, Corbett's view as a civilian historian was suspect as he carried the authority neither of an experienced seaman who had participated in fleet manoeuvres nor of an admiral who had experienced the weight of command. The outspoken naval officers who joined in this criticism of Corbett's interpretation were Admiral Sir Cyprian Bridge, Admiral Sir Reginald Custance, and Captain Mark Kerr, as well as James Thursfield of *The Times*. As a result of the continuing controversy, the First Sea Lord, Admiral Prince Louis of Battenberg, ordered an official inquiry.[76]

On 2 April 1912, the Admiralty appointed Admiral Sir Cyprian Bridge to chair a committee 'for the purpose of thoroughly examining and considering the whole of the evidence relative to the tactics employed by Nelson at Trafalgar'.[77] Although the initial complaints set naval officers against civilian scholars as to who should authoritatively adjudicate accuracy in naval history, the final composition of the committee provided an appropriate balance. The committee consisted of Admiral Custance, Charles H. Firth, the Regius Professor of Modern History at the University of Oxford, and W. G. Perrin, the Admiralty Librarian, as secretary of the committee. In addition, Captain Thomas H. Tizard, a former Assistant Hydrographer of the Navy, assisted the committee by examining and summarizing the ships' logs and creating the first known track charts drawn to scale of the battle. Along with the published material and manuscripts in the public records and private hands in Britain, the British naval attaché in Paris, Captain W. A. H. Kelley, facilitated the supply of copies of documents in the French archives. The committee submitted its final report to the Admiralty on 17 July 1913, and it was published and made public on Trafalgar Day 1913.

To the credit of the committee members, the conclusions of their formal report were quite the opposite—or at least extensively modified—from the personal assumptions they had held before their investigation. The committee's report created, for the first time, an authoritative track chart for the opening phase of the battle and finally laid to rest the century-old argument that Nelson had rashly rushed into action, finding in favour of the tactical analyses presented in Desbrière's and Corbett's recent books. Otherwise, the immediate and only practical result of the report was a recommendation to modify the scale model of the action on display at the Royal United Services Institute. With the First World War less than a year away, it certainly had no helpful effect on the tactics for the forthcoming conflict, but the emphasis on Trafalgar and the widespread interest in the subject at the time most likely added to the sense that the next war required its own Trafalgar.

Epilogue

In October 1921, Corbett took up the topic of Trafalgar again in his Creighton Memorial Lecture at King's College, London. It was one of the last lectures of his career and one in which he hoped to help revive the project of founding a school of naval history at the University of London. Bringing to bear his broad view of naval history, he began by pointing out that the subject was vast and neglected. It had become what he called 'a closed borough', with its commercial aspects separated from its military aspects. 'They are, in fact, twins that can never be quite happy apart.' Moreover, he wrote that the word 'naval' was not meant to refer just to the history of the Royal Navy but 'to connote the whole activities of our life at sea'. He thought that there were many areas of the subject that needed investigation, among them, 'Judged by the standards of modern historical scholarship, naval history between Trafalgar and Waterloo is a trackless desert.' So brilliant was Nelson's achievement at Trafalgar that an author with an eye for the dramatic naturally wanted to end the story there. 'Even Mahan, for all his philosophical outlook, could not resist the temptation. It is upon his works that intelligent appreciation of our sea-story mainly rests; and he stopped at Trafalgar, as though it had finally shattered Napoleon's sea-power.' Napoleon immediately began to develop a vision to restore his naval power. Britain built warships to check his advances. 'And so it was that, for years after Trafalgar, our navy and our army were absorbed in action to prevent Napoleon's dream being realized.' Providing a broad sketch of the naval war after Trafalgar, Corbett concluded, 'nearly every current belief about the later exhausting years of our struggle with Napoleon needs modification—even the cardinal belief, the effect of Trafalgar'. Corbett saw striking analogies between the Napoleonic War and the First World War that raised a wide range of questions. His study of the naval operations of 1914–16 led him to the conclusion that a decisive battle involved the intersection of naval, military, and economic forces and that victory in a naval battle was notably unimportant as long as the dominant naval power retained control of the sea and could effectively conduct economic warfare. His studies of both the Russo-Japanese War and the First World War underscored for him that the object of war and the prerequisite of peace was not the destruction of the enemy's armed forces.[78] Yet, limited by the state of historical knowledge in 1921, he could not yet answer the query that repeatedly came to his mind: 'What material advantage did Trafalgar give that Jutland did not give?'[79] Corbett did not live to complete *Naval Operations* or to revise *Some Principles* in order to put his later post-war thoughts on the limitations of battles into a comprehensive analytical form, but he left a powerful legacy for historians and maritime strategists.

Echoing Corbett's thoughts, the French naval theorist Admiral Raoul Castex concluded that 'Trafalgar and the sea mastery it brought were not mortal blows to France but only became so later when they were combined with ten years of struggle on the continent. Trafalgar was a necessary but not a sufficient condition for success. Only its intelligent exploitation could decide the victory and constitute a truly mortal blow.' Then, Castex pointedly went on to ask, 'But would it have proved sufficient for victory if the monumental mistakes called the War in Spain and the Russian Campaign had not been committed?'[80]

Except for the publication of Colonel Robert Holden Mackenzie's *The Trafalgar Roll* in 1913,[81] a listing of all ships and officers in the battle with brief biographies, Constance Eastwick's corrected version of Desbrière in 1933, Carola Oman's biography of *Nelson* in 1947,[82] and an academic article in 1980 on the Spanish view of Trafalgar,[83] there was little academic interest in the subject for more than eighty years. Several popular naval writers took a hand at writing about Trafalgar after 1913, but there were no new major historical interpretations during that period.[84] From the time of the battle until the early twentieth century, historians had tended to limit their focus to tactics and the details of the event. Mahan, Desbrière, Corbett, and Castex were among the first to suggest avenues for a broader understanding of the battle. Corbett's corrective dialogue with Mahan over the meaning of Trafalgar paved the way forward, but it would not bear fruit for many decades.

9

The Modern Historians' Trafalgar

In contrast to the centenary and its immediate aftermath, the Nelson Decade, between 1995 and 2005, which culminated in the bicentennial celebration, saw a massive output of new historical works relating to Nelson and the Battle of Trafalgar.[1] In several ways, the vision that Sir Julian Corbett had expressed for the field of naval history and for understanding Trafalgar in his 1921 Creighton Memorial Lecture was coming to fruition three quarters of a century later. Naval history had finally found an academic basis in universities as well as within navies. The conferences and activities during the Nelson Decade attracted a wide range of historians into the field of naval history, bringing with them a variety of skills and specializations that brought the subject into the broader sphere of political, economic, cultural, and social history, promoting multi-dimensional research and multi-disciplinary perspectives that have created a fundamental change to the subject beyond, but including, the specific topic of Trafalgar.[2]

One bibliographer made a selected list of 242 published items during the decade. Among them were eighteen new biographies of Nelson, while twelve older biographies appeared in reprint editions. Nine new volumes of collective biography for the period appeared with twelve additional items relating to Nelson's captains, his 'band of brothers'. In the same period, twenty-two new books appeared on the Battle of Trafalgar, and five older books were reprinted. In addition, three new works on HMS *Victory* appeared, with ten more devoted to other warships of the period.[3]

The sub-specialty of naval history, as well as the entire field of history, had undergone dramatic changes in the period since 1905.[4] No longer was naval history a field dominated by naval officers, amateurs, and newspaper correspondents who focused mainly on professional naval concerns. The old focus primarily lay on great admirals from the perspective of commissioned officers who sought to influence current naval policy and strategy. In contrast, the new naval historians were university-educated men and women with doctorates in history who had a much broader grounding in the study of history than their predecessors. They were historians first and specialists in naval history second. The new approach to naval history in the English-speaking world began to develop slowly and uneasily in the 1950s and 1960s. In 1953, the historian John Ehrman signalled the new approach when he famously wrote: 'If national history can be compared to the layers of a cake, the layers of which are the different aspects of national life, then naval history is not a layer, but a slice of that cake.'[5] Eventually, by the 1990s and the first decade of the new millennium, historians had come to a consensus that naval history was part of a much larger, multi-dimensional, and multi-disciplinary study that encompassed a new and broader concept of maritime history rather than an isolated, separate niche subject.

The essential historical insights during the Nelson Decade reflect a broader view of naval history than that of the nineteenth century. The fundamental contribution was N. A. M. Rodger's three-volume *A Naval History of Britain*, published between 1997 and 2024, which replaced William Laird Clowes's standard, century-old *History of the Royal Navy*. Rodger successfully established naval history as a central theme in British national history. Innovatively placing his subject within three broadly defined contexts—social, administrative, and operational history—he followed the subjects in separate chapters, weaving them together as interrelated threads. In his second volume, which appeared in 2004 and covered the period from 1648 to 1815, Rodger broadly outlined the social history of the officers and men who fought at Trafalgar, the significant prize money they earned, the essential effect that the victory had in redressing administrative deficiencies, and how the battle became the guarantor of British economic prosperity.[6] As one reviewer emphasized, Rodger effectively challenged old myths: 'The line of battle was never as rigid and as neat as the carefully drawn plans in the tactical textbooks have led us to believe. The late 18th-century navies were far more innovative tactically than old naval histories used to suggest. So, Nelson's battle plans were not the work of a lone revolutionary genius, but were the product of cumulative experimentation—as much by the French as by the British.'[7] Additionally, Rodger concluded that Trafalgar gave Britain 'an unchallenged command of the sea, in quantity and quality, materially and psychologically, over all her actual and potential enemies, which she had never known before.'[8] The battle allowed Britain to survive Napoleon's onslaught while simultaneously guaranteeing Britain's economic prosperity, enabling her to continue the war and subsidise her allies. Twenty years later, when describing the Second World War, Rodger noted that 'The Battle of Midway is sometimes presented as the U.S. Navy's Trafalgar, and in many respects this is a helpful comparison. Neither victory won the war, but both defeated dangerous enemy offensives, and significantly changed the nature of naval warfare in the following years.'[9] Rodger's narrative quickly became the broad standard narrative for British naval history, serving also as an inspiration for new research that delved further into his overview.

The Bicentenary Conferences

A relatively new feature in commemorating historical events emerged in the mid- to late twentieth century, particularly around significant anniversaries of historical events. This new feature involved the organization of conferences or lecture series by professional historians to provide new research and a critical examination of historical events rather than engaging in patriotic commemoration. Part of the concept for the Nelson Decade was to organize such conferences on each of Nelson's major battles. In this, the Trafalgar bicentenary was very unusual in that it spawned nine such events, all but one of which published its proceedings.[10]

Four of these conferences were in Spain, with the first taking place at the University of Cádiz in 2002. It produced a volume of collaborative scholarship in Spanish, *Trafalgar y el mundo atlántico,* edited by Agustín Guimerá and Alberto Ramos y Gonzalo Butrón, examining the context of Trafalgar and the Atlantic world.[11] This book is notable for the contributions of Marieta Cantos and Marianne Czisnik on the literary works that explain the nineteenth-century political, social, and cultural impact of the battle, as well as its consequences in Spanish historiography. Another conference held in Madrid in 2004 examined the entire century, from the Peace of Utrecht in 1714 to and including the Battle of Trafalgar.[12] In 2005, the International Congress of Military History held its 31st Congress in Madrid, devoted to *Land and Sea Power in the Age of the Battle of Trafalgar.*[13] The fourth 2005 conference in Spain was devoted to the *Technology of the Ships of Trafalgar.*[14]

The remaining four events took place in the United Kingdom. In October 2004, the Institute of Historical Research and the National Maritime Museum sponsored a series of lectures at the University of London on Nelson, the context of Nelson's life, and his legacy. These appeared in print the following July, edited by David Cannadine,[15] providing a range of important new insights regarding naval leadership, quality of seamanship, and fraternal relationships between officers, as well as the legacy of Nelson's mythology, his commemoration, and his place in the national pantheon. The following year, in 2005, a similar series of lectures was held, with the published volume again edited by Cannadine, titled *Trafalgar in History: A Battle and Its Afterlife.*[16] Both these collections of lectures were significant in applying new historical approaches drawn from fields outside of naval history to Nelson and the battle.

In October 2005, the Royal Naval Museum in Portsmouth hosted another conference, the proceedings of which were published as *A Great and Glorious Victory: New Perspectives on the Battle of Trafalgar*, edited by Richard Harding.[17] This conference also featured the perspectives of France and Spain. Once more, the issue of tactics in the battle arose. Validating, but going further than, Desbrière's work in 1907 and the 1913 Admiralty study, a group called the 'Inshore Squadron' used modern technology to create a computer animation of the individual ships' tracks for the entire engagement. They found that 'the traditional version of the battle as a heedless charge into action does not do justice to the tactical subtlety displayed by both Nelson and Collingwood ... The Spanish and French crews put up fierce resistance, but their efforts were limited by isolation and lack of cohesion, due to Nelson's plan.'[18] Another symposium took place at the British Academy in January 2006, a week after the bicentenary of Nelson's funeral. Holger Hoock edited these proceedings, which focused on the commemoration and national preoccupation with Trafalgar over the course of two centuries.[19]

New Accounts of the Battle of Trafalgar

Newly written accounts of the Battle of Trafalgar were central to the bicentenary. In that context, one of the first and most important of them appeared in French: Michèle Battesti's examination of the risks that Napoleon's naval strategy against Britain involved and which resulted in the battle.[20] The first major account in English was that by Tim Clayton and Phil Craig,[21] who presented a dramatic and evocative account that effectively used personal letters and gave views from various aspects of the battle. Roy Adkins's book *Nelson's Trafalgar* followed,[22] an introduction to the subject, and Adam Nicholson's *Seize the Fire*,[23] which used a dramatic description of the Battle of Trafalgar to meditate on more general ideas about heroism. Some of the most critical scholarly discussions on tactics and gunnery in the battle appeared in articles by Marianne Czisnik,[24] Michael Duffy, Agustín Rodríguez, and Remi Monaque.[25] Mark Adkin produced the most extensive and detailed reference work: *The Trafalgar Companion: A Guide to History's Most Famous Sea Battle and the Life of Admiral Lord Nelson*.[26]

In Spain, the most comprehensive publication about the battle was Rear Admiral José Ignacio González-Aller Hierro's massive two-volume, 1,880-page compilation of all known documents in the Spanish archives regarding the battle, including diagrams of actions and service biographies for the key naval officers.[27]

French Rear Admiral Rémi Monaque's *Trafalgar*[28] focused on the operational aspects of the battle, using extensive materials from French and Spanish archives. Based on these materials, Monaque concluded that while Trafalgar had a massive psychological effect and caused irreparable humiliation for the French, the battle had little direct effect in the short term. Napoleon had already cancelled his strategy to invade Britain before Trafalgar and had turned towards a plan that would culminate with his victory at Austerlitz two months later.

In 2002, La Fondation Napoléon began to publish an authoritative and comprehensive edition of the emperor's correspondence, completed in fifteen volumes with 40,500 letters in 2018 and since made available online with additional material. Of the total, 23,775 letters (58 per cent) were not included in the edition of the correspondence published during the Second Empire. A further 11,970 (29 per cent) were unpublished or only partially cited in other collections or monographs. Volume 5, which included the documents for 1805 and Trafalgar, first appeared in print in 2008.[29] It superseded the source for Napoleon's correspondence that historians generally used during the bicentennial. In 2010, using this and other sources, Jean-Claude Gillet placed Napoleon's navy in a larger context with his *La marine impériale: le grand rêve de Napoleon*.[30]

More recently, in 2023, Agustín Guimerá brought together a group of the leading Trafalgar experts from France, Britain, and Spain to provide a Spanish-language audience with a summary of the most up-to-date scholarship on Spain's glorious defeat at Trafalgar.[31]

The Nelson Biographies

In the decades leading up to the bicentenary period, the two standard biographies by A. T. Mahan[32] and Carola Oman[33] had been partially superseded, with Mahan's work still holding its own after a century as the best professional naval study and Oman's the best personal portrait. While a few new sources and insights had been published over the years, it was a series of biographical studies during the Nelson Decade that developed an entirely new approach, built on evidence independent of the older nineteenth-century traditional interpretations of the subject. Colin White's *The Nelson Companion*[34] was the first compilation of collective scholarship that laid the basis for a new beginning in this area. The contributors to that volume in 1995 laid out the agenda for the coming decade by their thematic examination of the legend, portraits, relics, commemorations, verifiable chronology, and manuscript sources, all of which suggested new perspectives and new interpretations of Nelson's life. Richard Walker followed his contribution to this volume with his book-length study of Nelson's portraits and iconography,[35] a masterful study in art history, which significantly contributed to biographical studies and studies on cultural and commemorative aspects of the Trafalgar period. The first edition of Colin White's *Nelson Encyclopaedia* followed,[36] a work that continued and complemented the initiatives of the *Nelson Companion* but with a broader range of topics. As new research and insights quickly followed, both works required revision and expansion in 2005.

The first new full biography to appear was Terry Coleman's *The Nelson Touch*,[37] in which the author portrayed Nelson as 'a paramount naval genius and a natural-born predator... In private life, as in war, he was ruthless when he had to be, and he could be pitiless.'[38] As the first to appear, Coleman's work became the spark for new and differing interpretations, leading those who followed to look for other primary sources and other aspects of Nelson's character to weigh. Coleman stressed the critical importance in his work of manuscript sources, citing the edited collections in print and original materials at the British Library, the National Maritime Museum, the National Archives, and the Nelson Museum in Monmouth, Wales.

Joel Hayward followed with a thematic examination of Nelson's way of warfare, which he constructed around themes, insights, and terminology from modern naval thinking.[39] Hayward made a unique contribution to the literature, focusing on Nelson's conception of his enemies, his spiritual beliefs, leadership, command, management, and war-fighting styles. While Hayward based his work on long-published material and the prevailing older biographical interpretations, his innovative use of modern professional thinking provided some intriguing insights for those serving in the armed forces at the beginning of the twenty-first century.

In 2003, Edgar Vincent published his extensive, vividly written biography,[40] which applied some unusual psychological insights into Nelson's charismatic personality, utilized the insights of a range of modern medical specialists to address various of Nelson's medical conditions, and benefited from the author's practical insights gained from his career in evaluating the character of candidates for senior management positions and placing them in suitable employment. Vincent's emphasis on Nelson's emotional make-up, his relationships, and his passion for fame provided a contrasting interpretation to Coleman's judgements. In emphasizing his reliance on original materials, Vincent highlighted his pioneering use of materials at the Huntington Library and the discovery of some seventy previously unknown Nelson letters.

In 2004, the publication of the first volume of John Sugden's two-volume biography made a significant contribution to the scholarly discourse unfolding at the time, and it had a profound influence on the works that followed.[41] Most impressive was the massive range of manuscript sources that Sugden utilized. Using what his publisher described as 'thousands of previously unused naval, military, diplomatic, and personal documents', Sugden listed three archival repositories in Canada, nine in the United States, and twenty in the United Kingdom, exploiting numerous previously untapped collections and archival series at the British Library, the National Maritime Museum, and the National Archives. Additionally, he listed a wide range of published materials. Sugden effectively utilized these widely scattered and diverse materials to dissect, analyse, and refute in detail the long-accepted mythology surrounding numerous events in Nelson's early life. In doing this,

Sugden's work became the most important recent research and the critical work to be superseded.

In 2004, Andrew Lambert published his study on Nelson, subtitled with Lord Byron's words as *Britannia's God of War*.[42] This important study had different origins than the others and, as a result, focused on different objectives for its contribution to the literature. As Lambert explained in his preface, he had long believed that Nelson's story had been 'so often told as to defy reinterpretation, but such thoughts were soon changed by the experience of trying to teach from the extant literature'.[43] His students sought to learn about aspects of his education, strategy, relationships with other senior officers, his significance, and the broader importance of Trafalgar that the existing biographical literature did not address. Lambert's book addresses these questions, which he links to interpreting Nelson in the context of understanding him today. Lambert's most original contribution was to explain how Nelson's life and achievements came to play a role in modern British national identity. As Lambert concluded his work, 'We need to understand Nelson because he, and the culture of his age, still define the way the British see themselves in the world and the way the world sees them.'[44]

As the bicentennial year approached, many works appeared nearly simultaneously. They fell into various categories that reflected some of the new evidence unearthed and utilized in several biographies. One of the most interesting discoveries occurred in 2002 when materials belonging to Alexander Davison, Nelson's close friend and prize agent, came to light. In an attractively written popular account, Martyn Downer related these events in the dramatic style of a detective story.[45] As the head of jewellery at Sotheby's in London, Downer shared his experience in authenticating the jewellery and other materials, which provided a remarkable range of new evidence and insights into Nelson's life. This popular account, directed at a broad audience, put in the spotlight one of the most serious issues for scholars and researchers working on Nelson: the problem of authenticating things that had belonged to Nelson amidst a vast range of widely distributed reproductions, fakes, falsely identified materials, and the numerous conflicting and unsubstantiated accounts surrounding them. Following the discovery of the Davison materials, Rina Prentice, a curator at the National Maritime Museum, published a significant corrective with her illustrated scholarly catalogue of all known surviving objects that Nelson had owned.[46] Prentice's work served not only curators and collectors grappling with questions of authenticity but also provided valuable insights for biographers and students of the period's material culture.

Nelson's correspondence has always been an essential source. Sir Nicholas Harris Nicolas (1799–1848) published the standard collection in seven volumes in the mid-nineteenth century, and this was republished in a paperback facsimile for the bicentenary.[47] Following this republication of a standard source, Nicholas Tracy made another beneficial contribution by publishing an indexed, five-volume abridgment of the forty volumes of the biannual *The Naval Chronicle* that originally appeared between 1799 and 1816.[48]

Roger Morriss's *Guide to British Naval Papers in North America* opened up broader uses for the often-neglected manuscript material on British naval history that had migrated to the United States and Canada.[49] As a result of this and other research efforts in Britain, many additional letters began to come to light and appeared in various publications. Joseph F. Callo used some of these to select quotations to introduce Nelson to American naval officers.[50] The most important work for historians and biographers was Colin White's continuing long-term effort to locate and transcribe all of Nelson's letters. His project, begun in 1999, had, by August 2004, revealed 1,300 previously unpublished letters in thirty different archives. In April 2005, White published a selection of 507 of these letters, arranged thematically to complement the biographies directly.[51] Yet, even before White published his volume, he had generously shared his findings with other scholars and reported key finds, such as his discovery of the Trafalgar battle plan,[52] in the press and through progress reports in scholarly journals.[53] In 2020, Marianne Czisnik published an authoritative volume on *Nelson's Letters to Lady Hamilton*.[54]

In the centenary year, Roger Knight published his major new biography, *The Pursuit of Victory*.[55] Appearing after Sugden's first volume and Lambert's biography, Knight's work could safely omit detailed explanations of why and how the traditional narrative about Nelson was wrong, nor did he need to feel obliged to focus on the meaning of Nelson's career for British identity. What Knight produced was notably different from all the works that preceded it. He presented an entirely new narrative picture by completely ignoring the traditional stories about Nelson and building anew entirely from archival sources. In addition, Knight was able to place Nelson's life within the context of his times, merging the particularistic biographical approach with a more general historical explanation. To supplement this, Knight added three valuable appendices to his work that included a chronology of Nelson's life based on documentary sources, short biographical sketches of the key individuals that explained their relationships to Nelson, and detailed data on each of the ships in which Nelson served—all this new material built upon the cumulative development of scholarship during the preceding decade.

Two additional biographies appeared during the bicentenary year to complete the new wave of publications. First, Colin White published *Nelson: The Admiral*,[56] a work mainly designed to attract and inform those early in their careers as modern naval officers. In this task, White was informed by all the latest and best scholarship but concentrated in this work on lucidly presenting those elements of leadership, command, and naval life that might inspire and interest young serving officers. Marianne Czisnik concluded the bicentenary biographical wave with her study of *Nelson: A Controversial Hero*.[57] Based on her recent doctoral thesis at the University of Edinburgh, it was an unusual work, not least for the fact that its German author wrote it in English but also for the fresh insights it offered in analysing the controversial aspects of Nelson's life in his involvement with the Neapolitan republicans and his relationship with Lady Hamilton. In addition, she made a significant original contribution to historical literature through her study of the Nelson legend as it appeared in French, Spanish, and German historical and literary works, as well as visual images.

Nelson's Fellow Naval Officers

One of the critical elements in understanding Nelson was an assessment of his place among his contemporaries and an understanding of the careers of naval officers. Making the transition between biographies of contemporaries and those of Nelson himself are two volumes that touch on medical practices. First, Lawrence Brockliss, John Cardwell, and Michael Moss used their biography of William Beatty, the surgeon who treated the dying Nelson,[58] as a study of the specific medical practice during the Battle of Trafalgar and the general medical situation in the Royal Navy. Following up on this theme, Dr Anne-Mary E. Hills's *Nelson: A Medical Casebook*[59] served as an examination of contemporary medical practice and a very specialized contribution to Nelson's biography.

One of the significant tools that provided initial help in the development of comparative biographical research was the 1994 publication of David Syrett's revision and correction of the list of *Commissioned Sea Officers of the Royal Navy*.[60] Initially compiled by David Bonner-Smith, the Admiralty had issued it in mimeographed form in 1954. Over the following decades, several scholars, including C. G. Pitcairn-Jones, Commander William May, and A. W. H. Pearsall, had annotated and corrected copies of this work. Syrett and DiNardo's work in updating this forty-year-old reference work made a significant contribution, providing the initial basis for the subsequent new assessments. It offered a useful starting point for many naval historians drawn into the project, initially known as the *New* (later, *Oxford*) *Dictionary of National Biography* project, after it began in earnest in 1992. This compilation of data was complemented for the Battle of Trafalgar with the electronic publication from 2001 of the *Ayshford Trafalgar Roll*,[61] which provided factual data on all 21,000 officers and ratings who served in British ships at Trafalgar. This resource complemented the similar electronic publication of *The Complete Navy List*, listing the 11,000 naval officers who served in the Royal Navy during the 1793–1815 period.[62] In the same genre, and just in time for the bicentenary, Nicholas Tracy published his selection of two hundred biographical sketches,[63] while Colin White and members of the 1805 Club compiled a short study on the memorials and grave sites for the thirty-eight officers who had commanded ships under Nelson at Trafalgar.[64]

The first of the significant new biographical studies to be published in the Nelson Decade that began to provide a comparative perspective with Nelson was Roger Morriss's study of Admiral Sir George Cockburn,[65] which emphasized entirely different theatres of the war from those in which Nelson dominated, showing the development of a younger officer who presided over the technological and political transitions that the navy faced in the post-Napoleonic War era. John E. Talbott's study followed with the contrasting figure of an older officer, Charles Middleton, who, as Lord Barham, served as First Lord of the Admiralty during the Trafalgar campaign.[66]

At the same time, the decade of collaborative scholarly work that went into the production of the sixty-volume *Oxford Dictionary of National Biography*[67] bore some early fruit for naval history even before that landmark reference work appeared in print in 2004, with some of the contributors to it producing early spin-off pieces for Peter Le Fevre and Richard Harding's volume *The Precursors of Nelson*,[68] the first of the significant new comparative biographical studies explicitly designed to place Nelson in the general context of the tradition he developed. Although this volume began with the distant opening years of the eighteenth century, Le Fevre and Harding's volume ranged through the century to include studies for the Nelson period, with Patricia Crimmins's study of St Vincent, Roger Morriss on Barham, and Brian Lavery on Keith. The essays in this volume collectively demonstrated that the basis for Nelson's achievements had developed over the preceding century and a half in the context of a flourishing maritime economy and that it was the application of money, administrative capabilities, manpower, and the development of Britain's professional naval officer corps that converted these raw materials into a formidable sea power.[69] Under these broad rubrics, the fundamental developments were the evolution of standardized systems and procedures for manning the fleet, maintaining the health and hygiene of sailors at sea, refining the design and technology of warships, creating the effective means of directing large numbers of ships in combat, and developing communications and understanding for this purpose. Moreover, the catalyst for these ingredients was applying, in an appropriate measure, the complementary elements of leadership and discipline throughout all levels of the naval organization to achieve these ends effectively. Such was the gradual and cumulative work over many generations that culminated in Nelson's unique achievements.

A significant number of valuable studies followed in succession, providing a greater range and depth to the comparisons with Nelson. Paul Krajeski's study of one of Nelson's contemporaries, Sir Charles Cotton, represented a much more typical type of flag officer as opposed to the exceptional character that Nelson represented.[70] Other valuable studies followed in succession to provide greater range and depth. One that directly touched on Trafalgar was Max Adams's study of Collingwood. It was the first in forty years and used several previously unused sources to provide new details.[71] Another was Hilary Rubenstein's study and volume of documents on one of Nelson's captains, Philip Durham, who had commanded HMS *Defiance* at the Battle of Trafalgar.[72]

A focus on Nelson's captains at Trafalgar raised a long-standing historical issue. In an important article published in 2005, Michael Duffy examined how Collingwood made no distinctions among officers in combat performance in his dispatch to avoid recriminations and distracting claims of personal valour.[73] Nearly two hundred years later, this had become a myth. As in any human endeavour, no one had performed to the same standards nor with the same success. The new biographical studies illustrated this in some detail, replacing myth with fact.

While some authors provided book-length, in-depth studies of their subjects that give differing personal perspectives on the period, Peter Le Fevre and Richard Harding gathered a second collection of biographical essays on Nelson's contemporaries that made a significant complementary contribution that illustrated the broad range of diversity among naval officers of Nelson's time as well as identified some of the critical elements of similar outlook and experience among them. Le Fevre and Harding's choice of subjects carefully focused on lesser-known admirals the editors felt deserved examination. Their choices fell not on the close circle of Nelson's captains, his 'band of brothers', but officers whose careers spanned the same years as Nelson's and involved the same broad pattern of war and peace. While they included some key individuals whose lives had been examined in the older literature or whose letters had been published—such as Collingwood, Pellew, and Saumarez, the last two just a year older than Nelson—others provided entirely new perspectives: Hotham, Duncan, Orde, Rainier, Knowles, Duckworth, Calder, Warren, Troubridge, Sir Samuel Hood, and Keats. Duncan, born in 1731, was the oldest of the group and twenty-seven years senior in age to Nelson, while Sir Samuel Hood, born in 1762, was just four years younger than Nelson. This collection demonstrates that Nelson's career pattern was not unique for his time and that many of his contemporaries had similar experiences, having joined the navy about the same age, were promoted after similar periods of service, had identical sea assignments, and shared the same concerns for the health and welfare of their seamen. In addition, a naval officer rose in his profession by his abilities and aptitude for the essential aspects of high naval command. Such a career path involved meticulous attention to detail in the managerial oversight of practical, routine, logistical, and operational aspects of large and complex organizations; it also extended to detailed diplomatic relations with foreign powers at overseas stations. Although it is commonly said that Nelson was not a typical individual in the naval officer corps of his time, his administrative experiences, his views about patriotism and the importance of the battle, his interest in prize money, his sensitivity to his honour, and his insistence on specific standards of conduct for a naval officer, were all things that that his contemporaries typically shared. Equally important, the collection highlighted the significance of various naval actions, not just climactic fleet battles. As Julian Corbett had pointed out so clearly in his 1911 theoretical work, *Some Principles of Maritime Strategy*, there is a range of naval operations to contest another naval power's ability to use the sea, among which naval battle is just one of several traditional means to achieve command of the sea over an enemy. Once command of the sea is achieved, a navy has an entirely different range of tasks to exercise that command.[74]

An officer rose in rank, typically seeing only a portion of these tasks, with repeated command experience in major fleet battles being the rarest and most unusual. More commonly, naval officers saw action against the enemy in various circumstances, typically on blockade duty or in frigates in small operations, such as raids, single-ship actions, and amphibious operations. Such operations provided relatively rare opportunities for an officer to show himself as a candidate for higher command. Richard Woodman[75] and Tom Wareham[76] examined this range of experiences with studies of frigate captains. Other authors examined the development of critical components of naval conflict, situating Trafalgar within the context of their themes. For example, Michael A. Palmer examined *Command at Sea: Naval Command and Control since the Sixteenth Century*,[77] while Geoffrey Till examined the concept of victory in naval operations from Trafalgar to the present.[78] Roger Knight examined the neglected yet essential procedure for protecting trade and maintaining the British economy in his study of *Convoys*.[79] Richard Hill delved into a further specific aspect of naval operations with his *Prizes of War*,[80] a study of the naval prize system and a subject of significant interest to Nelson and his fellow naval officers. Hill's analysis of the legal system and its procedures complemented and expanded on the understanding produced earlier through Henry Bourguignon's biography of Sir William Scott, the Judge of the High Court of Admiralty.[81]

Following the bicentennial, a new and innovative wave of scholarship emerged in the social history of naval officers during this period. Complementing the biographical approach, several works utilized statistical databases to create comparative patterns in officer careers and demonstrate the effects of Trafalgar on recruitment and promotion.[82] Approximately 6 per cent of the officers and men in British ships at Trafalgar were foreign-born, prompting historians to investigate the prevalence of foreign seamen and the presence of transnational networks of seamen within the Royal Navy during the Napoleonic Wars.[83] Among other studies of naval social life, Nelson's personal life gave rise to Margarette Lincoln's work on *Naval Wives and Mistresses*,[84] which Ellen Gill complemented with her *Naval Families, War and Duty in Britain, 1740–1820*.[85] Additionally, Anne Hawkins and Helen Watt documented insights from sailors on the lower decks in a thick volume of *Letters of Seamen in the Wars with France, 1793–1815*, which included several descriptions of Trafalgar.[86]

The Ships and the Battle

While the largest outpouring of significant research and writing focused on biographical studies, scholars also considered other approaches. They fall into two additional large categories: first, the ships and tactics of the Battle of Trafalgar, and second, the broader context of the battle, which included the history of the navy and the nation during this period.

The prevailing tendency for producing volumes of data and biographical studies of naval officers also extended to ships. In the genre of books of data on ships, the first important volume to appear was David Lyon's *The Sailing Ship Navy List*.[87] In 2002, Peter G. Goodwin published his detailed study of all the ships Nelson had served, effectively using ships' logbooks.[88] Goodwin then went on to publish *The Ships of Trafalgar*.[89] Just in time for the bicentenary, Rif Winfield made a significant contribution when he published his even more detailed compilation of data on all British warships for the period 1793–1817.[90] This compendium included information on dates of commissions, significant refit periods, changes of captains, when and on which stations vessels served, and details of noteworthy actions. Following the bicentenary, Winfield collaborated with others to produce additional studies of Spanish and French warships during the same period.[91]

While the compilation of detailed statistics about ships has been a traditional enterprise that has benefited from the work of generations of experts, a deeper understanding of how to calculate relative naval power from such lists and how to understand the development of ship design were aspects that have long needed detailed elaboration for the sailing ship period. Several works that appeared during the Nelson Decade benefited from the appearance in 1993 of Jan Glete's *Navies and Nations*.[92] His book offered a new approach that enabled a more nuanced quantification of national naval strength, linking it to Europe's broader state development process, the evolution of bureaucracy, and the various interest groups that supported the development of navies. Using ship tonnage, not the number of guns a ship carried, Glete drew samples every five years in peace and in war over three and a half centuries. Using his new paradigm, Glete summarized the situation by describing Napoleon's threat of invasion as a useful way to tie up British naval and military resources, sending large French and Spanish fleets to sea to make the threat more credible. This ended with the defeat at Trafalgar. 'In this battle and in its aftermath in early November, France and Spain lost 23 battleships of almost 70,000 tons, of which Great Britain added eight of 23,000 tons to her own navy. The result was that by the end of 1805, Great Britain had a comfortable superiority over France, Spain, and the Netherlands—570,000 tons against 360,000 tons.'[93] He noted that before Trafalgar, Britain and the three other navies had a battleship strength of around 330,000 tons each. After the battle, the British battle fleet of about 350,000 tons faced an allied force of just three quarters that strength. With its varied naval force, Britain firmly controlled European coastal waters through its ability to protect trade and support land warfare.[94]

There were also biographies of ships that had fought at Trafalgar, which provided helpful insights into how these highly technical warships operated. For this, Alan McGowan provided a new history of HMS *Victory*.[95] Additionally, David Cordingly provided a study of HMS *Bellerophon*,[96] and Sam Willis wrote on HMS *Temeraire*.[97] Willis also turned his attention to a much-needed understanding of how warships fought under sail in the eighteenth century, clearly elucidating the practical problems of wind, weather, and sea.[98] Complementing these volumes and directly focusing on the ships of Nelson's time, Brian Lavery's volume of documents on *Shipboard Life and Organization* presents an authoritative compilation that provides an essential reference for understanding naval life at sea in this period.[99]

With such a vast outpouring of new insights, the bicentenary led to a pressing need to place the Battle of Trafalgar within a broader perspective and to understand its relationship to the war against Napoleon. James Davey wrote two essential books that broached this subject: *The Transformation of British Naval Strategy: Seapower and Supply in Northern Europe*, in which he examined how the Royal Navy reformed itself after Trafalgar to focus on logistics and economic warfare in the Baltic Sea, with very different war aims than major fleet battles.[100] With his second study, *In Nelson's Wake: The Navy and the Napoleonic Wars*, Davey filled the significant void in historiography that Corbett had pointed out in 1921 and wrote a comprehensive history of the Royal Navy from 1803 to 1815 that placed Trafalgar in full perspective. Davey concluded that Trafalgar had been 'a powerful blow against the French navy (and a far more devastating one to the Spanish fleet), but it was by no means decisive, nor was Britain's subsequent naval superiority guaranteed to last'.[101] Napoleon's dominance on land ensured that the war would continue, while his attempts to rebuild the French fleet continued to worry Britain until the conflict's end. Rather than more major battles, Britain opted for a series of raids and amphibious assaults to thwart Napoleon's naval ambitions. 'It was these smaller, less famous actions against the navies of Denmark, Russia, Spain, Portugal, and, of course, the French fleets that were truly decisive,' Davey wrote.[102] Rather than winning battles, the most essential functions of the Royal Navy were its tenacious blockade of the French empire to weaken the French economy and protect British merchant shipping while buttressing a growing and increasingly wealthy British mercantile empire. At the same time, the Royal Navy played a crucial role in supporting military operations during the Peninsular War that followed Trafalgar.[103] 'While victory at Trafalgar exemplified the fighting spirit of the Royal Navy and cemented the reputation of its greatest commander, it was in Nelson's wake that the service showed its true strength, tenacity, and prowess,' Davey concluded. 'Looking beyond the great men and great battle reveals the people and events that ultimately defeated Napoleon.'[104]

One of the aspects operating beyond the great men and the battle was the administrative structure of the British state. Building further on Jan Glete's earlier insights and focusing on Britain, several innovative studies were completed that examined various aspects of administrative development within the British state, ranging from the Admiralty, contractors, and the Victualling Board to the Ordnance Board.[105] Subsuming these insights within the context of a much broader study, Roger Knight examined the entire British government and the full breadth of the war in his *Britain against Napoleon: The Organization of Victory, 1793–1815*.[106] He pointed out that the navy had used the largest amount of gunpowder and shot during the war. For example, there were 2,148 British cannon at Trafalgar, in contrast to ninety smaller-calibre cannon in Wellington's siege train at Vitoria.[107] After a period marked by scandal dominated by party politics, the Admiralty was able to establish a relatively efficient system of administration that functioned through effective delegation of authority. This was apparent in several areas relating to Trafalgar. Ship repair was an essential but often overlooked necessity to keep warships at sea. As the Second Secretary of the Admiralty, John Barrow, told Lord Melville in February 1806, 'It might be thought perhaps going too far to say that the battle of Trafalgar would not have taken place if the new mode of repairing ships had not been adopted... instead of 34 sailing of the line, the Mediterranean Fleet would not possibly have exceeded 24 of the line at the time the action happened... by the ordinary method of repairing ships.'[108] British ships enjoyed an additional advantage. While French and Spanish crews were unpaid for many months, and their food was scarce due to the British blockade of Cádiz, a succession of victualling convoys from Britain, along with ships carrying fresh meat and vegetables from Lisbon and North Africa, supplied the British crews. 'The result was that Nelson's seamen were better fed, and had greater energy and morale, than their French and Spanish enemies.'[109] After Nelson returned from the West

Indies in 1805, he was able to put to sea again in mid-September with refreshed ships to take command of Collingwood's squadron blockading Cádiz. Knight concluded in this context that 'With superior ships and sea-hardened crews, bolstered by leadership which stemmed from well-justified confidence, Nelson earned the overwhelming victory at Trafalgar on 21 October.'[110]

The cultural aspects of Trafalgar, the war, and its aftermath became a new area for historians to research. In 2002, Margarette Lincoln wrote a pioneering book examining the public perception of the navy and how the image of British sea power was constructed and deployed in the public sphere in her *Representing the Royal Navy: British Sea Power, 1750–1815*.[111] Emphasizing a multi-disciplinary approach, she showed, for example, how some members of the clergy became anxious about God's role in the victory. 'The battle is the Lord's; prayer is the nation's armour.'[112] Although Nelson's loss was significant, the clergyman argued, the navy was not left incapable of action. A former chaplain was even more critical. He believed that the navy and the nation had sunk into a kind of irreligion that shut out recognition of the superintending providence of God, which had led to the victory at Trafalgar.[113]

Timothy Jenks followed with his 2008 study, *Naval Engagements: Patriotism, Cultural Politics, and the Royal Navy, 1793–1815*.[114] His work highlighted the cultural divides within British patriotic political culture as he examined political, naval, social, art, and literary history. In the case of Trafalgar and Nelson's funeral, naval symbols were contested in the public arena in various ways, as heroism served as a counterpoint to the venality of the state.[115] Other authors followed with specific cultural themes. Geoff Quilley, an art historian, explored the battle between artists, both privately and publicly, over the appropriate way to commemorate Trafalgar and Nelson in either allegorical or realistic images in his *Empire to Nation*,[116] while James Davey and Richard Johns examined *Broadsides: Caricature and the Navy, 1756–1815*.[117] Nicolas Tracy wrote *Britannia's Palette: The Arts of Naval Victory*, providing the history behind the paintings of Trafalgar and other victories.

With the bicentennial of the Napoleonic Wars completed in 2015, historians sought to utilize all the new insights gained through the latest research and analysis provided by the commemorative events. One of the first to do this was Michael V. Leggiere's *Napoleon and the Operational Art of War*, which included chapters on the naval aspects of the war.[118] Alexander Mikaberidze followed with his *The Napoleonic Wars: A Global History*.[119] More recently, the three-volume, multi-author *Cambridge History of the Napoleonic Wars* appeared in 2022–3 and offered a comprehensive view and summary of the latest research with separate volumes devoted to politics and diplomacy,[120] fighting the wars,[121] and experience, culture, and memory.[122]

The Significance of Trafalgar in the Light of Modern Historical Insight

The scholarly focus on the Battle of Trafalgar during the bicentenary and afterward provided more than new insights and perspectives on the battle; it also offered stimulating and innovative approaches applicable to other periods of naval history. With all the latest scholarship and new approaches to thinking about the battle and those who participated in it, the fundamental question remained: what was the significance of the Battle of Trafalgar in light of these new insights? The long-standing answer for Britain—that the battle saved the country from invasion—clearly could no longer stand. That result was achieved in the summer of 1805, during the preceding campaign, not in the battle in October 1805.

For France and Spain, there was no strategic imperative for a major fleet battle off Trafalgar. Traditional French naval strategy had typically avoided risking battle, when possible, to focus on accomplishing an assigned mission. The Franco-Spanish fleet had a mission to enter the Mediterranean to support French military operations, but it was neither urgent nor vital. There were several instances when the French Navy waited for a gap in the British blockade to sail out to sea, carry out their mission, and avoid a battle. They could have done so here. It would have been a significant intelligence failure if the Franco-Spanish commanders had been unaware of Nelson and Collingwood's force just over the horizon when they put to sea. The evidence suggests that Villeneuve and his local Franco-Spanish war council deliberately chose to fight a battle. However, they had no orders to do so but took action as a point of honour to prove themselves to Napoleon, who was highly critical of his admirals.

Battle always presents risks and is subject to unexpected influences that can yield unintended consequences. At Trafalgar, Villeneuve appeared to be aware of what he could expect from Nelson but had not developed any innovative defensive tactics to counter the situation. The opposing ships fought the battle fiercely and courageously, but as typical of battle situations, some participants were more closely engaged than others. From a tactical perspective, the battle was a great British victory and a massive defeat for the Spanish and French. Backed by relatively more efficient administrative and logistical support from home, more effective mobilization of manpower, better-supplied British ships, and experienced seamen, Nelson used his effective leadership and tactics to defeat and nearly destroy the Franco-Spanish forces. The unexpected storm in the aftermath of the battle further exacerbated the devastation, depriving the British of most of their prizes and causing additional casualties. The battle was a decisive defeat in tactical terms, as it effectively eliminated the Franco-Spanish naval force; however, it was not a decisive victory in strategic terms.

The British victory at Trafalgar reset the balance of power in the midst of the war and allowed Britain to continue leveraging its sea power for another decade. While sea power could not end the war alone, it enforced the cumulative effects of blockades while undertaking a sequence of supporting military operations ashore and gaining naval command of the Baltic Sea as well as meeting the emerging threats from the French Navy as well as French attempts to use the Danish, French, Russian, Spanish, and Portuguese navies against Britain.

Trafalgar damaged French morale by leaving the French Navy with a lasting and profound sense of inferiority to the Royal Navy but had no direct, immediate effect on Napoleon's land campaigns on the European continent or the direction of the war. Nevertheless, Napoleon began to build a new navy to replace the losses sustained at Trafalgar, allowing France to continue posing a naval threat to Britain. At the same time, the battle and continuing British naval superiority contributed to Napoleon's decision to impose the Continental System on continental Europe in 1806, which aimed to block British trade. For that system to work, Napoleon had to force compliance with it in Russia and then in the Iberian Peninsula.

Spain was the most seriously injured participant in the battle. The loss of the Spanish Navy at Trafalgar made it impossible for Spain to maintain imperial control over her colonies in the Americas. Without a navy, Spanish colonies lost the connection to their metropole and independence movements were facilitated across Latin America. Defeat at Trafalgar contributed to the collapse of the already declining Bourbon monarchy in Spain. An agrarian crisis, combined with the French invasion, led to a revolt in 1808, creating an opportunity for Britain to deploy an army ashore that the Royal Navy could support logistically by sea. All this combined to develop a long-term national sense of Spain's decline that reached its nadir nearly a century later in the Spanish-American War of 1898.

Counterfactually, if the Franco-Spanish fleet had won the battle and destroyed Nelson and Collingwood's squadrons to a similar degree to what the British had done, it would neither have ended the war nor made the Royal Navy powerless. It would have seriously damaged British access to the Mediterranean and limited her freedom of the seas to trade in southern Europe, thereby damaging her economy. As it happened, the battle safeguarded British trade in the wider world, thereby supporting the continuing growth of the British war economy. Although the British victory at Trafalgar was not decisive in terms of the broader aspects of the war, it became an essential step in the cumulative and sequential naval strategies that eventually led to Napoleon's defeat.[123]

In the case of the Battle of Trafalgar, there is more to its significance than its tactical and strategic roles during the Napoleonic Wars. The new social and cultural histories have reinforced John Ehrman's point in the 1960s that naval history is a slice of the many-layered cake of national history. The navies at Trafalgar reflected their nations in all their strengths and weaknesses. As cultural and social historians have also pointed out, it is equally, if not more, important to consider the multiple roles that Trafalgar plays in the cultural afterlife that has developed around its memory and commemoration. For the French, Napoleon's victories on land dominated national memory. The Battle of Trafalgar is often overlooked, except for fascination with the French success in killing the great hero, Horatio Nelson, in combat.

In contrast, for Spain, it is the story of glorious defeat as some of the Spanish Navy's most famous officers fought against overwhelming odds. At the same time, it is a key part of the tragedy of Spain's imperial decline, which spans the nineteenth century. For the British, it is an epic story of sacrifice to duty as Nelson, dying at the moment of victory, utters his last words, 'Thank God, I have done my duty.' In this, there are clear cultural parallels to the Passion of Christ, the legendary sacrifice of Leonidas and his three hundred Spartans at Thermopylae to turn back the Persian invaders, and the enduring iconic stories of leaders who have fallen in battle, such as King Gustavus Adolphus of Sweden at the Battle of Lützen in 1632 or Britain's own General James Wolfe, who died at Quebec in 1756.[124]

Beyond Trafalgar's role in the separate national histories, there is a global dimension to Trafalgar's influence on naval culture worldwide. The story of the Battle of Trafalgar is inseparable from that of Admiral Horatio Lord Nelson. His legacy is much more than that of a British hero or a fleet commander who won a famous battle. He was a successful, humane, and beloved leader and one who thought innovatively about how to fight a naval battle effectively.

Even though navies today bear little resemblance to those in the age of fighting sail, Nelson remains a shared icon and a universal embodiment of the key virtues for a naval professional—Honor, Courage, and Commitment.

NOTES

Chapter 1

1. Andrew Roberts, *Napoleon: A Life* (New York: Viking, 2014), p. x.
2. Kenneth G. Johnson, 'Napoleon's War at Sea', in Michal Leggiere, ed., *Napoleon and the Operational Art of War* (Leiden: Brill, 2016), pp. 387–475, at p. 396.
3. 'Villeneuve est un misérable qu'il faut chasser ignominieusement. Sans combinasions, sans courage, sans intérêt general, il sacrifierait tout, pour qu'il sauve sa peau. Rien n'est comparable à l'ineptie de Villeneuve.' Quoted in Michèle Battesti, *Trafalgar: Les aléas de la stratégie naval de Napoleon* (Saint-Cloud: Fayard, 2004), p. 199, from *Correspondence de Napoléon 1er publiée par l'ordre de l'Empereur Napoléon III* (Paris: Imprimerie nationale, 1858–69), no. 9179, to Decrès, 4 September 1805.
4. Paraphrased from Decrès to Villeneuve, 14 Fructidor, An XIII [1 September 1805]: 'Sa Majesté veit éteindre cette circonspection qu'elle reproche à sa marine, ce système de defensive qui tue l'audace et qui double celle de l'ennemi. Cette audace, elle la veut dans tous ses amiraux, ses capitaines, officiers et marins, et, quelle que soit l'issue, elle promet sa considération et ses graces à ceux qui sauront la porter àl'excès, ne pas hésiter à attaquer des forces supérieures ou égales même, et avoir avec elle des combat d'extermination, voilà ce que veut Sa Majesté, elle compte pour rien la perte de ses vaisseaux, si elle les perd avec gloire; elle ne veut plus que ses escadres soient bloquées par un ennemi inférieur, et s'il se presente de cette manière devant Cadix, elle vous recommande et vous ordonne de ne pas hésiter à l'attaquer.' Quoted in Rémi Monaque, *Trafalgar: 21 octobre 1805* (Paris: Bibliothèque Napoléonienne, 2005), p. 226, from Service Historique de la Marine Vincennes, BB^4 230.
5. Monaque, *Trafalgar*, p. 227; Agustín Rodríguez González, 'The Spanish at Trafalgar: Ships, Cannon, Men and a Problematic Alliance', *Journal for Maritime Research*, vol. 7, no. 1 (2005), pp. 26–43.
6. Monaque, *Trafalgar*, pp. 65–85, 99. See also Rémi Monaque, *Latouche-Tréville 1745–1804): l'amiral qui défiait Nelson* (Paris: Éditions S.P.M.), 2000.
7. Quoted in Monaque, *Trafalgar*, p. 78, from Decrès to Napoleon, 14 Fructidor, An XII, from Archives National, AF IV 1210.

8. Rémi Monaque, 'Leadership in the French Navy during the Revolution and Empire: The Optimist and the Pessimist: Louis-René de Latouche-Tréville (1745–1804) and Pierre Charles de Villeneuve (1763–1806)', in Richard Harding and Agustín Guimerá, eds., *Naval Leadership in the Atlantic World: The Age of Reform and Revolution, 1700–1850* (London: University of Westminster Press, 2017), pp. 99–106.
9. Thanks to Ken Johnson for making these points on an early draft.
10. Battesti, *Trafalgar*, p. 92.
11. Ibid., p. 99.
12. Rodríguez González, 'The Spanish at Trafalgar', pp. 26–43; Paul W. Schroeder, *The Transformation of European Politics, 1763–1848* (Oxford: Clarendon Press, 1994), p. 257; N. A. M. Rodger, *The Command of the Ocean: A Naval History of Britain, 1649–1815* (London: Allen Lane, 2005), pp. 531–2.
13. 'Eh!, quelle triste perspective de faire battre les peuples pour qu'ils se battent! Le monde est aussi grand pour que nos deux nations puissent y vivre, et la raison a assez de puissance pour qu'on trouve les moyens de tout concilier, si de part et d'autre on en a la volonté.' Napoleon to George III, King of England, Paris, 11 Nivôse, An XIII [1 January 1805], Napoléon Bonaparte, *Correspondence générale*, vol. V: *Boulogne, Trafalgar, Austerlitz, 1805* (Paris: Fayard for the Foundation Napoléon, 2008), p. 21, Lettre 9484.
14. 'Il n'est pas juste ni conséquent que l'Espagne possède des meilleures colonies de l'Europe si elle ne veut ni montrer de l'énergie ni mettre en état des escadres.' Napoleon to Charles IV, King of Spain, 12 Nivôse, An XIII [2 January 1805]. Bonaparte, *Correspondance générale*, V, p. 23, Lettre 9486.
15. Napoléon to Decrès, 14 Nivôse, An XIII [4 January 1805]. Bonaparte, *Correspondance générale*, V, p. 24, Lettre 9488.
16. Julian S. Corbett, *The Campaign of Trafalgar* (London: Longmans, Green and Co., 1910), pp. 27–31; Battesti, *Trafalgar*, pp. 101–2.
17. Quoted in Roger Knight, *The Pursuit of Victory: The Life and Achievement of Horatio Nelson* (London: Allen Lane, 2005), p. 448.
18. Battesti, *Trafalgar*, p. 103; Monaque, *Trafalgar*, p. 90.
19. Knight, *Pursuit of Victory*, pp. 479–83.
20. 'Il était impossible de manoeuvrer, de là des vergues cassée, des voiles emportées, car toutes nos avaries, il y a bien autant de fautes de maladresse ou d'inexpérience que de défauts de qualité des objets délivrés par les arsenaux.' Quoted in Monaque, *Trafalgar*, pp. 91–2, at p. 92, from Villeneuve to Decrès, 2 Pluviôse, An XIII, Service Historique de la Defense, Vincennes, BB[4] 230.
21. Napoléon to Ganteaume and Napoléon to Villeneuve, 11 Ventôse, An XIII [2 March 1805], Bonaparte, *Correspondance générale*, V, pp. 92–4, 96–7, Lettres 9619, 9620, 9623.
22. Monaque, *Trafalgar*, pp. 96–9; Battesti, *Trafalgar*, pp. 109–22; René Monaque, 'La stratégie maritime de Napoléon en 1805', in Bonaparte, *Correspondance*

générale, V, pp. 1001–5; Jean-Claude Gillet, *La marine impériale: le grand rêve de Napoléon* ([Paris]: Bernard Giovanangeli, 2010), pp. 251–8.

23. Jan Glete, *Navies and Nations: Warships, Navies and State Building in Europe and America, 1500–1860*, 2 vols. (Stockholm: Almqvist & Wiksell, 1993), vol. 1, pp. 272, 276, 313.
24. Roger Knight, 'The Fleets at Trafalgar: The Margin of Superiority', in David Cannadine, ed., *Trafalgar in History: A Battle and its Afterlife* (Basingstoke: Palgrave Macmillan, 2005), p. 62; Jan Glete, *Navies and Nations: Warships, Navies and State Building in Europe and America, 1500–1860*, 2 vols. (Stockholm: Almqvist & Wiksell, 1993), vol. 1, pp. 272, 276, 313; Carla Rahn Phillips, '"The Life Blood of the Navy": Recruiting Sailors in Eighteenth Century Spain', *The Mariner's Mirror*, vol. 87, no. 4 (2001), pp. 420–45, at pp. 439–41; Gillet, *La marine impériale*, pp.16, 19.
25. Knight, 'The Fleets at Trafalgar', pp. 61–77; Roger Knight, *Britain against Napoleon: The Organization of Victory, 1793–1815* (London: Allen Lane, 2013), pp. 351–85.
26. The warships included in the first graph are rated warships, ranging from first rates of 100 guns to sixth-rate frigates of 20 guns. Sloops and other vessels with 18 guns or less are not included. There is no data for September 1804, so that month is omitted. The second graph of ships of the line displays the numbers of first rates through third rates, including ships with 100, 98, 90, and 74 guns. The data is drawn from TNA, ADM 8/87–90: Admiralty List Books. I am grateful to Roger Knight for providing me with the raw data that he used in constructing the graphs for his 'The Fleets at Trafalgar' in David Cannadine, ed., *Trafalgar in History*, p. 73.
27. Corbett, *Campaign of Trafalgar*, pp. 25–6.
28. Monaque, *Trafalgar*, pp. 93–4; Battesti, *Trafalgar*, pp. 148–9.
29. Battesti, *Trafalgar*, p. 124.
30. 'Une victoire navale dans cette circonstance ne conduire à rien. N'ayez qu'un seul but, celui de remplir votre mission. Sortez sans combat. Ce qui doit vous joindre est parti.' Napoléon to Ganteaume, La Malmaison, 2 Germinal, An XIII [23 mars 1805], Bonaparte, *Correspondance générale*, V, p. 154, Lettre 9732.
31. Battesti, *Trafalgar*, pp. 124–5; Monaque, *Trafalgar*, pp. 100–1; Quintin Barry, *Far Distant Ships: The Royal Navy and the Blockade of Brest, 1793–1815* (Solihull: Helion & Co., 2018), p. 254; Paul C. Krajeski, *In the Shadow of Nelson: The Naval Leadership of Admiral Sir Charles Cotton, 1753–1812* (Westport, CT: Greenwood Press, 2000), p. 40. John Leyland, ed., *Dispatches and Letters Relating to the Blockade of Brest, 1803–1805*, Publications of the Navy Records Society, vols. 14, 21 (London: Navy Records Society, 1899, 1902), vol. 2, pp. 199–224.
32. Battesti, *Trafalgar*, pp. 125–6; Monaque, *Trafalgar*, pp. 102–6; Knight, *Pursuit of Victory*, p. 483; John Sugden, *Nelson: The Sword of Albion* (London: Bodley Head, 2012), p. 735.
33. Nelson to Alexander Ball, 6 April 1805, quoted in Sugden, *Nelson*, p. 736.
34. Sugden, *Nelson*, pp. 735–6.

35. Sugden, *Nelson*, pp. 736–7; J. Ross Dancy and Evan Wilson, 'Sir John Orde and the Trafalgar Campaign: A Failure of Information Sharing', *Naval War College Review*, vol. 73, no. 2 (Spring 2020), pp. 141–71. For a biography of Orde, see Kathrin Orth, 'Sir John Order 1751–1824', in Peter LeFevre and Richard Harding, eds., *British Admirals of the Napoleonic Wars: The Contemporaries of Nelson* (London; Chatham Publishing, 2005), pp. 67–89 and 'Orde, Sir John, First Baronet (1751–1824)', *Oxford Dictionary of National Biography* https://oxfordindex.oup.com/view/10.1093/ref:odnb/20810.
36. Battesti, *Trafalgar*, p. 126; Monaque, *Trafalgar*, p. 105.
37. Dancy and Wilson, 'Sir John Orde and the Trafalgar Campaign', pp. 154–6.
38. 'Estado de ferza de la escuadra del mando del Exmo. Señor D. Federico Gravina…'. José Ignacio González-Aller Hierro, ed., *La campaña de Trafalgar (1804–1805): corpus documental conservado en los archivos españoles* (Madrid: Ministerio de Defensa, Armada Española, 2004), vol. 1, p. 545.
39. Battesti, *Trafalgar*, p. 127; Monaque, *Trafalgar*, pp. 105–6.
40. Monaque, *Trafalgar*, pp. 111–12.
41. Monaque, *Trafalgar*, pp. 114–15; Napoleon to Villeneuve, 24 Germinal, An XIII [14 April 1805], Bonaparte, *Correspondence générale*, V, pp. 207–28, Lettre 9842.
42. Vivian Stuart and George T. Eggleston, *His Majesty's Sloop-of-War Diamond Rock* (London: Robert Hale Ltd, 1978), pp. 133–49.
43. Monaque, *Trafalgar*, p. 116.
44. Rodger, *The Command of the Ocean*, pp. 534–5; James Davey, *In Nelson's Wake: The Navy and the Napoleonic Wars* (New Haven: Yale University Press, 2015), p. 84; John E. Talbot, *The Pen & Ink Sailor: Charles Middleton and the King's Navy, 1778–1813* (London: Frank Cass, 1998), pp. 149–50.
45. Piers Mackesy, *The War in the Mediterranean, 1803–1810* (Cambridge, MA: Harvard University Press, 1957), pp. 64–5; Knight, *Pursuit of Victory*, pp. 488, 489, 493; Sugden, *Nelson*, p. 739.
46. Sugden, *Nelson*, pp. 739–42; Jim Tildesley, 'The Influence of the Theories of John Clerk of Eldin on British Fleet Tactics, 1782–1805', *Mariner's Mirror*, vol. 106, no. 2 (May 2020), pp. 162–74; Brian Tunstall, *Naval Warfare in the Age of Sail: The Evolution of Fighting Tactics, 1650–1815*, edited by Dr Nicholas Tracy (Annapolis: Naval Institute Press, 1990), pp. 240–59. See also Michel Depeyre, *Tactiques et stratégies navales de la France et du Royaume-Uni de 1690 à 1815* (Paris: Economica, 1998), pp. 165–93; and Sam Willis, *Fighting at Sea in the Eighteenth Century: The Art of Sailing Warfare* (Woodbridge: Boydell, 2008).
47. Knight, *Pursuit of Victory*, p. 492; Sugden, *Nelson*, pp. 742–3; Desbrière, *Trafalgar*, vol. 1, pp. 54–5.
48. Rif Winfield, *British Warships in the Age of Sail, 1793–1817: Design, Construction, Careers and Fates* (London: Chatham Publishing and St Paul, MN: MBI Publishing, 2005), pp. 226, 386. The only other known 100 per cent loss was a Baltic convoy that Danish gunboats captured in 1810.

49. Monaque, *Trafalgar*, pp. 116–18, 121; Desbrière, *Trafalgar*, vol. 1, p. 34.
50. Knight, *Pursuit of Victory*, p. 493; Sugden, *Nelson*, pp. 744–5; Desbrière, *Trafalgar*, vol. 1, pp. 57–61.
51. John Knox Laughton, ed., *Letters and Papers of Charles, Lord Barham, Admiral of the Red Squadron, 1758–1813* (London, 1911), vol. 3, pp. xiv–xv.
52. Laughton, ed., *Barham Papers*, vol. 3, pp. 258–9: L.C.A. to Admiral Cornwallis, 9 July 1805; Knight, *Pursuit of Victory*, p. 495; Corbett, *Campaign of Trafalgar*, pp. 196–204.
53. Desbrière, *Trafalgar*, vol. 1, pp. 70–1; Barry, *Far Distant Ships*, pp. 264–6.
54. Corbett, *Campaign of Trafalgar*, pp. 217–25, gives the losses as British 41 killed, 158 wounded; Spanish 111 killed, 246 wounded; French 44 killed 95 wounded; Monaque, *Trafalgar*, p. 127, gives the losses as French 44 killed and 95 wounded, Spanish 11 killed and 21 wounded, but notes that these figures do not include the battle losses from the two ships that the British captured: *Firme*, 180 killed, 40 wounded; *San Rafael*: 20 killed, 80 wounded. Battesti, *Trafalgar*, p. 167 gives the French losses as 65 killed and 144 wounded and the Spanish casualties as 17 dead and 35 wounded.
55. Corbett, *Campaign of Trafalgar*, pp. 225–8; Monaque, *Trafalgar*, pp. 128–9; Battesti, *Trafalgar*, p. 127.
56. Corbett, *Campaign of Trafalgar*, map between pp. 204–5, 234–5; Knight, *Pursuit of Victory*, map on pp. 489–90.
57. Monaque, *Trafalgar*, pp. 130–5; Battesti, *Trafalgar*, p. 127.
58. Corbett, *Campaign of Trafalgar*, pp. 235–41; Monaque, *Trafalgar*, pp. 135–9.
59. Villeneuve to Decrès, 22 August 1805, quoted in Battesti, *Trafalgar*, p. 185.
60. Battesti, *Trafalgar*, pp. 184–5; Monaque, *Trafalgar*, p. 140; Desbrière, *Trafalgar*, vol. 1, p. 131.
61. Desbrière, *Trafalgar*, vol. 1, pp. 138–9.
62. Quoted in Battesti, *Trafalgar*, p. 188, from Jean Grivel, *Mémoires du vice-amiral baron Grivel. Révolution. Empire* (Paris: Plon Nourrit, 1914), p. 91.
63. Schroeder, *The Transformation of European Politics*, pp. 260–6; Alexander Mikaberidze, *The Napoleonic Wars: A Global History* (New York: Oxford University Press, 2020), p. 208; Sten Carlsson, *Den svenska utrikes politikens historia* (Stockholm: Norstedts, 1954), vol. 3.1: *1792–1810*, pp. 96–9.

Chapter 2

1. González-Aller Hierro, ed., *La campaña de Trafalgar*, vol. 1, pp. 835–6.
2. Corbett, *Campaign of Trafalgar*, pp. 269–70; Desbrière, *Trafalgar*, vol. 1, pp. 142–3; Edward Hughes, ed., *The Private Correspondence of Admiral Lord Collingwood*, Publications of the Navy Records Society, vol. 98 (London: Navy Records Society, 1957), pp. 161–3: Collingwood to his sister, 26 August 1805; G. L. Newnham Collingwood, ed., *A Selection from the Public and Private*

Correspondence of Vice-Admiral Lord Collingwood (London: James Ridgway, 1829), pp. 109–10: Collingwood to his wife, 21 August 1805. Sir James Gambier was a former army officer and a son of Vice-Admiral James Gambier (1723–89), as well as a cousin of Admiral Lord Gambier.

3. Desbrière, *Trafalgar*, vol. 1, pp. 146, note 3, 156.
4. Corbett, *Campaign of Trafalgar*, pp. 272–9; Desbrière, *Trafalgar*, vol. 1, pp. 144–57.
5. Laughton, ed., *Barham Papers*, vol. 3, pp. 312–15: Barham to Pitt with Enclosure and draft instructions to Nelson, 4 September 1805. This term is an early professional naval use of the phrase 'sea power', which is often attributed to A. T. Mahan, who popularized it in the 1890s.
6. Sugden, *Nelson*, pp. 764–5; Laughton, ed., *Barham Papers*, vol. 3, pp. 319–23: Bickerton to Barham, 4 October 1805; Nelson to Marsden, 6 October 1805; Monaque, 'La stratégie maritime de Napoléon en 1805', in Bonaparte, *Correspondence générale*, V, pp. 1001–5.
7. 'L'existence d'une squadron si considerable à Toulon aura des résultats incalculables; elle me fera une puissante diversion. Voilà le parti le plus utile que je puisse tirer de cette escadre dans ses circonstances', Napoléon to Vice-Amiral Decrès, Saint Cloud, 28 Fructidor, An XIII [15 September 1805], Bonaparte, *Correspondance générale*, V, p. 693, lettre 10,803. On the concept of the fleet in being, see Hattendorf, 'The Idea of the Fleet in Being in Historical Perspective', *Naval War College Review*, vol. 67, no. 1 (Winter 2014), pp. 43–60.
8. 'comme son pussillanimité l'empèchera de l'entreprendre', Napoléon to Vice-Amiral Decrès, Saint Cloud, 28 Fructidor, An XIII [15 September 1805], Bonaparte, *Correspondance générale*, V, p. 693, lettre 10,803.
9. Battesti, *Trafalgar*, pp. 201–3; Monaque, *Trafalgar*, p. 228.
10. Monaque, *Trafalgar*, pp. 222–3; Agustín Guimerá, 'Trafalgar: Myth and History', in Richard Harding, ed., *A Great and Glorious Victory: New Perspectives on the Battle of Trafalgar* (Barnsley: Seaforth, 2008), p. 43.
11. Battesti, *Trafalgar*, pp. 210–12; Monaque, *Trafalgar*, pp. 223–5; Lauriston to the emperor, 3 Fructidor, An XIII [21 August 1805], in Desbrière, *Trafalgar*, vol. 2, pp. 113–17; Guimerá, 'Trafalgar: Myth and History', p. 46.
12. Desbrière, *Trafalgar*, vol. 1, pp. 159–60; Napoleon to Vice-Amiral Rosily-Mesros, 30 Fructidor, An XIII [4 September 1805]: Bonaparte, *Correspondance Générale*, V, p. 708, lettre 10,829.
13. Villeneuve to Decrès, 8 October 1805. Desbrière, *Trafalgar*, vol. 2, pp. 104–5.
14. Minutes of Council of War, 8 October 1805. Desbrière, *Trafalgar*, vol. 2, pp. 105–7; Guimerá, 'Trafalgar: Myth and History', p. 49; Agustín Guimera, 'Gravina y el liderazgo naval de su tiempo', in Agustín Guimerá and Alberto Ramos y Gonzao Butrón, eds., *Trafalgar y el mundo atlántico* (Madrid: Marcial Pons Historia, 2005), pp. 233–56.
15. Michael Duffy, '... All Was Hushed Up: The Hidden Trafalgar', *The Mariner's Mirror*, vol. 91, no. 2 (May 2005), p. 218.

16. Vice-Admiral Lord Nelson's memorandum on how he proposed to fight the battle, 9 October 1805: John Hattendorf et al., eds., *British Naval Documents, 1204–1960*, Publications of the Navy Records Society, vol. 131 (Aldershot: Scolar Press for the Navy Records Society, 1993), pp. 424–6. See also Knight, *Pursuit of Victory*, pp. 505–8.
17. Villeneuve's final instructions, 29 Vendémiaire, An XIV [21 October 1805]: Desbrière, *Trafalgar*, vol. 2, pp. 129–33, quotation on p. 131.
18. Ibid.
19. Villeneuve to Decrès, 26 Vendémiaire, An XIV: Monaque, *Trafalgar*, pp. 232, quoted from SHM BB[4]230; English translation in Desbrière, *Trafalgar*, vol. 2, p. 182.
20. Napoleon to Villeneuve, 27 Fructidor, An XIII [4 September 1805]: Bonaparte, *Correspondance générale*, V, p. 690, lettre 10,797.
21. 'Log of Euryalus, 19 October 1805', in Sir Thomas Sturges Jackson, ed., *Logs of the Great Sea Fights, 1794–1805*, vol. 2, Publications of the Navy Records Society, vol. 18 (London, 1900), p. 145; Michael Duffy, *Touch and Take: The Battle of Trafalgar, 21 October 1805* (Shelton, Nottinghamshire, 2005), pp. 114–16.
22. Adkin, *Trafalgar Companion*, pp. 468–84; Battesti, *Trafalgar*, p. 238; Desbrière, *Trafalgar*, vol. 2, p. 138; Duffy, *Touch and Take*, p. 16; Knight, *Pursuit of Victory*, p. 511; Monaque, *Trafalgar*, pp. 236–7.
23. Agustín R. Rodríguez González, *Trafalgar y el conflicto naval Anglo-Español del siglo XVIII* (Madrid: Actas, 2005).
24. Battesti, *Trafalgar*, p. 239; Desbrière, *Trafalgar*, vol. 2, p. 138; Monaque, *Trafalgar*, pp. 237–8.
25. Robert Gardiner, 'Small Three-Deckers: A Second-Rate Solution', in F. Fernández-González, L. D. Ferreiro, and H. Nowacki, eds., *Technology of the Ships of Trafalgar* (Madrid: Escuela Técnica Superior de Ingenieros Navales, Universidad Politécnica de Madrid, 2006), pp. 16–112.
26. 'L'avantage de 3 vaisseaux à trois ponts contre une escadre qui n'avait pas équivaut à une différence de 8 vaisseaux, tous accoutumés à la mer et parfaitement exercés.' Napoléon to Ministre of Police Fouché, 21 Thermidor, An XIII [9 August 1805]: Bonaparte, *Correspondance générale*, V, p. 552, lettre 10,539.
27. Knight, *Pursuit of Victory*, pp. 512–13, quoting statistics from Goodwin, *Ships of Trafalgar*, p. 257; Adkin, *Trafalgar Companion*, 'The Trafalgar Fleets: A Balance Sheet', pp. 299–306; Rodríguez González, 'The Spanish at Trafalgar', pp. 26–43.
28. Villeneuve to Decrès, 15 November 1805: Desbrière, *Trafalgar*, vol. 2, p. 138.
29. Rodríguez González, *Trafalgar y el conflicto naval*, pp. 388–9.
30. For a discussion of whether the signal included the words 'the end of' as recorded in *Euryalus*'s log, see Duffy, 'Touch and Take', p. 22.
31. 'Log of *Euryalus*, 21 October 1805', in Jackson, ed., *Logs of the Great Sea Fights*, vol. 2, pp. 149–50.
32. Jackson, ed., *Logs of the Great Sea Fights*, vol. 2, pp. 149–50, 168.

33. Report of M. C.-C. Rigodit: Desbrière, *Trafalgar*, vol. 2, p. 175. He meant that the line curved away from the approaching British ships.
34. Report of Villeneuve: Desbrière, *Trafalgar*, vol. 2, p. 139.
35. Ibid.
36. William Beatty, M.D., *Authentic Narrative of the Death of Lord Nelson: Comprising Several Interesting Circumstances Preceding, Attending and Subsequent to, that Event*, 3rd edition (London: W. Mason, 1825), p. 28.
37. Duffy, *Touch and Take*, pp. 22–3; Adkin, *Trafalgar Companion*, pp. 483–6; Jackson, ed., *Logs of the Great Sea Fights*, vol. 2, pp. 168, 184–5, 197–8; James, *Naval History*, vol. 4, pp. 38–9.
38. Great Britain. Admiralty. Committee on Tactics of Nelson at Battle of Trafalgar. Navy (Trafalgar): *Report of a committee appointed by the Admiralty to examine and consider the evidence relating to the tactics employed by Nelson at the battle of Trafalgar.* Cd. 7120 (London, 1913), pp. xiii–xiv; Jackson, ed., *Logs of the Great Sea Fights*, vol. 2, pp. 149–50; Adkin, *Trafalgar Companion*, pp. 483–6; Taylor, 'Some New Aspects', p. 697; Duffy, 'All Was Hushed Up', p. 219.
39. Duffy, 'All Was Hushed Up', pp. 229, 232.
40. Adkin, *Trafalgar Companion*, p. 486.
41. Quoted in Michael Duffy, 'The Gunnery at Trafalgar: Training, Tactics or Temperament?', *Journal for Maritime Research*, vol. 7, no. 1 (2005), pp. 140–69, from Edward Fraser, *The Sailors Whom Nelson Led* (London: Methuen, 1913), p. 257.
42. Duffy, 'All Was Hushed Up', pp. 220, 234; Duffy, 'The Gunnery at Trafalgar', pp. 140–69.
43. The Inshore Squadron (Mark Barker, Alison Barker, Tony Gray, Malcolm Smalley), 'The Reconstruction of Trafalgar', in Harding, ed., *A Great and Glorious Victory*, pp. 16–18; Duffy, 'The Gunnery at Trafalgar', pp. 140–69.
44. Inshore Squadron, 'Reconstruction of Trafalgar', p. 20; Desbrière, *Trafalgar*, vol. 2, pp. 211–21: 'Report of Captain Lucas, Commanding the Redoubtable'.
45. Michael Duffy, 'Trafalgar: Myth and Reality', in Harding, *A Great and Glorious Victory*, p. 64.
46. Inshore Squadron, 'Reconstruction of Trafalgar', p. 20; Desbrière, *Trafalgar*, vol. 2, pp. 137–41: Report of Villeneuve, pp. 191–6: 'Report of Captain Magendie, Commanding the Bucentaure'.
47. Duffy, *Touch and Take*, p. 33; Adkin, *Trafalgar Companion*, p. 524.
48. Inshore Squadron, 'Reconstruction of Trafalgar', p. 21; Jackson, ed., *Logs of the Great Sea Fights*, vol. 2, pp. 203–4: journal—Vice-Admiral Collingwood; Guimerá, 'Trafalgar: Myth and History', p. 54.
49. Desbrière, *Trafalgar*, vol. 2, pp. 159–65; report of Rear-Admiral Dumanoir le Pelley, quote at p. 164; Inshore Squadron, 'Reconstruction of Trafalgar', pp. 26–7; Jackson, ed., *Logs of the Great Sea Fights*, vol. 2, pp. 279–80: Log of Orion.
50. Adkin, *Trafalgar Companion*, p. 524; Duffy, 'All Was Hushed Up', p. 235.
51. Desbrière, *Trafalgar*, vol. 2, p. 246: report of Commandeur Le Tourneur.

52. Desbrière, *Trafalgar*, vol. 2, p. 254: extract from the journal of Lieutenant Philibert, Magon's flag-lieutenant.
53. Desbrière, *Trafalgar*, vol. 2, pp. 418–42: Gravina's staff journal; log of *Principe de Asturias*, pp. 426–7; vol. 2, parte IV, pp. 1636–9 ; Goodwin, *Ships of Trafalgar*, pp. 212–14; Agustín Guimerá Ravina, 'Antonio Escaño, un héroe Olvidado', *La Aventura de la Historia*, vol. 7, no. 84 (Octubre 2005), pp. 66–71.
54. The statistics in the table are from Monaque, 'Trafalgar: A French View', in Harding, ed., *A Great and Glorious Victory*, p. 77. While there is consensus on British losses, there is no consensus on the exact number of French and Spanish casualties. Alternative statistics: Adkin, *Trafalgar Companion*, pp. 522–4, gives French killed 1,425, French wounded, 1,410, French drowned 2,296 for an overall total of 5,133 French casualties; Spanish killed 1,033, Spanish wounded 1,371, Spanish drowned 400 estimated for an overall total of 2,804 Spanish casualties, making an allied total of 7,935 casualties; British killed 458, British wounded 1,208. González-Aller Hierro, ed., *La campaña de Trafalgar*, vol. 2, Anexo 6, pp. 1380–1, gives Spanish killed 1,056 and Spanish wounded 1,385, Anexo 7, pp. 1382–3, provides French figures supplied by Monaque: French killed and drowned 3,499, French wounded 1,138, French prisoners held in Great Britain 2,200, French prisoners freed, 400. Battesti, *Trafalgar*, p. 286, gives French killed or drowned 3,370, French wounded 1,160; Spanish killed 1,038, Spanish wounded 1,385. Desbrière, *Trafalgar*, vol. 1, pp. 295–301, gives British killed 449; British wounded 1,214; approximate French losses: 3,370 French killed or drowned, 1,160 French wounded; Spanish officers killed or drowned 34, Spanish officers wounded 5, Spanish men killed or drowned 1,004, Spanish men wounded, 1,327; Duffy, *Touch and Take*, pp. 33–5, gives 458 British killed and 1,241 wounded for a total of 1,699; approximately 1,025 Spanish killed and 1,383 wounded; 3,370 French killed and 1,160 wounded, and some 4,000–5,000 taken prisoner.
55. Knight, *Pursuit of Victory*, p. 518 note; Sugden, *Nelson*, vol. 2, p. 831.
56. French and Spanish accounts differ in giving credit for the leadership in this event. See, for example, Guimerá Ravina, 'Antonio Escaño', p. 71; and Battesti, *Trafalgar*, pp. 291–2.
57. Jackson, ed., *Logs of the Great Sea Fights*, vol. 2, pp. 154–9: log of *Euryalus*; Knight, *Pursuit of Victory*, p. 522; Dennis Wheeler, 'The Weather of the European Atlantic Seaboard during October 1805: An Exercise in Historical Climatology', *Climate Change*, vol. 48 (2001), pp. 361–85. The Beaufort Scale was invented in 1805, but it was not used at Trafalgar. Its categories and descriptions have changed over time. The author cited here uses the modern terms in which Force 10 is a storm or whole gale with winds of 55–63 mph or 89–109 km/h, and a Force 11 is a violent storm with winds from 64 to 72 mph or 103–17 km/h; Guimerá Ravina, 'Antonio Escaño', pp. 66–71.
58. Roy Adkins, *Nelson's Trafalgar: The Battle that Changed the World* (New York: Viking Penguin, 2005), pp. 250–3.

59. Peter Hore, *HMS Pickle: The Swiftest Ship in Nelson's Trafalgar Fleet* (Stroud: The History Press, 2005), pp. 101–13; Jackson, ed., *Logs of the Great Sea Fights*, vol. 2, pp. 208–9: Collingwood's journal for 30 October 1805.
60. Desbrière, *Trafalgar*, vol. 2, pp. 334–44, 362–3: reports of Rear Admiral Dumanoir le Pelley and Sir Richard Strachan; 'Sir Richard Strachan's Dispatches', *Naval Chronicle*, vol. 14 (1805), pp. 426–7; Bartlett Library Researchers, National Maritime Museum, Cornwall, 'Gilding the Gingerbread: Sir Richard Strachan's Action, 3 November 1805' (2005), https://web.archive.org/web/20060928025209/http://www.nmmc.co.uk/images/uploaded/downloads/Trafalgar_Strachan.pdf.
61. Rif Winfield, *British Warships in the Age of Sail, 1793–1817* (London: Chatham Publishing, 2005), pp. 34, 86–7.
62. Monaque, 'Trafalgar: A French View', pp. 77–8.

Chapter 3

1. *The Examiner*, no. 15 (2–9 November 1710), p. 2, col. 1.
2. González-Aller Hierro, ed., *La campaña de Trafalgar*, vol. 2, pp. 1042–3, Document 971: Moreno to Prince of Peace, 22 October 1805.
3. Tim Clayton and Phil Craig, *Trafalgar: The Men, the Battle, the Storm* (London: Hodder & Stoughton, 2004), p. 363.
4. *Mercurio de España*, 15 Dicembre 1805, pp. 337 [25]–342 [30].
5. David G. Chandler, *The Campaigns of Napoleon: The Mind and Methods of History's Greatest Soldier* (New York: Macmillan, 1966), pp. 406–9.
6. 'Je reçoit votre lettre relative au combat de Cadix. J'attends les détails ultérieurs que vous m'annoncez avant de me former une opinion décisive sur la nature de cette affaire. En attendant, je m'empresse de vous faire connaître une que cela ne change rien à mes projets de croisières; je suis même fâché que tout ne soit pas prêt. Il faut qu'elles partent sans délai. Faites venir, par terre, toutes les troupes de terre qui sont à bord de l'escadre, elles attendront mes ordres à la première ville de France.' Napoléon to Decrès, Znaim, 27 Brumaire an XIV [18 Novembre 1805]. Bonaparte, *Correspondance générale*, V, p. 860. Lettre 11120.
7. 'Je ne puis être partout!' quoted in Battesti, *Trafalgar*, p. 302, from Joseph Fouché, *Mémoires de Fouché, duc du Otrante* (Paris: Imprimerie Nationale, 1992), p. 230.
8. Battesti, *Trafalgar*, pp. 301–2; Schroder, *Transformation of European Politics*, pp. 282, 284, 289.
9. 'Angleterre, 18 Novembre', *Le Journal de l'Empire*, 1 Décembre 1805, p. 1.
10. Battesti, *Trafalgar*, p. 302; Clayton and Craig, *Trafalgar*, p. 363.
11. Clayton and Craig, *Trafalgar*, p. 363.
12. *Le Journal de l'Empire*, 13 January 1806, p. 1.

13. 'Pendant 50 jours on a hésité si l'amputation de ses bras se serait ou non; il est enfin décidé qu'ils les conservera tous deux, ces bras dont il sait si bien se servir pour l'honneur de notre pavillon et l'exemple de nos marins.' *Le Journal de l'Empire*, 19 January 1806, p. 1.
14. 'Si tous mes vaisseaux s'étaient conduit comme ceux que vous commandiez, la victoire n'aurait été incertaine.' *Le Journal de l'Empire*, 6 May 1806, p. 2.
15. 'Je sais qu'il en est plusieurs qui ne vous ont pas imités, j'ai ordonné que des renseignements fussent recueillis à le regard. Les capitaines de vaisseaux qui, au lieu d'aborder l'ennemi, se sont tenus hors de la portée du canon, seront poursuivi, et s'il y a lieu, il en sera fait un exemple éclatant.' *Le Journal de l'Empire*, 6 May 1806, p. 2.
16. 'Aujourd'hui M. Pitt s'aperçoit qu'en se faisant une affaire personnelle de cette guerre, il est devenu personnellement responsable de tous les événements; tous les défaites sont tombées sur lui; l'humiliation le poursuit; et son nom qui a eu quelque temps un si grande crédit en Europe, va devenir dans notre pays même le plus sûr moyen de désigner l'ambitieux sans capacité.' *Journal de l'Empire*, 25 January 1806, p. 2.
17. 'Ce n'est ni a Trafalgar, ni au Cap de Bonne-Espérance qu'a pu décider le grand procès qui existe entre la France et l'Angleterre; et si nous ne voulons désormais signer de paix que celle qui abaisseront le prépondérance de notre ennemi, il faut nous résoudre à ébranler tous les états du Continent, qui sont à présent ou gagnés à sa cause, ou enchainés par sa puissance.' *Journal de l'Empire*, 12 March 1806, p. 2.
18. Adkins, *Nelson's Trafalgar*, pp. 275–6.
19. Jason R. Musteen, *Nelson's Refuge: Gibraltar in the Age of Napoleon* (Annapolis: Naval Institute Press, 2011), p. 41; Gibraltar Heritage Trust, *Trafalgar Cemetery* [information leaflet].
20. *Gibraltar Gazette*, 26 October 1805.
21. *Gibraltar Gazette, Supplement*, 2 November 1805.
22. *Gibraltar Gazette*, 9 November 1805.
23. *Gibraltar Gazette*, 9 November 1805.
24. Jackson, *Logs of the Great Sea Fights*, vol. 2, p. 208: Collingwood's Journal; Hore, *HMS Pickle*, pp. 103–5. The author is grateful to Captain Peter Hore, R.N. (ret.) for his advice and assistance in this and the following paragraph.
25. *Trewman's Exeter Flying Post or Plymouth and Cornish Advertiser*, Thursday, 21 November 1805.
26. Derek Allen and Peter Hore, *News of Nelson: John Lapenotière's Race from Trafalgar to London* (Brussels: SEFF Éditions, 2005), pp. 75–81; Hore, *HMS Pickle*, pp. 101–13, citing the quote from William Marsden, *A Brief Memoir of the Life and Writings of the Late William Marsden* (London, 1838), p. 116. An image of the Plymouth handbill is printed in Hore, *HMS Pickle*, between pp. 113–15.
27. Duffy, 'All Was Hushed Up', pp. 216–17, 235–6.

28. Hilary L. Rubinstein, *Trafalgar Captain: Durham of the Defiance* (Stroud: Tempus, 2005), p. 195.
29. Quoted in Duffy, 'All Was Hushed Up', p. 236, from Green's account of the battle in NMM, JOD/48; Robert Holden [Mackenzie], *The Trafalgar Roll: The Ships and the Officers* (London, 1913, reprinted Annapolis, 1989), p. 148. See also Jeremy B. Utt, 'Lieutenant William Pringle Green—Halifax, Nova Scotia', in Sean Heuvel and John Rodgaard, eds., *From across the Sea: North Americans in Nelson's Navy* (Warwick: Helion & Co., 2020), pp. 262–72.
30. *The London Gazette Extraordinary*, issue 15,858 (6 November 1805), pp. 1365–7. https://www.thegazette.co.uk/London/issue/15858/page/1365. The original, unredacted versions of Collingwood's dispatches of 22 and 24 October 1805 are printed in Sam Willis, *In the Hour of Victory: The Royal Navy at War in the Age of Nelson* (London and New York: W.W. Norton, 2014), pp. 257–73.
31. Contrast the narrative in Allen and Hore, *News of Nelson*, pp. 83–4, with Hore, *HMS Pickle*, pp. 118–20.
32. *Caledonian Mercury*, Saturday, 9 November 1805, p. 2.
33. *Saunders's News-Letter*, Monday, 1 November 1805, p. 1.
34. *Naval Chronicle*, vol. 14 (July–December 1805), p. 505.
35. For a general account, see Edward Fraser, *The Enemy at Trafalgar: Eye-Witness Narratives, Dispatches and Letters from the French and Spanish Fleets* (London: Hodder & Stoughton, 1906; reprinted London: Chatham, 2004), pp. 342–75.
36. *Portland Gazette and Maine Advertiser*, vol. 8, no. 35 (Monday, 16 December 1895), p. 3.
37. *Boston Gazette*, Thursday, 19 December 1805, vol. 19, no. 32, whole number 954, p. 2.
38. *Newport Mercury*, Saturday, 21 December 1805.
39. *New-York Gazette*, Tuesday 17 December 1805, vol. 18, no. 6179, p. 2; *The New York Evening Post*, Tuesday, 17 December 1805, no. 1270, p. 2; *Poulson's American Daily Advertiser*, Wednesday, 18 December 1805, [Philadelphia], vol. 34, no. 9059, p. 2; *Lancaster Intelligencer* [Lancaster, Pennsylvania], 20 December 1805, p. 2; *Eastern Shore General Advertiser* [Easton, Maryland], Tuesday, 24 December 1805, vol. 4, p. 3; *Hartford Courant* [Connecticut], 25 December 1805, p. 1; *Alexandria Daily Advertiser* [Virginia], Friday, 27 December 1805, vol. 6, no. 1482, p. 2; *National Intelligencer and Washington Advertiser* [District of Columbia], Friday, 20 December 1805, vol. 6, no. 814, p. 3; *Montreal Gazette*, 24 December 1805; *Quebec Gazette*, 25 December 1805; *Maryland Gazette* [Annapolis, Maryland], 26 December 1805, p. 2; *Newport Mercury*, Saturday, 28 December 1805, p. 1; *Rutland Weekly Herald* [Vermont], 28 December 1805, p. 2.
40. *St John's Gazette Extraordinary*, Monday, 30 December 1805.
41. Dudley W. Knox, ed., *United States Wars with the Barbary Powers: Naval Operations* (Washington: Government Printing Office, 1944), vol. 6, pp. 299–300: Captain Hugh Campbell to Secretary of the Navy, 30 October 1805.

42. Tuesday, 24 December in the New York City newspapers and copied in the *Alexandria Daily Advertiser*, Friday, 27 December 1805, vol. 6, no. 1482, p. 2.
43. *City Gazette* [Charleston, SC], Monday, 30 December 1805, p. 2.
44. *Barbados Mercury and Bridgetown Gazette*, Tuesday, 17 December 1805.
45. *Barbados Mercury and Bridgetown Gazette*, Saturday, 21 December 1805.
46. *Calcutta Gazette*, Thursday, 20 March 1806, p. 5; Thursday, 24 April 1806, pp. 6–7.
47. *Cape Gazette Extraordinary*, 26 January 1806, quoted in *Sydney Gazette and New South Wales Advertiser*, 13 April 1806, p. 5.
48. See Hore, *HMS Pickle*, p. 104.
49. 'The Battle of Trafalgar Celebration at Hobart Town in 1806', *The Mercury* [Hobart, Tasmania], Tuesday, 26 November 1872, p. 3.
50. Desbrière, *The Trafalgar Campaign*, vol. 2, is a compilation of British reports, with translations of the French and Spanish official reports and correspondence. British reports are also found in Jackson, ed., *Logs of the Great Sea Fights*, vol. 2. Spanish reports are also published in González-Aller Hierro, ed., *La campaña de Trafalgar*.
51. British Library, Add. Ms. 23207; Sam Willis, *In the Hour of Victory: The Royal Navy at War in the Age of Nelson* (London and New York: W.W. Norton, 2013), pp. 1–14.
52. Willis, *In the Hour of Victory*, pp. 243–98.
53. Willis, *In the Hour of Victory*, pp. 3–4; Inshore Squadron, 'The Reconstruction of Trafalgar', in Harding, ed., *A Great & Glorious Victory*, pp. 5–6.
54. Desbrière, *The Trafalgar Campaign*, vol. 2.
55. Monaque, *Trafalgar*, p. 289.
56. See Chapter 8.
57. Desbrière, *The Trafalgar Campaign*, vol. 2: reports of the Dumanoir courts of enquiry and court-martial, pp. 326–33, 364–9, 370–97.
58. Helen Watt and Anne Hawkins, eds., *Letters of Seamen in the Wars with France, 1793–1815* (Woodbridge: Boydell, 2016), pp. 240–1: Letter A113: Benjamin Thompson (alias Stevenson) to his sister, Portsmouth, 5 November 1805.
59. Ibid.
60. Watt and Hawkins, eds., *Letters of Seamen*, pp. 238–9: Letter A112: James West to his parents, off Cádiz, 4 November 1805.
61. Ibid.
62. Watt and Hawkins, eds., *Letters of Seamen*, pp. 232–3: Letter A109: Revd John Greenly to his father, off Cape St Mary's, near Cádiz, 28 October 1805.
63. Quoted without source in Peter Warwick, *Voices from the Battle of Trafalgar* (Newton Abbott: David & Charles, 2005), p. 169.
64. Tom Pocock, ed., *Trafalgar: An Eyewitness History* (London: The Folio Society, 2005), p. 112; Warwick, *Voices from the Battle of Trafalgar*, pp. 219–20.
65. Pocock, ed., *Trafalgar: An Eyewitness History*, pp. 126–7.

Chapter 4

1. David O'Brien, 'The Fine Arts and the Napoleonic Wars', in Alan Forrest, gen. ed., *The Cambridge History of the Napoleonic Wars* (Cambridge: Cambridge University Press, 2023), vol. 3, p. 302.
2. Allison Willow Yarrington, 'The Commemoration of the Hero, 1800–1864: Monuments to British Victors of the Napoleonic Wars', unpublished Ph.D. thesis, University of Cambridge, 1988; Timothy Jenks, *Naval Engagements: Patriotism, Cultural Politics, and the Royal Navy, 1793–1815* (Oxford: Oxford University Press, 2006), pp. 1–26; Christine Riding and Richard Johns, *Turner and the Sea* (London: Thames & Hudson in association with Royal Museums Greenwich, 2013), pp. 102–29; Roger Knight, *Pursuit of Victory: The Life and Achievements of Horatio Nelson* (London: Allen Lane, 2005), pp. 542–3.
3. For images of the early diagrams see, for example, Derek Allen and Peter Hore, *News of Nelson: John Lapenotière's Race from Trafalgar to London* (Brussels: SEFF Édition, 2005), illustration between pp. 16 and 17; anonymous pen and ink drawing dated 28 October 1805 in Richard Harding, ed., *A Great and Glorious Victory: New Perspectives on the Battle of Trafalgar* (Barnsley: Seaforth, 2008), p. 15; J. K. Laughton, ed., *Letters and Papers of Charles, Lord Barham, Admiral of the Red Squadron, 1758–1813*, Publications of the Navy Records Society, vol. 39 (London: Navy Records Society, 1911), vol. 3, diagram between pp. 324 and 325; Julian S. Corbett, *The Campaign of Trafalgar*, new edition (London: Longmans, Green, 1919), vol. 1, frontispiece; vol. 2, between pp. 426 and 427: 'Position of the Combined Forces of France & Spain', originally published 9 January 1806.
4. Holder Hoock, *The King's Artists: The Royal Academy of Arts and the Politics of British Culture, 1760–1840* (Oxford: Clarendon Press, 2003), p. 4.
5. David Cordingly, *Maritime Painting in England, 1700–1900* (New York: Clarkson N. Potter. 1973), pp. 14–15.
6. Eleanor Hughes, 'Nicholas Pocock: Accuracy and Agency', in Eleanor Hughes, *Spreading Canvas: Eighteenth-Century British Maritime Painting* (New Haven: Yale University Press, 2016), p. 73.
7. Geoff Quilley, *Empire to Nation: Art, History, and the Visualization of Maritime Britain, 1768–1829* (New Haven: Yale University Press, 2011), pp. 225–7.
8. David Cordingly, *Nicholas Pocock 1740–1821* (Annapolis: Naval Institute Press, 1986), p. 80; Colour Plate VII.
9. Nicholas Tracy, *Britannia's Palette: The Arts of Naval Victory* (Montreal: McGill-Queens University Press, 2007), p. 82.
10. Anya Lucas, Richard Johns, Sophie Stewart, and Stephan Paine, *The Painted Hall: Sir James Thornhill's Masterpiece at Greenwich* (London and New York: Merrell, 2019), p. 111; John Bold, *Greenwich: An Architectural History of the Royal Hospital for Seamen and the Queen's House* (New Haven: Yale University Press, 2000), pp. 187–8.

11. Tracy, *Britannia's Palette*, pp. 176–7, 310, 313; see also Cicely Robinson, 'The Apotheosis of Nelson in the National Gallery of Art', in Quintin Colville and James Davey, eds., *A New Naval History* (Manchester: Manchester University Press, 2019), pp. 151–74.
12. Tracy, *Britannia's Palette*, p. 176; Colin White, '"His dirge our groans—his monument out praise": Official and Popular Commemoration of Nelson in 1805–06', in Holger Hoock, ed., *Trafalgar, 1805–2005: History, Commemoration, and National Preoccupation* (Oxford: Oxford University Press for the British Academy, 2007), p. 41.
13. Willis, *In the Hour of Victory*, p. 262.
14. Tracy, *Britannia's Palette*, pp. 170–1; Barbara Tomlinson, *Commemorating the Seafarer: Monuments, Memorials and Memory* (Woodbridge: Boydell Press for the National Maritime Museum, 2015), p. 48.
15. Tracy, *Britannia's Palette*, pp. 173–4.
16. Riding and Johns, *Turner and the Sea*, pp. 103–7.
17. Joseph Farington, quoted in Tracy, *Britannia's Palette*, p. 285.
18. Quoted in Tracy, *Britannia's Palette*, p. 287, from *Review of Publications of Art* (June 1808), p. 83.
19. Riding and Johns, *Turner and the Sea*, pp. 107–14, 116, 123–9; Tracy, *Britannia's Palette*, pp. 290–1.
20. Riding and Johns, *Turner and the Sea*, pp. 124–9; Tracy, *Britannia's Palette*, pp. 301–3; Margarette Lincoln, ed., *Nelson and Napoléon* (London: National Maritime Museum, Greenwich, 2005), pp. 257–8.
21. *Morning Chronicle*, 7 May 1839, quoted in Riding and Johns, *Turner and the Sea*, p. 193.
22. Riding and Johns, *Turner and the Sea*, pp. 115, 193; Quilley, *Empire to Nation*, pp. 232, 249; Sam Willis, *The Fighting Temeraire: The Battle of Trafalgar and the Ship That Inspired J. M. W. Turner's Most Beloved Painting* (New York: Pegasus, 2010), pp. 229–46.
23. Pieter van der Merwe, 'Stanfield, Clarkson (1793–1867)', *Oxford Dictionary of National Biography* (online ed.), Oxford University Press, https://doi.org/10.1093/ref:odnb/26234.
24. Tracy, *Britannia's Palette*, pp. 332–6, 364–8; Riding and Johns, *Turner and the Sea*, pp. 122–3.
25. Quoted in Tracy, *Britannia's Palette*, p. 366.
26. Quoted in *Norwich Mercury*, Wednesday, 6 May 1863, p. 2.
27. Musée National de la Marine, Paris. Display label for Louis-Philippe Crépin, *Redoubtable at Trafalgar* (1806), inventory item 9 OA 120, as viewed by the author on 16 May 2025.
28. François Bellec, 'Artists: French', in John Hattendorf, ed., *Oxford Encyclopedia of Maritime History* (Oxford: Oxford University Press, 2007), vol. 1, pp. 171–3; Riding and Johns, *Turner and the Sea*, pp. 120–1; Battesti, *Trafalgar*, p. 347.

29. Prado Museum, Episodio de Trafalgar (boceto)—Colección—Museo Nacional del Prado (museodelprado.es).
30. María Jesús Piqueras Gómez, 'Rafael Monleón: el pintor del mar y su historia', *Ars longa: cuadernos de arte*, no. 2 (1991), pp. 49–52; Agustín Guimerá and Olivier Chaline, eds., *La Real Armada: la marine des Boorbons d'Espagne au XVIIIe siècle* (Paris: PUPS, 2018), pp. 364–5, cahier photo xxx–xxxi; Enrique Arias Angles, 'Artists; Spanish', in Hattendorf, ed., *Oxford Encyclopedia of Maritime History*, vol. 1, pp. 179–82.
31. Real Academia de la Historia, *Diccionario biográfico español*, https://dbe.rah.es/biografias/49523/angel-diaz-sanchez; Ronald J. Quirk, *Literature as Introspection: Spain Confronts Trafalgar*, Currents in Comparative Romance Languages and Literatures, vol. 57 (New York: Peter Lang, 1998), p. 39.
32. Prado Museum, Muerte de Churruca en Trafalgar—Colección—Museo Nacional del Prado (museodelprado.es).
33. Museo Naval de Madrid.
34. Roger Quarm and John Wyllie, *W. L. Wyllie: Marine Artist, 1851–1931* (London: Chris Bettles, Ltd, 1981), pp. 36–7, 42, 98–9, 110, 121–6; TNA ADM 1/8740/73: V. W. Baddeley, Sec. to Admiralty, to C-in-C Portsmouth, 31 May 1929.
35. Geoff Hunt, *The Marine Art of Geoff Hunt: Master Painter of the Naval World of Nelson and Patrick O'Brien* (Mystic, CT: Mystic Seaport, 2004), pp. 28–33, 68–71, 104–25.
36. Battesti, *Trafalgar*, pp. 345–57; https://www.paris-arc-de-triomphe.fr/en/discover/history-of-the-arc-de-triomphe; Battles on the Arc de Triomphe (frenchempire.net).
37. Memorial Battle of Trafalgar—Cádiz—TracesOfWar.com.
38. José Cervera Pery, *El Panteón de Marinos Ilustres* (Madrid: Ministerio de Defensa, Secretaría General Técnica, 2004), pp. 74–5, 162–3.
39. Trafalgar Cemetery Information Sheet from the Gibraltar Heritage Trust, https://gibraltarheritagetrust.org.gi/explore/places-to-visit/trafalgar-cemetery.
40. Yarrington, 'The Commemoration of the Hero', pp. xi–xiii; Tomlinson, *Commemorating the Seafarer*, p. 45.
41. Yarrington, 'The Commemoration of the Hero', pp. 1–83.
42. Yarrington, 'The Commemoration of the Hero', pp. 79–92; Tomlinson, *Commemorating the Seafarer*, p. 48; O'Brien, 'The Fine Arts', in Forrest, gen. ed., *The Cambridge History of the Napoleonic Wars*, vol. 3, pp. 313–14.
43. Yarrington, 'The Commemoration of the Hero', pp. 93–101; Tomlinson, *Commemorating the Seafarer*, p. 49.
44. Tomlinson, *Commemorating the Seafarer*, p. 51.
45. *The Times*, 11 June 1844; TNA, WORK 20/118: Trafalgar Square history.
46. Yarrington, 'The Commemoration of the Hero', pp. 277–325.
47. David Olusoga, *Black and British: A Forgotten History* (London: Pan Macmillan, 2016), pp. 20–1; https://www.theguardian.com/commentisfree/2017/aug/22/toppling-statues-nelsons-column-should-be-next-slavery.

48. [Robert Southey], *Letters from England by Don Manuel Alvarez Espriella* (London: Longman & Co, 1807), vol. 1, p. 312.
49. Peter Hore, *Nelson's Band of Brothers: Lives and Memorials* (Barnsley: Seaforth, 2015); Colin White, *The Trafalgar Captains: Their Lives and Monuments* (London: Chatham, 2005).
50. Mark Adkin, *The Trafalgar Companion* (London: Aurum Press, 2005), p. 542.
51. Andrew M. Shanken, *The Everyday Life of Memorials* (New York: Zone Books, 2022), pp. 324, 326–31.
52. Geoff Ward, 'Political Appeasement and the Erection of Nelson's Statue in Bridgetown', *The Journal of the Barbados Museum & Historica Society*, vol. 68 (December 2022), pp. 182–99.

Chapter 5

1. Dustin Kidd, *Popular Culture*. Oxford Bibliographies. DOI: 10.1093/OBO/9780199756384-0193.
2. Nicoletta Marini d'Armenia and Luigi Mascilli Migliorini, 'The Napoleonic Wars and Realms of Memory in Europe', in Alan Forrest, gen. ed., *The Cambridge History of the Napoleonic Wars*, vol. 3, pp. 588–609.
3. Quirk, *Literature as Introspection*, pp. 24–5.
4. *Octavas á la batalla naval del dia 21 de octubre de 1805, à la vista de Cadiz: entre la esquadra inglesa, y la combinada de Francia y España* (Reimpresas en México: Por don Mariano de Zúñiga y Ontiveros, calle del Espíritu Santo, 1806).
5. *Entrada pública del Almirante Nelson en la corte de Pluton el dia 23 de octúbre* (Cádiz: Manuel Ximénez Carreño, 1805), pp. 4–7, 9–12; translations from Marianne Czisnik, *Horatio Nelson: A Controversial Hero* (London: Hodder Arnold, 2005), p. 148.
6. Manuel Fernández Varela, *Oracion fúnebre: que en las exêquias generales celebradas el dia 23 de diciembre de 1805 á expensas y dovoción [sic] del Real Cuerpo de Marina del Departamento del Ferrol, por las ánimas de sus valerosos individuos y de todos los demás militares y marineros que han dado su vida por el rey y por la patria en el combate del 21 de octubre* (Mexico: Impreso en Madrid, y por su original en la Oficina de doña Maria Fernandez Jauregui, calle de santo Domingo, 1807).
7. Fernández Varela, *Oracion fúnebre*, pp. 1–4, 25–6.
8. Quirk, *Literature as Introspection*, pp. 20–1.
9. Lady Bourchier, *Memoir of the Life of Admiral Sir Edward Codrington with Selections from His Public and Private Correspondence* (London: Longmans, Green & Co., 1873), vol. 1, p. 73: Codrington to his brother William Bethell, *Orion*, 15 November 1805. In the 1875 one-volume edition, the letter is located on page 69.
10. *The Times*, 7 November 1805.
11. Timothy Jenks, *Naval Engagements: Patriotism, Cultural Politics, and the Royal Navy, 1793–1815* (Oxford: Oxford University Press, 2006), pp. 224–5.

12. White, 'His dirge our groans', p. 26.
13. Georgian Papers Online (http://gpp.rct.uk., January 2022), Royal Archives. GEO/ADD/15/8176: Princess Elizabeth to Lady Charlotte Finch, 6 November 1805.
14. Quoted in John Bew, *Castlereagh: Enlightenment, War and Tyranny* (London: Quercus, 2011), p. 212.
15. Extract of a letter from Lady Londonderry to her son-in-law, Lord Castlereagh, Mount Stewart, 13 November 1805, in Charles Ekins, *Naval Battles from 1744 to the Peace in 1814 Critically Reviewed and Illustrated* (London: Baldwin, Cradock, and Joy, 1824), p. 288.
16. *The Times*, 7 November 1805.
17. White, 'His dirge our groans', p. 27.
18. Ibid.
19. James Davey, *In Nelson's Wake: The Navy and the Napoleonic Wars* (New Haven: Yale University Press, 2015), pp. 106–8.
20. The three previous state funerals were Albemarle in 1670, Marlborough in 1722, and Chatham in 1772. Laurence Brockliss, John Cardwell, and Michael Moss, 'Nelson's Grand National Obsequies', *The English Historical Review*, vol. 121, no. 490 (2006), pp. 162–82.
21. Susan Amos and Louis Roeder, *Nelson's State Funeral, 1806: How to Bury a National Hero* (Cranbrook, Kent: Four Wents Publishing, 2020), *passim*.
22. Brockliss, Cardwell, and Moss, 'Nelson's Grand National Obsequies'; Timothy Jenks, 'Contesting the Hero: The Funeral of Admiral Lord Nelson', *Journal of British Studies*, vol. 39, no. 4 (2000), pp. 422–5; Jenks, *Naval Engagements*, pp. 231–6.
23. These items have seen a significant increase in value while remaining highly sought-after collectibles in the twenty-first century.
24. Marianne Czisnik, 'Nelson, Navy and National Identity', in Quintin Colville and James Davey, eds., *Nelson, Navy and Nation: The Royal Navy and the British People, 1688–1815* (London: Conway for the National Maritime Museum, 2013), pp. 188–207; John May, 'Nelson Commemorated', in Colin White, ed., *The Nelson Companion* (Thrupp: Sutton Publishing, 1995), pp. 81–98.
25. James Davey and Richard Johns, *Broadsides: Caricature and the Navy, 1756–1815* (Barnsley: Seaforth Publishing, 2012), pp. 27, 29; Colin White, 'Official and Popular Commemorations', in Hoock, ed., *Trafalgar*, pp. 30, 39, 46–7.
26. Laurence Halloran, 'The Battle of Trafalgar', transcript in Frank M. Snyder Collection, U.S. Naval War College, 'Trafalgar in Verse', p. 237.
27. Jenks, *Naval Engagements*, pp. 243–6.
28. Simon Bainbridge, *British Poetry and the Revolutionary and Napoleonic Wars: Visions of Conflict* (Oxford: Oxford University Press, 2003), pp. 162–3; see also George H. Hahn, *The Ocean Bards: British Poetry and the War at Sea, 1794–1915* (Oxford: Peter Lang, 2008).

29. C. H. Firth, *Naval Songs and Ballads*, Publications of the Navy Records Society, vol. 33 (London: Navy Records Society, 1908), pp. xcix–c.
30. Firth, *Naval Songs and Ballads*, p. c.
31. Firth, *Naval Songs and Ballads*, p. 301.
32. Alyson McLamore, '"Britannia Rule the Waves": Maritime Music and National Identity in Eighteenth Century Britain', in Eric Saylor and Christopher M. Scheer, eds., *The Sea in British Musical Imagination* (Woodbridge: Boydell, 2015), pp. 24–5.
33. *The Leeds Intelligencer and Yorkshire General Advertiser*, Monday 29 July 1822, p. 2; *The Nottingham Journal*, Saturday 18 January 1823, p. 2.
34. Knight, *The Pursuit of Victory*, pp. 542–3, 553.
35. C. I. Hamilton, 'Hagiography and the Victorian Hero', *The Historical Journal*, vol. 23, no. 2 (June 1980), pp. 381–98, quote at p. 392.
36. Quote in Dave Russell, '"We Carved our way to Glory": The British Soldier in Music Hall Song and Sketch, ca. 1880–1914', in John M. Mackenzie, ed., *Popular Imperialism and the Military, 1850–1950* (Manchester: Manchester University Press, 1992), p. 67.
37. *Les Annales politiques et littéraires*, 24 octobre 1886, pp. 266–7.
38. *Mémoires de Robert Guillemard, sergent en retraite, suivis de documens historiques... la plupart inédites, de 1805 à 1823* (Paris: Delaforest, 1826); Robert Guillemard, *Adventures of a French Serjeant during his campaigns in Italy, Spain, Germany, Russia, &c., from 1805 to 1823, written by himself* (London: H. Colburn, 1826).
39. Rémi Monaque, *Trafalgar: 21 octobre 1805* (Paris: Tallendrier, 2005), pp. 365–9; Fondation Napoléon, https://fondationnapoleon.org/en/oeuvre/t1_memoires-de-robert-guillemard-sergent-en-retraite-de-1805-1823-1826/.
40. Agustín Guimera, ed., *Trafalgar: una derrota gloriosa* (Madrid: Desperta Ferro Ediciones, 2023), p. x.
41. Marianne Cisnik, 'La interpretation del combate de Trafalgar más conocida: la novela de Benito Pérez Galdós', in Guimerá Ravina Agustín and Alberto Ramos y Gonzao Butrón, eds., *Trafalgar y el mundo Atlántico* (Madrid: Marcial Pons Historia, 2005), p. 362.
42. Quoted in Quirk, *Literature as Introspection*, p. 36. Author's translation.
43. Antonio Alcalá Galiano, *Recuerdos de un anciano* (Madrid: Librería de Perlado, Páez y Cª., 1907), p. 35.
44. Quoted in Quirk, *Literature as Introspection*, p. 46. Author's translation.
45. Benito Pérez Galdós, *Trafalgar* (Madrid: Imp. de J. Noguera, 1873). Digital copy at http://bdh-rd.bne.es/viewer.vm?id=0000206933&page=1.
46. *San Francisco Chronicle*, Sunday 22 June 1884, p. 6.
47. Quirk, *Literature as Introspection*, pp. 66–9; Cisnik, 'La interpretation del combate de Trafalgar más conocida', in Guimera et al., eds., *Trafalgar y el mundo*, pp. 359–74.

48. Benito Pérez Galdós, *Trafalgar: A Tale*, translated by Clara Bell (New York: William S. Gottsberger, 1884), p. 251.
49. Quirk, *Literature as Introspection*, pp. 69–70.
50. Guimerá, ed., *Trafalgar: una derrota gloriosa*, pp. 278–9.
51. Obituary of Friedrich Althaus, *Illustrated London News*, Saturday 17 July 1897, p. 76.
52. Friedrich Althaus, 'Admiral Nelson', in Rudolf von Gottschall, *Der Neue Plutarch: Biographien hervorragender Charaktere der Geschichte, Litteratur und Kunst*, Achter Teil (Leipzig: F. A. Brockhaus, 1880), p. 285.
53. Dermot Bradley, Hans H. Hildebrand, and Ernest Henriot, eds., *Deutschlands Admirale 1849–1945: Die militärischen Werdegänge der See-, Ingenieur-, Sanitäts-, Waffen- und Verwaltungsoffiziere im Admiralsrang* (Osnabrück: Biblio Verlag. Osnabrück, 1990), vol. 3: *P–Z*, pp. 536–7.
54. Reinhold Werner [later promoted to vice admiral in 1899, then ennobled in 1901 as Reinhold von Werner], *Berühmte Seeleute: Zweite Abtheilung. XVIII. und XIX. Jahrhundert* (Berlin: Otto Jahnke, 1884), pp. 116–344, devoted to Nelson.
55. Walter Parow, *Die Seeschlacht bei Trafalgar: Mit einer Tafel*, Wissenschaftliche Beilage zum Programm der Friedrichs-Werderschen Oberrealschule zu Berlin. Ostern 1890 (Berlin: n.p., 1890), p. 33.
56. Pieter van der Merwe. 'Views of the Royal Naval Exhibition, 1891', *Journal for Maritime Research*, vol. 3, no. 1 (2001), pp. 146–56; Marianne Czisnik, 'Commemorating Trafalgar: Public Celebration and National Identity', in David Cannadine, ed., *Trafalgar in History: A Battle and Its Afterlife* (London: Palgrave Macmillan, 2006), p. 142.
57. Quoted in W. Mark Hamilton. 'The "New Navalism" and the British Navy League, 1894–1914', *The Mariner's Mirror*, vol. 78, no. 1 (1978), pp. 37–44, at p. 41. See also Bradley M. Cesario, *New Crusade: The Royal Navy and British Navalism, 1884–1914* (Berlin and Boston: De Gruyter Oldenbourg, 2021), pp. 174–5.
58. Lord Charles Beresford and H. W. Wilson, *Nelson and His Times* (London: Harmsworth Brothers, 1898), p. iii.
59. Cesario, *New Crusade*, pp. 184–5.
60. Barbara Korte, 'Naval Heroism in the Mid-Victorian Family Magazine', in Quintin Colville and James Davey, eds., *A New Naval History* (Manchester: Manchester University Press with the National Maritime Museum, 2019), pp. 186–8.
61. Mary A. Conley, *From Jack Tar to Union Jack: Representing Naval Manhood in the British Empire, 1870–1918* (Manchester: Manchester University Press, 2009), p. 102, with reference to *Comrades*, vol. 1. no. 1 (17 January 1898).
62. George A. Henty, *By Conduct and Courage: A Story of Nelson's Days* (London: Blackie & Son, Ltd, 1904; New York: Charles Scribner's Sons, 1904).
63. Katherine Gazzard, *The Art of Naval Portraiture* (London: Royal Museums Greenwich, 2024), pp. 190–5.
64. Conley, *From Jack Tar to Union Jack*, pp. 164–5, 186.

65. 'Las Dos Marinas', *Revista contemporánea* (Madrid), vol. 110 (April–June 1898), p. 593.
66. *Chicago Tribune*, 30 May 1905. Cartoon reproduced in Rotem Kowner, *Tsushima*, Great Battles (Oxford: Oxford University Press, 2022), p. 150.
67. Quoted in Kowner, *Tsushima*, p. 153, from Elting E. Morison, ed., *The Letters of Theodore Roosevelt*, 8 volumes (Cambridge, MA: Harvard University Press, 1951–4), vol. 4, p. 1198.
68. *Punch*, 18 October 1905. Also reprinted in 1915 in a Special Issue, 'Punch & the Navy', for which this cartoon was used as an advertisement in many newspapers, for which see, for example, *Western Mail*, Wednesday 14 April 1915, p. 7; *Hartlepool Northern Daily Mail*, Wednesday 14 April 1915, p. 4.
69. Charles Villiers Stanford, *Songs of the Fleet, for Baritone Solo and Chorus, the Poems of H. Newbolt. Op. 117. No. 1 Sailing at Dawn. No. 2. The Song of the Sou'wester. No. 3. The Middle Watch. No. 4. The Little Admiral. No. 5. Fare well* (London: Stainer and Bell, 1910).
70. 'The Quarter-Gunner's Yarn', https://www.poetrynook.com/poem/quarter-gunners-yarn.
71. *South Wales Weekly Argus and Monmouthshire Advertiser*, Saturday 24 October 1914, p. 4.
72. *Liverpool Echo*, Saturday 21 October 1916, p. 4.
73. Marini d'Armenia and Luigi Mascilli Migliorini, 'The Napoleonic Wars and Realms of Memory in Europe', in Alan Forrest, gen. ed., *The Cambridge History of the Napoleonic Wars*, vol. 3, pp. 607–8.
74. Alan Aberg, 'Saving the Victory', *The Mariner's Mirror*, vol. 91, no. 2 (2005), pp. 358–8. DOI: 10.1080/00253359.2005.10656955; see also Alan McGowan, *HMS Victory: Her Construction, Career and Restoration* (London: Chatham Publishing, 1999).
75. Roger Quarm, 'Buying Nelson: Sir James Caird's Gifts to the National Maritime Museum', *The Mariner's Mirror*, vol. 91, no. 2 (2005), pp. 369–83. DOI: 10.1080/00253359.2005.10656956.
76. Kevin Littlewood and Beverly Butler, *Of Ships and Stars: Maritime Heritage and the Founding of the National Maritime Museum* (London: Athlone Press, 1998), pp. 21, 96.
77. John B. Hattendorf, *The Naval Novel: A Literary Genre in Historical Perspective* (Middletown, RI: Stone Tower Press, 2023), pp. 25–30.
78. Richard Woodman, *1805: A Nathaniel Drinkwater Novel* (London: John Murray, 1985); also Sue Parrill, *Nelson's Navy in Fiction and Film: Depictions of British Sea Power in the Napoleonic Era* (Jefferson, NC: McFarland & Co., 2009), pp. 249, 256–7.
79. Bernard Cornwell, *Sharpe's Trafalgar: Richard Sharpe and the Battle of Trafalgar, 21 October 1805* (London: HarperCollins, 2000); see also Mark Adkin, *The Sharpe Companion: The Early Years. A Guide to Bernard Cornwell's Richard Sharpe Novels* (London: HarperCollins, 2003), pp. 195–233.

80. Alan Villiers, *The Battle of Trafalgar: Lord Nelson Sweeps the Seas* (London: Collier-Macmillan Co., 1965), p. 85.
81. BBC News, 21 August 2002, http://news.bbc.co.uk/2/hi/entertainment/2208532.stm; https://web.archive.org/web/20040204074057/http://www.bbc.co.uk/history/programmes/greatbritons.shtml/.
82. The Nelson Society, https://nelson-society.com/; the 1805 Club, https://www.1805club.org/.

Chapter 6

1. Quoted in Battesti, *Trafalgar*, p. 311.
2. Battesti, *Trafalgar*, pp. 312–13.
3. Battesti, *Trafalgar*, pp. 306–10, quotation on p. 310.
4. Adkin, *The Trafalgar Companion*, pp. 518, 542–3; Monaque, *Trafalgar*, pp. 295–6.
5. González-Aller Hierro, ed., *La campaña de Trafalgar*, vol. 2, pp. 1551–629.
6. Jesús Chapela Rey, *Campaign Medals and Orders of Revolutionary and Napoleonic Wars (1792–1815)* (independently published, 2022), pp. 155, 190.
7. National Maritime Museum, Greenwich. https://www.rmg.co.uk/collections/objects/rmgc-object-40620; John Hayward, Diana Brich, and Richard Bishop, *British Battles and Medals*, 7th edition (London: Spink, 2006), pp. 44–43.
8. Adkin, *The Trafalgar Companion*, pp. 539–40.
9. Adkin, *The Trafalgar Companion*, pp. 537–8.
10. National Maritime Museum, Greenwich, https://www.rmg.co.uk/collections/objects/rmgc-object-40673; Hayward et al., *British Battles and Medals*, pp. 37–8.
11. National Maritime Museum Greenwich, https://www.rmg.co.uk/collections/objects/rmgc-object-40468; Hayward et al., *British Battles and Medals*, pp. 38–9.
12. National Maritime Museum Greenwich, https://www.rmg.co.uk/collections/objects/rmgc-object-39018.
13. Adkin, *Trafalgar Companion*, p. 539.
14. Hayward et al., *British Battles and Medals*, p. 135.
15. Quoted in Kenneth Douglas-Morris, *Naval General Service Medal Roll, 1793–1840* (Uckfield, East Sussex: Naval & Military Press, n.d.), p. xvi.
16. Douglas-Morris, *Naval General Service Medal Roll*, pp. xv–xxi.
17. National Maritime Museum, Greenwich, https://www.rmg.co.uk/collections/objects/rmgc-object-41276; Adkin, *The Trafalgar Companion*, p. 539. A complete list of all recipients is in Douglas-Morris, *Naval General Service Medal Roll*, pp. 98–126; Hayward et al., *British Battles and Medals*, pp. 45–8.
18. Charles Ekins, *Naval Battles, from 1744 to the Peace in 1814, Critically Reviewed and Illustrated* (London: Baldwin, Cradock, and Joy, 1824).
19. Evan Wilson, *The Horrible Peace: British Veterans and the End of the Napoleonic Wars* (Amherst and Boston: University of Massachusetts Press, 2023), pp. 90–106; Evan Wilson, 'The Limits of Naval Power: Britain after 1815', in

Paul Kennedy and Evan Wilson, eds., *Navies in Multipolar Worlds: From the Age of Sail to the Present* (London: Routledge, 2020), pp. 62–81.

20. National Maritime Museum, Greenwich, https://www.rmg.co.uk/collections/objects/rmgc-object-151538.
21. Katherine Gazzard, *The Art of Naval Portraiture* (London: Royal Museums Greenwich, 2024), pp. 155–9.
22. *London Evening Standard*, Wednesday, 23 October 1844.
23. Colin White, ed., *The Nelson Companion* (Stroud, Gloucestershire: Bramley Books, 1997), p. 17; *The Times*, 11 November 1805; Marianne Czisnik, 'Commemorating Trafalgar', in David Cannadine, ed., *Trafalgar in History: A Battle and Its Afterlife* (London: Palgrave Macmillan, 2006), p. 149.
24. Hilary L. Rubinstein, 'Trafalgar's Last Survivors', *The Trafalgar Chronicle*, New Series vol. 9 (2024), pp. 136–7.
25. Quoted in Rubinstein, 'Trafalgar's Last Survivors', p. 137.
26. Rubinstein, 'Trafalgar's Last Survivors', pp. 135–45; see also Adkin, *The Trafalgar Companion*, p. 538; 'Le Dernier de Trafalgar', *Le Petit Parisian*, no. 2629, 8 January 1884, p. 1. On the latter, see Clive L. Lloyd, *A History of Napoleonic and American Prisoners of War, 1756–1816: Hulk, Depot, and Parole* (Woodbridge: Antique Collectors' Club, 2007), p. 270.
27. Jaap R. Bruijn and Richard Unger, 'Ship Names and Naming', in John B. Hattendorf, ed.-in-chief, *The Oxford Encyclopaedia of Maritime History* (Oxford: Oxford University Press, 2007), vol. 3, pp. 606–8. See also Prince Louis Alexander of Battenberg, *Men of War Names: Their Meaning and Origin* (London: Stanford, 1907).
28. Rif Winfield, *British Warships in the Age of Sail, 1793–1817: Design, Construction, Careers and Fates* (London: Chatham Publishing and St Paul, Minnesota: MBI Publishing, 2005), p. 11–12.
29. Ships and stations named for Admiral Lord Nelson: HMS *Lord Nelson* (1800), storeship; HMS *Nelson* (1814), 120-first rate; HMS *Lord Nelson* (1906), Lord Nelson-class battleship; HMS *Nelson* (1876), Nelson-class armoured cruiser; HMS *Nelson* (1925), Nelson-class battleship, pennant number 28; and HMS *Nelson*, barracks in Portsmouth. In addition, there were three hired armed cutters named *Lord Nelson* in the Royal Navy. The first served from 1798 to 1801, the second from 1803 to 1804, and the third from 1807 to 1809.
30. Ships and stations named for Admiral Lord Collingwood: HMS *Collingwood* (1841), an 80-gun ship of the line, later converted to screw propulsion; HMS *Collingwood* (1882), the lead ship of the Admiral class of battleships; HMS *Collingwood* (1908), a St Vincent Class battleship; and HMS *Collingwood*, a shore establishment for recruits established in 1939 at Fareham, Hampshire, more recently the home for the Maritime Warfare School and other training establishments.

31. Oscar Parkes, *British Battleships: Warrior 1860 to Vanguard 1950* (London: Seeley, 1957).
32. Peter Hodges, *Battle Class Destroyers* (London: Almark, 1971).
33. *The Scotsman*, Friday, 19 October 2001, p. 8.
34. Admiralty Fleet Order (AFO) 2565/54 dated 1 October 1954.
35. Royal Navy Ships' Battle Honours, https://www.royalnavyresearcharchive.org.uk/Battle_hons.htm.
36. I am grateful to Agustin Guimerá and Carlos Alfaro Zaforteza for providing me with information on Spanish warships.
37. Jean-Michel Roche, *Dictionnaire des bâtiments de la flotte de guerre française de Colbert à nos jours* (Toulon: J. M. Roche, 2013).
38. For a detailed discussion, see, for example, John B. Hattendorf, 'In a Far More Thorough Manner: The Professionalization of the U.S. Navy at the Dawn of the Twentieth Century', in Hattendorf, *Talking about Naval History: A Collection of Essays* (Newport: Naval War College Press, 2011), pp. 245–54.
39. Charles E. Nowell, 'Sir Edward Creasy, 1812–1878', *Military Affairs*, vol. 15, no. 1 (Spring 1951), pp. 34–7; Dennis E. Showalter, 'Of Decisive Battles and Intellectual Fashions: Sir Edward Creasy Revisited', *Military Affairs*, vol. 52, no. 4 (October 1988), pp. 206–8.
40. Fletcher Pratt, *The Battles That Changed History* (Garden City: Hannover House, 1956), p. 12.
41. J. F. C. Fuller, *Decisive Battles: Their Influence upon History and Civilization* (New York: Charles Scribner's Sons, 1940).
42. J. F. C. Fuller, A *Military History of the Western World*, vol. 2: *From the Defeat of the Spanish Armada, 1588, to the Battle of Waterloo, 1815* (New York; Minerva Press), pp. 403.
43. J. K. Laughton, 'The Scientific Study of Naval History', *Journal of the Royal United Services Institution*, vol. 18 (1874), pp. 508–27; Andrew Lambert, *The Foundations of Naval History: John Knox Laughton and the Historical Profession* (London: Chatham, 1998), pp. 47–8.
44. J. K. Laughton, *Letters and Despatches of Horatio, Viscount Nelson, K.B. Duke of Bronte, Vice-Admiral of the White Squadron* (London: Longman's, 1886), unnumbered p. v. Lambert, *The Foundations of Naval History*, pp. 76–8.
45. Laughton, *Letters and Despatches*, pp. vi–xx; Lambert, *The Foundations of Naval History*, pp. 76–8.
46. John Leyland, ed., *Dispatches and Letters Relating to the Blockade of Brest, 1803–1805*, Publications of the Navy Records Society, vols. 14, 21 (London: Navy Records Society, 1899, 1902).
47. Sir Thomas Sturges Jackson, ed., *Logs of the Great Sea Fights, 1794–1805*, Publications of the Navy Records Society, vol. 18 (London; Navy Records Society, 1900).
48. Julian S. Corbett, *Fighting Instructions, 1530–1816*, Publications of the Navy Records Society, vol. 29 (London: Navy Records Society, 1905).

49. John Knox Laughton, ed., *Letters and Papers of Charles, Lord Barham, Admiral of the Red Squadron, 1758–1813*, Publications of the Navy Records Society, vols. 32, 38, 39 (London: Navy Records Society, 1907–11).
50. Lambert, *Foundations of Naval History*, pp. 97, 142–77.
51. Stephen B. Luce, 'On the Study of Naval History (Grand Tactics)' [1885], in John D. Hayes and John B. Hattendorf, eds., *The Writings of Stephen B. Luce* (Newport: Naval War College Press, 1975), pp. 84, 91, 93–4.
52. Stephen B. Luce, 'An Address Delivered at the United States Naval War College Narragansett Bay, R.I., June 2, 1903', in Hayes and Hattendorf, eds., *The Writings of Stephen B. Luce*, pp. 39–40.
53. John B. Hattendorf, 'Those Far Distant Storm-Beaten Ships upon Which the Grand Army Never Looked: The Influence of Sea Power, Alfred Thayer Mahan, and the U.S. Naval War College', in Hattendorf, *Reflections on Naval History: Collected Essays* (Newport: Naval War College Press, 2023), pp. 59–71.
54. Jon Tetsuro Sumida, *Inventing Grand Strategy and Teaching Command: The Classic Works of Alfred Thayer Mahan Reconsidered* (Baltimore: The Johns Hopkins University Press, 1997), pp. 35, 37–9, 44.
55. Nicholas Lambert, *The Neptune Factor: Alfred Thayer Mahan and the Concept of Sea Power* (Annapolis: Naval Institute Press, 2023); Paul M. Kennedy, *The Rise and Fall of British Naval Mastery* (London: Penguin, 1976, 2017).
56. Rolf Hobson. *Imperialism at Sea: Naval Strategic Thought, the Ideology of Sea Power and the Tirpitz Plan, 1875–1914*, Studies in Central European Histories (Boston and Leiden: Brill, 2002), pp. 96–109. For detailed studies of French naval thinking in this period, see also Arne Røksund, *The Jeune École: The Strategy of the Weak* (Leiden: Brill, 2007); and Martin Motte, *Une éducation géostratégic: la pensée naval française de la jeune école à 1914* (Paris: Economica, 2004).
57. A. Baudry, *The Naval Battle: A Study of the Tactical Factors* (London: Hugh Rees, Ltd, 1914), p. 6. Quoted in Jan S. Breemer, *The Burden of Trafalgar: Decisive Battle and Naval Strategic Expectations on the Eve of the First World War*, Newport Paper No. 6 (Newport: Naval War College Press, 1993), pp. 3–4.
58. Breemer, *The Burden of Trafalgar*, p. 4.
59. Dirk Bönker, *Militarism in a Global Age: Naval Ambitions in Germany and the United States before World War I* (Ithaca, NY: Cornell University Press, 2012), p. 256.
60. Holger Herwig, 'The Influence of A. T. Mahan upon German Sea Power', in John B. Hattendorf, ed., *The Influence of History on Mahan* (Newport: Naval War College Press, 1991), pp. 67–84; and 'Der Einfluß von Alfred Th. Mahan auf die deutsche Seemacht', in Werner Rahn, ed., *Deutsche Marinen im Wandel: Von Symbol nationaler Einheit zum Instrument internationaler Sicherheit* (Munich: Oldenbourg, 2004), pp. 127–42.
61. Arthur J. Marder, *Old Friends, New Enemies: The Royal Navy and the Imperial Japanese Navy*, vol. 1: *Strategic Illusions, 1936–1941* (Oxford: Clarendon Press, 1981), p. 285.

62. Marder, *Old Friends, New Enemies,* vol. 1, p. 341; David C. Evans and Mark Peattie, *Kaigun: Strategy, Tactics, and Technology in the Imperial Japanese Navy, 1887–1941* (Annapolis: Naval Institute Press, 1997), pp. 7–11.
63. John B. Hattendorf and Lynn C. Hattendorf, *A Bibliography of the Works of Alfred Thayer Mahan* (Newport: Naval War College Press, 1986), entries A2 Trans. d; A4 Trans. c; A6 Trans. b.
64. Evans and Peattie, *Kaigun,* p. 143; Bradley A. Fiske, *The Navy as a Fighting Machine,* with introduction and notes by Wayne P. Hughes, Jr., Classics of Sea Power series (Annapolis: Naval Institute Press, 1988), pp. 42, 52, 375–82.
65. Evans and Peattie, *Kaigun,* pp. 24, 134–44, 514–16.
66. Breemer, *The Burden of Trafalgar,* pp. 17–18.
67. Baudry, *The Naval Battle,* p. 7.
68. *The Memoirs of Admiral Lord Charles Beresford Written by Himself* (London: Methuen, 1914), vol. 2, p. 344.
69. Andrew Lambert, *The British Way of War: Julian Corbett and the Battle for a National Strategy* (New Haven: Yale University Press, 2021), p. 268.
70. Julian S. Corbett, *The Campaign of Trafalgar* (London: Longman's Green & Co., 1910), p. 452.
71. Eric Grove first published the two versions of this handout, from 1906 and 1909, in Julian S. Corbett, *Some Principles of Maritime Strategy,* with an introduction by Eric J. Grove, Classics of Sea Power series (Annapolis: Naval Institute Press, 1988), pp. 346ff.
72. Lambert, *The British Way of War,* pp. 156–7; Kurt von Maltzahn, 'Was lehrt das Buch des Generals von Clausewitz "Vom Kriege" dem Seeoffizier?', *Marine-Rundschau,* vol. 16 (June 1905), pp. 683–702; Admiral von Maltzahn, translated by W. H. Hancock, *What Lesson Has General von Clausewitz's Work, "On War," for the Naval Officer?* (Portsmouth: War College, 1906); see also Bönker, *Militarism in a Global Age,* pp. 262–3; and Christopher Bassford, *Clausewitz in English,* https://clausewitzstudies.org/readings/Bassford/CIE/Chapter11.htm.
73. Corbett, *Some Principles,* p. 163.
74. Corbett, *Some Principles,* p. 164.
75. Corbett, *Some Principles,* p. 167.
76. Julian S. Corbett, *Naval Operations,* History of the Great War, Based on Official Documents by Direction of the Historical Section of the Committee of Imperial Defence (London: Longmans, Green & Co., 1920), vol. 1, p. 2.
77. Corbett, *Naval Operations,* vol. 3, Introduction.
78. Andrew Gordon, *The Rules of the Game: Jutland and British Naval Command* (London: John Murray, 1996), pp. 180–202, 353–99, 562–600.
79. Quoted in Andrew Lambert, *The Crimean War: British Grand Strategy against Russia, 1853–56* (Manchester: Manchester University Press, 1990), p. 35. Also quoted in Bradley Cesario, '"Trafalgar Refought": The Professional and Cultural Memory of Horatio Nelson during Britain's Navalist Era, 1880–1914', unpublished MA thesis, Texas A & M University, December 2011, p. 64.

80. Andrew Lambert, 'The Magic of Trafalgar: The Nineteenth Century Legend', in Cannadine, ed., *Trafalgar in History*, p. 164. Also quoted in Bradley Cesario, 'Trafalgar Refought', p. 64.
81. Quoted in Gerald Jordan, 'Horatio Nelson: A Man to be Loved', in Jack Sweetman, ed., *The Great Admirals: Command at Sea, 1587–1945* (Annapolis: Naval Institute Press, 1997), pp. 200, 213 note 16.
82. Lambert, 'The Magic of Trafalgar', pp. 170–1.
83. W. S. Chalmers, *The Life and Letters of David, Earl Beatty* (London: Hodder and Stoughton, 1951), pp. 100–1, 422–3.
84. Gordon, *The Rules of the Game*, pp. 398, 431, 440, 498, 562–3, 600. For a recent, detailed study of the battle, see Michael Epkenhans, Jörg Hillmann, and Frank Nägler, *Jutland: World War I's Greatest Naval Battle* (Lexington, KY: University Press of Kentucky, [2015]).
85. See, for example, Vice-Admiral John Harper and Admiral Reginal Bacon, *The Jutland Scandal: The Truth about the World War's Greatest Sea Battle* (Barnsley: Frontline Books, 2015), pp. 9, 35, 82, 98, 109–10, 111–14, 119, 183. This 2015 book is a combined reprint of the two Jutland critiques that Harper published in 1927 and Bacon in 1933.
86. William Johnston, William G. P. Rawling, Richard H. Gimblett, and John MacFarlane, *The Seabound Coast: The Official History of the Royal Canadian Navy, 1867–1939* (Toronto: Dundurn Press, 2010), p. 167.
87. *The Labour Daily* (Sydney, New South Wales), Friday, 20 October 1933, p. 6.
88. Quoted in Daniel Owen Spence, *Colonial Naval Culture and British Imperialism, 1922–1967* (Manchester: Manchester University Press, 2015), p. 68.
89. *The Mercury* (Hobart, Tasmania), 25 October 1944, p. 2.
90. Spence, *Colonial Naval Culture*, pp. 71, 127, 185–9, 248.
91. Great Britain. Defence Council, *Fundamentals of British Maritime Doctrine. BR 1806* (London: HMSO, 1995); *British Maritime Doctrine*, 2nd edition (London: HMSO, 1999), p. 14; Andrew Lambert, *Nelson: Britannia's God of War* (London: Faber and Faber, 2004), p. 360.

Chapter 7

1. Bertrand Taithe, 'Remembering Victory—Commemorating Defeat: The Franco-British Trafalgar Centenary in 1905', in Holger Hoock, ed., *Trafalgar, 1805–2005: History, Commemoration, and National Preoccupation* (Oxford: Oxford University Press for the British Academy, 2007), pp. 49–64.
2. Fred T. Jane, 'Impressions of the French Fleet', *Graphic*, Saturday, 19 August 1905, p. 28.
3. Ibid.
4. *Hampshire Advertiser*, Saturday, 12 August 1905, p. 12; Steve R. Dunn, *The Power and the Glory: Royal Navy Fleet Reviews from Earliest Times to 2005* (Barnsley: Seaforth, 2021), pp. 156–61.

5. *The Spectator*, 12 August 1905, quoted in Dunn, *Power and Glory*, p. 160.
6. *Morning Post*, Saturday, 12 August 1905, p. 5.
7. Dunn, *Power and Glory*, p. 161.
8. David Shannon, *Nelson Remembered: The Nelson Centenary, 1905* ([Karawara, WA]: Broadsides Maritime Publications, in Association with the Nelson Society), 2007, pp. 18–20; Adam Oliver, '"In spite of lip service and tall columns he is half forgotten": A Brief Revisit to the Trafalgar Centenary Celebrations', *Trafalgar Chronicle*, no. 15 (2005), pp. 230–8.
9. Shannon, *Nelson Remembered*, pp. 20–1; Oliver, '"In spite of lip service"...', pp. 230–8.
10. Shannon, *Nelson Remembered*, pp. 25–8; Oliver, '"In spite of lip service"...', pp. 230–8; *Witney Gazette and West Oxfordshire Advertiser*, Saturday, 28 October 1905, p. 6.
11. *Isle of Wight Times*, Thursday, 26 October 1905, p. 5.
12. Ibid.
13. Ibid.
14. *Diss Express* [Norfolk], Friday, 13 October 1905, p. 6.
15. *The Times*, 15 October 1905.
16. *Norwich Mercury*, Wednesday, 25 October 1905, p. 5.
17. Shannon, *Nelson Remembered*, pp. 36, 66.
18. *Evening News* (Sydney, NSW), Tuesday, 24 October 1905, p. 4.
19. *Daily Record*, Monday, 23 October 1905, p. 5.
20. Shannon, *Nelson Remembered*, pp. 85–6.
21. *Daily Telegraph & Courier* (London), Monday, 23 October 1905, p. 12.
22. Roger Knight, *The Pursuit of Victory: The Life and Achievement of Horatio Nelson* (London: Allen Lane, 2005), p. 70.
23. *The Memoirs of Admiral Lord Charles Beresford Written by Himself* (London: Methuen & Co., 1914), vol. 2, pp. 513–14; *Daily Record*, Monday, 23 October 1905, p. 5.
24. Shannon, *Nelson Remembered*, p. 88.
25. Ibid.
26. TNA, CO 28/264, fo. 625: Carter to Lyttleton, 17 June 1905.
27. http://artinstamps.blogspot.com/2014/11lady-carter.html.
28. TNA, CO 28/264, fos. 625–7.
29. The statue, commissioned in 1806, stood at Bridgetown, Barbados, from 1813 until 2020, when the government removed it to the Barbados Museum. The statue also featured on three Barbadian postage stamps issued in 1950 and one in the 1953 Barbados Coronation issue. *Scott Standard Postage Stamp Catalogue* (Sidney, OH: Amos Media, 2023), vol. 1B, p. 207.
30. National Maritime Museum, Armold White Papers, WHI/118. *The Daily Graphic*, 18 September 1916.
31. *Birmingham Daily Post*, Friday, 21 October 1955, p. 19.
32. TNA, ADM 1/25917: Report of Commander Peter J. H. Hoare, RN, Festival Society Liaison Officer.

33. TNA, ADM 205/108, File 10E: Deputy Chief of Information to Secretary to First Sea Lord, 8 July 1955.
34. *Shields Daily News*, Friday, 21 October 1955, p. 12. The term 'splice the main brace' was originally an order to repair a key line controlling the mainsail but eventually came to mean, in nautical parlance, 'to serve out an extra allowance of grog in bad weather or after severe exertion'. W. H. Smythe, *The Sailor's Word Book* (London: Blackie & Son, 1867).
35. *Yorkshire Post and Leeds Intelligencer*, Saturday, 22 October 1955, p. 6.
36. TNA, ADM 205/108, File 10E: Handwritten note in green ink, Mountbatten to Permanent Secretary, from 10 Downing Street, 21 October 1955; Permanent Secretary to 1SL, 11 November 1955.
37. *Yorkshire Post and Leeds Intelligencer*, Saturday, 22 October 1955, p. 6.
38. *Portsmouth Evening News*, Friday, 21 October 1955, p. 4; TNA, ADM 205/108, File 10E: 150th anniversary of Trafalgar, 1955.
39. *The Scotsman*, Saturday, 22 October 1955, p. 7.
40. *Belfast News-Letter*, Saturday, 22 October 1955, p. 5; *The Sketch*, Wednesday, 2 November 1955, p. 25; *Illustrated London News*, Saturday, 29 October 1955, p. 17.
41. The Duke of Edinburgh, '"The Immortal Memory": Trafalgar Night, the Painted Hall, Greenwich, 150th anniversary, October 21, 1955', *Trafalgar Chronicle: The Year Book of the 1805 Club*, no. 15 (1805), pp. 1–4.
42. Ibid.
43. TNA, ADM 205/108, File 10E: 150th anniversary of Trafalgar, 1955. 'Make and mend' means providing time for sailors to attend to their personal needs by mending their clothing. In practice, it is an order that designates a portion of the day as a holiday, exempting employees from their required duties. For example, the order is often used on a royal birthday.
44. TNA, ADM 205/108, File 10E: CINC RN Norway, personal to 1SL; 1SL to Norwegian CinC, 21 October 1955, 211512Z Oct Admiralty to Norwegian Naval Headquarters.
45. *Birmingham Daily Post*, Monday, 24 October 1955, p. 18; *Cheshire Observer*, Saturday, 22 October 1955, p. 15; *Nantwich Chronicle*, Saturday, 29 October 1955, p. 4; *The Scotsman*, Monday, 24 October 1955, p. 5.
46. Richard Hill and Lt-Cdr W. J. R. Gardner, 'Society Records', *The Mariner's Mirror*, vol. 82, no. 3 (1996), pp. 350–4; Eugene L. Rasor, 'The Nelson Decade: A Survey of the Literature', *The Bicentennial Edition of the Nelson Dispatch* (December 2005), pp. 872–900. The institutions represented on the Official Nelson Commemoration [originally Celebration] Committee included the Society of Nautical Research, the National Maritime Museum, the Royal Naval Museum, the Nelson Society, the 1805 Club, the Ministry of Defence, the King George Fund, the Sea Cadets, the Royal Naval College, Greenwich, the Greenwich Foundation, HMS *Victory*, Lloyd's Naval Collection, Flagship Portsmouth, and the Nelson Museum, Monmouth.

47. Hattendorf, *The Naval Novel*, pp. 39–54.
48. Mark Connelly, 'Trafalgar: Back on the Map of British Popular Culture? Assessing the 2005 Bicentenary', in Hoock, ed., *Trafalgar, 1805–2005*, pp. 86–7.
49. *Broadside: Overview of the Year 2003–2004* (London: Royal Navy, 2004), p. 30, quoted in Connelly, 'Trafalgar: Back on the Map', p. 87.
50. Dunn, *Power and he Glory*, pp. 264–8, 300; Nick Slope, 'Photo Essay: The International Fleet Review, June 28, 2005, Portsmouth', *The Bicentennial Edition of the Nelson Dispatch* (December 2005), pp. 856–62.
51. Connelly, 'Trafalgar: Back on the Map', pp. 89–92.
52. *The Daily Telegraph*, Wednesday, 22 June 2005, p. 4.
53. Ibid.
54. *The Daily Telegraph*, Thursday, 20 October 2005, p. 12; Nigel Fordham, 'Nelson Stamps for the Bicentenary', *The Bicentennial Edition of the Nelson Dispatch* (December 2005), pp. 816–22; Scott Standard Postage Catalogue online, https://reader.scottonline.com/volumeset/library.html. Five postage stamps appear in a search for 'Admiral Nelson', twenty-three for 'Lord Nelson', and forty-eight for 'Horatio Nelson'.
55. Roy Clare, 'Introduction', in Lincoln, ed., *Nelson and Napoléon*, p. ix.
56. N. A. M. Rodger, 'Nelson and Napoleon: An Introduction', in Lincoln, ed., *Nelson and Napoléon*, p. 3.
57. *The Daily Telegraph*, Thursday, 20 October 2005, p. 14.
58. *The Independent*, Thursday, 20 October 2005, p. 53.
59. Court Circular, *The Daily Telegraph*, Thursday, 20 October 2005, p. 24.
60. Dunn, *Power and Glory*, p. 268; Connelly, 'Trafalgar: Back on the Map', pp. 88–9; Agustín Guimerá, ed., *Trafalgar: una derrota gloriosa* (Madrid: Desperta Ferro Ediciones, 2023), p. 274.
61. Dunn, *Power and Glory*, pp. 268–9, 301; *The Daily Telegraph*, Saturday, 22 October 2005, p. 4; *The Independent*, Saturday, 22 October 2005, p. 25; Colin White, *The Nelson Companion* (Stroud: Bramley Books, 1997), pp. 17–18; Colin White, ed., *The Nelson Encyclopedia: People, Places, Battles, Ships, Myths, Mistresses and Memorabilia* (London: Chatham Publishing, 2005), pp. 248–9.
62. The Right Rev. Richard Chartres, Bishop of London, 'The Trafalgar 200 Sermon, St Paul's Cathedral, October 23, 2005', in *Trafalgar Chronicle: The Yearbook of the 1805 Club*, no. 16 (2006), pp. 1–4; *The Daily Telegraph*, Friday, 28 October 2005, p. 22.
63. Derek Allen and Peter Hore, *News of Nelson: John Lapenotière's Race from Trafalgar to London* (Brussels: SEFF edition, 2005); Peter Hore, *HMS Pickle: The Swiftest Ship in Nelson's Fleet* (Stroud: The History Press, 2015), pp. 108–13; Joseph F. Callo, 'New York Pickle Night: 2004 Report', *The Bicentennial Edition of the Nelson Dispatch* (December 2005), pp. 852–5; The Trafalgar Way, https://www.thetrafalgarway.org/.

Chapter 8

1. John B. Hattendorf, 'Introduction', *The Oxford Encyclopedia of Maritime History* (Oxford: Oxford University Press, 2007), vol. 1, pp. xvii–xx; Richard Harding, *Modern Naval History: Debates and Prospects* (London: Bloomsbury, 2016), pp. 131–3.
2. Geoff Quilley, *Empire to Nation: Art, History, and the Visualization of Maritime Britain, 1768–1829* (New Haven: Yale University Press, 2011), p. 238; Stephen Bann, *The Clothing of Clio: A Study of the Representation of History in Nineteenth-Century Britain and France* (Cambridge: Cambridge University Press, 1984), pp. 8ff.
3. Andrew Lambert, ed. *Letters and Papers of Professor Sir John Knox Laughton, 1830–1915*, Publications of the Navy Records Society, vol. 143 (Aldershot: Navy Records Society, 2002), p. 32; Andrew Lambert, *The Foundations of Naval History: John Knox Laughton and the Historical Profession* (London: Chatham, 1998), p. 130.
4. John B. Hattendorf, 'The Study of War History in Oxford, 1862–1990', in Hattendorf and Malcolm Murfett, eds., *The Limitations of Military Power: Essays Presented to Professor Norman Gibbs on his 80th Birthday* (London: Macmillan, 1990), pp. 5–6. Peter R. H. Slee, *Learning and Education: The Study of Modern History in the Universities of Oxford, Cambridge and Manchester, 1800–1914* (Manchester: University of Manchester Press, 1986), p. 49.
5. The title varies slightly over several editions from 1825 to 1902. The most recent edition reproduces the 1836–7 edition: William James. *The Naval History of Great Britain from the Declaration of War by France in 1793 to the Accession of George IV. A New Edition, with Additions and Notes and an Account of the Burmese War and the Battle of Navarino by Captain Chamier, R.N.*, 6 vols. (London, 1836–7; reprinted with introductions by Andrew Lambert, London, 2002).
6. Brenton's title also changed over several editions. Although the book, in some editions, is in five volumes, the last edition, in 1837, contained only two but extended the subject to 1836: *The Naval History of Great Britain from the Year MDCCLXXXIII to MDCCCXXXVI: A New and Greatly Improved Edition*, 2 vols. (London, 1837).
7. Andrew Lambert, 'Introduction' to James, *The Naval History of Great Britain*, vol. 1, pp. viii–ix.
8. C. S. M. Phillipps reviewed the book in the *Edinburgh Review*, vol. 71 (April 1840), p. 121; Lambert, 'Introduction' to James, *The Naval History of Great Britain*, vol. 1, pp. iv–xv; vol. 2, pp. iv–xv; vol. 3, pp. iv–xviii.
9. Margrette Lincoln, *Representing the Royal Navy: British Sea Power, 1750–1815* (Aldershot: Ashgate in Association with the National Maritime Museum, 2002), p. 201.
10. Brenton, *The Naval History of Great Britain*, vol. 1, p. xvii.

11. Jahleel Brenton, *Memoir of Captain Edward Pelham Brenton, R.N., C.B., with Sketches of his Professional Life and Exertions in the Cause of Humanity, as Connected with the 'Children's Friend Society,' etc.; Observations upon his 'Naval History' and 'Life of the Earl of St Vincent'* (London: James Nisbet, 1842), p. 222.
12. Lincoln, *Representing the Royal Navy*, pp. 201–2.
13. Brenton, *The Naval History of Great Britain*, vol. 2, p. 62–90; James, *The Naval History of Great Britain*, vol. 4, pp. 23–108.
14. Brenton, *The Naval History of Great Britain*, vol. 2, pp. 68–9.
15. Ibid., p. 70.
16. James, *The Naval History of Great Britain*, vol. 4, p. 84.
17. Ibid., p. 101.
18. Charles Ekins, *Naval Battles from 1744 to the Peace in 1814 Critically Reviewed and Illustrated* (London: Baldwin, Cradock, and Joy, 1824), pp. 267–8.
19. Ibid., plate xxvii (50), pp. 267–8.
20. Ibid., p. 268.
21. James, *The Naval History of Great Britain*, vol. 4, p. 105.
22. Ibid., p. 106.
23. Ibid., p. 106; Quilley, *Empire to Nation*, p. 246.
24. Quilley, *Empire to Nation*, p. 247.
25. Willaim Laird Clowes, *The Royal Navy: A History from the Earliest Times to 1900* (London: Sampson, Low, Marston & Co., 1897–1903); Lambert, 'Introduction' to James, *The Naval History of Great Britain*, vol. 3, p. viii.
26. G. L. Newnham Collingwood, ed., A *Selection from the Public and Private Correspondence of Vice-Admiral Lord Collingwood: Interspersed with Memoirs of His Life* (England: James Ridgway, 1828).
27. Nicholas Harris Nicolas, ed., *The Dispatches and Letters of Vice Admiral Lord Viscount Nelson, with Notes by Sir N. H. Nicolas* (London: Henry Colburn, 1844).
28. Ibid., vol. 7, pp. 133–40, 142–368.
29. Robert Gildea, *The Past in French History* (New Haven: Yale University Press, 1994), p. 98; Andrew Lambert, 'Teaching by Example: Julian Corbett's *The Campaign of Trafalgar* of 1910', in Richard Harding and Agustin Guimerá, eds., *Sailors, Statesmen and the Implementation of Naval Strategy* (Woodbridge: The Boydell Press, 2024), p. 129 note 33.
30. Adolphe Thiers, *The Historical Works of M. Adolphe Thiers, Translated by Thomas W. Redhead, Esq* (London: A. Fullarton and Co, 1847), vol. 2, p. 514.
31. Ibid., p. 560.
32. Ibid., p. 560.
33. Ibid., p. 560.
34. Ibid., p. 560.
35. Ibid., p. 561.
36. Ibid., p. 561.
37. Edouard Jurien de la Gravière, *Guerres maritimes sous la république et l'empire* (Paris: Charpentier, 1847).

38. E. Jurien de la Gravière, *Sketches of the Last Naval War*, translated by the Hon. Captain Plunkett (London: Longman, Brown, Green, and Longmans, 1848).
39. Jurien de la Gravière, *Guerres maritimes*, vol. 2, pp. 241–2.
40. Ibid., p. 244. The reference is to Count Alexander Vasilyevich Suvorov-Rymnisky (1730–1800), the foremost imperial Russian general and theorist of the eighteenth century.
41. Manuel Marliani, *Combate de Trafalgar: vindicacion de la Armada española contra los aseretones injuriosas vertidas por Mr Thiers en su Historia del consulado y el imperio* (Madrid: Impreso de Orden Superior, 1850).
42. Agustín Guimerá, ed., *Trafalgar: una derrota gloriosa* (Madrid: Desperta Ferro Ediciones, 2023), p. 264; Manuel de Godoy y Álvarez de Faria Rios, *Memorias de Don Manuel Godoy, Príncipe de la Paz: o sea cuenta dada de su vida política para servir a la historia del reinado del Señor Don Carlos IV de Borbón* (Madrid: Librería Americana de Lecointe y Laserre, 1839–41).
43. Marliani, *Combate de Trafalgar*, p. viii.
44. Ibid., pp. viii–ix, 266.
45. See Guimerá, ed., *Trafalgar: una derrota gloriosa*, pp. 264–6.
46. O. Troude, *Batailles navales de la France* (Paris: Challamel aîné, 1867–8), pp. 361–412.
47. Napoleon I, Emperor of the French, *Correspondence de Napoléon Ier: publiée par ordre de l'empereur Napoléon III* (Paris: H. Plon, J. Dumaine, 1858–70), vol. 11.
48. Louis Édouard Chevalier, *Histoire de la marine sous le consulate et empire* (Paris: Hachette, 1886), vol. 3, bk 5, pp. 187–232.
49. A. T. Mahan, *The Influence of Sea Power upon the French Revolution and Empire, 1793–1812* (Boston: Little Brown, 1892), vol. 2, pp. 186–98.
50. A. T. Mahan, *The Life of Nelson: The Embodiment of the Sea Power of Great Britain* (Boston: Little Brown, 1897), vol. 2, pp. 337–97.
51. Captain Alfred Thayer Mahan, 'The Battle of Trafalgar. Read February 1, 1898', in Military History Society of Massachusetts, *Naval Actions and Operations against Cuba and Puerto Ricco, 1593–1815* (Boston: The Stillings Press, 1901), unpaginated. Some additional derivative pieces touching on Trafalgar by Mahan include the anonymous article attributed to Mahan: 'Tactics of Trafalgar', *Army and Navy Journal*, 29 July 1905, p. 708; 'The Centenary of Trafalgar: The Consistency of Nelson as a Tactician', *The Graphic*, 72 (21 October 1905), p. 514; and 'Nelson at Trafalgar', *Century Magazine*, 53 (March 1897), pp. 741–59.
52. José Ferrer de Couto, *Historia del combate naval de Trafalgar, precedida de la del renacimiento de la marina española durante el siglo XVIII* (Madrid: Imp. de W. Ayguals de Izco, 1851). Mahan's copy is in the U.S. Naval War College Library.
53. Nicholas Lambert, *The Neptune Factor: Alfred Thayer Mahan and the Concept of Sea Power* (Annapolis: Naval Institute Press, 2023), pp. 138–67; Jon Tetsuro Sumida, *Inventing Grand Strategy and Teaching Command: The Classic Works of Alfred Thayer Mahan Reconsidered* (Baltimore: The Johns Hopkins University Press, 1997), pp. 32–6.

54. Mahan, *The Influence of Sea Power upon the French Revolution and Empire*, vol. 2, pp. 196–7.
55. Ibid., p. 197.
56. Mahan, *The Life of Nelson*, vol. 2, pp. 337–97. See James R. Thursfield's 1898 review of *The Life of Nelson* in Thursfield, *Nelson and Other Studies* (New York: E. P. Dutton, 1909), pp. 82–132; Sumida, *Inventing Grand Strategy*, pp. 36–9.
57. P. H. Colomb, 'The Battle of Trafalgar', *United Services Magazine* (September 1899); reprinted in pamphlet form, P. H. Colomb, *The Battle of Trafalgar* (London: W. Clowes & Sons, Limited, 1905), p. 2.
58. Colomb, *The Battle of Trafalgar*, pp. 2–3.
59. Julian S. Corbett, *Fighting Instructions, 1539–1816*, Publications of the Navy Records Society, vol. 29 (London, 1905).
60. Thursfield, *Nelson and Other Studies*, pp. 56–68.
61. Edward Fraser, *The Enemy at Trafalgar: Eye-Witness' Narratives. Dispatches and Letters from the French and Spanish Fleets* (London: Hodder and Stoughton, 1906), reprinted with an introduction by Mariane Czisnik and Michael Nash (London: Chatham, 2004).
62. Edouard Desbrière, *1793–1805: projets et tentatives de débarquement aux îles Britanniques*, 4 vols. (Paris: R. Chapelot, 1900–2).
63. Édouard Desbrière, *Le blocus de Brest de 1793 à 1805* (Paris: Librairie militaire R. Chapelot, 1902); Desbrière, *La campagne maritime de 1805: Trafalgar* (Paris: Librairie militaire de R. Chapelot, 1907). Constance Eastwick translated and edited the latter, correcting the faulty transcripts in the original in Desbrière and Constance Eastwick. *The Naval Campaign of 1805: Trafalgar* (Oxford: The Clarendon Press, 1933).
64. John Leyland, ed., *Dispatches and Letters Relating to the Blockade of Brest, 1803–1805*, Publications of the Navy Records Society, vols. 14, 21 (London: Navy Records Society, 1899, 1902).
65. Desbrière's original 1907 preface is quoted from the translation in Desbrière and Eastwick, *The Naval Campaign of 1805*, pp. xi–xii.
66. *The Times*, 21 October 1913, p. 10; Corbett, *Fighting Instructions*, p, 298.
67. Desbrière and Eastwick. *The Naval Campaign of 1805*, p. 302.
68. For contemporary reviews of Eastwick's version, see the unsigned book review in U.S. Naval Institute *Proceedings*, vol. 60, no. 1, cumulative no. 371 (January 1934) and Robert G. Albion's review in the *Journal of Modern History*, vol. 7, no. 1 (March 1935), pp. 78–80.
69. Julian S. Corbett, *The Campaign of Trafalgar* (London: Longman's Green, 1910); Lambert, *British Way of War*, pp. 226–43.
70. Corbett, *The Campaign of Trafalgar*, vol. 1, p. vii.
71. Ibid., vol. 1, p. vii.
72. Ibid., vol. 2, p. 424.
73. Ibid., vol. 2, p. 395.
74. Ibid., vol. 2, p. 470.

75. Admiral Sir Cyprian Bridge, 'Nelson: The Centenary of Trafalgar', in *Sea Power and Other Studies* (London: Smith Elder & Co, 1910), pp. 206–26, quote at pp. 212–13.
76. Lambert, *British Way of War*, pp. 238–9, 241.
77. Great Britain. Admiralty. Committee on Tactics of Nelson at Battle of Trafalgar. Navy (Trafalgar): *Report of a committee appointed by the Admiralty to examine and consider the evidence relating to the tactics employed by Nelson at the battle of Trafalgar.* Cd. 7120. London, HMSO, 1913.
78. Lambert, *British Way of War*, pp. 406, 429.
79. Julian S. Corbett, 'Napoleon and the British Navy after Trafalgar', Creighton Memorial Lecture, *The Quarterly Review*, no. 237 (April 1922), pp. 238–55, reprinted in Andrew Lambert, ed., *21st Century Corbett: Maritime Strategy and Naval Policy for the Modern Era* (Annapolis: Naval Institute Press, 2017), pp. 130–46.
80. Raoul Castex, *Strategic Theories: Selections Translated and Edited with an Introduction by Eugenia C. Kiesling*, Classics of Sea Power (Annapolis: Naval Institute Press, 1994), p. 53. Quotations from the revised and expanded 2nd edition of vol. 1, *Théories stratégiques* (Paris: Société d'Editions Géographiques, Maritimes et Coloniales, 1937).
81. Robert Holden Mackenzie, *The Trafalgar Roll: Containing the Names and Services of All Officers Who Participated in the Victory* (London: George Allen, 1913).
82. Carola Oman, *Nelson* (London: Hodder and Stoughton, 1947).
83. Julian de Zulueta, 'Trafalgar: The Spanish View', *The Mariner's Mirror*, vol. 66, no. 4 (1980), pp. 293–318. DOI: 10.1080/00253359.1980.10659212.
84. See, for example, A. F. Fremantle, *Trafalgar* (London: Peter Davies, Ltd, 1933); Oliver Warner, *Trafalgar* (New York: Macmillan, 1959); John Terraine, *Trafalgar* (London: Sedgwick and Jackson, Ltd, 1975); Geoffrey Bennett, *The Battle of Trafalgar* (Annapolis: Naval Institute Press, 1977).

Chapter 9

1. This chapter is a revised and updated version of the parts that relate to Trafalgar in John B. Hattendorf, 'Whither with Nelson and Trafalgar? The Bicentenary Scholarship of the Nelson Era', in Hattendorf, *Talking about Naval History: A Collection of Essays* (Newport: Naval War College Press, 2011), pp. 143–63.
2. See, for example, the new approaches in Richard Harding, *Modern Naval History: Debates and Prospects* (London: Bloomsbury, 2016); John McAleer and Christopher Petley, eds., *The Royal Navy and the British Atlantic World, c. 1750–1820* (London: Palgrave Macmillan, 2016); Quinton Colville and James Davey, *A New Naval History*, Cultural History of Modern War (Manchester: Manchester University Press, 2019); Paul Kennedy and Evan Wilson, eds., *Navies in Multipolar Worlds: From the Age of Sail to the Present* (London: Routledge, 2020).

3. Eugene L. Rasor, 'The Nelson Decade: A Survey of the Literature', *The Bicentennial Edition of the Nelson Dispatch* (December 2005), pp. 872–900. See also Hattendorf, 'Whither with Nelson and Trafalgar?', pp. 143–63.
4. See, for example, A. D. Lambert, 'The Construction of Naval History 1815–1914', *The Mariner's Mirror*, vol. 97, no. 1 (February 2011), pp. 207–24.
5. John Ehrman, *The Navy in the War of William III, 1689–1697* (Cambridge: Cambridge University Press, 1953), p. xxii.
6. N. A. M. Rodger, *The Command of the Ocean: A Naval History of Britain, 1649–1815* (London: Allen Lane, 2004), pp. 420, 487–8, 508, 522, 537–43.
7. 'Putting the Sea back in Britain', *The Economist* (20 November 2004), p. 88.
8. Rodger, *Command of the Ocean*, p. 543.
9. N. A. M. Rodger, *The Price of Victory: A Naval History of Britain, 1815–1945* (London: Allen Lane, Penguin, in association with the National Maritime Museum, Greenwich, 2024), p. 468.
10. The only conference among the nine that did not publish its proceedings was 'The Trafalgar Bicentennial Conference: War at Sea in the Age of Nelson', held at Christ Church, Oxford, 4–9 September 2005.
11. Agustín Guimerá Ravina, Alberto Ramos, and Gonzalo Butrón, eds., *Trafalgar y el mundo Atlántico* (Madrid: Marcel Pons Historia, 2004).
12. Agustín Guimerá Ravina and Victor Peralta, eds., *El equilibrio de los imperios: de Utrecht a Trafalgar*, Actas de la VIII Reunión Científica de la Fundación Española de Historia Moderna. Madrid, 2–6 de junio de 2004, vol. 2 (Madrid: Fundación Española de Historia Moderna, 2005).
13. José María Blanco Núñez, Pablo de Castro Martín, and Enrique García Hernán, coord., *Poder terreste y poder naval en la época de la batalla de Trafalgar*, XXXI Congreso Internacional de Historia Militar (Madrid: Imprenta Ministerio de Defensa, 2006).
14. F. Fernández-González, L. D. Ferreiro, and H. Nowacki, eds., *Technology of the Ships of Trafalgar: Proceedings of an International Congress Held at the Escuela Técnica Superior de Ingenieros Navales, Madrid, and the Diputación Provincial, Cádiz, 3–5 November 2005* (Madrid: Escuela Técnica Superior de Ingenieros Navales Universidad Politécnica de Madrid, 2006).
15. David Cannadine, *Admiral Lord Nelson: Context and Legacy* (London: Palgrave Macmillan, 2005).
16. David Cannadine, ed., *Trafalgar in History: A Battle and Its Afterlife* (London: Palgrave Macmillan, 2006).
17. Richard Harding, ed., *A Great and Glorious Victory: New Perspectives on the Battle of Trafalgar* (Barnsley: Seaforth Publishing, 2008).
18. Ibid., p. 28.
19. Holger Hoock, ed., *History, Commemoration, and National Preoccupation: Trafalgar, 1805–2005* (Oxford: Oxford University Press for the British Academy, 2007).
20. Michèle Battesti, *Trafalgar: les aléas de la stratégie navale de Napoléon*, Bibliothèque Napoléonienne (Paris: Tallandier Éditions, 2004).

21. Tim Clayton and Phil Craig, *Trafalgar: The Men, the Battle, the Storm* (London: Hodder & Stoughton, 2004).
22. Roy Adkins, *Trafalgar: The Biography of a Battle* (London: Little Brown, 2004; Abacus, 2005); *Nelson's Trafalgar: The Battle that Changed the World* (New York: Viking Penguin, 2005).
23. Adam Nicholson, *Men of Honour: Trafalgar and the Making of the English Hero* (London: Harper Collins, 2005); *Seize the Fire: Heroism, Duty, and the Battle of Trafalgar* (New York: Harper Collins, 2005).
24. Marianne Czisnik, 'Admiral Nelson's Tactics at the Battle of Trafalgar', *History*, vol. 89, no. 4, no. 296 (October 2004), pp. 549–59.
25. Duffy, 'All Was Hushed Up', and 'The Gunnery at Trafalgar: Training, Tactics or Temperament', *The Journal for Maritime Research*, vol. 7, no. 1 (August 2005), pp. 140–69, DOI: 10.1080/21533369.2005.9668349; Rémi Monaque and R. Channon, RN, 'Trafalgar 1805: Strategy, Tactics, and Results', *The Mariner's Mirror*, vol. 9, no. 2 (2005), pp. 241–50, DOI: 10.1080/00253359.2005.1065694 7; Agustín R. Rodríguez González, 'The Spanish at Trafalgar: Ships, Cannons, Men and a Problematic Alliance', *Journal for Maritime Research*, vol. 7, no. 1 (2005), pp. 26–43, DOI: 10.1080/21533369.2005.9668343.
26. Mark Adkin, *The Trafalgar Companion: A Guide to History's Most Famous Sea Battle and the Life of Admiral Lord Nelson* (London: Aurum Press, 2005).
27. José Ignacio González-Aller Hierro, ed., *La campaña de Trafalgar (1804–1805): corpus documental conservado en los archivos españoles*, 2 vols. (Madrid: Ministerio de Defensa Armada Española, 2004).
28. Rémi Monaque, *Trafalgar: 21 Octobre 1805*, Bibliothèque Napoléonienne (Paris: Tallandier Éditions, 2005).
29. https://fondationnapoleon.org/en/2024/01/03/the-general-correspondence-of-napoleon-bonaparte-all-the-letters-are-now-available-on-napoleonica-les-archives/; Napoléon Bonaparte, *Correspondance générale*, vol. 5: *Boulogne, Trafalgar, Austerlitz, 1805* (Paris: Fayard, 2008), https://www.napoleonica.org/en/collections/correspondance/.
30. Jean-Claude Gillet, *La marine impériale: le grand rêve de Napoleon* (St Denis La Plaine: Bernard Giovanangeli, 2010).
31. Agustín Guimerá, ed., *Trafalgar: una derrota gloriosa* (Madrid: Desperta Ferro Ediciones, 2023). Contributors included Richard Harding, Rémi Monaque, Michael Duffy, Agustín Rodríguez González, Carlos Alfaro Zaforteza, Emilio La Parra, and María Baudot Monroy.
32. A. T. Mahan, *The Life of Nelson, the Embodiment of the Sea Power of Great Britain* (Boston: Little, Brown and Co., 1897).
33. Carola Oman, *Nelson* (Garden City, NY: Doubleday & Company, Inc., 1946; London: Hodder and Stoughton, 1947).
34. Colin White, ed., *The Nelson Companion* (Stroud: Bramley Books in Association with the Royal Naval Museum; Annapolis, MD: Naval Institute Press, 1995; Stroud: Royal Naval Museum Publications in association with Sutton, 2005).

35. Richard Walker, *The Nelson Portraits: An Iconography of Horatio, Viscount Nelson, K.B., Vice Admiral of the White* (Portsmouth: Royal Naval Museum, 1998). Walker has published addenda and corrections to this book in *The Trafalgar Chronicle: Year Book of the 1805 Club* for 2005 and 2006.
36. Colin White, *The Nelson Encyclopaedia: People, Places, Battles, Ships, Myth, Mistresses, Memorials, and Memorabilia* (London: Chatham Publishing; Mechanicsburg, PA: Stackpole Books, 2002; revised edition, 2005).
37. Terry Coleman, *The Nelson Touch: The Life and Legend of Horatio Nelson* (London: Bloomsbury, 2001, 2002; New York: Oxford University Press, 2002).
38. Ibid., p. 1.
39. Joel Hayward, *For God and Glory: Lord Nelson and His Way of War* (Annapolis, MD: Naval Institute Press, 2003).
40. Edgar Vincent, *Nelson: Love and Fame* (New Haven, CT, and London: Yale University Press, 2003).
41. John Sugden, *Nelson: A Dream of Glory* (London: Jonathan Cape, 2004; London: Pimlico, 2005); *Nelson: The Sword of Albion* (London: Bodley Head, 2012).
42. Andrew Lambert, *Nelson: Britannia's God of War* (London: Faber and Faber, 2004).
43. Ibid., p. xi.
44. Ibid., p. 361.
45. Martyn Downer, *Nelson's Purse: An Extraordinary Historical Detective Story Shedding Light on the Life of Britain's Greatest Naval Hero* (London: Bantam Press, 2004).
46. Rina Prentice, *The Authentic Nelson* (London: National Maritime Museum, 2005).
47. Sir Nicholas Harris Nicolas, ed., *The Dispatches and Letters of Vice Admiral Lord Viscount Nelson, with Notes*, foreword by Michael Nash (London: Chatham, 1997–8; Elibron Classics, Boston, MA: Adamant Media Corporation, 2003).
48. *The Naval Chronicle: The Contemporary Record of the Royal Navy at War, Prepared for General Use by Nicholas Tracy*, Consolidated Edition, 5 vols. (London: Chatham, 1998–9).
49. Roger Morriss with Peter Bursey, compilers, *Guide to British Naval Papers in North America* (London: Mansell, 1994).
50. Joseph F. Callo, ed., *Nelson Speaks: Admiral Lord Nelson in His Own Words* (Annapolis, MD: Naval Institute Press, 2001).
51. Colin White, ed., *Nelson: The New Letters* (Woodbridge: The Boydell Press in association with the National Maritime Museum and the Royal Naval Museum, 2005; paperback edition, 2007).
52. Colin White, 'Nelson's 1805 Battle Plan', *Journal for Maritime Research* (May 2002), http://www.jmr.nmm.ac.uk/server/show/conJmrArticle.32.
53. Colin White, 'The Nelson Letters Project', *Mariner's Mirror*, vol. 87 (November 2001), pp. 476–8; 'The New Nelson Letters: News of Remarkable Discoveries

Made by the Nelson Letters Project', *Mariner's Mirror*, vol. 89 (November 2003), pp. 464–6; '"Ever with real esteem...": Continuing the Nelson Letters Project', *Trafalgar Chronicle: Year Book of the 1805 Club*, vol. 16 (2006), pp. 44–8.

54. Marianne Czisnik, ed., *Nelson's Letters to Lady Hamilton and Related Documents*, Publications of the Navy Records Society, vol. 167 (London: Routledge for the Navy Records Society, 2020).
55. Roger Knight, *The Pursuit of Victory: The Life and Achievement of Horatio Nelson* (London: Allen Lane, 2005; Penguin Books Ltd, 2006; New York: Basic Books, 2005; Perseus Books Group, 2007).
56. Colin White, *Nelson: The Admiral* (Stroud: Sutton Publishing in Association with the Royal Navy and the Royal Naval Museum, 2005).
57. Marianne Czisnik, *Nelson: A Controversial Hero* (London: Hodder Arnold, 2005).
58. Lawrence Brockliss, John Cardwell, and Michael Moss, *Nelson's Surgeon: William Beatty, Naval Medicine, and the Battle of Trafalgar* (Oxford: Oxford University Press, 2005).
59. Anne-Mary E. Hills, *Nelson: A Medical Casebook* (London: Spellmount Publishers Ltd, 2006).
60. David Syrett and R. L. DiNardo, eds., *The Commissioned Sea Officers of the Royal Navy, 1660–1815*, Occasional Publications of the Navy Records Society, vol. 1 (Aldershot: Scolar Press for the Navy Records Society, 1994).
61. Pam and Derek Ayshford, *Ayshford Complete Trafalgar Roll*, CD-Rom. Available on the Internet at https://www.1805club.org/ayshford-trafalgar-roll. See also https://www.nationalarchives.gov.uk/aboutapps/trafalgarancestors/.
62. Patrick Marioné, *The Complete Navy List*, CD-Rom.
63. Nicholas Tracy, *Who's Who in Nelson's Navy: Two Hundred Heroes* (London: Chatham Publishing, 2005). A number of the biographies are based on the unpublished autobiographical sketches in TNA, ADM 9 series.
64. Colin White and the 1805 Club, *The Trafalgar Captains: The Lives and Memorials* (London: Chatham Publishing, 2005).
65. Roger Morriss, *Cockburn and the Royal Navy in Transition: Admiral Sir George Cockburn (1772–1853)* (Exeter: University of Exeter Press, 1997).
66. John E. Talbott, *The Pen and Ink Sailor: Charles Middleton and the King's Navy, 1778–1813* (London and Portland, OR: Frank Cass, 1998).
67. H. C. G. Matthew and Brian Harrison, eds., *Oxford Dictionary of National Biography: From the Earliest Times to the Year 2000* (Oxford: Oxford University Press in association with the British Academy, 2004).
68. Peter Le Fevre and Richard Harding, eds., *Precursors of Nelson: British Admirals of the Eighteenth Century* (London: Chatham, 2000).
69. Ibid., p. 8.
70. Paul Krajeski, *In the Shadow of Nelson: The Naval Leadership of Admiral Sir Charles Cotton, 1753–1812*, Contributions in Military Studies, no. 184 (Westport, CT: Greenwood Press, 2000).

71. Max Adams, *Admiral Collingwood* (London: Weidenfeld & Nicholson, 2005). Published in the USA as *Trafalgar's Lost Hero: Admiral Lord Collingwood and the Defeat of Napoleon* (Hoboken, NJ: John Wiley & Sons, 2005).
72. Hilary L. Rubenstein, *Trafalgar Captain: Durham of the Defiance* (Stroud: Tempus, 2004) and *The Durham Papers: Selections from the Papers of Admiral Sir Philip Charles Henderson Calderwood Durham, G.C.B. (1763–1845)*, Publications of the Navy Records Society, vol. 166 (London: Routledge, 2019). For other officer biographical studies, see Brian Vale, *The Audacious Admiral Cochrane: The True Life of a Naval Legend* (London: Conway Maritime Publishing, 2004); Iain Gordon, *Admiral of the Blue: The Life and Times of Admiral John Child Purvis, 1747–1825* (Barnsley: Pen & Sword, 2005); Victor T. Sharman, *Nelson's Hero: The Story of His 'Sea-Daddy' Captain William Locker* (Barnsley: Pen & Sword, 2005); Kevin D. McCranie, *Admiral Lord Keith and the Naval War against Napoleon* (Gainesville: University Press of Florida, 2006).
73. Duffy, 'All Was Hushed Up'.
74. Julian Stafford Corbett, *Some Principles of Maritime Strategy*, Classics of Sea Power series, with an introduction and notes by Eric J. Grove (Annapolis, MD: Naval Institute Press, 1988), the definitive edition of this work.
75. Richard Woodman, *The Sea Warriors: The Fighting Captains and Their Ships in the Age of Nelson* (London: Constable, 2001; London: Robinson, 2002).
76. Tom Wareham, *The Star Captains: Frigate Command in the Napoleonic Wars* (London: Chatham Publishing, 2001); *Frigate Commander* (London: Leo Cooper Ltd, 2004).
77. Michael A. Palmer, *Command at Sea: Naval Command and Control since the Sixteenth Century* (Cambridge, MA: Harvard University Press, 2005).
78. Geoffrey Till, *Understanding Victory: Naval Operations from Trafalgar to the Falklands* (Santa Barbara, CA: Praeger, [2014]).
79. Roger Knight, *Convoys: The British Struggle against Napoleonic Europe and America* (New Haven: Yale University Press, 2023).
80. Richard Hill, *The Prizes of War: The Naval Prize System in the Napoleonic Wars, 1793–1815* (Stroud: Sutton Publishing for the Royal Naval Museum, 1998).
81. Henry J. Bourguignon, *Sir William Scott, Lord Stowell: Judge of the High Court of Admiralty, 1798–1828* (Cambridge: Cambridge University Press, 1987, 2004).
82. S. A. Cavell, *Midshipmen and Quarterdeck Boys in the British Navy, 1771–1831* (Woodbridge: Boydell, 2012); Evan Wilson, *Social History of British Naval Officers, 1775–1815* (Woodbridge: Boydell, 2017); John Morrow, *British Flag Officers in the French Wars, 1793–1815: Admirals' Lives* (London: Bloomsbury, 2018); Evan Wilson, AnnaSara Hammar, and Jakob Seerup, *Eighteenth-Century Naval Officers: A Transnational Perspective* (Cham: Switzerland: Palgrave Macmillan, 2019).
83. Rodger, *Command of the Ocean*, p. 498; Sara Caputo, *Foreign Jack Tars: The British Navy and Transnational Seafarers during the Revolutionary and Napoleonic Wars* (Cambridge: Cambridge University Press, 2023), p. 30.

84. Margarette Lincoln, *Naval Wives and Mistresses* (London: National Maritime Museum, 2007).
85. Ellen Gill, *Naval Families, War and Duty in Britain, 1740–1820* (Woodbridge: Boydell, 2016).
86. Helen Watt with Anne Hawkins, eds., *Letters of Seamen in the Wars with France, 1793–1815* (Woodbridge: Boydell, 2016).
87. David Lyon, *The Sailing Ship Navy List: All the Ships of the Royal Navy–Built, Purchased, and Captured–1688–1860* (London: Conway Maritime Press, 1993, 1997).
88. Peter Goodwin, *Nelson's Ships: A History of the Vessels in Which He Served 1771–1805* (London: Conway Maritime, 2002).
89. Peter Goodwin, *The Ships of Trafalgar: The British, French and Spanish Fleets October 1805* (London: Conway Maritime Press, 2005).
90. Rif Winfield, *British Warships in the Age of Sail, 1793–1817: Design, Construction, Careers and Fates* (London: Chatham Publishing; St. Paul, MN: MBI Publishing Minnesota, 2005).
91. Rif Winfield and Stephen S. Roberts, *French Warships in the Age of Sail, 1786–1861: Design, Construction, Careers and Fates* (Barnsley: Seaforth, 2015); Rif Winfield, John Tredrea, Enrique García-Torralba Pérez, and Manual Blasco Felip, *Spanish Warships in the Age of Sail, 1700–1860: Design, Construction, Careers and Fates* (Barnsley: Seaforth, 2023).
92. Jan Glete, *Navies and Nations: Warships, Navies and State Building in Europe and America, 1500–1860*, Acta Universitatis Stockholmiensis, Stockholm Studies in History, vol. 48 (Stockholm: Almqvist & Wiksell International, 1993). See vol. 2, pp. 375–417, and tables on pp. 554, 568–70.
93. Ibid., vol. 2, p. 378.
94. Ibid., vol. 2, p. 378.
95. Alan McGowan, *HMS Victory: Her Construction, Career and Restoration* (London: Chatham Publishing, 1999).
96. David Cordingly, *The Billy Ruffian: The Bellerophon and the Downfall of Napoleon: The Biography of a Ship of the Line, 1782–1816* (London: Bloomsbury, 2003).
97. Sam Willis, *The Fighting Temeraire: The Battle of Trafalgar and the Ship That Inspired J. M. W. Turner's Most Beloved Painting* (New York: Pegasus, 2010).
98. Sam Willis, *Fighting at Sea in the Eighteenth Century: The Art of Sailing Warfare* (Woodbridge: Boydell, 2008).
99. Brian Lavery, *Shipboard Life and Organization, 1731–1815*, Publications of the Navy Records Society, vol. 138 (Aldershot, Brookfield, USA, Singapore, Sydney: Ashgate for the Navy Records Society, 1998).
100. James Davey, *The Transformation of British Naval Strategy: Seapower and Supply in Northern Europe, 1801–1812* (Woodbridge: Boydell, 2012).
101. James Davey, *In Nelson's Wake: The Navy and the Napoleonic Wars* (New Haven: Yale University Press, 2015), p. 313.

102. Ibid., p. 313.
103. Ibid., p. 314.
104. Ibid., p. 320.
105. Roger Morriss, *The Foundations of British Maritime Ascendancy: Resources, Logistics and the State, 1755–1815* (Cambridge: Cambridge University Press, 2011); C. I. Hamilton, *The Making of the Modern Admiralty: British Naval Policy-Making 1805–1927* (Cambridge: Cambridge University Press, 2011); Gareth Cole, *Arming the Royal Navy, 1793–1815* (London: Pickering & Chatto, 2012); Janet Macdonald, *Feeding Nelson's Navy: The True Story of Food at Sea* (London: Chatham; Mechanicsburg, PA: Stackpole Books, 2004); Roger Knight and Martin Wilcox, *Sustaining the Fleet, 1793–1815: War, the British Navy and the Contractor State* (Woodbridge: Boydell, 2010).
106. Roger Knight, *Britain against Napoleon: The Organization of Victory, 1793–1815* (London: Allen Lane, 2013).
107. Ibid., p. 372.
108. Quoted in ibid., p. 351.
109. Ibid., p. 175.
110. Ibid., p. 227.
111. Margarette Lincoln, *Representing the Royal Navy: British Sea Power, 1750–1815* (Aldershot: Ashgate, 2002).
112. Ibid., p. 114.
113. Ibid., p. 114.
114. Timothy Jenks, *Naval Engagements: Patriotism, Cultural Politics, and the Royal Navy, 1793–1815* (Oxford: Oxford University Press, 2006).
115. Ibid., p. 236.
116. Geoff Quilley, *Empire to Nation: Art, History and the Visualization of Maritime Britain 1768–1829* (New Haven: Yale University Press, 2011), pp. 219–49.
117. James Davey and Richard Johns, *Broadsides: Caricature and the Navy, 1756–1815* (Barnsley: Seaforth for the National Maritime Museum, 2012).
118. Michael V. Leggiere, *Napoleon and the Operational Art of War: Essays in Honour of Donald D. Howard* (Leiden and Boston: Brill, 2016; revised and extended edition, 2021).
119. Alexander Mikaberidze, *The Napoleonic Wars: A Global History* (Oxford: Oxford University Press, 2020).
120. Michael Broers and Philip Dwyer, eds., *The Cambridge History of the Napoleonic Wars*, vol. 1: *Politics and Diplomacy* (Cambridge: Cambridge University Press, 2022).
121. Bruno Colson and Alexander Mikaberidze, eds., *The Cambridge History of the Napoleonic Wars*, vol. 2: *Fighting the Napoleonic Wars* (Cambridge: Cambridge University Press, 2023).

122. Alan I. Forrest and Peter Hicks, eds., *The Cambridge History of the Napoleonic Wars*, vol. 3: *Experience, Culture and Memory* (Cambridge: Cambridge University Press, 2022).
123. For the concept of cumulative and sequential strategy, see J. C. Wylie, *Military Strategy*, Classics of Sea Power (Annapolis: Naval Institute Press, 1989), pp. 22–7.
124. Beatrice G. Heuser and Athena S. Leoussi, *Famous Battles and How They Shaped the Modern World*, 2 vols. (Yorkshire and Philadelphia: Pen and Sword, 2018).

SELECT BIBLIOGRAPHY

Archival Sources

The National Archives, Kew.
U.S. Naval War College, Newport, Rhode Island.
Captain Frank M. Snyder, USN, Papers. Manuscript Coll. 137, Box 25, Folder 9: 'Trafalgar in Verse: The Battle Is Won, but Nelson Is Dead', poems compiled and edited by Frank M. Snyder, 2005.

Published Primary Sources

Beatty, William, M. D. *Authentic Narrative of the Death of Lord Nelson: Comprising Several Interesting Circumstances Preceding, Attending and Subsequent to, that Event.* 3rd edition. London: W. Mason, 1825.
Beresford, Admiral Lord Charles. *The Memoirs of Admiral Lord Charles Beresford Written by Himself.* 3rd edition. London: Methuen & Co. Ltd, [1914].
Bonaparte, Napoléon. *Correspondance générale*, vol. 5: *Boulogne, Trafalgar, Austerlitz, 1805*. Paris: Fayard, 2008.
Bourchier, Lady [Jane]. *Memoir of the Life of Admiral Sir Edward Codrington with Selections from his Public and Private Correspondence.* 2 volumes. London: Longmans, Green & Co., 1873.
Collingwood, G. L. Newnham, ed. *A Selection from the Public and Private Correspondence of Vice-Admiral Lord Collingwood.* London, 1829.
Corbett, Julian S. *Fighting Instructions, 1530–1816*. Publications of the Navy Records Society, vol. 29. London: Navy Records Society, 1905.
Cowie, Leonard W. *Lord Nelson, 1758–1805: A Bibliography*. Westport: Meckler, 1990 [pp. 155–7: bibliography of published eyewitness accounts of Trafalgar].
Desbrière, Édouard. *Trafalgar: The Naval Campaign of 1805*, translated and edited by Constance Eastwick. 3 volumes. Oxford: Clarendon Press, 1933.
Firth, C. H. *Naval Songs and Ballads*. Publications of the Navy Records Society, vol. 33. London: Navy Records Society, 1908.
Fraser, Edward. *The Enemy at Trafalgar: Eye-Witness Narratives, Dispatches and Letters from the French and Spanish Fleets.* London, 1906, reprinted with an introduction by Marianne Czisnik and Michael Nash. London and Mechanicsburg, PA: Chatham Publishing and Stackpole Books, 2004.

Fraser, Edward. *The Sailors Whom Nelson Led: Their Doings Described by Themselves.* London, 1913.

González-Aller Hierro, José Ignacio, ed. *La campaña de Trafalgar (1804–1805): corpus documental conservado en los archivos españoles.* 2 volumes. Madrid: Ministerio de Defensa, Armada Española, 2004.

Hattendorf, John B., R. J. B. Knight, A. W. H. Pearsall, N. A. M. Rodger, and Geoffrey Till, eds. *British Naval Documents, 1204–1960.* Publications of the Navy Records Society, vol. 131. Aldershot: Scolar Press for the Navy Records Society, 1993.

Hughes, Edward, ed. *The Private Correspondence of Admiral Lord Collingwood.* Publications of the Navy Records Society, vol. 98. London: Navy Records Society, 1957.

Jackson, Sir Thomas Sturges. *Logs of the Great Sea Fights, 1794–1805.* Publications of the Navy Records Society, vol. 18. London: Navy Records Society, 1900.

Lambert, Andrew, ed. *Letters and Papers of Professor Sir John Knox Laughton, 1830–1915.* Publications of the Navy Records Society, vol. 143. Aldershot: Navy Records Society, 2002.

Laughton, John Knox, ed. *Letters and Despatches of Horatio, Viscount Nelson, Duke of Bronte, Vice Admiral of the White Squadron.* London: Longman's, 1886.

Laughton, John Knox, ed. *Letters and Papers of Charles, Lord Barham, Admiral of the Red Squadron, 1758–1813.* Publications of the Navy Records Society, vols. 32, 38, 39. London: Navy Records Society, 1907–11.

Leyland, John, ed. *Dispatches and Letters Relating to the Blockade of Brest, 1803–1805.* Publications of the Navy Records Society, vols. 14, 21. London: Navy Records Society, 1899, 1902.

Lincoln, Margarette, ed. *Nelson and Napoléon.* London: National Maritime Museum, Greenwich, 2005.

Lloyd, Christopher, ed. *The Keith Papers, Selected from the Papers of Admiral Viscount Keith,* vol. 3. Publications of Navy Records Society, vol. 96. London: Navy Records Society, 1955.

Napoleon I, Emperor of the French. *Correspondence de Napoléon Ier: publiée par ordre de l'empereur Napoléon III.* Paris: H. Plon, J. Dumaine, 1858–70.

Nicolas, Sir Nicholas Harris, ed. *The Dispatches and Letters of Vice Admiral Lord Viscount Nelson with Notes.*7 volumes. London: Henry Colburn, 1844–6.

[Southey, Robert]. *Letters from England by Don Manuel Alvarez Espriella.* London: Longman & Co, 1807.

Willis, Sam. *In the Hour of Victory: The Royal Navy at War in the Age of Nelson.* New York and London: W. W. Norton, 2014.

Printed Government Documents

Great Britain. Admiralty. Committee on Tactics of Nelson at Battle of Trafalgar. Navy (Trafalgar): *Report of a Committee Appointed by the Admiralty to Examine and Consider the Evidence Relating to the Tactics Employed by Nelson at the Battle of Trafalgar.* Cd. 7120. London, HMSO, 1913.

Contemporary Newspapers and Periodicals

Barbados Mercury and Bridgetown Gazette
City Gazette [Charleston, SC]
Gazette Nationale ou Le Moniteur Universel
Gibraltar Gazette
Le Journal de l'Empire
Le Journal de Paris
The London Gazette
Mecurio de España
The Mercury [Hobart, Tasmania]
The Naval Chronicle
The Times [London]

Contemporary Pamphlets and Broadsheets

Entrada pública del Almirante Nelson en la corte de Pluton el dia 23 de octúbre. Cádiz: Manuel Ximénez Carreño, 1805.

Fernández Varela, Manuel. *Oracion fúnebre: que en las exêquias generales celebradas el dia 23 de diciembre de 1805. á expensas y dovoción [sic] del Real Cuerpo de Marina del Departamento del Ferrol, por las ánimas de sus valerosos individuos y de todos los demás militares y marineros que han dado su vida por el rey y por la patria en el combate del 21 de octubre*. Mexico: Impreso en Madrid, y por su original en la Oficina de doña Maria Fernandez Jauregui, calle de santo Domingo, 1807.

Octavas á la batalla naval del dia 21 de octubre de 1805, à la vista de Cadiz: entre la esquadra inglesa, y la combinada de Francia y España. Reimpresas en México: Por don Mariano de Zúñiga y Ontiveros, calle del Espíritu Santo, 1806.

Secondary Sources

Aberg, Alan. 'Saving the Victory', *The Mariner's Mirror*, vol. 91, no. 2 (2005), pp. 358–68.

Adkin, Mark. *The Sharpe Companion: The Early Years. A Guide to Bernard Cornwell's Richard Sharpe Novels*. London: HarperCollins, 2003.

Adkin, Mark. *The Trafalgar Companion: A Guide to the Most Famous Sea Battle and the Life of Admiral Lord Nelson*. London: Arum Press, 2005.

Adkins, Roy. *Nelson's Trafalgar: The Battle That Changed the World*. New York: Viking, 2005.

Alcalá Galiano, Antonio. *Recuerdos de un Anciano*. Madrid: Libreriá de Perlado, Páez y C[a], 1907.

Allen, Derek, and Peter Hore. *News of Nelson: John Lapenotiere's Race from Trafalgar to London*. Brussels: SEFF edition, 2005.

Amos, Susan, and Louis Roeder. *Nelson's State Funeral, 1806: How to Bury a National Hero*. Cranbook, Kent: Four Wents Publishing, 2020.

Bainbridge, Simon. *British Poetry and the Revolutionary and Napoleonic Wars: Visions of Conflict*. Oxford: Oxford University Press, 2003.

Bann, Stephen. *The Clothing of Clio: A Study of the Representation of History in Nineteenth Century Britain and France*. Cambridge: Cambridge University Press, 1984.

Bartlett Library Researchers, National Maritime Museum, Cornwall. 'Gilding the Gingerbread: Sir Richard Strachan's Action, November 3rd 1805' (2005). https://web.archive.org/web/20060928025209/http://www.nmmc.co.uk/images/uploaded/downloads/Trafalgar_Strachan.pdf.

Battesti, Michèle. *Trafalgar: les aléas de la stratégie naval de Napoléon*. Saint-Cloud: Napoléon 1er Éditions, 2004.

Baudry, A. *The Naval Battle: A Study of the Tactical Factors*. London: Hugh Rees, Ltd, 1914.

Beresford, Lord Charles, and H. W. Wilson. *Nelson and His Times*. London: Harmsworth Brothers, 1898.

Blanco Núñez, José María, Pablo de Castro Martín, and Enrique García Hernán, coord. *Poder terreste y poder naval en la época de la batalla de Trafalgar*. XXXI Congreso Internacional de Historia Militar. Madrid: Imprenta Ministerio de Defensa, 2006.

Bold, John. *Greenwich: An Architectural History of the Royal Hospital for Seamen and the Queen's House*. New Haven: Yale University Press, 2000.

Bönker, Dirk. *Militarism in a Global Age: Naval Ambitions in Germany and the United States before World War I*. Ithaca, NY: Cornell University Press, 2012.

Breemer, Jan S. *The Burden of Trafalgar: Decisive Battle and Naval Strategic Expectations on the Eve of the First World War*. Newport Paper No. 6. Newport: Naval War College Press, 1993. Republished in *Journal of Strategic Studies*, vol. 17, no. 1 (March 1994), pp. 33–62.

Brenton, Edward Pelham. *The Naval History of Great Britain from the Year MDCCLXXXIII to MDCCCXXXVI. A New and Greatly Improved Edition*. 2 volumes. London, 1837.

Brockliss, Laurence, John Cardwell, and Michael Moss. 'Nelson's Grand National Obsequies', *The English Historical Review*, vol. 121, no. 490 (2006), pp. 162–82. http://www.jstor.org/stable/3806244.

Cannadine, David, ed. *Admiral Lord Nelson: Context and Legacy*. London: Palgrave Macmillan, 2005.

Cannadine, David, ed. *Trafalgar in History: A Battle and Its Afterlife*. London: Palgrave Macmillan, 2006.

Castex, Raoul. *Strategic Theories: Selections Translated and Edited with an Introduction by Eugenia C. Kiesling*. Classics of Sea Power. Annapolis: Naval Institute Press, 1994.

Castex, Raoul. *Théories stratégiques*. Paris: Société d'Editions Géographiques, Maritimes et Coloniales, 1937.

Cervera Pery, José. *El panteón de marinos ilustres: trayectoria histórica, reseña biográfica*. Madrid: Ministerio de Defensa, Armada. Secretaría General Técnica, 2004.

Cesario, Bradley M. *New Crusade: The Royal Navy and British Navalism, 1884–1914*. Berlin and Boston: De Gruyter Oldenbourg, 2021.

Chapela Rey, Jesús. *Campaign Medals and Orders of Revolutionary and Napoleonic Wars (1792–1815)*. Independently published, 2022.

Chevalier, Louis Édouard. *Histoire de la marine sous le consulate et empire*. Paris: Hachette, 1886.

Clayton, Tim, and Phil Craig. *Trafalgar: The Men, the Battle, the Storm*. London: Hodder & Stoughton, 2004.

Clowes, William Laird. *The Royal Navy: A History from the Earliest Times to 1900*. London: Sampson, Low, Marston & Co., 1897–1903.

Colomb, P. H. *The Battle of Trafalgar*. London: W. Clowes & Sons, Limited, 1905.

Colville, Quintin, and James Davey, eds. *Nelson, Navy and Nation: The Royal Navy and the British People, 1688–1815*. London: Conway for the National Maritime Museum, 2013.

Colville, Quintin, and James Davey, eds. *A New Naval History*. Manchester: Manchester University Press with the National Maritime Museum, 2019.

Conley, Mary A. *From Jack Tar to Union Jack: Representing Naval Manhood in the British Empire, 1870–1918*. Manchester: Manchester University Press, 2009.

Corbett, Julian S. *The Campaign of Trafalgar*. London: Longman's Green & Co., 1910.

Corbett, Julian S. 'Napoleon and the British Navy after Trafalgar'. The Creighton Memorial Lecture. *The Quarterly Review*, no. 237 (April 1922), pp. 238–55.

Corbett, Sir Julian S. *Naval Operations*. History of the Great War Based on Official Documents by Direction of the Historical Section of the Committee of Imperial Defence. London: Longmans, Green & Co., 1920.

Corbett, Julian S. *Some Principles of Maritime Strategy*, with an introduction and notes by Eric J. Grove. Classics of Sea Power series. Annapolis: Naval Institute Press, 1988.

Cordingly, David. *Maritime Painting in England, 1700–1900*. New York: Clarkson N. Potter, 1973.

Cordingly, David. *Nicholas Pocock 1740–1821*. Annapolis: Naval Institute Press, 1986.

Cornwall, Bernard. *Sharpe's Trafalgar: Richard Sharpe and the Battle of Trafalgar, 21 October 1805*. London: Harper Collins, 2000.

Czisnik, Marianne. *Horatio Nelson: A Controversial Hero*. London: Hodder Arnold, 2005.

Dancy, J. Ross, and Evan Wilson. 'Sir John Orde and the Trafalgar Campaign: A Failure of Information Sharing', *Naval War College Review*, vol. 73, no. 2 (Spring 2020), pp. 141–71.

Davey, James. *In Nelson's Wake: The Navy and the Napoleonic Wars*. New Haven: Yale University Press, 2015.

Davey, James, and Richard Johns. *Broadsides: Caricature and the Navy, 1756–1815*. Barnsley: Seaforth Publishing, 2012.

Depeyre, Michel. *Tactiques et stratégies navales de la France et du Royaume-Uni de 1690 à 1815*. Paris: Economica, 1998.

Douglas-Morris, Kenneth. *Naval General Service Medal Roll, 1793–1840*. Uckfield, East Sussex: Naval & Military Press, n.d.

Duffy, Michael. ' "...All Was Hushed Up": The Hidden Trafalgar', *The Mariner's Mirror*, vol. 91, no. 2 (May 2005), pp. 216–40.

Duffy, Michael. 'The Gunnery at Trafalgar: Training, Tactics or Temperament?', *Journal for Maritime Research*, vol. 7, no. 1 (2005), pp. 140–69.

Duffy, Michael. *Touch and Take: The Battle of Trafalgar, 21 October 1805*. Shelton, Nottinghamshire: The 1805 Club, 2005.

Dunn, Steve R. *The Power and the Glory: Royal Navy Fleet Reviews from Earliest Times to 2005*. Barnsley: Seaforth, 2021.

Ekins, Charles. *Naval Battles from 1744 to the Peace in 1814 Critically Reviewed and Illustrated*. London: Baldwin, Cradock, and Joy, 1824.

Epkenhans, Michael, Jörg Hillmann, and Frank Nägler. *Jutland: World War I's Greatest Naval Battle*. Lexington, KY: University Press of Kentucky, [2015].

Evans, David C., and Mark Peattie. *Kaigun: Strategy, Tactics, and Technology in the Imperial Japanese Navy, 1887–1941*. Annapolis: Naval Institute Press, 1997.

Fernández-González, F., L. D. Ferreiro, and H. Nowacki, eds. *Technology of the Ships of Trafalgar: Proceedings of an International Congress Held at the Escuela Técnica Superior de Ingenieros Navales, Madrid, and the Diputación Provincial, Cádiz, 3–5 November 2005*. Madrid: Escuela Técnica Superior de Ingenieros Navales, Universidad Politécnica de Madrid, 2006.

Ferrer de Couto, José. *Historia del combate naval de Trafalgar, precedida de la del renacimiento de la marina española durante el siglo XVIII*. Madrid: Imp. de W. Ayguals de Izco, 1851.

Fiske, Bradley A. *The Navy as a Fighting Machine*, with introduction and notes by Wayne P. Hughes, Jr. Classics of Sea Power series. Annapolis: Naval Institute Press, 1988.

Forrest, Alan, gen. ed. *The Cambridge History of the Napoleonic Wars*. 3 volumes. Cambridge: Cambridge University Press, 2023.

Fraser, Edward. *The Enemy at Trafalgar: Eye-Witness' Narratives. Dispatches and Letters from the French and Spanish Fleets*. London: Hodder and Stoughton, 1906. Reprinted with an introduction by Mariane Czisnik and Michael Nash. London: Chatham, 2004.

Gazzard, Katherine. *The Art of Naval Portraiture*. London: Royal Museums Greenwich, 2024.

Gillet, Jean-Claude. *La Marine impériale: le grand rêve de Napoléon*. Paris: Bernard Giovanangeli Éditeur, 2010.

Glete, Jan. *Navies and Nations: Warships, Navies, and State Building in Europe and America, 1500–1860*. 2 volumes. Stockholm: Almqvist & Wiksell, 1993.

Godwin, Peter. *The Ships of Trafalgar: The British, French, and Spanish Fleets, 21 October 1805*. Annapolis: Naval Institute Press, 2005.

Gordon, Andrew. *The Rules of the Game: Jutland and British Naval Command*. London: John Murray, 1996.

Guimerá Ravina, Agustín. 'Antonio Escaño, un héroe Olvidado', *La Aventura de la Historia*, vol. 7, no. 84 (October 2005), pp. 66–71.

Guimerá Ravina, Agustín, and Victor Peralta, eds. *El equilibrio de los imperios: de Utrecht a Trafalgar*. Actas de la VIII Reunión Científica de la Fundación Española de Historia Moderna. Madrid, 2–6 de junio de 2004. Madrid: Fundación Española de Historia Moderna, 2005.

Guimerá Ravina, Agustín, Alberto Ramos, and Gonzao Butrón, eds. *Trafalgar y el mundo atlántico*. Madrid: Marcial Pons Historia, 2005.

Guimerá, Agustín, ed. *Trafalgar: una derrota gloriosa*. Madrid: Desperta Ferro Ediciones, 2023.

Hahn, George H. *The Ocean Bards: British Poetry and the War at Sea, 1794–1915*. Oxford: Peter Lang, 2008.

Hamilton, C. I. 'Hagiography and the Victorian Hero', *The Historical Journal*, vol. 23, no. 2 (June 1980), pp. 381–98.

Hamilton, W. Mark. 'The "New Navalism" and the British Navy League, 1894–1914', *The Mariner's Mirror*, vol. 78, no. 1 (1978), pp. 37–44.

Harding, Richard, ed. *A Great and Glorious Victory: New Perspectives on the Battle of Trafalgar*. Barnsley: Seaforth Publishing, 2008.

Harding, Richard. *Modern Naval History: Debates and Prospects*. London: Bloomsbury, 2016.

Harding, Richard, and Agustín Guimerá, eds. *Sailors, Statemen and the Implementation of Naval Strategy*. Woodbridge: The Boydell Press, 2024.

Harper, Vice Admiral John, and Admiral Reginal Bacon. *The Jutland Scandal: The Truth about the World War's Greatest Sea Battle*. Barnsley: Frontline Books, 2015.

Hattendorf, John B. *The Naval Novel: A Literary Genre in Historical Perspective*. Middletown, RI: Stone Tower Press, 2023.

Hattendorf, John B., ed.-in-chief. *The Oxford Encyclopedia of Maritime History*. Oxford: Oxford University Press, 2007.

Hattendorf, John B. *Reflections on Naval History: Collected Essays*. Newport: Naval War College Press, 2023.

Hattendorf, John B. *Talking about Naval History: A Collection of Essays*. Newport: Naval War College Press, 2011.

Hattendorf, John B., and Lynn C. Hattendorf. *A Bibliography of the Works of Alfred Thayer Mahan*. Newport: Naval War College Press, 1986.

Hattendorf, John B., and Malcolm Murfett, eds. *The Limitations of Military Power: Essays Presented to Professor Norman Gibbs on His 80th Birthday*. London: Macmillan, 1990.

Hattendorf, John B., B. M. Simpson, and John R. Wadleigh. *Sailors and Scholars: The Centennial History of the Naval War College*. Newport: Naval War College Press, 1984; revised and expanded as *Sailors and Scholars: The History of the Naval War College, 1884–2009*, 2025.

Hayward, John, Diana Birch, and Richard Bishop. *British Battles and Medals*. 7th edition. London: Spink, 2006.

Heuser, Beatrice G., and Athena S. Leoussi. *Famous Battles and How They Shaped the Modern World*. 2 volumes. Yorkshire and Philadelphia: Pen and Sword, 2018.

Heuvel, Sean, and John Rodgaard, eds. *From across the Sea: North Americans in Nelson's Navy*. Warwick: Helion & Company, 2020.

Hobson, Rolf. *Imperialism at Sea: Naval Strategic Thought, the Ideology of Sea Power and the Tirpitz Plan, 1875–1914*. Studies in Central European Histories. Boston and Leiden: Brill, 2002.

Hoock, Holger. *The King's Artists: The Royal Academy of Arts and the Politics of British Culture, 1760–1840*. Oxford: Clarendon Press, 2003.

Hoock, Holger, ed. *History, Commemoration, and National Preoccupation: Trafalgar, 1805–2005*. Oxford: Oxford University Press for the British Academy, 2007.

Hore, Peter. *Nelson's Band of Brothers: Lives and Memorials*. Barnsley: Seaforth, 2015.

Hore, Peter. *HMS Pickle: The Swiftest Ship in Nelson's Fleet*. Stroud: The History Press, 2015.

Hughes, Eleanor. *Spreading Canvas: Eighteenth Century British Maritime Painting*. New Haven: Yale University Press, 2016.

Hunt, Geoff. *The Marine Art of Geoff Hunt: Master Painter of the Naval World of Nelson and Patrick O'Brien*. Mystic, CT: Mystic Seaport, 2004.

James, William M. *The Naval History of Great Britain from the Declaration of War by France in 1793 to the Accession of George IV. A New Edition, with Additions and Notes and An Account of the Burmese War and the Battle of Navarino by Captain Chamier, R.N.* 6 volumes. London, 1836–7; reprinted with introductions by Andrew Lambert. London Conway Maritime Press and Mechanicsburg, PA: Stackpole Books, 2002.

Jenks, Timothy. 'Contesting the Hero: The Funeral of Admiral Lord Nelson', *Journal of British Studies*, vol. 39, no. 4 (2000), pp. 422–53. http://www.jstor.org/stable/175858.

Jenks, Timothy. *Naval Engagements: Patriotism, Cultural Politics, and the Royal Navy, 1793–1815*. Oxford: Oxford University Press, 2006.

Johnson, Kenneth G. 'Napoleon's War at Sea', in Michal V. Leggiere, ed., *Napoleon and the Operational Art of War*. Leiden: Brill, 2016; revised and extended, 2021).

Johnston, Wiliam, William G. P. Rawling, Richard H. Gimblett, and John MacFarlane. *The Seabound Coast: The Official History of the Royal Canadian Navy, 1867–1939*. Toronto: Dundurn Press, 2010.

Jordon, Gerald, and Nicholas Rogers. 'Heroes: Patriotism and Liberty in Hanoverian England', *Journal of British Studies*, vol. 28, no. 3 (July 1989), pp. 201–24.

Jurien de la Gravière, Edouard. *Guerres maritimes sous la République et l'Empire*. Paris: Charpentier, 1847.

Kennedy, Paul M. *The Rise and Fall of British Naval Mastery*. London: Penguin, 1976, 2017.

Kennedy, Paul, and Evan Wilson, eds. *Navies in Multipolar Worlds: From the Age of Sail to the Present*. London: Routledge, 2020.

Knight, Roger. *Britain against Napoleon: The Organization of Victory, 17893–1815*. London: Allen Lane, 2013.

Knight, Roger. *The Pursuit of Victory: The Life and Achievement of Horatio Nelson*. London: Allen Lane, 2005.

Kowner, Rotem. *Tsushima*. Great Battles. Oxford: Oxford University Press, 2022.

Lambert, Andrew. *The British Way of War: Julian Corbett and the Battle for a National Strategy*. New Haven: Yale University Press, 2021.

Lambert, Andrew. *The Crimean War: British Grand Strategy against Russia, 1853–56*. Manchester: Manchester University Press, 1990.

Lambert, Andrew. *The Foundations of Naval History: John Knox Laughton and the Historical Profession*. London: Chatham, 1998.

Lambert, Andrew. *The Last Sailing Battlefleet: Maintaining Naval Mastery 1815–1850*. London: Conway, 1991.

Lambert, Andrew. 'Teaching by Example: Julian Corbett's *The Campaign of Trafalgar* of 1910', in Richard Harding and Agustin Guimerá, eds., *Sailors, Statesmen and the Implementation of Naval Strategy*. Woodbridge: The Boydell Prees, 2024, pp. 120–40.

Lambert, Andrew, ed. *21st Century Corbett: Maritime Strategy and Naval Policy for the Modern Era*. Annapolis: Naval Institute Press, 2017.

Lambert, Nicholas. *The Neptune Factor: Alfred Thayer Mahan and the Concept of Sea Power*. Annapolis: Naval Institute Press, 2023.

Laughton, J. K. 'The Scientific Study of Naval History', *Journal of the Royal United Services Institution*, vol. 18 (1874), pp. 508–27.

LeFevre, Peter, and Richard Harding, eds. *British Admirals of the Napoleonic Wars: The Contemporaries of Nelson*. London: Chatham Publishing, 2005.

Lincoln, Margarette, ed. *Nelson and Napoléon*. London: National Maritime Museum, 2005.

Littlewood, Kevin, and Beverly Butler. *Of Ships and Stars: Maritime Heritage and the Founding of the National Maritime Museum*. London: Athlone Press, 1998.

Lloyd, Clive L. *A History of Napoleonic and American Prisoners of War, 1756–1816: Hulk, Deport and Parole*. Woodbridge: Antique Collectors' Club, 2007.

Lucas, Anya, Richard Johns, Sophie Stewart, and Stephan Paine. *The Painted Hall: Sir James Thornhill's Masterpiece at Greenwich*. London and New York: Merrell, 2019.

Mace, Rodney. *Trafalgar Square: Emblem of Empire*. London: Lawrence and Wishart, 1976, reprinted 2005.

Mackenzie, John M., ed. *Popular Imperialism and the Military, 1850–1950*. Manchester: Manchester University Press, 1992.

Mackenzie, Robert Holden. *The Trafalgar Roll: The Ships and the Officers*. London: George Allen, 1913; reprinted Annapolis: Naval Institute Press, 1989.

Mackesy, Piers. *The War in the Mediterranean, 1803–1810*. Cambridge, MA: Harvard University Press, 1957.

Mahan, Alfred Thayer. 'The Battle of Trafalgar. Read February 1, 1898', in Military History Society of Massachusetts, *Naval Actions and Operations against Cuba and Puerto Ricco, 1593–1815*. Boston: The Stillings Press, 1901.

Mahan, A. T. *The Influence of Sea Power upon the French Revolution and Empire. 1793–1812*. Boston: Little Brown, 1892.

Mahan, A. T. *The Life of Nelson: The Embodiment of the Sea Power of Great Britain*. Boston: Little Brown, 1897.

Maltzahn, Kurt von. 'Was lehrt das Buch des Generals von Clausewitz "Vom Kriege" dem Seeoffizier?', *Marine-Rundschau*, vol. 16 (June 1905), pp. 683–702; Admiral von Maltzahn, trans. W. H. Hancock, *What Lesson Has General von Clausewitz's Work, 'On War', for the Naval Officer?* (Portsmouth: War College, November 1906).

Marder, Arthur J. *Old Friends, New Enemies: The Royal Navy and the Imperial Japanese Navy*, vol. 1: *Strategic Illusions, 1936–1941*. Oxford: Clarendon Press, 1981.

Marliani, Manuel. *Combate de Trafalgar: vindicacion de la Armada española contra los aseretones injuriosas vertidas por Mr Thiers en su historia del consulado y el imperio*. Madrid: Impreso de Orden Superior, 1850.

McCranie, Kevin D. 'Through the Lens of Sea Power and Maritime Strategy: Alfred T. Mahan and Julian S. Corbett on the Napoleonic Wars', *The Northern Mariner*, vol. 33, nos. 3–4 (Fall–Winter 2023), pp. 335–52.

McGowan, Alan. *HMS Victory: Her Construction, Career and Restoration*. London: Chatham Publishing, 1999.

Mikaberidze, Alexander. *The Napoleonic Wars: A Global History*. New York: Oxford University Press, 2020.

Monaque, Rémi. *Trafalgar: 21 octobre 1805*. Paris: Tallendier Bibliothèque Napoléonienne, 2005.

Musteen, Jason R. *Nelson's Refuge: Gibraltar in the Age of Napoleon*. Annapolis: Naval Insititute Press, 2011.

Nicolson, Adam. *Men of Honour: Trafalgar and the Making of the English Hero*. London: HarperCollins, 2005.

Oliver, Adam. '"In spite of lip service and tall columns he is half forgotten": A Brief Revisit to the Trafalgar Centenary Celebrations', *Trafalgar Chronicle*, no. 15 (2005), pp. 230–8.

Oman, Carola. *Nelson*. London: Hodder and Stoughton, 1947.

Orth, Kathrin. 'Sir John Orde, 1751–1824', in Peter LeFevre and Richard Harding, eds., *British Admirals of the Napoleonic Wars: The Contemporaries of Nelson*. London: Chatham Publishing, 2005, pp. 67–89.

Parkes, Oscar. *British Battleships: Warrior 1860 to Vanguard 1950*. London: Seeley, 1957.

Parow, Walter. *Die Seeschlacht bei Trafalgar…Mit einer Tafel*. Wissenschaftliche Beilage zum Programm der Friedrichs-Werderschen Oberrealschule zu Berlin. Ostern 1890. Berlin: n.p., 1890.

Parrill, Sue. *Nelson's Navy in Fiction and Film: Depictions of British Sea Power in the Napoleonic Era*. Jefferson, NC: McFarland & Co., 2009.

Pérez Galdós, Benito. *Trafalgar*. Madrid: Imp. de J. Noguera, 1873. Digital copy at http://bdh-rd.bne.es/viewer.vm?id=0000206933&page=1.

Pérez Galdós, Benito. *Trafalgar: A Tale*. Translated by Clara Bell. New York: William S. Gottsberger, 1884.

Phillips, Carla Rahn. '"The Life Blood of the Navy": Recruiting Sailors in Eighteenth Century Spain', *The Mariner's Mirror*, vol. 87, no. 4 (2001), pp. 420–45.

Pratt, Fletcher. *The Battles That Changed History*. Garden City: Hannover House, 1956.

Quarm, Roger. 'Buying Nelson: Sir James Caird's Gifts to the National Maritime Museum', *The Mariner's Mirror*, vol. 91, no. 2 (2005), pp. 369–83.

Quarm, Roger, and John Wyllie. *W. L. Wyllie: Marine Artist, 1851–1931*. London: Chris Bettles, Ltd, 1981.

Quilley, Geoff. *Empire to Nation: Art, History, and the Visualization of Maritime Britain, 1768–1829*. New Haven: Yale University Press, 2011.

Quirk, Ronald J. *Literature as Introspection: Spain Confronts Trafalgar*. Currents in Comparative Romance Languages and Literatures, vol. 57. New York: Peter Lang, 1998.

Riding, Christine, and Richard Johns. *Turner and the Sea*. London: Thames & Hudson in association with Royal Museums Greenwich, 2013.

Roberts, Andrew. *Napoleon: A Life*. New York: Viking, 2014.

Rodger, N. A. M. *The Command of the Ocean: A Naval History of Britian, 1649–1815*. London: Allen Lane, Penguin, in association with the National Maritime Museum, Greenwich, 2004.

Rodger, N. A. M. *The Price of Victory: A Naval History of Britian, 1815–1945*. London: Allen Lane, Penguin, in association with the National Maritime Museum, Greenwich, 2024.

Rodríguez González, Agustín R. 'The Spanish at Trafalgar: Ships, Cannons, Men and a Problematic Alliance', *Journal for Maritime Research*, vol. 7, no. 1 (2005), pp. 26–43. DOI: 10.1080/21533369.2005.9668343.

Rodríguez González, Agustín R. *Trafalgar y el conflicto naval anglo-español del siglo XVIII*. Madrid: ACTAS, 2005.

Rubinstein, Hilary L. *Trafalgar Captain: Durham of the Defiance*. Stroud: Tempus Publishing Ltd, 2005.

Rubenstein, Hillary L. 'Trafalgar's Last Survivors', *The Trafalgar Chronicle*, New Series, vol. 9 (2024), pp. 135–45.

Runn, Steve. *The Power and the Glory: Royal Navy Fleet Reviews from Earliest Times to 2005*. Barnsley: Seaforth, 2021.

Russell, Wiliam Clark. *Nelson and the Naval Supremacy of England*. London: G. P. Putman, 1890.

Sainsbury, A. B. *The Centenary of the Navy Records Society, 1893–1993*. London: Navy Records Society, 1993.

Saylor, Eric, and Christopher M. Scheer, eds. *The Sea in British Musical Imagination*. Woodbridge: Boydell, 2015.

Schroeder, Paul W. *The Transformation of European Politics, 1763–1848*. Oxford: Oxford University Press, 1994.

Shanken, Andrew M. *The Everyday Life of Memorials*. New York: Zone Books, 2022.

Shannon, David. *Nelson Remembered: The Nelson Centenary, 1905*. [Karawara, W. Australia]: Broadsides Maritime Publications, in Association with the Nelson Society, 2007.

Slee, Peter R. H. *Learning and Education: The Study of Modern History in the Universities of Oxford, Cambridge and Manchester, 1800–1914*. Manchester: University of Manchester Press, 1986.

Spence, Daniel Owen. *Colonial Naval Culture and British Imperialism, 1922–1967*. Manchester: Manchester University Press, 2015.

Sumida, Jon Tetsuro. *Inventing Grand Strategy and Teaching Command: The Classic Works of Alfred Thayer Mahan Reconsidered*. Baltimore: The Johns Hopkins University Press, 1997.

Sweetman, Jack, ed. *The Great Admirals: Command at Sea, 1587–1945*. Annapolis: Naval Institute Press, 1997.

Talbot, John E. *The Pen and Ink Sailor: Charles Middleton and the King's Navy, 1778–1813*. London: Frank Cass, 1998.

Taylor, Rear-Admiral A. H. Taylor. 'Some New Aspects of the Battle of Trafalgar', *The Journal of the Royal United Services Institution*, vol. 82, no. 528 (November 1937), pp. 690–712.

Thiers, Adolphe. *The Historical Works of M. Adolphe Thiers, Translated by Thomas W. Redhead, Esq*. London: A. Fullarton and Co, 1847, vol. 2.

Tildesley, Jim. 'The Influence of the Theories of John Clerk of Eldin on British Fleet Tactics, 1782–1805', *Mariner's Mirror*, vol. 106, no. 2 (May 2020), pp. 162–74.

Todorov, Nicola. 'La non-défaite de Trafalgar'. https://theconversation.com/la-non-defaite-de-trafalgar-78295.

Tomlinson, Barbara. *Commemorating the Seafarer: Monuments, Memorials and Memory*. Woodbridge: Boydell Press for the National Maritime Museum, 2015.

Tracy, Nicholas. *Britannia's Palette: The Arts of Naval Victory*. Montreal: McGill-Queens University Press, 2007.

Troude, O. *Batailles navales de la France*. Paris: Challamel aîné, 1867–8.

Tunstall, Brian. *Naval Warfare in the Age of Sail: The Evolution of Fighting Tactics, 1650–1815*, edited by Dr Nicholas Tracy. Annapolis: Naval Institute Press, 1990.

Van der Merwe, Pieter. 'Views of the Royal Naval Exhibition, 1891', *Journal for Maritime Research*, vol. 3, no. 1 (2001), pp. 146–56.

Villiers, Alan. *The Battle of Trafalgar: Lord Nelson Sweeps the Seas*. London: Collier-Macmillan, 1965.

Ward, Geoff. 'Political Appeasement and the Erection of Nelson's Statue in Bridgetown', *The Journal of the Barbados Museum and Historical Society*, vol. 68 (December 2022), pp. 182–99.

White, Colin, ed. *The Nelson Companion*. Stroud, Gloucestershire: Bramley Books, 1997.

White, Colin, ed. *The Nelson Encyclopedia: People, Places, Battles, Ships, Myths, Mistresses and Memorabilia*. London: Chatham Publishing, 2005.

White, Colin, and the 1805 Club. *The Trafalgar Captains: Their Lives and Monuments*. London: Chatham, 2005.

Willis, Sam. *Fighting at Sea in the Eighteenth Century: The Art of Sailing Warfare*. Woodbridge: Boydell, 2008.

Willis, Sam. *The Fighting Temeraire: The Battle of Trafalgar and the Ship That Inspired J. M. W. Turner's Most Beloved Painting*. New York: Pegasus, 2010.

Wilson, Evan. *The Horrible Peace: British Veterans and the End of the Napoleonic Wars*. Amherst and Boston: University of Massachusetts Press, 2023.

Winfield, Rif. *British Warships in the Age of Sail, 1793–1817: Design, Construction, Careers and Fates*. London: Chatham Publishing and St Paul, MN: MBI Publishing, 2005.

Winfield, Rif, and Stephen Roberts. *French Warships in the Age of Sail, 1786–1861: Design, Construction, Careers and Fates*. Barnsley: Seaforth and Annapolis: U.S. Naval Institute Press, 2015.

Winfield, Rif, John Treadrea, Enrique García-Torralba Pérez, and Manuel Blasco Felip. *Spanish Warships in the Age of Sail 1700–1860: Design, Construction, Careers and Fates*. Barnsley: Seaforth and Annapolis: U.S. Naval Institute Press, 2023.

Woodman, Richard. *1805. A Nathaniel Drinkwater Novel*. London: John Murray, 1985.

Zulueta, Julian de. 'Trafalgar: The Spanish View', *The Mariner's Mirror*, vol. 66, no. 4 (1980), pp. 293–318. DOI: 10.1080/00253359.1980.10659212.

Unpublished Theses

Cesario, Bradley M. '"Trafalgar Refought:" The Professional and Cultural Memory of Horatio Nelson during Britain's Navalist Era, 1880–1914'. Unpublished M.A. thesis, Texas A & M University, December 2011.

Yarrington, Allison Willow. 'The Commemoration of the Hero, 1800–1864: Monuments to British Victors of the Napoleonic Wars'. Unpublished Ph.D. thesis, University of Cambridge, 1988.

Digital Online Resources

Biblioteca Nacional de España (https://www.bne.es). Digital Periodical and Newspaper Library

Biblioteca Digital Hispánica (http://bdh-rd.bne.es)

Bibliothèque Nationale de France. RetroNews. (https:/retronews.fr)

The British Newspaper Archive (https://www.britishnewspaperarchive.co.uk/)

Georgian Papers Online (http://gpp.rct.uk)

Historical Newspapers (https://www.newspapers.com)

Real Academia de la Historia, *Diccionario biográfico español* (https://dbe.rah.es)

The Trafalgar Way (https://www.thetrafalgarway.org/)

ILLUSTRATION ACKNOWLEDGEMENTS

DIAGRAM 1.1. © 2025, Mappa Mundi Cartography.
DIAGRAM 1.2. © 2025, Mappa Mundi Cartography.
DIAGRAM 1.3. © 2025, Mappa Mundi Cartography.
DIAGRAM 2.1. © 2025, Mappa Mundi Cartography.
GRAPH 1.1. Admiralty List Books. TNA, ADM 8/87–90. With thanks to Roger Knight, who supplied the raw data he also used in 'The Fleets at Trafalgar: The Margin of Superiority', in Canadine, ed., *Trafalgar in History*, p. 73.
GRAPH 1.2. Admiralty List Books. TNA, ADM 8/87–90. With thanks to Roger Knight, who supplied the raw data he also used in 'The Fleets at Trafalgar: The Margin of Superiority', in Canadine, ed., *Trafalgar in History*, p. 73.
TABLE 1.1. Monaque, 'La stratégie maritime', in Bonaparte, *Correspondance générale*, V, pp. 1003–4.
TABLE 1.2. Monaque, 'La stratégie maritime', in Bonaparte, *Correspondance générale*, V, pp. 1003–4.
TABLE 1.3. Edward Pelham Brenton, *The Naval History of Great Britain*, 2 vols. (London: Henry Colburn, 1837), vol. 2, Appendix VIII, pp. 700–5: Commanders in Chief on Home and Foreign Stations, 1783–1823.
FIGURE 1.1. The Print Collector/Alamy Images; INTERFOTO/Alamy Images; MUSEO NAVAL/Alamy Images.
FIGURE 2.1. Fuente: Museo Naval de Madrid / Biblioteca Virtual de Defensa.
FIGURE 3.1. National Maritime Museum, Greenwich: NMM (Greenwich Hospital Collection) WPN 1045.
FIGURE 4.1. The Picture Art Collection/Alamy Images.
FIGURE 4.2. IanDagnall Computing / Alamy Stock Photo.
FIGURE 4.3. The Picture Art Collection/Alamy Images.
FIGURE 4.4. Fuente: Museo Naval de Madrid / Biblioteca Virtual de Defensa.
FIGURE 4.5. Heritage Image Partnership Ltd/Alamy Images.
FIGURE 4.6. Chronicle / Alamy Stock Photo.
FIGURE 4.7. David Osborn / Alamy Stock Photo.

FIGURE 4.8. https://commons.wikimedia.org/wiki/File:Nelson%27s_Pillar,_Sackville-Street,_Dublin_RMG_PU3914.tiff.
FIGURE 5.1. images@rmg.co.uk - Sept 24.
FIGURE 5.2. © Look and Learn / Bridgeman Images.
FIGURE 5.3. Look and Learn / Illustrated Papers Collection / Bridgeman Images.
FIGURE 5.4. https://commons.wikimedia.org/wiki/File:%271805-1905_Admiral_Lord_Nelson_%27My_Ships_have_Passed_Away,_But_The_Spirit_of_My_Men_Remains%27_Punch,_October_18,_1905%27_RMG_PT0098.tiff.
FIGURE 5.5. John Frost Newspapers / Alamy Stock Photo.
FIGURE 6.1. The Print Collector/Alamy Images.
FIGURE 6.2. National Maritime Museum, Greenwich: NMM, Med0159.
FIGURE 6.3. PjrStudio / Alamy Stock Photo.
FIGURE 6.4. Public Domain, Library of Congress.
FIGURE 6.5. Chronicle/Alamy Images.
FIGURE 6.6. Chronicle / Alamy Stock Photo.
FIGURE 6.7. Alamy 2C875W1.
FIGURE 6.8. Public Domain. Library of Congress Prints and Photographs Division Washington, D.C. 20540.
FIGURE 6.9. eSales@awm.gov.au - Sept 24.

INDEX

For the benefit of digital users, indexed terms that span two pages (e.g., 52–53) may, on occasion, appear on only one of those pages.

INDEX

INDEX

INDEX